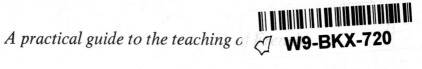

A practical guide to the teaching of W9-BKX-720

A practical guide to the teaching of
FRENCH

WILGA M. RIVERS

Harvard University

New York
OXFORD UNIVERSITY PRESS
London   1975   Toronto

Permission to reprint copyright material is hereby gratefully acknowledged:

To Roch Carrier, for "Les Mots qu'il faudrait...," from K. Brearley and R.-B. McBride, *Nouvelles du Québec*. Copyright © 1970 by Prentice-Hall of Canada Ltd.

To Editions Gallimard, for selections from C. Audry, *Derrière la baignoire*, 1962; J. Delais, *Idoles, idoles;* R. Queneau, *Zazie dans le métro*, 1959; and for A. Camus, "L'Hôte" from *L'Exil et le royaume*, 1957, and P. Eluard, "Je ne suis pas" from *Choix de poèmes*, 1941; all © Editions Gallimard.

To Ginn and Company Ltd., for material from D. Grayson, *A La Page*, 1964.

To Harcourt Brace Jovanovich, for material from *A-LM French*, Level I, Second Edition. Copyright © 1969 by Harcourt Brace Jovanovich, Inc. and reprinted with their permission.

To Macmillan Publishing Co., for material from R. Ortali, *Entre Nous*. Copyright © 1972 by Macmillan Publishing Co., Inc.

Printed in the United States of America

Preface

Foreign-language teaching is an interesting and exciting occupation. Since the nature of language and its complex operations is still a matter of controversy, and since the psychologists have still much to learn about how language is acquired—the native language as well as a second or third language—foreign-language teachers have an open field. They are free to experiment and innovate. They can appropriate what has proved successful in other times and other places. They can repeat and refine what they have found to be effective in their own circumstances with their own students. They can share successes and explore failures with their colleagues, learning much from each other.

Learning to use a language freely and fully is a lengthy and effortful process. Teachers cannot learn the language for their students. They can set their students on the road, helping them to develop confidence in their own learning powers. Then they must wait on the sidelines, ready to encourage and assist, while each student struggles and perseveres with autonomous activity. Some students learn the language well, even while the teacher observes. For those who find the task more difficult, we should at least make every effort to ensure that their language-learning is an enjoyable and educational experience.

As foreign-language teachers we must remain optimistic. Rarely will we see the fully developed product—the autonomous, confident language-user —although we will often be stimulated by the enthusiasm of those we have started along that path. Let us not be discouraged by the jeremiads of those who tell us our task is an impossible one in the time at our disposal. Our colleagues in mathematics and physics do not produce batches of Einsteins after three or four years of study, and Stravinskys are rare in the music room. Students interested in language and uninhibited in using the little they have assimilated will have a foundation on which to build when the opportunity presents itself. Surely all true education is beginnings. It is the hope of the author that this book and its companion volumes will play some part in stimulating imaginative and resourceful teaching which will arouse and sustain effective self-motivated learning.

In these books we do not provide final answers. What we have written is intended to provoke lively discussion. This is clearly an age when flexibility is a prime attribute for the young teacher. As prospective and practicing teachers consider the many techniques we have described and understand the rationale behind them, recognizing their strengths and weaknesses, they will be establishing a solid basis for choice when they are faced in a local situation with a wide variety of students of different ages and personal objectives. Ultimately, their selection should accord with their educational ideals, their own personality potential, and the needs and learning preferences of their students. The one all-sufficient answer for the classroom teacher is an alluring panacea but as illusory and unattainable as the philosopher's stone.

Method books for the preparation of foreign-language teachers abound. Some students using this book may have a background in general methodology such as is provided in *Teaching Foreign-Language Skills**** and books of a similar nature. The range of material in that book, however, is not considered in detail in this one. Rather, many ideas implicit and explicit in the earlier book have been developed in practical detail in the light of more recent emphases in the various branches of linguistics and the psychology of language. (Teachers are provided with much information without the confusions of overly technical language.) Stress is laid throughout on using language from the earliest stages for the normal purposes of language. Attention is also paid to contemporary developments in the study of the French language.

For all of the volumes in the series, the basic theoretical discussion and the elaboration of techniques remain parallel but for every exercise or activity, and for the types of study materials discussed, examples are supplied in the language the student will be teaching. The books are, therefore, appropriate for simultaneous use in a multiple-language methods class as well as for language-specific courses in foreign-language departments, whether for future high school teachers or for those preparing for

---

* Wilga M. Rivers, 1968. Chicago: The University of Chicago Press.

a future in undergraduate instruction. The material will also be useful for in-service training courses and institutes, enabling teachers of different languages to consider general problems together while penetrating to the heart of the matter through the language with which each is most familiar. The books will also provide a treasury from which practicing teachers can draw many ideas for individualized learning packets and for small-group activity, as well as for stimulating learning in a more conventional classroom.

A few additional explanations may facilitate the use of the book. Although there is some detailed discussion of points of French syntax and phonology, these are subordinate to the discussion of the preparation of teaching and testing materials and the elaboration of techniques; no attempt has been made to treat them systematically or exhaustively. Other books are available to meet this need. On the other hand, material used in the examples has been selected with a view to opening up discussion of areas of language about which the non-native speaker of French may not be quite clear, particular emphasis being laid, in a number of places, on the differences between spoken and written language. Examples, as given, are not intended to be complete but rather to be illustrative of technique. The suggested exercises, indicated by an asterisk (*), then draw the application into other areas of possible confusion or difficulty. One cannot teach what one does not fully understand oneself. Teachers in training will thus have a further opportunity to clarify matters which have worried them in the past.

It should be noted, at this point, that it is the intention of the author that the asterisked activities be assigned, so that students actively participate in creation of new materials and in the adaptation and refinement of those provided in current textbooks. The close examination and judicious adaptation of text, test, and taped materials should be part of every trainee teacher's experience, along with the trying out in actual teaching situations of what has been developed (whether in micro-lessons or in practice teaching with a class). Students should be encouraged during their training period, to begin a permanent indexed file of personally culled teaching materials, together with ideas for activities and projects. They should keep on file reading passages, cultural information, poems, scenes from plays, songs, and games appropriate for various ages and levels, informal visual aids, interesting and amusing variations of techniques, practical activities in which their students can use the language informally and spontaneously, and sources of information and supplementary assistance. If students share what they gather during this important period of preparation, they will not approach their first year of full-time teaching empty-handed.

The artificiality of dealing with various aspects of language use in separate chapters is apparent (e.g., the separation of listening and acceptable production of sounds from communicative interaction and both of these from knowledge of the rules of grammar). Students will need to hold certain questions in abeyance until they can see the whole picture. For those who wish to consider questions in a different order from that supplied, numerous cross-references are included in the text, in addition to the comprehensive information in the detailed list of contents and the index. To facilitate the finding of examples dealing with particular aspects of language use, initial-letter classifications have been used throughout different sections, viz., C: Communicating, both speaking and listening; G: Grammar; S: Sounds; R: Reading; and W: Writing.

Examples go beyond the elementary course. Although it is difficult to establish a level of difficulty in the abstract, E has been used to indicate the elementary level (first or second year of high school, first or second semester of beginning college study), I for intermediate level (second or third year of high school, second or third semester of college), and A for advanced level (fourth or fifth year of high school, fourth semester or above in college). This classification is non-scientific and indicative only. It will be for the instructor, the student, or the practicing teacher to adjust the interpretation of levels of difficulty to particular situations.

In conclusion, the author wishes to thank most warmly the numerous persons, scholars and teachers in the field, who have contributed to the development of her thinking through discussion, demonstration, or published work. Special thanks must, however, go to the editors at Oxford University Press, John Wright and Stephanie Golden, for their constant encouragement and meticulous assistance in production; to Arlene Vander-Werff, whose careful and intelligent preparation of the manuscript, tactful requests for clarification, and devotion to our joint endeavor have kept the work on an even keel; to Fred Jenkins, whose suggestions for improvement have been incorporated in Chapter 5; to Paulette Pelc, Roz Kaplan, Gloria Russo, Tobie Kranitz, and René Coppieters, who added their labors at various stages; to Harriett Weatherford, whose help was given in subtle ways; and to Michèle Leroux who kindly read the entire manuscript. I also wish to express my appreciation of the material help in the realization of the task which was accorded by the Research Board and Center for Advanced Study of the University of Illinois at Urbana-Champaign.

Cambridge, Massachusetts   W.M.R.
November 1974

Contents

A practical guide to the teaching of French

I
COMMUNICATING

Communication acts

In Part I, speaking and listening are discussed in separate chapters, although in a communication act one clearly complements the other. The reader will bear in mind that being able to speak a language without understanding what is being said by native speakers is of limited use, while being able to understand a language but not speak it can have specialized utility (for the enjoyment of foreign-language films, broadcasts, plays, and songs, or for professional monitoring purposes) but is very frustrating in normal communication situations. Being able to speak comprehensibly does not necessarily ensure ability to comprehend normal native speech; on the other hand many people develop a very high level of aural comprehension without being able to express themselves freely. Both areas require serious attention.

In a well-rounded program, success in each will be recognized as a separate achievement and given equal importance in the eyes of the students. Nevertheless, practice of each should normally be in relation to the other if communicating is the ultimate goal.

Developing skill and confidence in communication

When selecting learning activities, we must always remember that our goal is for the students to be able to interact freely with others: to understand what others wish to communicate in the broadest sense, and to be able

3

to convey to others what they themselves wish to share (whether as a reaction to a communication or as an original contribution to the exchange). To do this effectively, however, the students must understand how the French language works and be able to make the interrelated changes for which the system of the language provides mechanisms.

The following schema will help us to see the essential processes involved in learning to communicate.

C1 Processes involved in learning to communicate

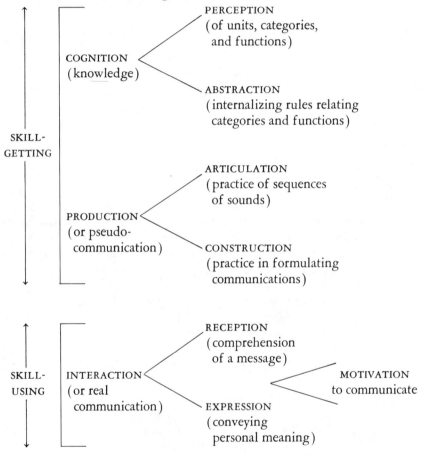

Note: 1. This is not a sequential but a parallel schema, in the sense that skill-getting and skill-using[1] are continually proceeding hand in hand. There is genuine *interaction from the beginning,* with students exploring the full scope of what is being learned.

2. *Bridging the gap* between skill-getting and skill-using is not automatic. Skill-getting activities must be so designed as to be already *pseudo-communication,* thus leading naturally into spontaneous communication activities.

3. The terminology of this schema will be used in discussing appropriate activities for skill-getting and skill-using.

Knowledge and intensive practice (skill-getting) are not enough to ensure confident interaction. The latter requires practice in actual, purposeful conversational exchange with others. In Chapter 1 we shall discuss linguistic aspects of the spoken language with which the students need to be familiar if their communication is not to be stilted and various types of bridging activities (e.g., the many uses of dialogues, Cummings devices, and action chains); in Chapter 2, ways of involving students in real interaction.[2] In Chapter 3 the problems of understanding the spoken language are considered in depth. Chapters 4 and 5 give the rationale for techniques and activities for perception, abstraction, articulation, and construction.

1
Structured interaction

Opposing views on the development of speaking skill

According to the *progressive development* view, ability to speak the language derives from the systematic study of grammar, phonology, and lexicon. This is the approach of grammar-translation texts, where it is assumed that accuracy in expressing oneself orally is dependent on prior study of language forms through reading and written exercises; of audio-lingual or aural-oral texts where oral imitation, memorization, and drilling techniques precede attempts to speak spontaneously (although in this case the latter is attempted much sooner than in traditional grammar-translation texts); and of texts which begin with narrative and conversational reading passages.

The *immediate communication* view holds that speaking skill is developed from the first contact with the language. The student may be encouraged to express himself in simple ways under the guidance of the teacher (*Qu'est-ce que c'est? C'est un livre; Où est le livre? Le livre est sur la table*). Alternatively, in a simulation of the total immersion experience of the foreigner in another culture, he may be expected to use for the expression of his own message anything he has acquired of the language from hearing it, supplemented by gestures, pantomime, or the showing of objects, with the teacher suggesting words and expressions only when the student falters.

This chapter takes a *middle position* between these two approaches,

6

advocating that students be encouraged to express themselves freely in the language from the beginning, through experiences and games which provide them with a framework for spontaneous communicative creation while presupposing they will use what they have been learning through an orderly progression of study and practice. The Type B exercises described in Chapter 4 prepare students to use the language for expressing their own meanings[1] and are paralleled from the beginning with extensive opportunities for autonomous interaction of the type discussed in Chapter 2. If students are to develop as uninhibited communicators who seize opportunities to use the language with native speakers, they must early overcome their timidity and the fear of being embarrassed when they express themselves simplistically or awkwardly, as they will often do when their knowledge of the language is at an elementary stage.

Differences between spoken and written French

Much of any foreign language learned at school is acquired from books. Even where conversations and dialogues appear, they are often unrepresentative of authentic speech. Tapes and records attempt to bring the oral language into the classroom, but some of these are no more than stilted oral recitations of written forms of the language. If students are to learn to use authentic speech, their teachers must be aware of the features which differentiate the spoken language from the conventional written forms, and particularly from the literary usages to which they have become accustomed in their own advanced studies.

For conciseness and precision of meaning the French usually employ in written material more complicated structures and a wider vocabulary than in speech. This is one reason why learning to write French well is an advanced art. In one sense, written French is *less redundant* than the spoken form of the language (that is, it contains fewer signals of the same aspect of meaning) in that repetitions and duplications are avoided and the additional clues provided by such things as rising and falling intonation and tone of voice are absent. In another sense it is more redundant, in that it contains many signals to meaning which are completely lost when the written form is presented orally: for example, indicators of the person and number of the verb (rends-le; ils portent); of plurality (de bons fromages); and of gender in certain environments (tout autre: toute autre; quelle bonne amie).

C2 Analysis of two sentences from a modern short story highlights a number of differences between the written and spoken codes in French.

Un accident survenu à ma roue avant, à deux ou trois cents mètres du village, m'obligea à poursuivre la route à pied. Chemin faisant, j'aperçus à quelques pas d'un bouquet de noisetiers, au bord du fossé, un vieux paysan en contemplation devant un champ de blé.   M. AYMÉ, "Le Décret."[2]

If recounted orally this incident might have been expressed as follows:

Je n'étais pas loin du village, tu vois—à deux ou trois cents mètres, pas plus. Mais je ne pouvais pas continuer, ça c'était évident. Quelque chose était arrivé à ma roue—la roue avant, d'ailleurs. Je n'avais pas le choix; j'étais obligé de faire le reste du trajet à pied. Un peu plus loin, j'ai remarqué un paysan au bord du fossé. C'était à quelque pas d'un bouquet de noisetiers. Lui, le vieux, contemplait un champ de blé.

Commentary

1. Not only would the second version when spoken contain more clues to meaning (that is, to be more redundant) because of the prosodic features of intonation and pitch, and the expressive features of tone of voice, gesture, and facial expression with which it would be accompanied, but it is expressed in simple declarative sentences, with considerable repetition of semantic detail (*pas loin du village—à deux ou trois cents mètres, pas plus; ma roue—la roue avant; je n'avais pas le choix—j'étais obligé de*); with grammatical substitutions with the same referent (*un paysan—lui; au bord du fossé—c'était; ça c'était*); and with expletives and conversational tags and clichés like *tu vois, d'ailleurs, ça c'était évident,* which add little to the message but give the speaker time to organize the succeeding segment for production.

2. *Assimilation:* The speaker would probably pronounce *je ne pouvais pas* as /ʒənpuvɛpa/, *suppressing the ə caduc of ne,* or as /ʃpuvɛpa/, *omitting the ne* as is frequently done in rapid familiar speech and, as a consequence, assimilating the voiced /ʒ/ to the unvoiced /p/ as /ʃp/.

3. The tendency in a rapid, familiar style of speech to reduce the two parts of the negation (*ne . . . pas*) to one (*pas*), giving, for instance, *je pouvais pas continuer,* may seem at first sight to contradict the statement that spoken language is more repetitious than written language. Note, however, that in a similar expression in a more purely literary (written) context the *pas* of *je ne pouvais pas* would not appear, giving *je ne pouvais continuer.* If transferred to rapid speech this would result in /ʒənpuvɛ/, the disappearance of the *ə caduc* of *ne* in the unstressed position between two consonants making the negation barely obvious. The inclusion of *pas* in *je ne pouvais pas continuer* is a characteristic feature of spoken language (and informal writing), the negation being thus fortified by placing

the irreducible element *pas* in a semi-stressed position in the utterance, making it possible to express the negation quite clearly even when the abbreviated form /n/ is omitted, as in *je pouvais pas continuer.* (The *pas* is frequently in a fully stressed position, as in *Non, je ne peux pas,* which, with the reduction characteristic of rapid speech, becomes *Non, je peux pas* /nɔ̃ ʃpøpa/, the negative element *pas* being quite distinctly articulated.)

The *position of stress* is most important in influencing the structure of spoken French, as we shall see in a moment. It should be fully understood by the teacher. Useful references are Pierre R. Léon, *Prononciation du français standard,* pp. 17–18, and P. and M. Léon, *Introduction à la phonétique corrective,* pp. 64–66.

4. *Liaison:* In colloquial spoken language fewer liaisons are made than in formal speech and far fewer than in the reading aloud of poetry or literary prose. Even in such combinations as *était arrivé* and *étais obligé* in the second passage above, the liaison is frequently not made in informal speech, although these would normally be linked in formal speech.

✱ Be sure that you know the rules for inserting and deleting the ə *caduc* and modern usage with regard to *liaison.* (Léon explains these rules clearly in *Prononciation du français standard,* Chapters I.21 and III, giving many examples which show the distinctions for formal and informal use.)

Effects of the position of stress
PHRASES SEGMENTÉES

C3 Many of the characteristics of spoken French have been demonstrated by Céline in his description of New York as first glimpsed from an immigrant ship.

> Figurez-vous qu'elle était debout leur ville, absolument debout. New York c'est une ville debout. On en avait déjà vu nous des villes bien sûr, et des belles encore, et des ports et des fameux même. Mais chez nous, n'est-ce pas, elles sont couchées les villes, au bord de la mer ou sur les fleuves, elles s'allongent sur le paysage, elles attendent le voyageur, tandis que celle-là l'Américaine, elle ne se pâmait pas, non, elle se tenait bien raide.   L. F. CÉLINE, *Voyage au bout de la nuit.*[3]

Commentary

The syntax of spoken French is strongly influenced by the position of stress which comes at the end of the *groupe rythmique.* If any word is to be

stressed, it must normally be brought to the end of a *groupe rythmique*.
As a result, spoken French contains frequent *phrases segmentées* which
permit more words to appear in the position of stress. In *leur ville était
debout*, the word *debout* only would be stressed; in *elle était debout / leur
ville* two *groupes rythmiques* have been created by the use of the substitute
elle, and now both *debout* and *ville* can be stressed. (The two *groupes
rythmiques* together form one *groupe de souffle*.)

   Notice the difference in effect in speech of the following pairs:

New York est une ville de*bout*.
New *York*, c'est une ville de*bout*.

Les villes sont cou*chées*.
Elles sont cou*chées*, les *villes*.

L'Américaine ne se pâmait *pas*.
Celle-*là* l'Améri*caine*, elle ne se pâmait *pas*.

On avait déjà vu des *villes*.
On en avait déjà *vu nous* des *villes*.

✱ Practice taking simple statements or questions and rephrasing them in
phrases segmentées to emphasize different elements in the utterance, e.g.:

Ton frère est *parti?*
Il est *parti*, ton *frère?*
Il est *parti*, ton frère *à toi?*

TOURS PRÉSENTATIFS

   Another device of speech which brings particular words into the position
of stress is the *tour présentatif: c'est . . . qui (que)*.

C4 Compare:

Il l'a *fait*.
C'est *lui* qui l'a *fait*.

Je lui ai donné la *lettre*.
C'est à *lui* que j'ai donné la *lettre*.

✱ Use either *tours présentatifs* or *phrases segmentées* to replicate the emphasis of the following in French:

I wrote that letter.
I *wrote* that letter myself.

I wrote *that* letter.

I wrote that *letter* (but not the address on the envelope).

Notice that both of these common patterns of speech make the spoken utterance more redundant than a simple written declarative sentence would be. This fact is significant for the aural comprehension of fleeting combinations of sounds.

Even though we would not normally teach our students to express themselves in quite such a familiar register as is used by Céline's poor immigrant, writing such as this dramatically illustrates certain basic tendencies of spoken French which spring from the prosodic features that do not appear in writing. The mere inclusion of expletives and clichés does not transform formal language into conversational language. The teacher must be aware of these basic patterns and encourage students to use them when expressing themselves orally in French. (The writer recalls a small French child, one of whose earliest sentence patterns was "Il est parti, mon papa," which was imitated by her younger sister as "Parti papa.")

Style of language (register or level of discourse)

We use different styles of language in diverse situations—when we are speaking to a person in an official position, to an acquaintance, to a close friend, or within the family circle. Students should be made conscious of this fact and learn to recognize, and eventually use, French in these different styles. They should be able to distinguish *langue surveillée* or *langue soignée* from *langue familière* or *relâchée*. They should be able to understand rather than use *langue populaire* and *langue vulgaire*. (These distinctions also help them to recognize the author's intent in conversational material in written French.) The *Précis de syntaxe du français contemporain* of W. von Wartburg and P. Zumthor gives a useful "description de l'état actuel du français et de ses variétés" (p. 9), making clear what syntactical usages are acceptable at the different levels of language. The Larousse *Dictionnaire du français contemporain* and *Le Petit Robert* perform the same service for the lexicon.

Joos distinguishes for English five styles: intimate, casual, consultative, formal, and frozen. Applying the criteria set out by Joos in *The Five Clocks*[4] we may develop the following sequence in French for a similar situation treated at the five levels.

C5 In an *intimate* situation, a parent may say to a child who is embarrassingly present and has shown some reluctance to leave: *Allez hop!* (According to Joos, in intimate style the utterance contains no information that is known to the participants.) This is *langue familière*.

In a *casual* style the parent may say: *Laisse-nous enfin!* (Once again complete information is not supplied, and this style involves the use of well-known formulas.) This is *langue relâchée* and employs the *tutoiement*.

Consultative style, the style of standard exchange between strangers, would require rather: *Quittez la pièce un moment, s'il vous plaît.* (Since consultative style is used for persons outside the intimate circle, the *tu* form would not be used. Consultative style supplies all necessary background information.) In such a situation one would use *langue surveillée*.

A *formal* situation, on the other hand, may require: *Auriez-vous l'obligeance de vous absenter pendant quelques instants.* (In formal style, the speaker often does not refer to himself and he does not anticipate any immediate participation on the part of the person addressed.) Here *langue formelle* is used.

Frozen or printed style may be observed on a notice outside a door: *Prière de ne pas interrompre la conférence.* This is usually *langue administrative.*

Compare the following:

Et le sel?; passe-le-moi, veux-tu?; passez-moi le sel, s'il vous plaît; voudriez-vous être assez aimable pour me passer le sel; prière de ne pas monopoliser le sel.

* Try constructing a similar series on the themes: "Please do not talk" and "Write to me about it."

C6 In the light of the above discussion on styles of language, examine the following passage from *Zazie dans le métro* by R. Queneau:[5]

Gridoux déjeunait sur place, ça lui évitait de rater un client, s'il s'en présentait un; il est vrai qu'à cette heure-là il n'en survenait jamais. Déjeuner sur place présentait donc un double avantage puisque comme nul client n'apparaissait asteure, Gridoux pouvait casser la graine en toute tranquillité. Cette graine était en général une assiette de hachis parmentier fumant que Mado Ptits-pieds lui apportait après le coup de feu, à l'environ d'une heure.

— Je croyais que c'était des tripes aujourd'hui, dit Gridoux en plongeant pour attraper son litron de rouge planqué dans un coin.

Mado Ptits-pieds haussa les épaules. Tripes? Mythe! Et Gridoux le savait bien.

— Et le type? demanda Gridoux, qu'est-ce qu'il branle?

— I finit de croûter. I parle pas.

— Il pose pas de questions?

— Rien.

— Et Tulandot, il lui cause pas?

— Il ose pas.

— Il est pas curieux.

— C'est pas qu'il est pas curieux, mais il ose pas.

— Ouais.

Gridoux se mit à attaquer sa pâtée dont la température avait baissé jusqu'à un degré raisonnable.

— Après? demanda Mado Ptits-pieds, ce sera quoi? Du brie? du camembert?

— Il est beau le brie?

— Il va pas très vite.

— Alors de l'autre.

Comme Mado Ptits-pieds s'éloignait, Gridoux lui demanda:

— Et lui? qu'est-ce qu'il a croûté?

— Comme vous. Gzactement.

* Discuss in the above passage: indications of rapid speech; structures commonly used in *langue familière;* words which are particularly indicative of *langue familière* and *langue populaire;* and allusions which reflect typically French customs. (Consult the Wartburg and Zumthor grammar and the Larousse *Dictionnaire du français contemporain* or *Le petit Robert* when in doubt.)

The style of language in dialogues of the sort found in textbooks may not always be used consistently.

C7 Madame Martin rencontre une amie en ville.

MADAME MARTIN	Bonjour, chère madame. Comment allez-vous?
MADAME LEBRUN	Je vais bien, merci.
MADAME MARTIN	Et votre fils?
MADAME LEBRUN	Pas mal.

Commentary

1. If Madame Lebrun were really an *amie* of Madame Martin, she would normally say: *"Bonjour, Lucille"* and probably (not necessarily) use the *tu* form. By the tone of her address, Madame Lebrun is more probably a *connaissance* or a *voisine*.

2. In response to Madame Martin's very polite greeting, Madame Lebrun should add to her reply an inquiry after Madame Martin's health: *"Et vous?"*

3. Madame Lebrun's *"Pas mal"* after Madame Martin's polite enquiry is very brusque and out of keeping with the general tone of the exchange. If the son has not been well, *"Il va assez bien, merci"* would have been more polite.

* Examine dialogues in current textbooks to see if they use different levels of discourse appropriately and consistently.

Bridging activities

All that we can teach students in a foreign language is how to construct the appropriate framework, in all its detail, for the expression of meaning. We cannot teach students to express their own meaning; we can provide opportunities which stimulate motivation for this personal activity to take place and we can help the student to improve the framework so that it can really carry the message intended. We can develop activities where the student constructs various types of frameworks and help him try them out to see if they will carry effectively the meanings he intends. Searle calls language "rule-governed intentional behavior."[6] We can help the student internalize the rules; we cannot supply the intention, although we can stimulate it by contriving situations and encounters. One way in which we help students try out frameworks of varying degrees of complexity and subtlety (that is, to perform "speech acts"[7]) is by providing practice in *pseudo-communication.* This is communication in which the content is structured by the learning situation, rather than springing autonomously from the mind and emotions of the student. *We bridge the gap to true communication by encouraging the student to use these structured practices for autonomous purposes from the early stages.* In this way, the average student acquires confidence in his ability to function on his own. (Linguistically gifted students will always develop confidence in their own way, with or without special guidance.)

The concept of *individualization of instruction* has to be very carefully analyzed in relation to the development of communication skills: it can mean small-group practice and interaction, but not independent study, because communication by definition involves someone other than the communicator. Students also learn a great deal from listening to the way other people formulate their communications. At the other extreme, communication cannot be efficiently practiced in large groups. For a discussion of suitable groupings of students for communication practice, see Wilga M.

Rivers *et al.,* "Techniques for the Development of Proficiency in the Spoken Language" in H. B. Altman and R. L. Politzer, eds., *Individualizing Foreign Language Instruction* (Rowley, Mass.: Newbury House, 1971), pp. 165–74.

RULE-GOVERNED BEHAVIOR

In language use, we fit our meaning into a framework which conforms to many types of rules, or recurring regularities: not only syntactic, morphological, and phonological, but also semantic and cultural. Once we have an intention to express, not only do we have to select the "right words" for our purpose, but these choices entail other lexical selections within the sentence which we must respect, but which function according to rules at present only vaguely understood. Semantics also dictates our choices in syntax,[8] and syntactic selection forces certain morphological adjustments. We cannot operate effectively in speech or writing until we have understood the possibilities the rules afford and are able to put into operation the sheer mechanics of the language at the level of verb endings for person and tense, required agreements, conventional word order, and so on.[9] Cultural expectations come into play as well; that is, rules of relationships and obligations in interpersonal communication within a society, expressed in part through registers or levels of discourse, but also through expected and implied questions and reactions, social taboos, and the mutually understood references of words used in certain associations.

C8 Il m'a empêché de faire ce que je voulais.
Il a entravé la réalisation de mes projets.[10]

The decision to express this intention at a more formal level in the second sentence motivated the choice of *entraver* instead of *empêcher,* and this lexical choice entailed other lexical choices and a different syntactic framework from that in the first sentence.

Je regrette de ne pouvoir vous accompagner mais c'est la fête de ma marraine.

Comprehension of this sentence is dependent on comprehension not merely of the individual words but of certain extra-family relationships and obligations of French society.

Supplying the student with a basic corpus

The first problem we face in teaching students to speak a foreign language is how to plunge them into using natural language when they know little or nothing of the new tongue. Proponents of the grammar-translation approach have usually maintained that conversing in the language should not be attempted until students control the essentials of the syntactic and morphological systems intellectually and in graphic form and have acquired through reading and memorization an extensive vocabulary, at which stage they can learn to express themselves orally quite rapidly by drawing on what they have learned. But with the modern emphasis on the importance of oral communication and the present generation's greater familiarity with aural-oral rather than graphic presentations of information, this approach can be discouraging for many students.

A number of approaches have been proposed at different times for plunging the student into active language use. All have proved effective in the early stages when intelligently and imaginatively implemented. We need some way of supplying the student with a basic corpus with which to work.

We can identify four main approaches to this problem: the object centered, the melody and rhythm centered, the verb centered, and the situation centered.

OBJECT CENTERED

In this approach, students begin by discussing objects in the classroom in imitation of the teacher. The grammatical structures introduced are demonstrable in relation to these objects, so that students hear and practice them in a realistic setting.

C9 Voici le livre. Voilà la fenêtre . . . Qu'est-ce que c'est? C'est le livre. C'est la fenêtre . . . Où est le livre? Le livre est sur la table . . . Le livre est vert . . . C'est le livre de Pierre . . .

The class then goes on to discuss persons in the classroom in much the same terms:

Pierre est un élève. Il est grand.
Marie est une élève. Elle est petite.
C'est la sœur de Pierre.

Variant: Teachers sometimes use the contents of a handbag or shopping basket instead of classroom objects. Later, pictures of houses, gardens, airports, farms are used to expand the environment for purposes of description and discussion. Sometimes these pictures are in the textbook. Otherwise, use is made of commercially available wall-pictures, full- or double-page scenes cut from magazines, or projected slides. Students often construct posters, with items labeled in French, to illustrate these environments, and these are posted on the bulletin board so that students can assimilate the vocabulary casually through frequent contact. (Unless the teacher is watchful, however, an overemphasis on acquiring names for a multiplicity of objects may develop.)

This approach sometimes limits students to accurate production of very trite sentences which they would not conceivably wish to use in spontaneous conversation: *C'est un livre. Il est vert. Il est sur le bureau du professeur. C'est le livre du professeur.* Modern students find this approach boring and trivial. It is well to remember that in real conversation we rarely comment on things which are visible unless the situation is exceptional: *La chaise est sur le bureau du professeur! Pourquoi ça?* A little whimsy will help to enliven the exchanges and keep the students alert.

MELODY AND RHYTHM CENTERED

In a quite different approach, only one noun is used for quite a long time: *une réglette* (a rod). Called "the silent way"[11] by Gattegno, its originator, this method concentrates at the beginning on developing sensitivity to the melody and flow of the language. Students listen to tapes of a number of languages trying to recognize which of the speeches they hear is in the language they have been studying.[12] Gattegno considers that

since babies learn to talk their mother tongue first by yielding to its "music," we can . . . trace the first elements of the spirit of a language to the unconscious surrender of our sensitivity to what is conveyed by the background of noise in each language. This background obviously includes the silences, the pauses, the flow, the linkages of words, the duration of each breath required to utter connected chunks of the language, the overtones and undertones, the stresses as well as the special vowels or consonants belonging to that language.[13]

The teacher works with only about thirty words in the initial lessons, mainly the feminine articles *la* and *une* for use with *réglette,* pronouns in the direct and indirect object forms (*la, les, moi, lui*), some color adjectives in the feminine form,[14] possessives (*ma, notre, votre*), a few numerals, some forms of *avoir* and *être* (*ai, avons, avez, ont; est, sont*), the imperative forms of *donner* and *prendre,* the preposition *à,* the conjunction *et, oui, non,* and a few adverbs like *aussi, là, ici.* Using a box of colored rods, the teacher induces the student to utter fluent sentences with nativelike facility, while talking as little as possible himself. There is a minimum of imitation of the teacher and a maximum of concentration by the student on constructing sentences with the help of the rods. The teacher does not explain grammatical features but encourages the students to think about what they hear and to try to construct utterances which conform to the rules they have discovered for themselves.

C10   Types of sentences practiced with the rods:

Prenez une réglette bleue (rouge, verte).
Donnez-la-moi.
Prenez une réglette jaune et donnez-la à Robert.
Prenez deux réglettes vertes et donnez-les-moi.

The rods continue to be used for learning such things as comparatives, temporal relationships, and tenses.

Later, through the technique of *visual dictation*,[15] students are given practice in recognizing the printed equivalents of the words they have been using orally as they created situations with the rods, and also in the fluent construction of sentences using these words. Here the teacher points silently and rapidly, but only once, to a succession of words on a chart of scrambled words with phonic color coding, and in a short time students are able to produce with acceptable diction long sentences like: *Prenez une réglette bleue et une réglette verte et donnez la réglette bleue à Robert et donnez-moi la réglette verte* and to demonstrate through action that they have understood what they are saying.

Gattegno claims to be "rejecting the learning of vocabularies and grammar . . . and replacing it with as thorough a penetration of the spirit of a language as possible."[16]

VERB CENTERED

One of the best-known devices under this head is the *Gouin series*.[17] Gouin had observed the way his child commented on his own actions, and he developed from this the idea of an *action series* or *action chain*. He divided common events into five general series: the home, man in society, life in nature, science, and occupations. These were subdivided and re-subdivided into shorter series centering around the verb, which, according to Gouin, is "the generating element of the sentence."[18] The language was then taught through a series of commonly performed actions, first orally, then in writing. A different verb was used in each statement, and students were expected to acquire the situational vocabulary along with the verb through performing or miming the actions while they described what they were doing. The teacher first demonstrated the series in the native language and then, when the students had understood it clearly, in the foreign language. The students next repeated the actions under the guidance of the teacher or of other students, describing what they were doing in the foreign language as they were doing it. (Gouin advocated peer teaching, saying that "in Nature, one child can and does teach another child to talk."[19])

While the students were trying to reproduce the series the teacher would make encouraging remarks in the language. After this aural-oral phase, the series would be read and then written out by the students.

C11 The example Gouin himself gives[20] is the following (the verb is emphasized orally in the initial demonstration) :

marche	Je marche vers la porte.
m'approche	Je m'approche de la porte.
arrive	J'arrive à la porte.
m'arrête	Je m'arrête à la porte.
allonge	J'allonge le bras.
prends	Je prends la poignée.
tourne	Je tourne la poignée.
tire	Je tire la porte.
cède	La porte cède.
tourne	La porte tourne sur ses gonds.
lâche	Je lâche la poignée.

We may be surprised at the amount of specialized vocabulary this method entailed. Gouin considered that general terms were infrequently used in comparison with specific vocabulary. His emphasis was, of course, on the verb, but the verb in complete sentences.

This approach can be extended to provide practice in all persons and in different tenses.

C12

STUDENT A	Qu'est-ce que je fais?
STUDENT B	Tu ouvres la porte.
STUDENTS A & B	Nous écrivons sur le tableau.
TEACHER	Qu'est-ce qu'ils font?
STUDENT C	Ils écrivent sur le tableau.
STUDENTS A & B	Qu'est-ce que nous faisons?
STUDENT C	Vous écrivez sur le tableau.
TEACHER	Qu'est-ce qu'ils ont fait?
STUDENT C	Ils ont écrit sur le tableau.
STUDENT A	Regardez ce que je ferai la semaine prochaine (miming action).
STUDENT B	Tu feras tes valises.
STUDENT C	Elle fera ses valises.

Through mime the variety of the actions can be expanded considerably and the activity becomes a competitive game, with students describing each movement and then guessing what is being mimed. This may be a completely student-to-student activity in an individualized or group work program.

C13   (I)   In another variation, the student is given an order or a series of orders (of increasing complexity) by the teacher or another student:

Allez[21] à la porte; ouvrez la porte; mettez le livre dans le tiroir du bureau; prenez le livre dans le tiroir du bureau, ouvrez le livre à la page vingt et lisez la première phrase à haute voix.

The student obeys the order saying what he is doing or, if he is learning the *passé composé,* what he has done. If he makes a mistake another student can describe what he actually did and what he should have done. (*Il a pris le livre sur le bureau. Il aurait dû prendre le livre dans le tiroir du bureau.*) This provides a useful situational context for learning the difficult expression *aurait dû faire* or the useful *au lieu de faire.*

Recent revivals of this type of activity learning have been called the *strategy of the total physical response*[22] (in which students respond physically to commands in the foreign language of increasing morphological and syntactical complexity) and *Situational Reinforcement*[23] (which uses the techniques of C12).

The Gouin approach can be developed in considerable detail beyond these simple examples and can be the basis for factual learning about the geography of France, the monuments of Paris, activities at festivals, matters of etiquette, and so on.

C14   (I)   A map of France is drawn, as a cooperative project, on the floor of the classroom, and students are asked to undertake journeys. (A posted map and pointer may be substituted, but this reduces the physical response to a symbolic one.)

TEACHER OR ANOTHER STUDENT   En partant de Paris, traversez la Seine. Approchez-vous de Chartres. N'y entrez pas mais continuez sur la route de Tours.

The student addressed then describes his journey in the *passé composé* with personal embellishments.

STUDENT   Je suis parti de Paris où il faisait très chaud. J'ai traversé la Seine à neuf heures du matin. Je me suis approché de Chartres mais je n'y suis pas entré parce qu'il pleuvait. J'ai continué sur la route de Tours où j'ai déjeuné.

Recognizing its debt to Gouin and to the subsequent work of Emile de Sauzé of Cleveland, whose influence can still be perceived in many a modern textbook, is the *verbal-active approach,* which has also been called "a rationalist direct method."[24] Yvone Lenard says, "The sentence arranges itself around the verb" and "it is, therefore, imperative that the student learn to listen for the verb in the sentence, recognize its form, and answer immediately with the appropriate form."[25] In essence, this echoes Gouin, although Lenard's method adds a question-answer sequence to the action series. Since this is a direct method, unlike the Gouin approach it excludes the native language from the classroom and the textbook.

In this approach, grammar is learned inductively and through action rather than through deductive grammar rules. Diller says, "Knowing a rule and being able to act on it is quite independent of being able to formulate the rule adequately. The rule can be psychologically real without any formulation of it. . . . Rules for action are best learned in conjunction with demonstration and practice of the action."[26] Both Diller and Lenard emphasize the necessity for the learning stage to develop into opportunities for innovative sentence creation on the part of the student. Quoting de Sauzé's viewpoint, Lenard says, " 'Language is invention.' It has no existence apart from the speaker or the writer who recreates, reinvents the language for his own needs each time he uses it."[27] She lays great stress on the daily oral composition as "the most important exercise of the verbal-active method in building the elements of which fluency is composed."[28] In these oral compositions, prepared in advance in writing but delivered orally in front of their fellows, students try to use only what everyone else is learning, thus cultivating "originality, free invention, and personal expression within a strictly controlled structural framework."[29] (Note that the verbal-active method moves from listening and speaking to writing before reading, another deviation from Gouin which is traceable to de Sauzé.)

C15 *Verbal-active action series*

Déclaration et Question	*Réponse*
Le matin, je me réveille de bonne heure. A quelle heure *vous réveillez-vous?*	*Je me réveille* à sept heures.
Je me lève tout de suite. *Vous levez-vous* tout de suite?	Non, *je* ne *me lève* pas tout de suite. Je n'*aime* pas *me lever* tout de suite.

Ensuite, je fais ma toilette: *je me lave* (avec   Oui, *je me peigne.*
de l'eau et du savon), *je me brosse les dents*
(avec une brosse à dents) et *je me brosse les*
cheveux (avec une brosse à cheveux). Et
puis *je me peigne. Vous peignez-vous?*

Un homme *se rase* le matin (probablement   Oui, *je me rase,* mais *je me*
avec un rasoir électrique). *Vous rasez-vous,*   *laisse pousser* des pattes et
Monsieur? [30]   la moustache.

SITUATION CENTERED

For many centuries, situationally based dialogues have been in and out of
fashion for providing students with a corpus of foreign-language words
and expressions with which to work. [31] They are very frequently found in
present-day textbooks. The situations chosen may be experiences common
to both the native and the foreign culture, or may introduce the student
to typically French ways of interacting and reacting. Sometimes they are
printed with a parallel idiomatic translation; at other times students are
expected to comprehend the meaning through action or through simple
French explanations.

Dialogue construction can be indicative of diverse philosophies. Some
dialogues are designed to *demonstrate grammatical rules,* and examples of
rules in use and the variations of paradigms are introduced systematically
in the exchanges.

C16   PAULE   Où vas-tu ce soir?
      MADELEINE   Je vais en ville avec ma famille. Nous allons au cinéma.
           PAULE   Qu'est-ce que vous allez voir?
      MADELEINE   *Zazie dans le Métro.* Mes cousins vont voir le même film
                   demain.

The aim of grammar-demonstration dialogues is to lead students to inductive recognition of the rule or the paradigm. These dialogues need not be
memorized: they can be studied and discussed in French, dramatized, and
used as a basis for recombinations. They lead naturally to grammatical
explanations and intensive practice exercises through which the operation
of the rule, or paradigm, becomes clear to the student, enters his active
repertoire, and is then used by him in a genuinely communicative interchange.

Other dialogues, which we shall call *conversation-facilitation dialogues,*
are intended primarily to provide students with a stock of useful expressions (clichés of conversation, frequently used expressions, conventional

greetings, expletives, and rejoinders) with which to practice conversing, while the teaching of the grammar proceeds as a parallel but distinct activity.

C17   JACQUES   Salut, Georges. Comment vas-tu?
     GEORGES   Pas mal. Et toi?
     JACQUES   Bien, merci. Tu viens en ville?
     GEORGES   D'accord. Tout de suite?

Students memorize the segments, which have been selected because of their potential usefulness, and then practice using them in recombinations to form new dialogues involving different personalities.

Many dialogues combine both of these functions: grammar demonstration and conversation facilitation. It is important to recognize the type of dialogue with which you are dealing so that it may be used for the purpose for which it was constructed.

A third type of dialogue we may call *recreational*. This is the familiar skit or *saynète*. This activity has always been popular with students and teachers in an orally oriented approach.[32] It is a true bridging activity which provides for spontaneous creation within the limits of what is being learned. It is discussed under *Dialogue Exploitation*, p. 36.

Dialogue construction and adaptation

You should be able to recognize the good and bad features of dialogues for several reasons:

—so that you can select well-written materials for use in classroom teaching or in individualized learning packets;

—so that you can rewrite poorly constructed dialogues when you are forced to use materials selected by others;

—so that you can write dialogues yourself, if you wish to supplement available materials (e.g., you may decide to prepare a dialogue based on a story which has been read).

GRAMMAR-DEMONSTRATION DIALOGUES

C18   1. MARIE   Où irez-vous demain?
     2. LOUISE   J'irai voir mon amie Jacqueline qui demeure dans un petit village.
     3. MARIE   Que ferez-vous là-bas?
     4. LOUISE   Nous visiterons la vieille abbaye et nous ferons des promenades dans la forêt.

5.	MARIE	Qu'y a-t-il à voir dans un petit village?
6.	LOUISE	Beaucoup de choses—de vieilles maisons, des jardins, des animaux, et une école.
7.	MARIE	Resterez-vous plusieurs jours?
8.	LOUISE	Bien entendu. Je ne rentrerai pas avant la semaine prochaine.
9.	MARIE	Préférez-vous un petit village ou une grande ville?
10.	LOUISE	Je préfère un petit village.
11.	MARIE	Et moi, j'aime mieux une grande ville.

Commentary

1. As a sustained exchange between two friends, this dialogue is very artificial and stilted. It has been laboriously constructed to include various persons of the future tense of regular -er verbs and of certain common irregular verbs, as well as plural forms of the partitive article.

2. *Contemporary usage.* Certain features of authentic modern speech have been completely ignored.

a. Two friends of school age would use the *tu* form. There is some controversy about the usefulness of the *tu* form for foreign students. Some say that foreigners rarely reach a stage of intimacy where the use of *tu* is acceptable and may offend by using it too freely. It is, of course, commonly used among students in France and it is becoming much more acceptable in many situations of contemporary French life, especially among the younger generation. Offense can be caused by the person who is insensitive to the right moment for using *tu* as well as by the person who uses it inappropriately. Furthermore, students who have not experienced through use the different relationships which *tu* and *vous* imply in various situations will miss many nuances in their later reading. It is the teacher's role to train students in correct use of the two forms. See also C56.

b. *Tenses.* In sentence 1, the *present tense* would certainly be used in conversation for a project so close at hand, instead of the future tense which pushes the action into a more remote, less certain domain: *Où allez-vous demain?* (Contrast: *Que ferez-vous l'année prochaine?*)

This choice of present tense in the question would attract a response in the *immediate future* form in 2: *je vais voir mon amie.* The immediate future would also be used in 3: *Que vas-tu faire . . . ,* in 4: *nous allons visiter . . . nous allons faire,* and in 7: *Vas-tu rester . . .*

In 8: *je ne rentrerai pas avant la semaine prochaine,* the future tense would be retained because it demonstrates the use of this tense for a not-too-distant future for which plans are not absolutely definite. This indefiniteness is here reinforced by the use of the negative: *je ne rentrerai pas.*

c. In 3 and 7, the inversion form of the *question* with the pronoun is acceptable: *Que vas-tu faire . . . ?* and *Vas-tu rester . . . ?* Other possibilities in common use which should be practiced and which could have been included to give the passage a more authentic flavor are: *Qu'est-ce que tu vas faire . . . ? Est-ce que tu vas rester . . . ?* or merely *Tu vas rester . . . ?* with rising intonation. (Practice in the latter form, which is in very frequent use in conversation, is often neglected in the classroom.)

d. *Demeure* in sentence 2 is an old-fashioned word in this sense; *habite* would be used in contemporary French.

3. *Weaknesses in the construction of the dialogue*

a. In sentence 4, unfamiliar vocabulary and difficulties of pronunciation coincide quite unnecessarily in *vieille abbaye* /vjɛjabei/. The simpler, familiar word *église* is a perfectly good substitute in this context.

b. Sentence 6 is incredibly trite, constructed with the obvious intent of introducing certain forms of the partitive article.

c. Certain questions which seem clearly to have been introduced into the dialogue because of their usefulness for an unimaginative question-answer period in class add to the artificiality of the dialogue: *Préferez-vous un petit village ou une grande ville? J'aime mieux . . . Préférez-vous la vie à la campagne ou dans une grande ville? Préférez-vous des vacances à la campagne ou au bord de la mer?* (Similarly: *Qu'y a-t-il à voir . . . ?*)

C19 *Rewritten,* with sentences shortened and language and usage modernized, this dialogue might read as follows:

MARIE-FRANCE	Où vas-tu demain?
ANNICK	Je vais voir mon amie Jacqueline. Elle habite un petit village pas loin d'ici.
MARIE-FRANCE	Qu'est-ce que tu vas faire là-bas?
ANNICK	Nous allons visiter la vieille église et nous ferons peut-être quelques promenades dans la forêt.
MARIE-FRANCE	Tu vas rester plusieurs jours?
ANNICK	Bien sûr. Je ne rentrerai pas avant la semaine prochaine.

Commentary

This shorter dialogue demonstrates the use of the immediate future and the future tense in the matrix of a possible conversation which could be exploited in various ways apart from its grammatical purpose. Clearly the complete morphology of the future tense cannot be appropriately taught through a dialogue, but this short version which includes three persons of the immediate future and two forms of the future tense, one of which is irregular, provides a basis for discussion of the contemporary uses of these forms. In C18, four irregular and three regular forms of the future tense appear in a very unrealistic dialogue, with no use of the immediate future. Not only is there no clear demonstration of appropriate use, but the student is given a very false view of conversational possibilities.

* Find some grammar-demonstration dialogues in textbooks in current use, comment on their good and bad features, and practice rewriting the least effective of them.

CONVERSATION-FACILITATION DIALOGUES

Many textbooks include dialogues purely for the purpose of providing students in the early stages with *useful utterances and exclamations* which, with variations of vocabulary, can be recombined in all kinds of personal ways to make possible active classroom conversation and creative skits. Well written and presented, such dialogues can provide the student with a fund of very authentic expressions for use at a stage when his overall knowledge of the language is still quite minimal. This ability to put together something meaningful encourages him with a sense of progress.

C20 1. JEAN-MARC   Bonjour, Pierre.
     2.   PIERRE   Bonjour, Jean-Marc. Où vas-tu? Au cinéma?
     3. JEAN-MARC   Non. J'ai faim. Je vais déjeuner.
     4.   PIERRE   Tiens! J'ai faim aussi, moi.
     5. JEAN-MARC   Viens avec moi, si tu veux.
     6.   PIERRE   D'accord. Où allons-nous?
     7. JEAN-MARC   Il y a un bon petit restaurant près de la gare.
     8.   PIERRE   Ah ça alors! Voilà Marie-Claude qui arrive! Je ne veux pas la voir.
     9. JEAN-MARC   Moi non plus. Vite, on s'en va!

Commentary

1. With this type of dialogue, students are expected to memorize the sentences (through active role-playing) so that they can produce them quickly in new situations. This provides practice in the rhythm of the phrase and in specific intonation patterns.

2. The dialogue would be learned and practiced in sections (1-3, 1-7, 1-9). In other words, the dialogue is open-ended.

3. Utterances are short or are easily divided into short, meaningful segments (*j'ai faim, près de la gare, on s'en va*). The aim of the memorizing is for the students to be able to use these segments freely in new combinations, and to learn to vary segments semantically, not to know the sixteen utterances by heart so that they can produce them parrot-fashion in the original sequence.

4. Students will learn short utterances like these easily by acting out the dialogue in small groups. The memorization and recall process are aided by visuals: flashcards, stick figures, flannel board, puppets, vanishing techniques (where the dialogue is written on the chalkboard with major elements of the phrase being obliterated one by one until students know the complete utterance thoroughly).

5. Small groups will perform their version of the dialogue for the others. Meaningful deviations from the original wording and paraphrases will be welcomed as indications that the students have indeed assimilated the material in a more than superficial way. The students will be encouraged to develop new situations, including as often as possible material learned in other dialogues or in other classwork. (See *Dialogue Exploitation,* below.)

6. Conversation-facilitation dialogues do not follow a question-answer, question-answer sequence. This is not the natural mode of ordinary conversation. C20 consists of greeting, greeting returned, question, question, answer, explanation, statement, exclamation, statement, suggestion, acceptance, question, oblique answer, exclamation, statement, statement, suggestion.

7. Items are not exploited grammatically or paradigmatically as they would tend to be in a grammar-demonstration dialogue. Here students are familiarized, in a meaningful context, with constructions which they may not study systematically for some time (e.g., *je ne veux pas la voir*) but which are immediately useable in their present form and in semantic variants (*je ne veux pas la casser, je ne veux pas le lire*).

8. Many modern textbook writers would consider C20 too long for an early dialogue. The material in it can easily be rewritten as a spiral series.

SPIRAL SERIES OF DIALOGUES

Short dialogues are usually more useful than longer dialogues. The interrelated content of two response pairs is more easily remembered than the development of thought in six response pairs. One response pair (A to B) allows little scope for an interesting mini-situation, although it is used as the basic unit in the Cummings device illustrated in C29.

Sometimes several short dialogues develop a continuing theme, each in succession using some of the linguistic material from the one preceding. Such a succession of dialogues is called a spiral series. As students exploit each section, they are consolidating material already learned, and the now-familiar material makes the learning of the new material more meaningful. Dialogue C19 could be developed spirally as follows:

C21   1. MARIE-FRANCE   Où vas-tu demain, Annick?
            ANNICK   Je vais voir mon amie Jacqueline.
        MARIE-FRANCE   Où habite-t-elle?
            ANNICK   Elle habite un petit village pas loin d'ici.

    2. MARIE-FRANCE   Qui vas-tu voir demain?
            ANNICK   Mon amie Jacqueline qui habite un petit village.
        MARIE-FRANCE   Est-ce loin d'ici?
            ANNICK   Non, c'est ce petit village avec la vieille église.

    3. MARIE-FRANCE   Quand est-ce que tu vas voir ton amie Jacqueline?
            ANNICK   Demain. Nous allons visiter une vieille église dans son village.
        MARIE-FRANCE   C'est ce village près de la forêt de Fontainebleau, n'est-ce pas?
            ANNICK   C'est ça, et nous ferons peut-être quelques promenades dans la forêt pendant mon séjour.

    4. MARIE-FRANCE   Est-ce que tu vas faire quelques promenades dans la forêt avec ton amie Jacqueline?
            ANNICK   Bien sûr. Je resterai chez elle plusieurs jours.
        MARIE-FRANCE   Tu vas visiter aussi la vieille église de Saint-Séverin?
            ANNICK   Oui, j'aurai largement le temps. Je ne rentrerai pas avant la semaine prochaine.

Commentary

Practice with expanding dialogues gives students the confidence for making up their own recombinations and original skits and provides a useful link with writing. The spiral sequence above gives experience with immediate future and future tenses, different types of questions, and the varied possibilities of use of simple adverbial phrases.

✳ Rewrite C20 as a spiral series.

Many textbook writers are criticized for writing dialogues which are culturally neutral, that is, which deal with situations like the one in C20 which could take place in any culture.

Some critics would argue that C20 would convey a feeling for French everyday culture if its content were more like the following:

C22 JEAN-MARC Bonjour, Pierre.
          PIERRE Bonjour, Jean-Marc. Où vas-tu en ce moment?
      JEAN-MARC J'ai une lettre à mettre à la poste, mais je n'ai pas de timbre.
          PIERRE Il y a un bureau de tabac tout près d'ici. Veux-tu que je te montre le chemin?

This dialogue conveys the useful piece of information for a visitor to France that he should look for a tobacconist's shop if he wants to buy stamps for his postcards, whereas in most other countries he would expect to buy them in a post office. This kind of superficial difference in social organization has no deep significance and, if such snippets of information are over-emphasized by repetition and exploitation in dialogues, students may well develop the attitude that the French persist in doing things in odd ways for no apparent reason. This type of factual information can also become outdated overnight as a result of a shift in social organization or habits. (Note, for instance, the recent radical changes in the French educational system, and the influence of the increasing number of refrigerators and supermarkets on the French housewife's traditional routine.)

True cultural understanding means an appreciation of basically different attitudes and values which are reflected in the things people do, but are not necessarily explicitly stated. It is difficult to work such concepts into short situational exchanges without oversimplifying and stereotyping social behavior.

The following dialogue,[33] obviously for students with some experience in reading, does convey a basic French value which is reflected in many aspects of individual and social life.

C23 Le père Dubois, restaurateur, s'entretient avec un de ses clients.
          DUBOIS Alors? Ça vous plaît?
      LE CLIENT Votre cuisine est absolument délicieuse. Tous mes compliments. Je ne connais personne qui sache faire la bouillabaisse comme vous.
          DUBOIS Quand le client est content, je suis content aussi.

LE CLIENT   Mais, dites-moi un peu. Pourquoi n'agrandissez-vous pas
              votre restaurant? Vous auriez une clientèle monstre et on
              serait moins serré.

DUBOIS   Je n'en suis pas tellement sûr. Les temps peuvent changer,
              vous savez.

LE CLIENT   Ne me dites pas que les touristes deviennent moins nom-
              breux.

DUBOIS   Peut-être pas. Mais, voyez-vous, si je voulais recevoir plus de
              clients, il faudrait construire, embaucher un autre cuisinier.
              J'aurais toutes sortes d'ennuis, quoi!

LE CLIENT   Mais une fois que ce serait fait, vous pourriez vous croiser
              les bras.

DUBOIS   Ma cuisine ne serait plus la même si elle était produite en
              série. Vous ne voudriez tout de même pas que je sacrifie la
              qualité à la quantité, non?

LE CLIENT   Vous avez raison. Je n'avais pas envisagé la question sous cet
              angle-là.

DUBOIS   Alors, encore un peu de bouillabaisse?

LE CLIENT   Non. Mais réservez-moi une table demain.

DUBOIS   Entendu. Je vous préparerai une spécialité à moi. Vous m'en
              direz des nouvelles.

✻ Examine some textbook dialogues which purport to convey some understanding of French culture. Analyze the cultural content in the following
terms: Is the cultural content of a superficial nature, reflecting interesting
but insignificant aspects of behavior or social organization, or are the features portrayed surface indicators of deeper attitudes and values?

CHECKLIST FOR ORIGINAL OR REWRITTEN DIALOGUES

1. Do I intend this to be a grammar-demonstration, a conversation-
facilitation, or a recreational dialogue?

2. Is the conversation interesting and natural? Do the participants say
something worthwhile? Have I avoided the question-answer-question-
answer format?

3. What points of grammar (or conversational items) do I wish students to assimilate?

4. Is my list so ambitious that it has made the dialogue stilted and un-
natural? (What can I omit while still achieving my purpose? See C18.)

5. Can I increase the redundancy to make the conversation more
natural? (See C2.)

6. Can I include more expletives and rejoinders to make it sound more spontaneous? (See Chapter 4: G44.)

7. Are the levels of language I have used appropriate and consistent? (See C5.)

8. Is the dialogue of a reasonable length for classroom use and exploitation? (Is it open-ended? Should I rewrite it as a spiral series?)

9. Are individual utterances short enough to be assimilated or, alternatively, do they break naturally into useful segments?

10. Have I reentered lexical items, idioms, and grammatical structures from previous dialogues to refresh the students' memory?

11. In how many ways can this dialogue be exploited? (See below.)

12. Does the situation lend itself naturally to interesting or amusing recombinations? Is it likely to stimulate students to produce their own recreational dialogues or skits?

Dialogue exploitation

The dialogue as a teaching technique has come in for much criticism because it has been used unimaginatively and its full potential ignored. There is more than one way to use a dialogue. In fact, the possibilities are so extensive that one could actually exploit each dialogue differently for a whole semester, if one wished.

DIALOGUE MEMORIZATION

The most criticized way of teaching through dialogues has required of each student that he memorize every dialogue completely and thoroughly (and this often for dialogues of fifteen or twenty sentences) and that he be able to recite the whole sequence on demand. This type of activity is time-consuming and tedious and gives indefensible importance to a particular sequence of utterances. As a result, students are at a loss when they do not hear the precise cue they are expecting. They become discouraged and exasperated by the mistakes they make in recalling memorized materials— mistakes which have nothing to do with their comprehension and assimilation of the material.

As has been noted earlier, there is no need for memorization of *grammar-demonstration dialogues*. A certain amount of repetition to ensure correct, fluent production is sufficient. Thorough exploitation with variety, in the ways suggested below, paralleled by as much grammatical explanation as the students need, will ensure understanding of the principles behind the structures used, while judicious practice in their meaningful use in all kinds of variations of their original setting will prepare students to use them perceptively in utterances of their own creation.

Similarly, vocabulary will be retained more thoroughly if used frequently in various contexts.

Conversation-facilitation dialogues, which are short and full of expressions of wide applicability, may be memorized to the point where the useful segments, rather than the original sequence, are immediately available for use. Meaningful variations of the sequence will be welcomed as signs of real assimilation of the material. Recall may be aided by the use of a series of pictures on film, flashcards, or transparencies for overhead projection. Some teachers in the early stages like to have an English translation readily available when the student momentarily forgets the sequence of the dialogue; others reject this aid, preferring to concentrate on direct association of utterance and action.

WAYS OF PRESENTING AND LEARNING FROM THE DIALOGUE

With imagination the teacher can vary ways of presenting the dialogue. There are *five aspects* of the dialogue activity which need to be provided for if the energy expended is to yield any fruit in terms of the students' growing ability to function freely in the language.

1. Some *setting of the scene* to arouse student interest in the content of the dialogue and facilitate comprehension of the language used.

For example: acting out the conversation first of all in English or in mime, with appropriate props; discussion of the content of the dialogue with the help of pictures, slides, flashcards, projected diagrams, maps, plans; discussion of some aspect of life or some social situation for which the dialogue will supply a cultural contrast; some classroom language activity of the direct method or Gouin type (C11–13) which relates to the content of the dialogue; some preparing of the semantic area through discussion or through a competition or game; the recounting in the foreign language of an incident or anecdote of related interest, or the showing and discussion in English of a cartoon or a series of stick figures related to the theme. For a *grammar-demonstration* dialogue: raising some questions about the grammatical problem to arouse interest in its manifestations in the script and as a stimulus to the students to find out for themselves how the rule works.

2. Some technique for *focusing student attention* on the meaning of the interchange.

For example: students may be asked to listen to the whole dialogue on tape several times as a listening comprehension exercise, with opportunity between each hearing for group piecing together of the meaning; students may listen to the dialogue as they watch a series of slides, or look at a series of sketches illustrating the content of the interchange; students may be supplied ahead of time with a set of questions for which they should find answers as they listen to the dialogue; sometimes, for variety, students may be given the written script of the dialogue to peruse and ask questions about before listening to it without the script.

3. Some *familiarization* of students with the actual utterances in the dialogue through an activity which makes cognitive demands on them.[34]

For example: as students in the initial stage repeat the lines of the dialogue to develop fluency in their production, they take roles, group speaking to group or class to teacher, until they can handle the material with reasonable efficiency; after hearing an utterance two or three times, students try to reconstruct it as a group endeavor; the teacher writes the material on the board and gradually erases sections to see if students are repeating meaningfully and can supply the erased portions (erasures increase in length). For a *conversation-facilitation* dialogue: some students mime the dialogue while the class supplies the words; students go off in pairs and practice taking roles, testing each other on knowledge of the material; students act out the roles on an individual basis or as group presentations.

4. Some *formal manipulation* of the material in the dialogue, exploiting the useful expressions in a *conversation-facilitation* dialogue or the morphological and syntactic items in a *grammar-demonstration* dialogue.

For example: directed dialogue or guided conversation (see C24); group recombinations for similar but slightly different situations; chain dialogue (see C25). For *grammar-demonstration* dialogues: analysis of rules demonstrated in the material, leading into intensive practice through the various kinds of oral exercises described in Chapter 4. For *conversation-facilitation* dialogues: items of the dialogue may be used as personal questions to students who either answer for themselves or pretend through their answers to be someone else (the teacher or other students guess who they are); the teacher, or a student, establishes a situation by a remark and another student responds with a suitable expletive or rejoinder (*riposter du tac au tac* is the French expression for this type of activity):

A Je ne peux pas déjeuner avec toi.
 Je n'ai plus d'argent.
B Dommage! (*or* Sans blague?);

for a given expletive, the student creates an utterance:

A *Tiens!* B Tiens! Voilà ta cousine qui arrive!
A *Pardon* B Pardon, où est la rue de la Paix?

5. Some ways in which the dialogue material can be used in the *creation of new utterances and new dialogue* expressing the students' own

whims, feelings, and imaginings. The suggestions below encourage students to draw on anything they know from previous dialogues, from group conversation, or from reading, in preparing their versions. (They should, however, be discouraged from seeking extra vocabulary in dictionaries at this stage.)

For example: the creation of a similar situation in another setting (the irate shopper demanding money back for a faulty appliance becomes the irate air traveler demanding a refund for a ticket, or a householder trying to get rid of a door-to-door salesman becomes a television viewer trying to cut off a telephone advertiser); group preparation, using a series of pictures of a different setting and a climactic utterance (*Mais elle est cassée!*) as a basis for a dialogue with a similar dénouement to the one already studied. See also suggestions for *Recreational Dialogues,* below.

DIRECTED DIALOGUE OR GUIDED CONVERSATION

The teacher prompts pairs of students to reproduce sections of the dialogue. Directed dialogue may be conducted in several ways.

C24 (Working from C20)

a. TEACHER TO STUDENT A

>Ask B where he's going.

STUDENT A Où vas-tu, Michel?

TEACHER TO STUDENT B

>Tell him you're going to lunch.

STUDENT B Je vais déjeuner.

b. TEACHER TO STUDENTS A & B You meet each other in the corridor and one of you asks the other where he's going. The other replies he's going to lunch.

STUDENT A Où vas-tu, Michel?

STUDENT B Je vais déjeuner.

c. TEACHER TO STUDENT A

>Demande(z) [21] à Michel où il va.

STUDENT A Où vas-tu, Michel?

TEACHER TO STUDENT B

>Réponds (Répondez) à Pierre que tu vas (vous allez) déjeuner.

STUDENT B Je vais déjeuner.

Commentary

Directed dialogue is more difficult than most teachers realize because it involves a transformation of the teacher's cue for which students must be well prepared. Any potential usefulness is often negated by the amount of time devoted to the pure mechanics of the performance. *It is sometimes helpful to perform the operation several times in English to accustom the students to the procedure before using any of the approaches suggested.*

d. TEACHER TO STUDENTS A & B Vous vous rencontrez dans le couloir et l'un d'entre vous demande à l'autre où il va et l'autre répond qu'il va déjeuner.

STUDENT A Où vas-tu, Michel?
STUDENT B Je vais déjeuner.

Commentary

Here the language of the directions is more complex than the language, possibly memorized, of the response. This can make the exercise confusing and difficult for an elementary-level student.

CHAIN DIALOGUE

This is a challenging and amusing way for students to practice retrieval of many expressions and structures they have learned. It can begin with very recent material (for instance, a response pair from C20), but should soon develop into a competition to think up questions and answers of all kinds.

C25 TEACHER TO A Où vas-tu, Michel?
          A Je vais déjeuner.
    A TO B Viens avec moi, si tu veux.
          B D'accord.
    B TO C Où allons-nous?
          C Au cinéma.
    C TO D Aimes-tu les films?
          D Non, je préfère la télévision.
    D TO E Quel âge as-tu?
          E J'ai quatorze ans.
    E TO F Et toi?

Rubbishing the dialogue

As a variation of the chain dialogue, but with a similar aim of developing flexibility by drawing on all kinds of expressions which the students have acquired, one team of students (Jacques) undertakes to keep to the utterances in the dialogue recently studied, the other team (Pierre) thinks up possible responses other than those learned. (Later the teams exchange roles.) Students try to remain within the bounds of what they have learned but may ask the teacher occasionally for a few new expressions, thus adding to their repertoire things they would like to say. (Since this is a satirical approach there is no need for the resulting sequence to be semantically probable.)

C26 (Based on C20.)

JACQUES Bonjour, Pierre.

PIERRE Bonjour, monsieur. Est-ce que je vous connais? (*or* Je ne comprends pas, monsieur; *or* Pardon, vous me parlez?)

JACQUES Où vas-tu? Au cinéma?

PIERRE Non, je reste ici. (*or* Non, je vais me coucher; *or* Ça ne vous regarde pas; *or* Qu'est-ce que c'est qu'un cinéma?)

JACQUES Viens avec moi, si tu veux.

PIERRE Quelle idée! (*or* Ah! ça alors; *or* Non, je ne veux pas; *or* D'accord, si tu paies le billet!) . . .

THE DIALOGUE AS A CULMINATING ACTIVITY

It has become customary to think of the dialogue as an introductory teaching technique, but it can also come at the end of a unit of study, whether dialogues are or are not used as a technique in the body of the lesson. In this case, it demonstrates in operation in a realistic situation what has been studied analytically. It is then enjoyed as an opportunity to express oneself in language and structures which are now familiar. This is the place for the *recreational dialogue, skit,* or *saynète.*

As a bridging activity, the *recreational dialogue* should have as its starting point a situation for which the student has some vocabulary and expressions available to him. "Situation" here is used in its broadest sense: a person alone in a house who hears a strange noise outside the window experiences a similar nervous reaction to a person watching a spider weave its web from the ceiling to a shelf of his bookcase and may very well exclaim in the same fashion: "Mon dieu! qu'est-ce que je vais faire!"

Most students need the stimulus of seminal ideas such as the following, which take them from the shelter of the cove further and further into the open sea.

1. Skits may be based on an adaptation of the type of situation in a dialogue they have just been studying: two people discussing their meal in a restaurant become the seven dwarfs grumbling about the meal Snow-White has prepared; two people meeting in a supermarket become a boy meeting a girl at the school dance.

2. Students are given one side of a conversation which is not explicit and are asked to create a dialogue. Different groups act out their versions.

C27   A   Pardon, qu'est-ce que vous avez là?

B   . . . .

A   Mais, je n'en ai jamais vu comme ça!

B   . . . .

A   Il (Elle) vous plaît quand même?

B   . . . .

A   Excusez-moi. Malheureusement, j'ai du travail à faire.

3. Students are given a response-pair beginning: *A: Qui t'a dit ça? Ta sœur? B: Pas du tout. Elle n'était pas à la maison.* They extemporize a response-pair completion (or prepare a longer completion). Students should not strive each time for wit, which requires fairly sophisticated manipulation of language, but rather for a sensible conclusion.

C28   ANDRÉ   Qui t'a dit ça? Ta sœur?

BERNARD   Pas du tout. Elle n'était pas à la maison.

ANDRÉ   Mais je l'ai vu sur le balcon!

BERNARD   Non, c'était ma mère. Elles se ressemblent.

4. Students are given a punch line and different groups work out short skits leading up to it. (*Mais il est déjà parti!* or *Non, non, non! pas moi! pas moi!*)

5. Skits are based on a list of words providing basic elements (*train, vieille dame, deux étudiants en vacances, frontière, douanier, petite enveloppe blanche, le lendemain*).

6. Students prepare puppet plays using the particular settings of recent dialogues (*restaurant; banque; chez la grand'mère*). Timid or reticent students will often express themselves in the voice of a puppet.

7. Students create original dialogue arising from an ambiguous picture, or a cartoon without caption. The pictures chosen should show an obviously emotional situation, a predicament involving two or more people, or some incongruity.

8. Students invent dialogues based on problems caused by differences in everyday living in France; e.g., a foreign visitor to a French home finds himself looking at a plate of *escargots;* problems of two tourists trying to

find a French acquaintance in an apartment building (*sonnette, concierge, minuterie, ascenseur, premier étage*).

The Cummings device [35]

One attempt to link structural practice and lexical exploration to communication is Stevick's Cummings device, based on the two-utterance communication. Stevick says, "The shorter a dialog, the less unexplained, confusing clutter it contains." [36] As a technique for moving from manipulation of structures to communication at each learning step, the Cummings device merits a place in this section on bridging activities.

"Cummings device" is Stevick's preferred term for what he earlier called his "microwave cycle." He describes the device as follows:

The . . . format itself, in what we may a little wryly call its "classical form," contained a basic utterance (usually but not always a question) and from four to eight potential answers or other appropriate rejoinders. If the basic utterance and the rejoinders are well chosen, they can lead to almost immediate real or realistic . . . conversation in class, and are also likely to find use in real life outside of class. At the same time, new structures and new vocabulary can be kept to a minimum.

A . . . "cycle" was divided into an M-phase and a C-phase. *M* stood for *m*imicry, *m*anipulation, *m*echanics and *m*emorization, and *C* for *c*ommunication, *c*onversation, and *c*ontinuity. Within the M-phase, the first section usually introduced the answers or rejoinders, often in the form of a substitution drill with a separate column for cue words. The second section contained the question(s) or other basic utterance(s). The C-phase combined the elements of the M-phase with each other and, ideally, with material from earlier lessons, to form a short sample conversation. [37]

The C series is so designed that lexical items are easily substitutable (substitutable items being placed in parentheses as a guide). As Stevick explains,

it is only through this kind of "delexicalization" that one can get away from content words chosen either at the whim of the textbook writer, or for their high frequency in the language as a whole, and that one can insure the use of the content words that are of high frequency in the student's immediate surroundings. In this way, through localization and personalization of vocabulary, we improve the likelihood that language *study* will be replaced by language *use*, and that language *use* will become a part of the group life of the students. [38]

The usefulness of this technique is that the teacher who has mastered the principle can derive Cummings devices, as need and interest suggest, from any materials—lessons in books, newspaper articles, material heard on tape, radio, or film track, or ongoing communicative activities. As with any device, it is intended, not as the whole of the course, but as one among the many possible activities which provide variety for student learning.

C29 *The Cummings device*

M-1   Jean travaille en ville.

Nous   Nous travaillons en ville.

Annick et Pierre   Annick et Pierre travaillent en ville.

tous les jours   Annick et Pierre travaillent tous les jours.

huit heures par jour   Annick et Pierre travaillent huit heures par jour.

Vous   Vous travaillez huit heures par jour.

Jacqueline   Jacqueline travaille huit heures par jour.

dans un bureau   Jacqueline travaille dans un bureau.

aujourd'hui   Jacqueline travaille aujourd'hui.

Nous   Nous travaillons aujourd'hui.

M-2   Est-ce que vous travaillez tous les jours?

Non, je ne travaille pas tous les jours.

M-3   Où est-ce que vous travaillez?

Quand est-ce que vous travaillez?

Combien de temps est-ce que vous travaillez?

C-1   A   Est-ce que vous travaillez dans (un bureau)?

      B   Non, je ne travaille pas dans un bureau.

      A   Est-ce que Camille travaille dans (un bureau)?

      B   Non, elle travaille dans (un magasin).

      A   Est-ce que vous travaillez (aujourd'hui)?

      B   Oui, je travaille (tous les jours)...

C-2   A   Où est-ce que vous (travaillez)?

      B   Je travaille (en ville).

      A   Est-ce que vous travaillez (à Chicago)?

      B   Oui, je travaille (là).

      A   Quand est-ce que vous (travaillez)?

      B   Je travaille (tous les jours).

      A   Combien d'(heures) est-ce que Robert (travaille) par (jour)?

      B   Il travaille (huit) (heures) par (jour).

      A   Combien de (jours) est-ce que vous (travaillez) par (semaine)?

      B   (Cinq) (jours) par (semaine).

C-3   A   (Vous) travaillez (à Chicago)?

      B   Oui, (je) travaille là.

B   (On) travaille (huit) (heures) par (jour) ici?
C   Non, (nous) travaillons (sept) (heures) par (jour).

Note that in the C (Communication) phases the questions will be per-sonalized: names and activities used will be those of members of the class.

Stevick warns his readers that the device "is not a theory, nor a method, but only a format," [39] that there are a number of pitfalls to be avoided in writing individual cycles (these are discussed in Chapter 6 of Stevick, 1971), and that no course should consist of just one format. "Procedures and systems and approaches," he says, "supplement one another more than they supersede one another." [40]

THE CUMMINGS DEVICE AND CULTURAL INFORMATION

In C29, questions and answers refer to general activities of daily life in any society. The device can also be used to interest students in differences between daily activities in their own country and in France. The following types of information could be incorporated in a Cummings device based on question forms.

C30   En France on achète des timbres dans un bureau de tabac.
En France est-ce qu'on achète des enveloppes dans une pharmacie?
Où est-ce qu'on achète des boîtes de peinture? (Dans une droguerie.)

✱   Try to construct a Cummings device incorporating the type of information in C30.

Oral reports

Up to this point most of the bridging activities discussed have involved questions and answers, short statements and comments, requests, and ex-clamations. Another important facet of communicating includes describing, narrating, and explaining, all of which involve more sustained speech. Very early in the language course, students should have opportunities to practice these skills, taking as topics whatever suggests itself in the course of their reading or classroom activities. Reading passages, dialogues, sets of pictures, films, magazines, or class discussions of aspects of the country, its achievements, and the people who live in it provide basic vocabulary and ideas from which the students fan out in a creative way.

1. Reports at first are *short* (four or five sentences), later expanding as the students gain in confidence and experience. Students are always encouraged to ask the presenter questions about details of the report.

2. Initial efforts may be combined ones. Students in small groups con-

struct their reports orally, with one student writing the group production on a chalkboard while the others criticize and improve on it until all are satisfied. When the class is next reassembled, a spokesman for the group gives the description or narration orally, without referring to a script, and students from other groups ask questions. (The role of presenter is taken by different members of the group on successive occasions.)

3. In Lenard's verbal-active method, oral compositions play an important role.[41] She reiterates to her students the slogan: "Une excellente composition est originale, imaginative, correcte. Dictionnaire? Non, non, absolument non."[42] After the composition has been thoroughly discussed and worked over orally in class, it is written out and corrected by the teacher. "There is no point," Lenard says, ". . . in permanently recording . . . anything that has not reached its best possible form."[43]

We may add that, at least by the intermediate level, teachers need to give students help in the effective use of the dictionary, and some oral reports can then be devised as demonstrations of successful dictionary search. (See Chapter 9: *Exploring the Dictionary*.) In these cases, presenters explain in simple French paraphrases any specialized vocabulary they have used, thus developing another useful skill.

4. Early reports may be guided in a number of ways.

a. A sequential series of questions is provided on what has been read, viewed, or discussed, or on a similar, but personalized, situation.

C31 (Based on R38.)

Vous êtes à Paris. Où désirez-vous aller? Pourquoi? Quel moyen de transport choisissez-vous? Décrivez-le. Un homme en uniforme vous parle. Qui est-ce? Qu'est-ce qu'il vous demande? Qu'est-ce qu'il vous donne? Où descendez-vous? Qu'est-ce que vous voyez?

With an undefined series such as this, the students' answers become very diverse: they may be drawn directly from the text or may deviate considerably from it; e.g., instead of going to the Quartier Latin by bus, the student may decide to go to Chartres by train to see the cathedral, or to the Place de la République by *métro*.

b. The student is given a series of pictures with no questions attached, the interpretation being left entirely to his imagination or invention.

c. A framework of key words forms a skeleton outline.

C32 Vous allez partir en avion.

Préparatifs — voiture — stationnement — bagages — billet — consigne — salle d'attente — journal — deux jeunes amoureux — garçon qui est désagréable — deux matelots — annonce — embarquement — départ.

d. Persons, places, or things in the students' own environment lead to mystery descriptions for which the other students guess the referent.

5. A simple form of oral report is a regular *Show and Tell* (*Montrer-raconter*) session, where students of their own volition share with their classmates things they have discovered about France, French Canada, Haiti, Tahiti, or French-speaking Africa, and show objects imported from these countries, stamps, postcards, maps, menus, objets d'art, and bric-à-brac brought back by touring relatives.

6. Oral reports are an essential part of learning about the great figures and artistic, scientific, and social achievements of the people as well as their pleasures and aspirations in daily living; students prepare individual and group presentations as a culmination to their research on specific topics.

7. At more advanced stages, many opportunities arise for students to explain and discuss what they have been reading, hearing, or seeing in films, or to discuss topics of general interest arising from these or from current events in the news.

Situation tapes

Cartier[44] reports experimentation with situational conversations on tape for individual practice. The student hears the voices of two or more persons who are ostensibly conversing with him; spaces are left for him to record his parts of the interchange. The conversations are so designed that the student is led to make replies consistent with their drift, although what he actually says and how he says it are his own choice. The interlocutors call each other by their names and soon the student feels that he knows them and that they are actually speaking to him. After he has recorded his responses, he listens to the completed conversation and then re-records it as often as he wishes until he is satisfied with his part. (After all, we always think of that clever response after the crucial moment has passed.) The context can also be filled in with visuals. No monitoring or correction is supplied, the student being perfectly free to express himself to the best of his ability. In this way, the less confident student is able to practice real communication without the embarrassment of expressing himself inadequately in front of others.

C33 Pierre et Jacques vous rencontrent devant le cinéma.

The student is shown a picture of the cinema, with the name of the film being shown and a notice stating the times at which it will be shown. Italicized speeches are on the tape. A blip* indicates when the student is expected to reply.

PIERRE	*Salut, mon vieux. Tu viens voir ce film aussi?**
ÉTUDIANT	Oui, on dit que c'est un bon film.
or	Oui, je n'ai rien d'autre à faire.
or	Non, je passais par ici tout simplement.
JACQUES	*Ma sœur m'a dit que c'est un film excellent.*
PIERRE	*Personnellement, moi, je n'en sais rien. Et toi?**
ÉTUDIANT	J'ai des camarades qui l'ont vu.
or	Moi, je n'en sais rien, non plus.
or	Non, je n'en ai jamais entendu parler . . .
PIERRE	*Qu'est-ce que tu vas faire maintenant, Jacques?*
JACQUES	*Rien. Je flâne un peu.*
PIERRE	*Nous t'accompagnons, si tu veux. Tu attends quelqu'un peut-être?**
ÉTUDIANT	Oui, j'attends une amie (un copain).
or	Non, je suis tout seul.
JACQUES	*Nous avons du temps. Tu as soif, Pierre? Si on prenait un café ici à côté?*
PIERRE	*C'est une bonne idée. A quelle heure est-ce que le film va commencer?**
ÉTUDIANT	Dans dix minutes, je crois.
or	A vingt heures, paraît-il.
or	Il va commencer tout de suite . . .

* Imagine you are on the beach at St. Tropez. Try to make up a series of taped utterances for a situation tape. Then see whether different kinds of responses can be inserted without destroying the coherence of the sequence.

2
Autonomous interaction

Returning to the schema C1, we observe the gap between skill-getting and skill-using. Some indications have been given of ways in which production or pseudo-communication activities can become bridging activities, facilitating and stimulating autonomous interaction. (See also Chapter 4: Oral Practice, Type B exercises, p. 130.)

The crossing from bridge to shore, however, will not necessarily take place without encouragement. Many students will remain on the bridge, rather than face the unprotected autonomy of real communication, unless they are given opportunities very early to develop confidence and self-reliance through frequent, pleasant incursions into autonomous territory. In other words, the student will prefer the safety of the structured exercise and develop a nervous attitude toward the unstructured which will be hard to change. He must learn early to express his personal intentions through all kinds of familiar and unfamiliar recombinations of the language elements at his disposal. "The more daring he is in . . . linguistic innovation, the more rapidly he progresses."[1] This means that priority must be given to the development of an adventurous spirit in trying to convey one's meaning to others in the foreign language.

How can we develop this necessary confidence and self-reliance? We must create, and allow to develop naturally, opportunities for our students to use the foreign language for the normal purposes of language in relations with others—as Birkmaier puts it, "to use language in a natural, useful way, in a significant social setting."[2] Such activities link listening and speaking, since, without ability to comprehend the speech of others, "communication" becomes an uninteresting and frustrating one-way street. In some approaches, activities such as those described in this section are the chief preoccupation. Even where this is not so, they must be given time and place if students are to communicate in uninhibited freedom.

Categories of language use

The student needs situations where he is on his own (that is, not supported by teacher or structured exercise), trying to use the foreign language to exchange with others messages of real interest to him. Yet we cannot send students off in groups or pairs and tell them to interact. *Motivation to communicate* must be aroused in some way. We must propose, or encourage students to develop, activities which have an intrinsic interest for them—activities in such natural interactional contexts as the following: (1) establishing and maintaining social relations, (2) expressing one's reactions, (3) hiding one's intentions, (4) talking one's way out of trouble, (5) seeking and giving information, (6) learning or teaching others to do or make something, (7) conversing over the telephone, (8) solving problems, (9) discussing ideas, (10) playing with language, (11) acting out social roles, (12) entertaining others, (13) displaying one's achievements, (14) sharing leisure activities.

These types of interactional activity lend themselves to various patterns of individualization, with students naturally seeking out partners with whom they feel at ease. Maslow[3] has shown that each individual has a hierarchy of needs to be satisfied, rising from physiological needs through the needs for feelings of security, belongingness, esteem (of others and for oneself), and self-realization. These are reflected in complex interrelationships within any group. Since genuine interaction springs from the depths of the individual personality, all of these needs affect student reactions in a truly autonomous situation. For these reasons, only the student himself knows whether he feels more at ease with a fluent speaker who can help him along, a less fluent speaker whose lesser ability encourages him in his own efforts, or a good listener who inspires him with confidence. Some students, by their nature, interact very fully with few words. Students thus form their own small, natural-affinity interactional groups which select or generate activities as the group becomes a compatible unit.

An imaginative teacher and involved students will think of many absorbing and exciting interactional activities. Listed below are some expansions, by no means exhaustive, of the possibilities for language use within each category and some sample activities which would lead to the use of language in the terms of the category. Naturally, once an activity becomes truly autonomous the student automatically draws on elements from other categories; e.g., while making something (category 6), he overturns a container of paint and apologizes (category 1), then solves a problem by suggesting how such a situation could be avoided by a different arrangement of working space (category 8).

All of the activities suggested will obviously not be possible for all students from the earliest stage of learning. The teacher will *select and graduate activities to propose* from these categories, so that the attitude of seeking to communicate is developed early in an activity which is within the student's growing capacity. An impossible task, which bewilders and discourages the student too early in his language learning, is just as inhibiting of ultimate fluency as lack of opportunity to try what he can do with what he knows. The sample activities within each category are broadly labeled E (Elementary), I (Intermediate), and A (Advanced). This is obviously not a hard-and-fast guide since the maturity, capabilities, and goals of groups are so diverse.

1. ESTABLISHING AND MAINTAINING SOCIAL RELATIONS

(E) Greetings between persons of the same and different age and status, introductions, wishes for special occasions, polite enquiries (with attention to the permissible and the expected questions in the culture), making arrangements, giving directions, apologies, refusals; (I) excuses, mild rebukes, conventional expressions of agreement and polite disagreement, encouraging, discouraging, and persuading others; (A) expressing impatience, surprise, dismay, making promises, hedging (the gentle art of non-communication), teasing.

Conversation capsules or *mini-incidents* can be developed by interaction groups to demonstrate how to handle various situations. These need not be lengthy. Students learn appropriate gestures as they enact the situations.

(E) Answering the door and politely getting rid of an unwanted caller; calling on the phone with birthday greetings, congratulations on a successful achievement, an enquiry about the health of a friend, or to make some arrangements; enacting urgent situations (fire, drowning, street attack) which require quick vocal responses with set phrases; (I) welcoming visitors at home, customers in a shop, or clients in an office.

(A) These uses become inextricably interwoven within other activities. Reality is achieved when students are able to greet, escort, and entertain a French-speaking visitor to the school or the town, interact in French with an exchange student, or participate in a visit abroad or an informal activity of category 14.

2. EXPRESSING ONE'S REACTIONS

The student can be put in real or simulated situations where he has to react verbally throughout a television show, at an exhibition of pictures or photographs, during a friendly sharing of slides, or at a student fashion show. (In these cases the clever or amusing remark, instead of being frowned upon as presumptuous, is welcomed, as long as it is in French.)

3. HIDING ONE'S INTENTIONS

(I) Each student may be given a mission which he must not reveal under any provocation, but which he tries to carry out within a given period of time. This activity carries purposeful use of the language beyond course hours as students try to discover each other's missions. (E) Selekman[4] has developed for this category a game called *Super Spy* (*Super-espion*). One group forms a team of spies who decide on a mission. Each spy goes to a different group, the members of which try to find out his mission through astute questioning. The group which is successful first then explains how their spy's mission was discovered. This activity also involves (5), (8), and (13).

4. TALKING ONE'S WAY OUT OF TROUBLE

Simulated or real situations of increasing verbal difficulty should be set up, where the student must use his wits to extract himself from his dilemma; e.g., giving non-answers to an inquisitive neighbor anxious to know the origin of a loud noise he heard in the middle of the night; redirecting the course of an awkward or embarrassing conversation; answering the complaint: *"Je t'ai téléphoné hier soir, comme convenu, mais personne n'a répondu"* without revealing where one was or what one was doing.

5. SEEKING AND GIVING INFORMATION

a. *Seeking information* on subjects for which students have some basic vocabulary. (A) Finding out specialized vocabulary for a special interest can be part of this type of interaction, particularly in connection with (6). (I) Students may be sent to find out specific information from a monolingual French speaker or an informant who pretends to be monolingual, or the students seek the information from other French speakers outside of the course or the school. The information may be useful for activities in categories (1), (6), (8), or (12).

b. *Giving information:* (E and I) about oneself, one's family background, the area where one lives, one's career aspirations, vacation preferences, pet peeves; (I and A) about some subject in which one is proficient (the student may be giving information to other students learning to do or make something, perhaps explaining what he is doing while he is doing it).

Combining (a) and (b). (E and I) All kinds of classroom opportunities arise for students to wonder why and ask the teacher or each other. Students should be encouraged to ask questions in French about what they are to do and to seek information about French customs and institutions. If a new student has joined the class, if there is a new baby in the family, if some student has returned from a vacation or a summer job, or if someone saw an accident on the way to school, other activities should be suspended while students ask about it in French. *Simulated settings* like bank or airline counters, customs desks, workshops, or restaurants may be used to expand the school setting. Advertisements from magazines can give an initial fillip to the interaction, with students enquiring about advertised services. Students may use French air schedules, customs forms, menus, or maps (often brought home by traveling relatives or the teacher) as a basis for asking and answering questions or giving directions. The *interview technique* also combines these two aspects of information-sharing. (A) The interview may be based on social roles adopted by the participants, thus linking (5) with (11). The results of the interview may be written up for a wall newspaper, as a link with writing practice.

6. LEARNING OR TEACHING HOW TO DO OR MAKE SOMETHING

Here, language is associated with action. The possibilities for increasing the interest and motivation of students of all kinds of abilities and interests are limitless. It is the basic technique of foreign-language camps and should be incorporated automatically into the programs of foreign-language clubs. On a smaller scale it can become part of a regular course. The pressure of intensive courses is certainly relieved by sessions in the foreign language where students actually work with real-life materials and activities (sports, hobbies, crafts, physical exercise, dances).

7. CONVERSING OVER THE TELEPHONE

This is always difficult in a foreign language because of the distortions of sound, interference, and lack of situational, facial, and body language clues to meaning. It should, therefore, be practiced early. The students should learn to use a phone book from the country where the language is spoken, and, where this is possible, make actual calls enquiring about goods, services, or timetables for transport.

The help of monolingual, or presumed monolingual, contacts outside the course should be enlisted. Some incapacitated persons, older persons living alone, and retired teachers would enjoy participating in this type of activity. They should be instructed to act strictly as monolinguals[5] and should be informed of the specific nature of the student's assignment. Where none of these are available, teachers will act as informants for A students from their colleagues' classes, and A students will act as informants for E and I students.

The telephone practice is usually associated with (6) or (8).

8. PROBLEM SOLVING

The problem should require verbal activity for its solution. It may involve (5) or (6), even (3), (4), (9), or (10).

a. (E) Such well-known games as *Vingt et une questions, Identification, Animal-minéral-végétal,* and their derivatives are popular. One student thinks of something (or someone, or an historical incident . . .), the others try to guess what it is with the fewest possible yes-no questions. (See G43.) (I and A) These games can become very sophisticated as versions of television panel series like *Pas de secrets, Qui dit la vérité?* (where three people pretend to be the person who performed some particular acts and the students try to decide which one is telling the truth), and *Devinez mon métier* (where the questioners try to decide the occupation of the one being questioned).

b. (E and I) Selekman has experimented with a game called *Guilty Party*[6] (*Le Coupable*), where one student is accused by the group of an unspecified crime which he must discover through a series of questions (When did I do this? Where did I do it? Why did I do it? Did anyone help me? . . .) After he has discovered his crime, the accused must attempt to defend himself to seek an acquittal. (A) This game can follow a study of the French legal system and incorporate relevant features of French justice.

c. (E and I) Lipson,[7] in an attempt to focus the students' attention on the *content* of the sentences they are producing, has worked out materials which take up the principle of this well-known type of puzzle:

A, B, and C live on X, Y, and Z streets.
A works in an office.
B is a lawyer.
C stays home while his wife goes to work.
The people on X street all work in factories.
The people on Y street are all single.
The people on X street all own their own businesses downtown.

On which streets do A, B, and C live?

Lipson's materials are about hooligans who steal in factories, conduct themselves badly in parks, like to smoke on trolley buses, and are often uncultured people (uncultured people never wash). Later we find out that hooligans are of two types: those who conduct themselves badly in parks never wash, while those who steal in factories like to smoke on trolley buses. The plot thickens when we find out that there are two gangs of hooligans, Borodin's and Gladkov's: Borodin steals at Gladkov's factory and Gladkov at Borodin's. This complicated background leads to questions such as the following:

Which hooligans often wash?	Hooligans who steal at factories
	OR
	hooligans who don't conduct themselves badly in parks . . .
When does Borodin steal at his own factory?	He never steals at his own factory.
Why not?	Borodin steals at Gladkov's factory.
What does Gladkov do when Borodin is not stealing?	As far as I know, Gladkov steals at Borodin's factory.

Both Selekman[8] and Lipson[9] report that students become so involved in these problem-solving activities that their verbal participation becomes really creative and personally meaningful. As Lipson puts it: "What often happens is that members of the class start arguing with each other, and the teacher steps aside and lets the argument run."

d. (A) Problem-solving activities may be associated with some project for another course. Students may want to find answers to such questions as the following:

i. Why are the French wary of German leadership in the European Economic Community? Why did they oppose the entry of Britain into the European Community for so long?

ii. Why does my French dressing not taste French?

The answer to (i) may be sought through library research, listening to speeches, interviews with French visitors, reading of newspapers and magazines, and finally classroom discussion of what each student has gleaned, thus interweaving (5), (8), (9), and (13). Question (ii) may require some of the same procedures, along with experimentation in the kitchen (6).

9. DISCUSSING IDEAS

(E and I) Factual details of things read, seen, or heard provide a basis for discussion. Mystery stories are useful. Cultural differences are most likely to provoke lively discussion. Since students at the E and I stages are at a disadvantage in such discussions because of the teacher's wider command of the language, the teacher must refrain from taking over and doing all the talking. At these levels, topics for discussion are normally kept to areas for which the students know some vocabulary and expressions. Otherwise, they come after a project of research into the area; or, students are provided with some written or recorded material from which they can acquire the necessary French terms for use in the discussion.

(A) Students decide on controversial subjects they wish to discuss, prepare their points for discussion, but make their remarks without a written script; two groups prepare the same topic and discuss it with each other while students from other groups ask questions; one student takes a viewpoint and tries to convince other students that this viewpoint is tenable.

Stevick's *microtexts*[10] are useful as starters. A short text in French on any subject may be selected by teacher or students. This text is distributed, shown on the overhead projector, or written on the chalkboard; students then discuss and elaborate on the details of the text and any implications of it. The text should not be more than fifty words in length, or, if delivered orally, should not take longer than thirty seconds to relate. With experience, teachers and students can draw an astonishing amount of interesting discussion from almost any text. Possible microtexts are: (E) a menu, a concert program, an airline timetable, selections from letters from French correspondents, or a paragraph from a newspaper about the official activities of the President of the Republic; (I) newspaper accounts of the dog that saved its master during a fire, a bank robbery, two children lost in the mountains, a recent French Nobel Prize winner, a swing in fashions for dress or hair styles, or selected letters from the *Courrier du cœur;* (A) accounts of recent decisions on French domestic or foreign policy (editorial comments from two different French newspapers or from a French- and an English-language newspaper may be compared), new developments in the French educational system, the latest approaches to the drug problem in Europe, letters to the editor raising interesting questions.

10. PLAYING WITH LANGUAGE

Newspapers and magazines have for years published regularly all kinds of word games (crossword puzzles, acrostics and double-crostics, vocabulary expansion quizzes). Books on language enjoy a perennial popularity, and magic and esoteric words continue to mesmerize devotees. From early childhood people are fascinated by language. This natural love of language can be exploited in the foreign-language class.

(E, I, A) *Scrabble* games geared to the letter frequencies of different languages are obtainable.

(E) Nonsense and counting rhymes may be learned by heart and recited for fun. Songs with repetitive refrains are popular. Students like to learn onomatopoeic expressions (animal cries, rain dripping, doors banging) and these can be used in games and classroom drama.

(I) Oral construction in groups of crossword and other language puzzles can stimulate much discussion in the language, particularly when the construction becomes complicated in the final stages. *Charades* provide amusing themes for classroom dramatization. Students take a two-syllable word (*chaussure*) and for each syllable they improvise a short episode which brings in the word it represents (*chaud/sûr* or *sur*). They then act out an episode which brings in the complete word (*chaussure*) and students guess which word it is. (Other possibilities are: *banque/route/ banqueroute; pour/boire/pourboire;* or two segments: *main/tenir/ maintenir,* or three syllables: *mon/nu/ment/monument.*)

(A) Students may seek out and discuss word origins, word histories, and borrowings. They may examine French popular magazines like *Paris Match* to see the extent of contemporary French borrowings from English (what Etiemble has called *Franglais*[11]). At this level too, students may begin to take an interest in regional differences in the French language (e.g., the accent and common expressions of the Midi or Québec as contrasted with standard Parisian French).

11. ACTING OUT SOCIAL ROLES

Psychologists point out that we are constantly taking on different roles and the style of language which goes with them.

Dramatic improvisation is an excellent technique for eliciting autonomous interaction. Situations and participating characters are suggested in a very sketchy fashion. Students are allowed a short time to plan what they will do before they enact the scene, improvising the dialogue as they proceed. Several groups or pairs may improvise the same situation with very different results. Even inhibited students feel free to express themselves when they are being someone else in a recreational activity.

(E) Students act out roles in which they can use expressions learned in (1).

(I and A) Situations are proposed which represent various social settings, with characters of different occupations, relationships, and levels of authority:

a. The job interview with a timid (or overconfident) applicant.

b. The overbearing bureaucrat and the applicant for a visa extension.

c. The *concierge* trying to find out all about the reticent new *locataire* on the fourth floor.

d. The hippie son asking his very proper father for money.

e. The cocktail party at the *Ambassade de France:* the vapid female talking about nothing at great length or echoing what other people say (*C'est la première fois que je suis invitée à l'Ambassade. / Ah oui? Vous êtes ici pour la première fois?*); the boastful type (*Moi, je suis l'auteur de vingt romans qui ont eu un succès fou! Vous avez sûrement lu* Demain à Venise?); the parallel monologue (A: *Ma fille vient de se marier ce matin même.* B: *Vraiment? Moi, je n'ai que des fils.* A: *Elle a épousé un ingénieur des P. et T.*[12] B: *Ah oui? Mon fils aîné fait ses études de médecine*); the ignoramus talking to the Nobel Prize winner . . .

f. Situations based on proverbs.

g. Well-known political figures or characters in films or television programs may be mimicked in familiar situations.

12. ENTERTAINING OTHERS

The student should be given the opportunity to use his natural talents for singing, making music, or acting as host for a radio call-in program or a TV talk show. Groups of students may prepare and present radio or TV commercials. (These may involve more or less talking interspersed with mime, and are, therefore, very suitable for the early stages of a course.) A complete radio or TV program with news, situation comedy, commercials, weather report, interview, give-away show, sports, song and dance routine, and *La Marseillaise* may be prepared for presentation to another class, for a *Quatorze Juillet* celebration, for an Open Day, or for a school assembly.

13. DISPLAYING ONE'S ACHIEVEMENTS

(E, I, and A) Students may tell the group about what they did in (3), (4), (5), (6), or (8), or present and explain special projects, which will often be interdisciplinary (e.g., the study of an aspect of French art, music, architecture, or history). (A) As a climax to (9), groups may present their different viewpoints in a full-scale debate.

Some kind of public presentation can become a regular culminating activity to draw together many individualized interaction projects.

14. SHARING LEISURE ACTIVITIES

Students should have the opportunity to learn, and become proficient in, the games and diversions of the French people. They should be able to participate in verbal competitions. Where there are special activities traditionally associated with festivals or national holidays, students should be able to engage in them at the appropriate time (*veillées de Noël et du Nouvel-An, santons provençaux, Fête de la Chandeleur, Fête des Rois, la Sainte-Catherine, la Saint-Nicolas, le premier mai, le Quatorze Juillet . . .*).

Much autonomous interaction takes place at French clubs, French tables, class picnics, or at French camps. Visits are arranged to see exhibitions of French paintings, eat at French restaurants, see French films, or attend performances by visiting theatrical companies. Groups within a class may take turns preparing a French meal and inviting the others. Schools should investigate possibilities for inviting French exchange students and *assistants*. French-speaking residents of the district or visitors passing through should be invited to talk with French classes on a formal or informal basis. Students should undertake to show their town or their school to French-speaking visitors or tourists on a regular basis.

At the advanced level students often opt for *purely oral courses* to perfect their ability to communicate. For these courses, activities such as those described above which plunge students into normal uses of language are essential.

✱ Take three of the categories listed and for each try to think of three more activities which would lead to these particular normal uses of language. If you are studying this book in a class group, have a brain-storming session to see what you can add to the suggestions given.

Perfectionnement, *not perfection*
CORRECTION OF ERRORS IN AUTONOMOUS INTERACTION

It is during intensive practice exercises, or construction practice, that immediate corrections may be made. Even then, we should not jump in before our students have had time to think and often to correct themselves. Our task is to make our students conscious of possible errors and to familiarize them to such a degree with acceptable, rule-governed sequences that they are able to monitor their own production and work toward its improvement in spontaneous interaction. In interaction practice we are trying to develop an attitude of innovation and experimentation with the new language. Nothing dampens enthusiasm and effort more than constant correction when the student is trying to express his ideas within the limitations of his newly acquired knowledge of the language. Teachers who are non-native speakers of the language know that they are very often fully conscious of a mistake they have just made, even mortified by it, but unable to take it back. We should be happy when our students have reached the same level of awareness of acceptable usage, since it means they are becoming autonomous learners as well as autonomous speakers.

The best approach during interaction activities is for the instructor silently to note consistent, systematic errors (not slips of the tongue and occasional lapses in areas where the student usually acquits himself well). These errors will then be discussed with the student at a time when the instructor is helping him evaluate his success in interaction, with particular attention to the types of errors which hinder communication. The instructor will then use his knowledge of the areas of weakness of a number of students as a basis for his emphases in instruction and in review. In this way, we help students focus on what are problem areas for them as they learn from their mistakes. Steady improvement will come only from individual motivation and purpose—that personal desire to perfect one's communicative effectiveness which is stimulated by genuine interest in what one is doing.

WHAT LEVEL OF CORRECT SPEECH CAN WE EXPECT FROM OUR STUDENTS?

The first question we must ask ourselves is: How does a native speaker frame his utterances when he is thinking only of expressing his meaning?

C34 De même que, je me permets, tenez, excusez-moi, une idée qui me vient à laquelle je tiens assez, il existe un Français, un Français moyen, Français moyen, de cette région en particulier, mettez un Français de Paris, un Français est toujours un être double, on a dû vous enseigner ça en civilisation française, c'est toujours un être double, pourquoi, pourquoi à votre avis, pourquoi sommes-nous doubles dans le tempérament, dans la façon de penser, pourquoi est-ce que un Français est toujours un être double? Il y a plus ou moins de ceci et plus ou moins de cela . . . et tous les Français on a un, entre nous une dose plus ou moins grande d'homme du nord et d'homme du midi, voyez-vous.[13]

This passage, transcribed from a taped conversation, shows clearly how we feel our way toward the most effective framework for expressing our meaning, leaning heavily on hesitation and transition expressions (*je me permets, tenez, excusez-moi* . . .) and repetitions (*un Français, un Français moyen, Français moyen* . . .), changing our minds in mid-stream about choice of words (*on a un, entre nous une dose* . . .) and about the type of sentence which will best express our meaning (*de même que, je me permets, excusez-moi, une idée qui me vient à laquelle je tiens assez, il existe un Français . . . moyen . . .*). Note that we do not make basic errors in morphology or syntax. (In *"on a un,"* the word *un* acts as a transition expression while the speaker chooses the precise noun he needs to express his meaning—*une dose; est-ce que un Français* . . . indicates hesitancy in formulating the sentence.) The repetitions also help the listener to process each segment at the speed of utterance by providing redundancy to reinforce the meaning he is extracting.

It is clear that we cannot expect our students to speak French always in well-formed sentences in the heat of personal expression, when they do not do so in their native language. We must also expect students to hesitate, restructure sentences, and make sudden changes of lexical choice which may temporarily affect agreements of person and gender in the immediate vicinity. These imperfections are important only if they affect comprehensibility.

THE SI LINE

Stevick draws to our attention an interesting fact about simultaneous interpreters. "These remarkable individuals," he observes, "perceive both lexical meaning and grammatical form, and come out with their own reformulations in the other language after only a few seconds delay. Even as they speak, they are taking in new data for interpretation. . . . But if they are to continue, there is a line that they dare not cross: they must not become personally involved in what they are saying. Once the content of the message begins to make a difference to them, they lose the power of speaking and listening at the same time."[14] Stevick calls this boundary the SI (simultaneous interpretation) line: "Above it," he says, "lie grammatical form and dictionary meaning; below it lies everything that matters to speaker and listener."[15]

In view of this psychological phenomenon we have no reason to be surprised that students engaging in genuine interaction make many slips which we know they would not make in structured activities. Correcting them immediately and frequently will force students, for self-protection, to keep their attention above the SI line and will result in speech which is more carefully correct but which never goes beyond the banal and the obvious. This is surely not our goal.

INDIVIDUAL DIFFERENCES

Because of the personal nature of autonomous interaction, the participation of a particular student will naturally be consistent with his personality. Some people are temperamentally incapable of interacting by means of a babble of words; to expect them to do so is to force them back into pseudo-communication and into mouthing memorized phrases. The quality of the interaction will be judged by other criteria: ability to receive and express meaning, to understand and convey intentions, to perform acceptably in all kinds of situations in his relations with others. The means by which the student attains these desirable goals will be a function of his personal learning strategies. We can allow these full play through the provision of a wide choice of activity options, but we cannot determine for him what they shall be.

THE INDIVIDUAL TEACHER

Some non-native teachers feel inadequate to the demands of autonomous interaction activities because of insufficiencies of training or a long period of time away from foreign-language teaching. Just like their students, such teachers grow in skill and confidence as they participate. In a non-authoritarian approach the teacher accepts and acknowledges his weaknesses, drawing on his strengths as an *animateur* to compensate. The students then accept him as a member of a group which is learning together. From year to year his control of the language improves, especially if he uses tapes of authentic native speech regularly to supplement his teaching and seizes every opportunity to listen to the language on the radio or on the sound tracks of films and to speak it in his contacts with colleagues in the school, at professional meetings, and *especially in his own classroom.* He also reads for pleasure modern books and plays in the language to keep him in contact with its contemporary spoken form. What he does not know, he encourages his students to find out, or, better still, he and his students find it out together. He also makes every effort to join in professional visits to French-speaking areas, or he goes on his own. If finances are the problem here, he organizes a group of students for such a visit and covers his expenses by accompanying them as guide and host. Many a poorly prepared teacher has overcome his inadequacies. The essential is the determination to do so.

3
Listening

Essential to all interaction is the ability to understand what others are saying. Even in the native language many people are poor listeners, whether through weak powers of concentration, egocentrism, or short auditory memory. Yet it has been estimated that, of the time adults spend in communication activities, 45 per cent is devoted to listening, only 30 per cent to speaking, 16 per cent to reading, and a mere 9 per cent to writing (and these data are from a pre-television, pre-talking-picture, pre-dictaphone era).[1] Apart from communicative interaction, much of the enjoyment in foreign-language use comes from listening activities—watching films and plays or listening to radio broadcasts, songs, or talks by native speakers. Even in class students learn a great deal from listening to their teacher, to tapes or records, or to each other.

It is noteworthy that some students who do not excel in other areas of foreign-language use achieve a very high level of success in understanding spoken messages. It has been suggested by some researchers that there is a special listening comprehension factor,[2] but this has not yet been fully characterized. Even in life situations many people become skilled, in their own or a foreign language, in understanding registers, dialectal variations, and complexities of structure which they cannot produce in their own speech. Troike[3] has called this a difference between receptive and productive competence. Students with special skill in listening comprehension should be encouraged and given opportunities to go beyond others in this area, which is especially suitable for individualized work. They should also be rewarded in final grading with full consideration for this skill in which they excel.

Listening is a complex operation, integrating the distinct components of perception and linguistic knowledge in ways which are at present poorly understood.[4] Psychologists have tried to explain this phenomenon from several viewpoints, each of which can give us some clues to our students' problems in listening to a foreign language and suggest ways of structuring effective materials for practice and enjoyment.

The schema C1 brings out the cognitive nature of listening, which involves *perception* based on *internalized knowledge* of the rules of the language. Students have to learn to abstract from a stream of sound units which machines cannot as yet be programmed to identify, to assign these to categories, and to attribute to them functions in relation to other units, so that an intelligible message may be constructed from what they are hearing. While they are doing this, they are anticipating the import of the message, holding segments already identified in their immediate memory, and readjusting their interpretation of earlier segments in accordance with the final message *as they understand it.*

In this context the phrase "as they understand it" is basic, because listening is not a passive but an *active process of constructing a message* from a stream of sound with what one knows of the phonological, semantic, and syntactic potentialities of the language. Even in our own language we often "hear" what was never said. This becomes an even more frequent occurrence in a language we are still learning. It is this active process of message construction which has been labeled *reception* (or comprehension of the message) in C1. The two terms *perception* and *reception* represent the two levels[5] of practice required to improve systematically the student's skill in interpreting messages intended by speakers.

Models of listening processes

Some linguists[6] maintain that knowledge of the same system of grammatical rules of a language is basic to both listening and speaking. Some psychologists, on the other hand, believe the rules we apply are different and that we employ perceptual strategies[7] for surface scanning of what we are hearing, stopping to penetrate to underlying relations only to resolve ambiguities or untangle complexities. Despite their theoretical divergence, interesting insights can be derived from various linguistic and psychological schools of thought, each of which emphasizes a different facet of the complicated processes of listening and receiving messages.

In this section, we will discuss in detail (A) the role of uncertainty and redundancy in Cherry's theory of communication, (B) Neisser's active processing of a message, and (C) Bever's strategies of perceptual segmentation (with which we will link Schlesinger's semantic-syntactic decoding).

A. *The uncertainties of a spoken message*

Cherry[8] says, "Communication proceeds in the face of a number of uncertainties and has the character of . . . numerous inductive inferences being carried out concurrently."

He lists these uncertainties as:

1. Uncertainties of speech sounds, or acoustic patterning. Accents, tones, loudness may be varied; speakers may shout, sing, whisper, or talk with their mouths full.

2. Uncertainties of language and syntax. Sentence constructions differ; conversational language may be bound by few rules of syntax. Vocabularies vary; words have many near-synonyms, popular usages, special usages, et cetera.

3. Environmental uncertainties. Conversations are disturbed by street noises, by telephone bells, and background chatter.

4. Recognition uncertainties. Recognition depends upon the peculiar past experiences of the listener, upon his familiarity with the speaker's speech habits, knowledge of language, subject matter, et cetera.

Here we have in a nutshell many of the problems our students face in the comprehension of speech, each of these being compounded where a foreign language is involved. "Yet," Cherry continues, "speech communication works. It is so structured as to possess redundancy at a variety of levels, to assist in overcoming these uncertainties."[9] In C2 we examined some of the redundancies of spoken, as opposed to written, French. It is time now to examine a specimen of completely unedited, authentic speech, uttered in a natural situation by a person who had no idea that what she said would ever serve any pedagogical purpose. (This passage will reinforce the impressions gained from C34.)

EDITED AND UNEDITED LISTENING COMPREHENSION MATERIALS

In preparing materials and activities for listening comprehension we do not give enough consideration to the differences between edited, or artificially constructed, messages and an authentic output of speech in natural interaction. As a result we make the listening comprehension materials we record, or present to the students orally in class, much more difficult to comprehend than we realize. The difference is like that between listening to a prepared and polished scholarly paper read verbatim and the free interchange of unprepared discussion which follows the paper and usually makes the speaker's ideas seem much clearer.

C36-37

The following edited and unedited discussions of the same subject will illustrate this difference. The unedited version is taken from a tape made by B.E.L.C. in 1968 at Orléans.[10]

The speakers (*délégués syndicaux*) are discussing the characteristics of their fellow workers in Orléans. The following remarks have already been made by various speakers:

L'Orléanais est quand même assez froid. Il n'est pas expansif. Il garde ses sentiments pour lui. . . . Il est méfiant. . . .

C35 Edited content of the remarks of a woman delegate:

Mais cette méfiance est fonction de l'évolution de la vie et des conditions de travail. On ne peut pas dire que l'Orléanais est très différent des habitants d'une autre ville. En campagne les habitants sont beaucoup plus ouverts. Ils ont davantage le temps de fréquenter les autres, tandis que maintenant en ville c'est presque impossible, à part les femmes qui ne travaillent pas. Mais une femme qui travaille n'a pas le temps le soir en rentrant d'aller voir ce qui se passe chez la voisine. Le tempérament change en fonction du mode de vie.

C36 The following passage, transcribed from the original tape, shows how the same ideas were expressed in authentic interaction. Slashes indicate the position of the pauses in delivery. No attempt has been made to insert punctuation, which is a convention of written language.

Mais c'est / ça c'est aussi fonction / de l'évolution de la vie / parce que / du mode de vie / on ne peut pas dire que le / l'Orléanais a un tempérament plus ou moins / qu'une / que les habitants d'une autre ville / je crois que c'est surtout / fonction / des / conditions de vie et de travail par exemple en / en campagne les habitants sont quand même beaucoup plus ouverts / ils ont davantage le temps d'ailleurs de fréquenter / toute personne / tandis que maintenant en ville c'est / c'est presque impossible à part / euh quelques exceptions et puis / chez les femmes qui ne travaillent pas / mais une maman qui travaille enfin / si elle n'est pas maman bon bien / elle travaille elle n'a pas le temps le soir en rentrant / d'aller voir chez la voisine / ce / ce qui se passe / ça c'est aussi fonction du / le tempérament change je pense / en fonction du mode de vie /

C37 If we set C36 and C35 out in parallel columns we see much more strikingly how much verbal redundancy has been eliminated even in such a colloquially expressed version as C35. For C36 a separate line has been allotted to each breath group.

C36	C35
Mais c'est	Mais (cette méfiance)
ça c'est aussi fonction	est fonction
de l'évolution de la vie	de l'évolution de la vie
parce que	et des conditions de travail.
du mode de vie	
on ne peut pas dire que le	On ne peut pas dire que
l'Orléanais a un tempérament plus ou moins	l'Orléanais est très différent
qu'une	
que les habitants d'une autre ville	des habitants d'une autre ville.
je crois que c'est surtout	
fonction	
des	
conditions de vie et de travail par exemple en	
en campagne les habitants sont quand même beaucoup plus ouverts	En campagne les habitants sont beaucoup plus ouverts.
ils ont davantage le temps d'ailleurs de fréquenter	Ils ont davantage le temps de fréquenter
toute personne	les autres.
tandis que maintenant en ville c'est	tandis que maintenant en ville
c'est presque impossible à part	c'est presque impossible,
euh quelques exceptions et puis	
chez les femmes qui ne travaillent pas	à part les femmes qui ne travaillent pas.
mais une maman qui travaille enfin	Mais une femme qui travaille
si elle n'est pas maman bon bien	
elle travaille elle n'a pas le temps le soir en rentrant	n'a pas le temps le soir en rentrant
d'aller voir chez la voisine	d'aller voir ce qui se passe chez la voisine.
ce	
ce qui se passe	
ça c'est aussi fonction du	
le tempérament change je pense	Le tempérament change
en fonction du mode de vie	en fonction du mode de vie.

Commentary

Although the edited version C35 retains the colloquial flavor of C36, it eliminates synonymous expressions which merely repeat the thought content or elaborate it in minor ways (*une maman qui travaille enfin / si elle n'est pas maman bon bien / elle travaille*); function words indicating a direction of sentence structure which is not followed through (*ça c'est aussi fonction du / le tempérament change je pense / en fonction du mode de vie*); hesitation expressions (*bon bien*), conversational tags and formulas (*d'ailleurs, je pense*), and false starts (*qu'une / que les habitants*). It also regularizes syntax which does not observe the accepted constraints (*on ne peut pas dire que le / l'Orléanais a un tempérament plus ou moins / qu'une / que les habitants d'une autre ville*). Thus, in a well-meaning attempt at improving the "disorderly" output of C36, the editor has provided in C35 a version which would demand much more concentrated effort in listening than the authentic speech of C36. *As with speaking, we may well be demanding more of our foreign-language listeners in the exercises we present than is demanded in native-language listening.*

Authentic materials of the type illustrated are unfortunately not easy for classroom teachers to obtain. The following suggestions should be implemented:

1. When visiting French speakers and French exchange students are temporarily at hand, teachers should seize the opportunity to tape-record general conversation with the visitors. Suitable excerpts from the tapes should then be shared among groups of schools.

2. French cultural services should be bombarded with requests for tapes of radio discussions, informal chats, and film sound tracks, until an awareness is created that these are the types of materials our students need.

3. Exchanges of tapes should be encouraged between twinned classes in French- and English-speaking schools. Both classes should be encouraged to send unedited tapes—not of prepared talks, but of free discussion among members of the class on aspects of their daily lives and their likes and dislikes. To obtain such tapes requires a change of attitude on the part of teachers who often expect a class exchange tape to be a perfectly orchestrated performance.

4. Individual students should be encouraged to begin tape exchanges with correspondents in France, along the lines of the more conventional letter exchanges.

Listening to authentic tapes recorded by native speakers who are not teachers provides one of the best opportunities for students to have real contact with the life and thought of French-speaking people, whether from metropolitan France, French-speaking Canada, Haiti, Senegal, or New

Caledonia. Through these tapes, they encounter the normal and the natural, even the trivial, much more than in the reading of newspapers, magazines, novels, plays, and short stories, all of which tend to choose as subjects the exceptional, the sensational, the idealized, or the eccentric in order to arouse and maintain interest.

RECOGNITION UNCERTAINTIES

The listener constructs a message from what he is hearing according to certain expectations[11] based on:

—what he knows of the language, not only syntax and lexicon, but usage in these areas for different styles of language (see C5);

—his familiarity with the subject under discussion;

—the knowledge of the real world that he shares with the speaker (through which he can assume certain things which have not been expressed);

—his acquaintance with or assumptions about the personal attitudes and interests of the speaker;

—his observation and interpretation of the circumstances of the utterance, including what has preceded it;

—his understanding of the cultural context in which it occurs;

—his reading of paralinguistic cues (speed of speech, length of pauses, loudness, pitch, facial expressions), gestures, and other body language which differ from culture to culture.[12]

The listener imposes a syntactic structure on what he is hearing and this arouses further expectations about what is to come. Sometimes a succeeding segment proves to be incongruous with his syntactic expectations and this forces him to reconsider and project a different syntactic structure; in other words, to resolve the ambiguity.

For these reasons ability to receive messages aurally becomes more refined as knowledge of the potentialities of the grammatical system increases.

C38   1. *Quels soldats commandent ces officiers?*

Commentary

a. On hearing the interrogative adjective (*quels*) + noun, the listener anticipates the order subject-verb-object, as in the question: *Quels voyoux du quartier ont attaqué ce pauvre vieillard?*

b. His experience of the real world (normally, officers are in charge of soldiers) makes him restructure the message he is extracting.

c. His knowledge of French syntax confirms this restructuring: when a question centers on the object of a sentence with a noun-subject, inversion of subject and verb takes place—either simple inversion of verb and noun-subject, as in (1), or complex inversion through the use of a noun substitute, or pronoun, as in:

2. *Quels soldats ces officiers commandent-ils?*

3. *Quel chien déteste ton chat?* is truly ambiguous because either *chien* or *chat* could be the spontaneous enemy in the real world.

In these cases, the listener must hold the utterance in his immediate memory while comparing it with the context or the circumstances of the utterance before assigning it a disambiguating structure.

* Discuss the two possible syntactic structures of the following:

C39 J'ai trouvé ce livre intéressant.
L'homme reçoit le livre du garçon.
J'ai fait porter ce message à Pierre.
Hélène aime mieux Marc que Bernard.[13]

Find other examples of ambiguities of structure in French.

Ignorance of the cultural context can be an impediment

C40 (A) Jean-Pierre rencontre Anne-Marie à la terrasse du Café de Flore.

JEAN-PIERRE   Vive l'anarchie! On ne t'a pas vu depuis la Saint-Germain-des-Prés!

ANNE-MARIE   (vivement) On croirait que tu parles de la Saint-Barthélemy! Moi, j'ai d'autres choses en tête.

Commentary

A student could well understand every word of this interchange without having any real idea of its meaning and its emotional overtones. Full comprehension of it requires knowledge in various domains:

1. *The setting.* Two students meeting in Paris. The area around *Saint-Germain-des-Prés* is much frequented by students from the *Quartier Latin,* and the *Flore* is a *café* where Jean-Paul Sartre and Simone de Beauvoir often did their writing. *Tu* is commonly used among students.

2. *The subject matter.* The student demonstrations in Paris in 1968, usually referred to in French as *les événements de mai, 1968,* when the black flags of the anarchists were raised over the Sorbonne, the oldest

building of the University of Paris, where the Faculté des Lettres et
Sciences Humaines (now called Paris IV) is located.[14] It was in confrontations at the Carrefour Saint-Germain-des-Prés that the police first used
tear gas against students who were throwing *pavés* taken from the surface
of the road.

3. *The historical allusion* is clear to all Frenchmen: *la Saint-Barthélemy*
was the night of the twenty-fourth of August, 1572, when King Charles
IX ordered the massacre of all Huguenots in Paris. The massacre began
when the bells were rung at Saint-Germain-l'Auxerrois. Anne-Marie's
remark draws a parallel between the police attacks on students during the
1968 confrontations and this notorious historical confrontation between
the state authorities and the Protestant Huguenots.

4. *Syntax.* a. Anne-Marie obviously thinks Pierre is exaggerating the
gravity of the occasion by his use of *la Saint-Germain-des-Prés,* the abbreviated form of *la fête de Saint-Germain-des-Prés,* which gives it the
status usually accorded a special national or religious day (*la Fête Nationale, la Saint-Nicolas*).

b. One use of the conditional in the main clause (*on croirait*) is to
express strong emotional rejection of the idea.[15] She is saying: "You talk
as though it were the *Saint-Barthélemy.* It doesn't seem like that to me."
In spoken form, tone of voice would convey some of this significance. If
the person speaking were visible (on film, for instance) facial expression
and movements would help in the interpretation, which is supported by
her declaration that she has more important things to do than spend her
time demonstrating.

C41 (A) *Informations: France Inter*[16]

La nouvelle la plus intéressante qui me soit parvenue ce soir vient d'Alger.
En effet, l'Algérie a décidé de suspendre sans délai l'immigration de ses
travailleurs en France, à la suite des récents attentats et d'un communiqué,
tant que les conditions de sécurité et de dignité ne seront pas garanties.
C'est une mesure qui sera peut-être provisoire, mais en attendant elle est
prise. Et le communiqué fait état de ce qu'il appelle "la situation devenue
dramatique des travailleurs algériens en France." C'est le Conseil de la
Révolution et le Conseil des Ministres d'Algérie qui ont pris cette décision. . . . Les assassinats de nord-africains dans plusieurs grandes villes de
France ont fait le plus mauvais effet à Alger et, ne l'oublions pas, ces
crimes ont été commis au moment même où l'Algérie réunissait le Tiers-
Monde.

Commentary

1. This news report is in a mixture of *formal* and *consultative styles*. Since the announcer wishes his listener to feel he is being addressed, he intersperses among more formal announcements (e.g., *l'Algérie a décidé de suspendre sans délai l'immigration de ses travailleurs en France, à la suite des récents attentats et d'un communiqué, tant que les conditions de sécurité et de dignité ne seront pas garanties*) more personal forms of address (e.g., *La nouvelle la plus intéressante qui me soit parvenue ce soir; ne l'oublions pas*), and less formal sentence structure (*C'est le Conseil de la Révolution et le Conseil des Ministres d'Algérie qui ont pris cette décision*).

2. News broadcasts like this are more difficult to follow linguistically than the natural, informal speech of C36, because many of the rephrasings which provide redundancy of content have been eliminated and a more specialized vocabulary is employed (e.g., *attentats, mesure . . . provisoire, Conseil des Ministres, Tiers-Monde*). On the other hand, they are delivered in a more deliberate tone, with clearer enunciation, and distinct pauses at major syntactic boundaries.

3. Radio commentaries are often easier to follow than newscasts because they pursue a single subject for some time, whereas a complete newscast moves rapidly from one context to another.

4. *Place names and personal names* given orally can hinder recognition considerably. Students need instruction in the recognition of names in the news. /ɛzenɔvɛrɛmɔːr/ is not easily recognized by an American student as *Eisenhower est mort*. In C41, /alʒe/ will not necessarily be identified quickly by the student as the more familiar Algiers. If newscasts are made available within the week in which they were broadcast, familiarity with recent events of international significance will provide conceptual background for recognition of many of the names of people and places.

World geography lessons with French wall maps and guessing games with names of famous persons in the accepted French oral form[17] are helpful as associated activities when newscasts are being used as listening comprehension material. The students and the teacher should also keep a file of clippings from French newspapers and magazines which give background information, with the requisite specialized vocabulary, for the current national and international preoccupations of France and French-speaking areas.

5. The difficulties faced by the students on first hearing a newscast can

be diminished by encouraging them to relisten to the recording of the broadcast until they have comprehended the gist of the discussion.

❋ What knowledge of history, contemporary French life and attitudes, and present-day international developments would a student need to have in order to fully comprehend the import of the C41 news item from Paris?

Equally important for the comprehension of radio broadcasts is *recognition of dates and numbers,* as in the following:

C42 (A) *Informations: France Inter*[18]
Les vaccinations sont efficaces. Le ministère de la Santé publique le rappelle aujourd'hui dans une note. La plupart de ces vaccinations ont permis une régression spectaculaire des maladies infectieuses graves. Quelques exemples: en 1961: 207 décès dus à la coqueluche; en 1971: 29; en 1961: 126 décès dus à la poliomyélite; 10 ans plus tard: 9 décès seulement.

Rapid recognition of numbers and dates is indispensable to modern communication. One has only to think of common situations like asking the operator for telephone numbers, requesting airline and train schedules, changing travel plans, and understanding prices, rates for service, final accounts, bank balances, exchange rates, current dates, dates of birth, times for performances, or document numbers. With the multiplication of computerized services, more and longer numbers are becoming a part of everyday life, the latter often involving also rapid recognition of the *names of letters of the alphabet.*
Practice in attentive listening to numbers is provided by games like Bingo (*Lotto*), in dictation of series of numbers of increasing complexity, and in competitions where events must be selected from lists of multiple-choice items to correspond with dates given orally. The alphabet should be learned early and students should become adept at recognizing the oral spelling of new words and names letter by letter—a skill which is also useful for a foreigner in many communication situations.

PRACTICAL APPLICATIONS

1. Activities to *prepare the learner conceptually* for the type of content in a listening exercise are valuable in helping students develop expectations and project possible meanings.
2. Listening comprehension materials should preferably be well *integrated thematically* with the rest of the learning program; otherwise, *discussions of a related subject* may be necessary to stimulate the student's

thinking. For example, discussion of the differences between city and country dwellers in way of life and in attitudes toward neighbors would prepare for listening to C36; a study of student life and attitudes in contemporary Paris would bring to life a listening tape of which C40 was a part; discussion of some aspects of the French educational system makes comprehensible a conversation among students waiting for the *examen oral* of the *baccalauréat;* at a more elementary level, practice in telling time in French prepares for a tape where several prospective travelers are making enquiries at an airline counter.

3. Students may be encouraged to project, to think ahead to reasonable completions, by games which test their alertness in detecting tricks in the completion of sentences.

Contrôlez le narrateur is a team game which forces the student to think of the meaningful use of learned phrases or facts by dislodging them from their familiar settings. It may be given orally or on tape.

At the elementary stage, simple narratives may capitalize on common errors in meaning which students are making in everyday phrases they have learned in dialogues or classroom conversation. (For instance, elementary students often confuse *Comment allez-vous?* and *Quel âge avez-vous?* or *il a* and *il est*). Groups of students can prepare these narratives to try out on other groups. The team preparing the narrative gets points for each item missed by the opposing team.

One, or two, narrators read the prepared narrative expressively, not pausing or indicating in any other way where there are anomalies. When a student interrupts to point out an anomaly and is able to give an appropriate replacement, his team scores a point.

C43 (E) With anomalies italicized:

Ce matin je sors seule. Mon frère *qui m'accompagne* me demande:

— *Mademoiselle,* quel âge avez-vous?
— *Très bien, merci.* Et toi, quelle heure est-il?
— *J'ai onze ans,* répond-il.

Commentary

If each utterance begins, as in the last three utterances, with an inappropriate segment, the position of the error becomes predictable. Students preparing narratives should be alerted to avoid clues such as positional regularity, alternation of correct/incorrect, and so on.

(I) Attention to detail to overcome the lulling effects of expectation can also be encouraged in listening to factual material. In C44 below, some of the facts will be known to the students from a lesson in French geography; the effect of this lesson will be to create expectations which may make it difficult for them to "hear" some of the discrepancies. Once again a point is awarded to the team of the student who detects a fantastic or incorrect fact and can supply a suitable replacement for the offending segment.

C44 (I)

Statements read	*Replacements*
Bordeaux est un port de mer important situé	à cinq cents kilomètres
à cinq kilomètres de Paris.	*or* à une grande distance
	or loin . . .
Peu de bateaux entrent dans le port de Bordeaux.	Beaucoup
Tous les jours aussi de grands *châteaux* sortent du port.	bateaux
Ils sortent *de la porte* de Bordeaux pour aller dans toutes les parties *de la lune*.	du port
	du monde

Commentary

The narrator must be careful not to accentuate slightly the incorrect word or look for a response. Because of the phonetic similarity in some cases (*châteaux/bateaux*) and the fact that other words belong to the same semantic field (*beaucoup/peu*), student expectations will often result in their thinking they have heard what makes sense in the context.

B. *The active process of constructing a message: stages of perception* [19]

1. PERCEIVING A SYSTEMATIC MESSAGE

In listening comprehension *we first learn to perceive that there is a systematic message rather than accidental noise in a continuous stream of sound*. We learn to recognize a characteristic rise and fall of the voice, varying pitch levels, and recurrences of certain sound sequences which may seem somewhat like those of our own language, yet strangely different. At this stage, we make an elementary segmentation of what we hear in order to retain it in our memory. Even with gibberish or an utterance in a completely unknown tongue, we must segment in some way in order to repeat or memorize it. Many of the amusing things little children say result from their idiosyncratic segmentation of what they do not fully understand. (This is the stage called *Identification* in the chart of activities for listening comprehension, C67.)

Prolonged listening as an introduction to language study

Students are often plunged into trying to produce utterances in a new language too soon. As a result, they approximate these to the phonological system of their own language, without having any feeling for the distinctiveness of the new language.

It has been suggested by some that foreign-language learning should begin with a prolonged period of listening to the language without attempting to produce it. Prolonged listening to a strange language which is not associated with visuals, action, writing, or some intellectual exercise to help in identification of meaning, can become boring and will not necessarily lead to advantageous results. A baby hears a great deal of language around him for a long time before he speaks, but always associated with persons, places, objects, and bodily needs, so that he gradually focuses on segments of it which are functional in his living space.

The *total physical response* approach encourages early attentive listening with physical action to demonstrate comprehension, but with no attempt at production.[20]

C45 (E) In the form of the game Simon Says (*Jacques a dit*), this approach has always been with us:

TEACHER OR STUDENT   Levez la main.
Students do not react.
TEACHER OR STUDENT   Touchez la tête.
Students do not react.
TEACHER OR STUDENT   Jacques a dit: Touchez la tête.
Students touch their heads . . .

C46 In its more developed form, students learn to perform progressively more complicated series of actions, still without any attempt at production. This has been shown to produce a high rate of retention.[21]

Students move from simple imperatives (*écrivez; levez-vous*) to short directions (*allez à la porte; écrivez sur le tableau noir*), then to more complex directions (*allez au bureau du professeur et déposez la craie*), and finally to novel directions combining utterances already heard (*allez à la fenêtre, prenez le livre, déposez le livre sur le bureau du professeur, et asseyez-vous sur la chaise*).

Some practice of this type should be included in all early lessons, no matter what approach is being used.

Discriminating sounds which change meaning

1. Gattegno, it will be remembered, encourages early listening to tapes and disks of different languages, so that the student gradually comes to

recognize characteristics of the language he is learning. This is useful practice in identification. The classroom teacher can introduce this element without much difficulty by playing tapes of French songs and readings of poetry as background in the elementary classroom—in intervals before classes begin, while students are engaged on projects, over amplifiers to set the atmosphere for the beginning of a language laboratory session, or in a listening room or a listening corner of the classroom. This strategy encourages individual students to listen for the pleasure of the sounds. Some students will pick up parts of the songs, particularly refrains, purely by imitation as some opera singers do, thus learning to segment what they are hearing. This is pure perception, not reception of a message. Documentary films may be shown with the original French sound track, even before students can be expected to understand it, to familiarize the ear with the sound-aura of the language. After hearing a great deal of the language in this way, students will be far less inhibited about pronouncing words so that they really sound French.

2. Various types of *aural discrimination* exercises are given in Chapter 5. Some of these exercises can be worked into aural discrimination games and into competitions which involve listening practice. They should be continued at the intermediate level to keep students alert to sound distinctions which affect meaning.

C47 *Corrigez-moi*

Groups of students, or the teacher, prepare stories into which they work words which are inappropriate in the context but could be confused with the appropriate word if the listeners were not paying careful attention to sound distinctions. The student who has the best pronunciation or the teacher tells the story orally. A point is awarded to each student who notices an inappropriate word and is able to give the appropriate substitute with correct pronunciation.

In the sample text below, incorrect words are italicized and correct words are given in parentheses.

(I) Un jour je me promenais dans la *roue* (rue) en vélo. J'avais *femme* (faim) et je n'avais rien *boue* (bu) depuis le matin. *Au-dessous* (au-dessus) le soleil brillait dans le ciel bleu et le vent *d'eau* (doux) de l'automne me caressait les *jeux* (joues). Les feuilles *jeunes* (jaunes) tombaient des *sables* (arbres) le long de la route. Ma petite sœur *Jean* (Jeanne) me souriait de l'autre côté de la route et son petit *chêne* (chien) remuait *le cœur* (la queue) au plaisir de me *raconter* (rencontrer).

2. IMPOSING A STRUCTURE

In the second stage of perception, we identify in what we are hearing segments with distinctive structure—segments which seem to cohere. These segments may not be distinguishable by machine, because it is at this stage that *we impose a structure on what we are hearing according to our knowledge of the grammatical system of the language.* The more we know of a language the more easily we can detect meaningful segments, such as noun phrases, verb phrases, or adverbial phrases. Our experience with our own language makes us expect such structural segmentation. For this reason, we may segment incorrectly at first with a language with a very different structure. (It is interesting to note that in psychological experiments subjects rarely report hearing ungrammatical sentences, and when asked to repeat ungrammatical utterances they correct them, which indicates that they are imposing known structures in constructing a message from the sound signal.)

This early segmentation determines what we will remember of the actual sound signal. It is a process of *selection.* The identification of "chunks,"[22] or syntactic groupings, reduces the load on our memory. Just as it is easier to remember nine numbers in three groups (382 965 421), so it is easier to remember *Je le vois / juste en face / dans son jardin* as three syntactic groupings, or meaningful chunks, rather than as nine separate words, even if we are not sure of the lexical meanings of some of the words.

If we have segmented incorrectly or heard inaccurately, we will retain what we think we have heard, because we will have no further access to the sound signal after echoic memory has faded. (Echoic memory is estimated to last a few seconds only. It is during this interval that we can still readjust our segmentation, as discussed in C38.)

Practical application

Except in specialized courses, listening comprehension is not usually practiced in isolation from other language-learning activities. Some common classroom techniques help students develop their ability to hear language in organized chunks (or to segment according to syntactic groupings).

1. The *backward buildup* technique is frequently used in the memorization of conversation-facilitation dialogues. Each utterance to be memorized is divided into syntactically coherent segments. Students learn the last segment with correct end-of-utterance intonation, then the second-last followed by the last, and so on.

C48 Utterance 7 of C20 would be memorized in imitation of the model as follows:

près de la gare.

un bon petit restaurant près de la gare.

Il y a un bon petit restaurant près de la gare.

In this way students move from a new segment to a segment they already know, making for more confident recitation.[23]

2. *Dictation* is useful, when well integrated with other learning activities. Dictation also involves listening to language segmented in meaningful chunks. Students in the early stages should be encouraged to repeat the segments to themselves before trying to write what they think they have heard. This gives the student practice in imposing a construction on the segment before he writes it, thus increasing his short-term retention of the segment.

3. Oral exercises which require students to vary syntactic segments purposefully provide practice in "hearing" language in syntactically coherent chunks. (See Chapter 4: G9–G21.)

4. *Information Search (Renseignez-vous),* a kind of spot dictation, gives practice in detecting syntactic cues to segmentation. In this activity, students are asked to listen to a sequence of sentences, writing down only the segments which answer certain questions with which they are supplied beforehand. The passage is given orally several times, and students write down the segments which answer particular questions as they comprehend them, that is, after the first, the second, or the third hearing. This encourages attentive listening for specific segments that fulfill certain syntactic functions, e.g., who? where? what?

C49 (E) C'est le premier avril. Il est huit heures moins cinq. Marie-Lise est à l'école. Elle est à sa place au troisième rang. Devant elle il y a son amie, Anne-Marie. La classe va bientôt commencer. Marie-Lise sort de sa poche un petit poisson en papier argenté. Tout doucement elle l'attache au tablier d'Anne-Marie.

Questions supplied	*Segments to be written*
1. Quel jour est-ce?	le premier avril
2. Quelle heure est-il?	huit heures moins cinq
3. Où est Marie-Lise?	à l'école
4. Où est sa place?	au troisième rang
5. Qui est devant elle?	son amie, Anne-Marie
6. Est-ce que la classe commence?	Non, la classe va commencer
7. Qu'est-ce que Marie-Lise sort de sa poche?	un petit poisson en papier argenté
8. Où est-ce qu'elle l'attache?	au tablier d'Anne-Marie

5. *Faire ou ne pas faire.* Inexperienced students need practice in listening for certain *syntactic signals* which must be recognized automatically in rapid speech because their presence or absence crucially affects meaning. One of these is the signal of *negation*. Students need to recognize that *ne . . . que* merely modifies meaning, whereas *ne . . . pas, ne . . . plus,* and *ne . . . jamais* reverse it. Since in rapid speech the *ne* is frequently omitted,

the attention of students should be directed toward the second part of the negation.

In this game, which can be devised at quite an elementary level, students listen to a narration and mime or do not mime actions according to whether they are described affirmatively or negatively. The narration is given at normal speed, with the elisions and omissions (e.g., *e caduc*) of familiar style. Students who make the wrong movements are progressively eliminated, until only one student remains.

C50   (E and I) Based on C15.

Le matin, je n(e) me lève pas d(e) bonne heure.
Je dors jusqu'à huit heures.
Je m(e) réveille enfin et je r(e) garde par la f(e) nêtre.
Je n(e) me lave pas tout d(e) suite tous les jours.
Quelquefois je m(e) brosse les ch(e) veux pendant dix minutes.
Je n(e) me rase jamais parce que j(e n)'ai pas de barbe.
Je n(e) me brosse les dents que l(e) soir.
Après quelque temps j(e ne) fais plus ma toilette.
J'ouvre la f(e) nêtre et je r(e) garde les oiseaux.

A variation of this game, *Aujourd'hui ou demain?*, draws attention to *signals of tense*. Students mime an action in the present tense, but clap or tap with a pencil when they hear the *r* of futurity or the auxiliary use of *aller* in the immediate future. Students making wrong reactions are progressively eliminated.

C51   (E and I) Based on C15 and C50.

Nous n(e) nous lèv(e) rons pas d(e) bonne heure.
Nous dormons souvent jusqu'à huit heures.
Nous nous réveill(e) rons enfin et nous regard(e) rons par la f(e) nêtre.
Moi j(e) vais m(e) laver tout d(e) suite mais je n(e) me bross(e) rai pas les ch(e) veux.
Je m(e) brosse les dents l(e) matin; mais je n(e) me rase pas avant le p(e) tit déjeuner.
Ma sœur f(e) ra sa toilette plus tard.

*   Work out a game to train for recognition of the various question forms and interrogative intonation patterns.[24]

3. RECIRCULATING, SELECTING, RECODING FOR STORAGE

At the third stage of perception we recirculate material we are hearing through our cognitive system to relate earlier to later segments and *make the final selection* of what we will retain as the message. In this way, we follow a "line of thought." We then *recode what we have selected for storage in long-term memory.*

Rehearsal or recirculation of material perceived

1. Unfamiliar language elements which are being held in suspension and recirculated while decisions are being made as to the composition of the entire message impose a *heavy load on the short-term memory.* Sometimes the short-term memory becomes overloaded, and some of these segments have to be discarded in order to leave room for the absorption of new segments. It should not surprise us, therefore, if inexperienced listeners, at an elementary or even intermediate stage, declare that they understood everything as they were listening but are unable to recall what they understood. At this stage students may be able to recognize from multiple-choice items or true-false questions details of what they heard, whereas they would not be able to give a full account of the message without this help.

2. *Many different aspects of a listening text may be retained* by students, and these may not always be those elements the teacher expected. Students often need some guidance as to the facets of a message on which they should concentrate for the purpose of the exercise. This guidance in selection, which relieves the memory of some of the burden of detail, can be supplied by preliminary discussion or questions (given orally, or in writing).

3. At the elementary stage, students may be provided with questions with multiple-choice items *before* they begin listening. They should be encouraged to mark a tentative choice during the first hearing and confirm this on the second or third hearing. Teachers should remember that this method combines listening with reading. They should take care to see that the multiple-choice items supplied are short and expressed in language simple enough for the level of the students concerned. The items should not reproduce verbatim any sections of the material for listening practice, since this makes the task merely one of recognition, not comprehension.

4. Although some people consider that providing written questions is a *mixing of modalities* which raises doubts as to whether one is testing listening comprehension only, several other facts must be kept in mind.

a. *Oral questions* cannot be absorbed during the process of listening to other materials. (Psychological studies show that we filter out competing oral stimuli when the material to which we are listening demands careful attention.)

b. Oral questions given before or after the listening material add a further aural exercise to the one being evaluated. (Students may have understood the exercise, but not the questions on it.)

c. Oral questions asked *after* a listening exercise of some length require the retention of details over a period of time. They therefore test not only immediate comprehension, but long-term retention. The same observation may be made about oral questions asked *before* listening to an oral narrative, or dialogue, as a guide to selection. These will need to be repeated after the material has been heard. Otherwise, we are evaluating not only listening comprehension but also retention and recall. The use of oral questions is, therefore, more appropriate at the intermediate level. (For the special problems of short listening-comprehension items, see *Designing Multiple-Choice Items for Listening Comprehension,* below.)

d. At the elementary level, the problem of oral versus written questions is often solved by the *use of pictures*. Students are asked to circle the letter corresponding to the picture which best represents what they are hearing. They may also be asked to complete a diagram, or picture, according to oral directions or to mime what they are hearing.

5. When the attention of students is directed to particular aspects of the listening task, they will not retain in their memory material they do not require for this specific purpose, except incidentally. With C47, for instance, students may very well comprehend as they proceed and make correct decisions about the inappropriate items and appropriate replacements, yet still not be able to say at the end what the complete narration was about. After the C47 exercise has been completed, the passage should be read as a whole, with the appropriate replacements, as practice in comprehension of a complete narrative.

Note that since *the processes involved in fluent reading and in listening are similar,*[25] students will have the same problem in reading. A common test of reading has been to ask students to read a passage aloud with careful attention to diction, phrasing, and intonation. A student performing well on this task will not necessarily be able to answer questions on the content of what he has just read, without first being given the opportunity to reread the passage silently. With his attention concentrated on identifying meaningful segments, interrelating these in sentences distinguished by certain intonational patterns, and pronouncing individual words and groups of words comprehensibly, the student may have engaged his cognitive system in too much activity to be able also to recirculate segments and recode them for long-term storage.

6. When students have selected segments for the construction of the message they are extracting, they will no longer have access to the rejected segments (unless these were recirculated as alternatives and retained because the student was in doubt). If students have misunderstood the tenor of the message, the solution is not to question them further in an attempt to extract the correct message. They should be given some indication of where they misinterpreted the message and the opportunity to hear it again, so that they can construct a new version of it.

7. It is a mistake to make all listening comprehension exercises tests

with strict limitations. Students should be *allowed to listen to material as often as they need to* until they are able to "hear" and retain the content. Relaxed conditions, with no feelings of apprehension, are essential, since emotional tension greatly affects our ability to "hear" a message. Students should have frequent opportunities to listen to material purely for the pleasure of comprehension without the threat of grading.

8. *The recirculation of material in the memory takes place during the pauses in speech,* so the pauses are vital. In normal speech, pauses are lengthened by hesitation expressions (*euh . . . ah . . .* etc.), whereas in edited speech, or careful speech, these extensions of the pauses are missing. This allows less processing time for the listener. Speech which appears "too fast" to the inexperienced listener should be "slowed down" by lengthening slightly the pauses between segments, rather than by slowing down the delivery within the segments. The latter procedure distorts the natural sounds of the language by lengthening vowels, creating diphthongs, eliminating customary linking, and so on.

Recording of material for storage in long-term memory

We store what we hear in long-term memory in a simplified form. In common parlance, *we retain the gist of what was said,* that is, the basic semantic information, rather than the actual statements with all their complications of structure.

C52 We may hear the following discussion of grading systems in France and the United States.

RAY Je propose que nous disions un mot pour finir—ou presque—du système des notes qui est très différent en France et aux Etats-Unis. Aux Etats-Unis, quand on compte sur cent, il est très mauvais de donner à un étudiant une note inférieure à, disons, soixante-dix. En France, par contre, si je me réfère à une statistique récente qui a fait beaucoup de bruit, certains étudiants n'étaient pas très contents de la moyenne de leurs notes au baccalauréat. Cette moyenne était légèrement supérieure à 8/20. Le ministre a expliqué que la moyenne de 8/20, c'est une chose à peu près normale! Aux Etats-Unis par contre, la moyenne sur cent, c'est quelque chose comme quatre-vingts. C'est assez curieux![26]

C53 If asked what this passage was about, a student might come up with a series of statements like these:
Ray parle du système des notes.
Le système des notes est très différent en France et aux Etats-Unis.
Aux Etats-Unis on compte sur cent.
Aux Etats-Unis une note inférieure à soixante-dix est très mauvaise.

Récemment en France certains étudiants de baccalauréat étaient mécontents de la moyenne de leurs notes.

La moyenne de leurs notes était légèrement supérieure à 8/20 (huit sur vingt).

Le ministre a trouvé cette moyenne normale.

Aux Etats-Unis la moyenne des notes est plutôt quatre-vingts sur cent.

Cette différence est curieuse.

Commentary

1. In reducing what he heard to a set of factual statements, the student has produced *a series of simple active affirmative declarative sentences* (SAAD's to the psychologist). This is the basic type of sentence in most grammars. Facts in this form are the easiest to recall because all relationships are reduced to subject-verb-object, with some adverbial modifications.

2. A set of basic utterances like these is quite *redundant* in that much information is repeated from sentence to sentence, thus providing associational tags which make it easier to retrieve all the information about any one aspect, as in the following questions:

C54 Comment est le système des notes *aux Etats-Unis?*

Le système des notes aux Etats-Unis est différent du système français. On compte sur cent. Une note inférieure à soixante-dix est très mauvaise. La moyenne des notes est plutôt quatre-vingts sur cent.

Or: Est-ce que *la moyenne des notes* est la même en France et aux Etats-Unis?

Non, le système des notes est différent en France et aux Etats-Unis. En France on compte sur vingt et une moyenne de huit sur vingt est normale. Aux Etats-Unis on compte sur cent et la moyenne est plutôt quatre-vingts.

3. Note that *a certain amount of the information in the original has been dropped.* Without looking back to check the details, our reader, like the student listener, will probably not recall, for instance, that the French information was based on *une statistique récente qui a fait beaucoup de bruit* or that Ray was proposing a comparison of the grading systems in the United States and France as a subject of discussion. In preparing questions which require retrieval of information from long-term memory, teachers should keep in mind how this information is stored and *focus on the central line of thought and the basic facts,* rather than on peripheral detail.

Where there is ambiguity, the listener, by reducing the message to its basic elements, clarifies interpretatively relationships between what he has assimilated and what he is hearing.

C55 The listener hears:

Marie-Jeanne propose à son fiancé de faire des photos dans le jardin.

He recodes this information for long-term storage as:

A. Marie-Jeanne propose quelque chose à son fiancé.
    Elle va faire des photos dans le jardin.
or B. Marie-Jeanne propose quelque chose à son fiancé.
    Il va faire des photos dans le jardin.

If he has selected interpretation A for recoding for storage, this is what he will recall and he may even argue forcefully that this is exactly what was said, as listeners often do in native-language communication situations. After he has constructed interpretation A from what he has heard, interpretation B will be accessible to him only if a contiguous segment forces him to readjust interpretation A while he is still recirculating what he heard through his short-term memory.

Since psychological experiments and empirical intuition seem to indicate that recoding is basic to long-term memory storage, *we can help our students develop efficiency in listening comprehension,* and in retention and recall, by:

1. presenting them with an outline of the main ideas in basic SAAD sentences before they listen to a structurally complicated version;

2. by asking them to state in basic SAAD sentences what they have retained of a listening comprehension exercise;

3. by asking questions on the text which require SAAD sentences as answers.

The teacher's expectations

We cannot expect students to extract and retain from foreign-language listening material more than they do in the native language. Experiments have shown that average-ability adults recall a very low percentage of the possible information from broadcast talks (about 20 per cent when they were not aware that they were to be tested, 28 per cent when they knew they were to be tested). Other studies suggest that college students comprehend about half of the basic matter of lectures. The degree of listening efficiency on any particular occasion depends, of course, on the type of material and its organization, the interest the material holds for the listener, the way it is presented (speed, audibility, variations in tone of voice, situational relevance), and even such factors as the acoustics of the room and the emotional state or physical fatigue of the listener. Nevertheless, "evidence on the ability of people to be trained in listening makes it clear that many people listen below capacity"[27] in the native language. We may expect a higher degree of concentrated attention to a foreign-language listening exercise because students are aware of its difficulty for them, but *we must not look for total or near-total recall of detail*. In order to correct any unrealistic expectations, it is often useful to try a listening comprehension exercise out on a native speaker before giving it to foreign-language learners.

* Reduce the basic facts in the following text to SAAD sentences and write some questions which would extract from the listener this series of related facts, rather than a few isolated details.

C56   *Tu*[28]

RAY   Comment tutoyez-vous? Quand tutoyez-vous? Qui tutoyez-vous?

MARTINE   Eh bien, ça dépend de l'environnement . . . Si je suis au milieu de gens d'une certaine tenue, d'une certaine réserve, je les *vouvoie* automatiquement. . . .

JOËL   En général, une personne que l'on respecte ou que l'on est censé respecter, on la vouvoie. Par le mot *censé*, j'entends qu'il y a une certaine politesse, certaines conventions, qui font que vous devez vouvoyer. . . .

JEAN-CLAUDE   Pour moi, tutoyer quelqu'un c'est l'inclure dans son groupe. Moi, ça ne me gêne pas tellement—pas du tout même—de te tutoyer ici, bien qu'étant plus âgé que moi, parce qu'en ce moment on est dans un groupe, dans un même ensemble. Dans le travail, c'est différent . . . Actuellement, là où je travaille, il y a un chef de service qui a mon âge, qui est très *sympa* . . . mais je le vouvoie parce que je sais que ça serait choquant si je lui disais tu. Ça serait une sorte de barrière franchie en quelque sorte. Pour moi, le vouvoiement est social.

MARTINE   Je voudrais dire quand même que le fait de vouvoyer quelqu'un n'est pas automatiquement une marque de respect. Je peux respecter tout autant une personne que je tutoie. . . .

RAY   Au fond, c'est une espèce de sympathie envers quelqu'un, qui fait passer par dessus les marques habituelles de politesse. . . .

MARTINE   Il y a aussi le fait que, parmi les jeunes surtout, on peut tutoyer quelqu'un même si on ne le connaît pas; ça arrive très fréquemment. Il y a une certaine *vogue* du tutoiement . . . Mais il faut dire que ça n'est pas vrai dans tous les milieux. Par exemple, j'ai travaillé pendant un mois, l'été dernier, dans l'entreprise où travaille mon père; j'étais au service de traduction. Il y avait dans ce service quatre filles qui avaient entre vingt et vingt-cinq ans et qui toutes se vouvoyaient; et moi, ça m'a énormément choquée. . . .

NICOLE   Moi, je crois que toute la subtilité entre le tu et le vous, c'est une question de sentiment.

RAY   C'est bien la raison pour laquelle il est si difficile aux grammaires françaises de l'expliquer!

C. Strategies of perceptual segmentation

For the psychologist Bever, "the internal logical relations are a major determiner of perceptual segmentation in speech processing."[29] This view aligns well with that of the linguist G. Lakoff of the generative semantics group, that logical categories and logical classes provide the natural basis for grammar and, therefore, ultimately of language use.[30] In other words, since our experience of the real world has taught us to expect such functions as agents, actions, objects, and place, time, and manner modifications,[31] we identify these in what we hear.

Bever has identified four strategies[32] which we seem to employ in the perception of speech.

1. First of all, we tend to segment what we hear into sequences which could form *actor-action-object . . . modifier* relations. This segmentation strategy Bever calls Strategy A. Clearly, for this elementary segmentation, we need to be able to identify, at least approximately, syntactic groups. Fortunately, languages generally supply a certain number of surface indicators of function, or syntactic cues which we use to separate out different clauses within the sentence.[33] This aspect of perceptual segmentation has already been discussed as stage two of the active process of constructing a message, and exercises have been proposed for developing this ability in a foreign language.

2. In English at least, we learn to expect *the first N . . . V . . . (N)*

(that is, noun . . . verb . . . optional noun) *to be the main clause* (that is, to set out the overriding idea of the sentence) unless morphemes like *if, when,* or *before* warn us that we are dealing with a subordinate clause. This segmentation Strategy B carries over to French, for the most part, although this would not necessarily be so for all languages. The student needs to learn to interpret rapidly such cues as *si, quand, avant que, quoique,* which indicate subordination, and, at the advanced level, to recognize such deviations from the usual pattern as the not uncommon sentence opening segment *noun phrase + past participle,* which he might encounter in more formal listening materials, e.g., *le congrès terminé, il a pris le chemin de Moscou; la mesure prise, on attend la suite.*

3. In applying Strategy C, we seek the meaning by *combining the lexical items in the most plausible way.* Thus, *the dog bit the man* is easily comprehended, whereas *the man bit the dog,* not being consistent with our normal experiences of the real world, gives us pause. We may "hear" it as *the man was bitten by the dog,* but be forced to reprocess it as subject-verb-object when later segments make it clear that something unusual has happened. Alternatively, we may ask the speaker to repeat his statement.

4. Sometimes there is no specific semantic information to guide us in assigning relationships. We then fall back on a primary functional labeling strategy, based on the apparent order of lexical items in a sentence— Strategy D. We assume that any *noun-verb-(noun), NV(N),* sequence represents the relations *actor-action-object.* It is for this reason that we understand the active construction *the dog chased the cat* more quickly than the passive form *the cat was chased by the dog.* Since the latter allows semantically for reversal of roles, it will often be heard as *the cat chased the dog,* especially by children. In a continuing message, later information which does not support this interpretation will cause us to pause and reprocess the utterance syntactically. We then search for cues (passive form of the verb, agent *by-*phrase) which indicate to us the order *logical object–verb–logical subject.*

SEMANTIC-SYNTACTIC DECODING

Schlesinger has called the process of relying at first on semantic expectations and resorting to syntactic processing only in doubtful cases *semantic-syntactic decoding.*[34] In summary, we perceive the semantic cues and rapidly assign these such roles as actor (or experiencer or instrument), action, object, or modifier according to our knowledge of the real world. It is when our initial interpretation does not fit into the developing message that we pause to analyze syntactic cues to function.

Because of this initial tendency in listening to take the easier road of

semantic decoding, students with an *extensive vocabulary* can often interpret a great deal of what they hear by sheer word recognition and logical
reasoning. A person listening to a news broadcast might identify the following lexical items:

C57 ... jeune femme ... vingt-cinq ans ... avion ... Air France ... liaison Paris-
Nice ... menace ... armes ... obligé ... pilote ... Marseille ... quatre heures
... série ... exigences ahurissantes ... Finalement ... aéroport ... Marseille
... brigade anti-commando ... décidé ... intervenir ... trois hommes déguisés ... stewards ... montés ... appareil ... abattu ... pirate de l'air.

With this basic information, his knowledge of similar situations, and
his powers of inference, the student would probably have little difficulty
deducing the following facts:

C58 Une jeune femme de vingt-cinq ans s'est emparée d'un avion d'Air France
effectuant la liaison Paris-Nice. Sous la menace de ses armes, elle a obligé
le pilote à mettre le cap sur Marseille et pendant quatre heures elle a
formulé une série d'exigences ahurissantes ... Finalement, à l'aéroport
de Marseille la brigade anti-commando a décidé d'intervenir: trois hommes
déguisés en stewards sont montés dans l'appareil. Ils ont abattu la pirate
de l'air.[35]

* As an exercise in introspection, try to remember which of Strategies A–D
you employed in your perception of the meaning of C57.

AURAL RECOGNITION VOCABULARY

Since combining lexical items in a plausible way plays such an important
role in listening comprehension, attention should be given to building an
extensive aural recognition vocabulary.

For many students, particularly above the elementary level, the greater
part of their vocabulary is acquired in association with reading and writing. It is not surprising, therefore, that many of them have problems in
recognizing by ear the words they already know in graphic form. They
also have difficulty recognizing words derived from these, and even the
cognates and the rapidly disseminated vocabulary of contemporary tech-
nology, science, politics, and social diversions (*le pipeline, la bombe
hydrogène, le missile-gap, le pop et le rock*). Many of these terms are
pronounced in a sufficiently different fashion in French to appear novel to
the inexperienced ear. In C58, for instance, even /katrœr/ when spoken
at normal speed may not be obvious to a visually trained person, while

words like /pirat/ and /stiwart/ may elude recognition, and /egziʒɑ̃s/ may not be recognized as a derivative of /egziʒe/.

To develop confidence in aural recognition of words originally encountered in graphic form, students need to understand and apply constantly the rules of sound-symbol correspondence in French. Although these rules may at times seem a little complicated (see R27), they are, on the whole, very regular. Knowledge of such rules often helps a student to visualize the probable spelling of a seemingly new word and so to relate it to what he knows. This is an ability which is important to a person who has been accustomed to learning the language graphically or who by modality preference is visually oriented.

All kinds of practice techniques and competitions can foster transfer from visual to aural recognition and from aural to visual.

1. Clearly *comprehensible pronunciation of all new words* should be expected as they are encountered, so that the students' ears are kept tuned to a high pitch. This is particularly important beyond the elementary level, where students and teacher often relax their efforts in this regard. It is no wonder that such students fail to recognize words pronounced so differently from the classroom norm.

2. Flashcards should be made of *groups of words which follow certain rules* of sound-symbol correspondence and competitions organized with points allotted to the first person who gives the correct pronunciation for the series, e.g.:

sain, main, pain;
bon, pont, allons;
sein, nain, daim.

Later, more rigorous competitions can be conducted with the words isolated from the series and presented in short sentences.

3. Conversely, students should hear words in short sentences and be asked to *identify* which of the *spellings* on three cards represents the word they heard, e.g.:

/rjɛ̃/ rein, riant, rien;
/bɔrne/ bonnet, borné, bonté.

4. Students should be shown cards of words in *special problem groups* and drilled in their pronunciation, e.g.:

/sjɔ̃/ nation, révolution, incarnation;
/ɛj/ soleil, sommeil, orteil.

5. Spelling bees (*concours d'orthographe*) may be conducted to arouse enthusiasm for a high level of performance. Words are given in sentences, then repeated in isolation, or in short word-groups, for the student to write down, e.g.:

il lit les deux quotidiens — *quotidiens*
Il reste dans le palais présidentiel — *le palais présidentiel.*

Those making mistakes are progressively eliminated until a champion is found.

6. These may be paralleled by pronunciation bees (*concours de prononciation*). Sentences are flashed on the screen or wall by overhead projector, or are shown on flashcards, and elimination contests are conducted for acceptable pronunciation, e.g.:

Où est *la Pologne?* /lapɔlɔɲ/

Note: Items for both 5 and 6 should be kept to words students may be expected to meet. Common words with irregular pronunciation will be introduced, e.g., *il l'a* eu. Any unfamiliar word which follows regular sound-symbol correspondence rules is admissible, e.g., *crépuscule, extinction, rognon, piétiner.* Teams may work out elimination lists to try on each other.

7. *Spot dictation* is useful at the elementary level (see R26); continuous dictation passages at higher levels.

8. Students should be trained in the changes in pronunciation as one moves *from a root word through various derivatives and compounds.* Once again, each series admissible must follow regular sound-symbol correspondence rules, e.g.:

   bon, bonne, bonté, bonnement, bon garçon, bon enfant;
   /bɔ̃/ /bɔn/ /bɔ̃te/ /bɔnmã/   /bɔ̃garsɔ̃/   /bɔnãfã/
   beau, belle, beauté, embellir.
   /bo/ /bɛl/ /bote/ /ãbɛlir/

Students may work out series of this type by dictionary search and then dictate them to each other.

9. Students should be given regular practice in finding and interpreting *pronunciations in dictionaries.* Teaching phonetic symbols for recognition purposes can arouse interest in this exercise.

10. If students are to understand radio newscasts and documentary films, they should be given regular training in the aural identification of the *contemporary vocabulary for matters of international preoccupation,* e.g., /lapɔlysjɔ̃dlɛr/ *la pollution de l'air,* /lərsiklaʒ/ *le recyclage.*

Some people will object that the above recommendations relate the aural too closely to the graphic and that aural vocabulary should be learned only by ear. This may be advisable for specialized aural courses, although, even in this case, student modality preferences must be allowed some play. Most intermediate and advanced foreign-language classes have multiple aims. Students who have been trained to depend on visual information need the liberating realization that there are predictable relationships between the pronunciation of a word and its written form. In this way, what they have learned in one modality can become available to them in the other, and the students' limited processing capacity will be used more economically and efficiently.

Macro or Micro?

With listening, as with all other aspects of language learning, we must keep in view the final goal of *macro-language use* (the ability to use language holistically for normal life-purposes). *Micro-language learning* (the learning of elements of language and their potential combinations) is only a means leading to this end.

In the macro context, listening can be evaluated only by response: How does the listener react emotionally? How does he respond—verbally or by action? Does he do what he has been asked or told? Does he use the information offered? Does he fill the supportive role of the listener? (In other words, does he utter, at appropriate intervals, agreeing or consoling interpolations, exclamations of surprise, or tut-tutting noises—such expressions in French as *Ah bon? Ah oui? Non, non! Oh la la! Vraiment? Ça alors!*) Does he laugh or smile at the right moments? Is he absorbed by what he is hearing?

Because micro-language learning is more easily assessed than macro-language use, there is a tendency to think of the evaluation of listening comprehension in terms of multiple-choice and true/false items. Certainly these can play a useful part in directing the students' efforts in listening and helping them assess the accuracy of their comprehension. The importance of understanding fine detail at crucial points in some aural tasks cannot be ignored, since puzzlement can cause an emotional or cognitive block, which overloads channel capacity so that the student loses the thread. On the other hand, there are students who tackle aural comprehension almost heuristically with considerable success. Students who can cope with macro-language use practically from the start may be wasting their time on micro-tests of detail. Other students need the developmental, step-by-step approach, and their needs should not be neglected. Even for the latter, however, functional comprehension in real situations must be the ultimate criterion.

For these reasons, listening comprehension is particularly suited to individualized arrangements, with students working at their own level and their own pace. Teachers should assemble all the materials they can find into *developmental listening kits,* each containing micro-training exercises for particular purposes, but culminating in a macro-activity. Students should be encouraged to work their way through a series of these kits in their own manner and at their own pace. Taking one's own time is important in listening, where individuals require differing lengths of time for processing. Students who are capable of doing so should be encouraged to jump from macro-activity to macro-activity, until listening to the foreign language becomes for them natural and effortless. Eventually most students will reach the stage where their listening is completely integrated with communication activities of the kind outlined in Chapter 2.

ASSESSMENT OF MACRO-LANGUAGE USE

We must place the student in a situation where listening comprehension plays an essential role, then see how he copes. Macro-language evaluation should be related to the normal uses of listening in life-situations:

1. as part of a purposeful communicative interchange;
2. for receiving direction or instructions;
3. for obtaining information;
4. for the pleasure of an activity like watching a play, a film, a TV show, or a fashion parade, or listening to a sports commentary, a newscast, or group discussion on the radio;
5. for participating in social gatherings (listening to small talk, listening to others conversing, and so on).

Any items in the B and D sections of the *Chart of Listening Comprehension Activities,* C67, are appropriate for macro-language assessment.

ASSESSMENT OF MICRO-LANGUAGE LEARNING

Many aspects of micro-language learning have already been discussed in this chapter (discrimination of sounds which change meaning; recognition of intonation patterns, syntactic segments, and word groups with high frequency of occurrence; aural vocabulary recognition). Any activities in the A and C sections of the *Chart of Listening Comprehension Activities,* C67, can be adapted to micro-language testing.

One of the commonest forms of assessment of this developmental phase of listening comprehension is the use of *multiple-choice questions,* yet the preparation of this type of test holds many pitfalls for the inexperienced.

The test items often consist of *short questions or comments in isolation,* like those in C59, for which students choose appropriate rejoinders (sometimes completions) from multiple-choice options.

C59 1. Où allez-vous ce matin?
     2. Quelle heure est-il?
     3. Qu'est-ce qu'il y a là-bas?

In natural interaction, there is a context for such short utterances which helps in the interpretation of the fleeting sounds, e.g., place, time, relationship of the person speaking to the person addressed, previous utterance, gesture of pointing or eyes turned in a certain direction, facial expression of exasperation, surprise, or expectancy. If the person addressed is taken off-guard, the interlocutor frequently makes a circumstantial comment before repeating the question, thus bringing it into focus, e.g.,

C60   A. Où allez-vous ce matin?
        B. Vous dites?
        A. Il est très tôt. Où allez-vous ce matin?

Materials writers often seem not to realize that isolated short utterances are more difficult to "hear" correctly than longer, contextualized segments.

In real life, the responses which would actually occur to such short, non-contextualized utterances may well be some of the options considered "incorrect" by the writer of the multiple-choice exercise. Choosing the "appropriate" response then becomes a question of reading the mind of the item-writer or the corrector of the exercise.

C61   Circle the letter corresponding to the most appropriate response to the question you hear.

     Recorded voice: Où allez-vous ce matin?
       A. Je rentre tout juste de la gare.
       B. A la messe. Tu viens aussi?
       C. Moi, je vais écrire des lettres.
       D. J'attends un ami.

Any of the above is an "appropriate response" in a certain context.

     A. *Je rentre tout juste de la gare.* (I may be walking along the street, but I'm not *going* anywhere. I'm *coming back.*)

     B. *A la messe. Tu viens aussi?* (The "appropriate response" anticipated.)

     C. *Moi, je vais écrire des lettres.* (I'm not going anywhere this morning. I've got far too much to do here at home.)

     D. *J'attends un ami.* (I may look as if I'm waiting for the lights to change so that I can cross the road, but I'm not.)

As any experienced teacher knows, students who dispute the grading of such short multiple-choice items can often justify their choices quite logically. Some kind of context should be built into every listening item.

C62   (Cf. C59.)
     1. Vous mettez votre manteau! Où allez-vous ce matin?
     2. J'ai faim! Quelle heure est-il, s'il te plaît?
     3. Qu'est-ce qu'il y a là-bas? De l'autre côté de la rue?

Students should also be given opportunities from time to time to select more than one "appropriate response," adding a brief note indicating a possible context. This encourages projection of expectations of the kind provided also in *Situation Tapes* (C33).

The following fully contextualized passage for listening would actually be easier than a short, non-contextualized utterance (if we exclude clichés and sentences students have heard over and over again in class):

C63 (I) *Recorded voice:*

Il faisait très chaud et l'eau était fraîche. Partout on voyait des gens qui se baignaient. Pierre était étendu sur le dos à l'ombre d'un rocher; il laissait passer du sable entre ses doigts. Dans le lointain un bateau partait pour l'Angleterre. Que faisait Pierre?

Choices supplied: A. Il s'embarquait sur un bateau.
B. Il se baignait dans la mer.
C. Il se reposait sur la plage.
D. Il construisait un château de sable.

The recorded passage contains a number of associated concepts which provide clues to the correct answer. The student who has understood some parts clearly, but not all, has more opportunity in a longer passage like this to reconstruct by conjecture those sections he did not comprehend fully.

DESIGNING MULTIPLE-CHOICE ITEMS FOR LISTENING COMPREHENSION

Many of the problems of multiple-choice items discussed in Chapter 7, in the section *Assisting and Assessing Reading Comprehension* (p. 217) apply also to multiple-choice items for assessing listening comprehension. There must be no ambiguity in the choices. The correct choice should not repeat word for word some sentence in the listening text. The correct choice should not depend on comprehension or non-comprehension of one unusual vocabulary item. Where there is a series of questions on one passage, the correct choices should not form an obvious sequence which students can detect without understanding the passage (a later item can sometimes supply the answer sought in an earlier question). Care must be taken to see that the items do not test powers of logical deduction, or ability to recognize exact paraphrases, rather than actual comprehension of the passage.

Apart from the general problems of preparing multiple-choice questions, items for listening comprehension present problems peculiar to this modality. The items have to be prepared in such a way that they give a clear indication of what the student "heard," that is, constructed per-

sonally from the sound signal. The item-writer must be able to imagine himself in the place of the neophyte and reconstruct what the latter may be "hearing." For these reasons, it is difficult for a native speaker to construct suitable choices for foreign-language listeners, unless he has had long experience with their particular problems.

It is useful to analyze the types of confusions one is anticipating on the part of the listeners by the choices one proposes. If there is no predictable rationale for a certain choice, it can be considered a "donkey item" which will be chosen only by a student who interpreted almost nothing of the sound signal. There should never be more than one "donkey item" in each set and this particular item must be very plausible, if it is to be selected at all. Unless it has some obvious relationship to the rest of the set, or reechoes closely what was heard, even the donkeys will shy away from it.

C64 (E) *Recorded voice:* Est-ce que vous vous êtes couché de bonne heure hier soir?

A. Non, nous avons soupé à sept heures hier soir.
B. Oui, je me couche à onze heures tous les soirs.
C. Oui, je me suis mis au lit à huit heures du soir.
D. Oui, vous vous couchez à la même heure chaque soir.

Commentary

A. The student who chooses A identifies

1. the question form *Est-ce que* and the pronoun *vous,* requiring the answer *je* or *nous;*

2. the lexical item *heure* and the expression *hier soir* (which provides some associative context); and

3. the /u/ in /kuʃe/ which he recognizes again in *soupé.*

4. A student weak enough to choose this item may well pronounce *onze* as /ɔnz/ and so interpret /bɔnœr/ as /ɔnzœr/. Having decided that *soupé* is what he heard and considering *onze heures* to be a late hour for this activity, he selects *Non* and Choice A with a more appropriate hour.

B. The student who chooses B identifies

1. the question form *Est-ce que* and the pronoun *vous,* requiring the answer *je* or *nous;*

2. *heure* in a context which somewhat resembles *onze heures;*

3. the word *coucher,* which is repeated in this item;

4. *hier soir,* or at least *soir,* which is reechoed in this item.

The student has not, however, understood the question. He chooses an item which assembles all of these elements in a plausible statement.

C is the correct response.

It expresses the main concept in nearly synonymous terms (*se coucher—se mettre au lit*), thus testing the apprehension of meaning, and contains a response element which is consistent with the question element (*de bonne heure hier soir—à huit heures du soir*). This avoids the possibility that the student is not comprehending but selecting the choice with the most items in identical form.

D. The student has not understood the question, but the D response matches his audial image of parts he perceived (*couché . . . heure . . . soir*) and seems plausible, so he chooses D, which is a "donkey item" in that it makes no pretense at answering the question.

C65 (I) Tout le monde sait que la France est célèbre pour sa cuisine. Il ne faut pas croire, pourtant, que les Français mangent tous les jours du lapin en sauce et du canard à l'orange. En effet, chez lui, le Français moyen prend volontiers un simple bifteck avec des frites. Il suffit que le tout soit bien fait. Il y a des cuisiniers américains qui pensent que pour faire de la bonne cuisine française, il suffit d'ajouter de la sauce ou du vin à tous les plats. Quelle erreur!

Qu'est-ce que vous avez appris sur la cuisine française?

A. Les Français aiment les plats simples quand ils sont bien préparés.
B. Il suffit d'ajouter du vin ou de la sauce à tous les plats pour faire de la cuisine française.
C. Les Français mangent du canard et du lapin tous les jours.
D. Les Français aiment manger dans la cuisine.[36]

Commentary

An additional source of error in this example may be the student's lack of knowledge of the French way of life.

A. The correct choice draws elements from several sentences and requires comprehension of a sequence of ideas.

B. This choice echoes a complete sentence the student has heard and reflects a common misconception about the subject. If the student has not related what he is hearing at this point with what he has heard previously, he may select this item.

C. The student who chooses C has heard clearly a statement like this but has not noted the structural interrelationships (in this case, the influence of *il ne faut pas croire . . . que* on the meaning supplied by the subordinate clause). He has also not recognized the modifying effect of the logical opposition word *pourtant*.

D. The student choosing D has not followed the line of thought, but has recognized the names of various foods and the lexical item *cuisine* which he learned early in his studies meant *kitchen*. Since this type of student has a rather elementary knowledge of French, this choice is deliberately constructed by using only words commonly found in elementary courses.

* *Analyze* in similar fashion the anticipated reactions of the students who will choose the various alternatives in the following listening comprehension exercise.

C66 Comment! Il est déjà parti! A six heures du matin!
   A. Oui, il va nous quitter bientôt.
   B. Oui, la partie a continué toute la nuit.
   C. Oui, tu comprends, il travaille très loin d'ici.
   D. Non, je ne pars pas à six heures du matin.

C67 *Chart of listening comprehension activities* [37]

In the following chart, the activities are divided into four learning stages:

A. *Identification:* perception of sounds and phrases; identifying these directly and holistically with meaning.

B. *Identification and selection without retention:* listening for the pleasure of comprehension, extracting sequential meanings, without being expected to demonstrate comprehension through active use of language.

C. *Identification and guided selection with short-term retention:*[38] students are given some prior indication of what they are to listen for; they demonstrate their comprehension immediately in some active fashion.

D. *Identification and selection with long-term retention:* students demonstrate their comprehension, or use the material they have comprehended, after the listening experience has been completed; or they engage in an activity which requires recall of material learned some time previously.

Elementary level (E)

A. IDENTIFICATION (E)
Macro

1. Listening to tapes of various languages to detect the language one is learning.

2. Listening to songs and poems for the pleasure of the sounds (in classroom, listening room, or listening corner).

3. Songs and poems amplified in language laboratory for atmosphere.

4. Hearing original sound tracks of documentary films before being able to understand them.

Micro

5. Aural discrimination exercises.

6. Short-phrase discrimination with pictures.

7. Listening to segments of dialogue to be learned.

8. Responding with miming actions to segments from dialogue learned or from classroom conversation.

9. Responding with flashcards to names of letters of the alphabet.

10. Backward buildup in imitation of a model (C48).

B. IDENTIFICATION AND SELECTION WITHOUT RETENTION (E)

11. Games involving miming of words and phrases learned.

12. Listening to conversation-facilitation dialogues, songs, or poems already learned.

13. Listening to retelling of stories already read, reacting in some way to variations from the original.

14. Listening to a conversation which is a variant of a dialogue studied.

15. Listening to an anecdote based on reading material studied.

16. Teacher gives some background information on a topic, then tells an anecdote, or describes an experience.

With visual

17. Listening to description of pictures or slides.

18. Listening to an anecdote, story, or dialogue illustrated with a flannelboard (*tableau de feutre*).

19. Listening to a *Show and Tell* oral report (*Montrer-raconter*).

With action

20. Total physical response activity or *Jacques a dit* (C45–46).

21. Obeying classroom instructions.

22. Listening to simple narration, raising hands whenever a color (or occupation, or kind of food, etc.) is mentioned.

23. *Letter Bingo:* Letters of alphabet called randomly; each student checks against word in front of him; first student with complete word wins.

24. *Number Bingo (Lotto):* Numbers called randomly; students check numbers on their cards; first student with all numbers correctly checked wins.

C. IDENTIFICATION AND GUIDED SELECTION WITH SHORT-TERM
RETENTION (E)
With visual

25. Discrimination of numbers, dates, and times of day by pairing with multiple-choice items, clockfaces, lists of famous events, or flight schedules.

26. Learning a dialogue with vanishing techniques (see *Dialogue Exploitation* in Chapter 1, p. 33).

27. True/false questions supplied beforehand; student listens to variation of dialogue or story read and checks answers.

28. Multiple-choice answers supplied beforehand; student listens to dialogue or story using recombinations of vocabulary and structures learned, and checks appropriate answers.

With action

29. Miming the actions in story being narrated.

30. Obeying complex classroom instructions for class exercises and tests.

31. Completing a diagram according to instructions.

32. *Faire ou ne pas faire* (C50): miming affirmative, but not negative, statements.

With speaking

33. Directed dialogue (C24).

34. Group piecing together of a new dialogue from initial hearings.

35. Participating in Cummings device (C29).

36. Participating in Gouin series (C11–13).

37. Participating in verbal-active series (C15).

38. *Qui est-ce? Qu'est-ce que c'est? Où est-ce?* (guessing who, what, or which place is being described by teacher or student).

39. Intensive practice exercises varying syntactic segments (see Chapter 4).

40. Running commentary: listening to a story and giving the gist at the end of each sentence in SAAD's (see C52–53).

With writing

41. Writing down words which are dictated letter by letter.

42. Writing from dictation series of numbers of increasing length and complexity.

43. *Information Search* (*Renseignez-vous,* C49) : writing down segments which answer particular questions.

44. Dictation: students repeat to themselves what they think they heard before they write it.

45. Spot dictation (R26).

D. IDENTIFICATION, SELECTION, AND LONG-TERM RETENTION (E)

46. Listening to a continuation of a story (with same vocabulary area, same setting, and same characters).

47. Listening to a story different from, but with similar vocabulary to, one already read.

48. Listening to a conversation similar to one studied.

49. Listening to skits prepared by other students.

50. Listening to dramatizations of stories read.

51. Listening without the text to the expressive reading (on tape, by the teacher, or by a student) of a poem already studied.

52. Listening to other students reciting poems in a poetry competition.

53. Checking answers to aural questions given before or after a passage for listening.

54. Checking appropriate choices for multiple-choice continuations (or rejoinders) given orally after a listening passage.

With speaking

55. Listening to a story, then giving the gist at the end in SAAD's (see C52–53).

56. Answering questions orally on a passage just heard.

57. Responding to others in spontaneous role-playing.

58. Listening to and discussing oral reports of other students.

59. Chain dialogue (C25).

60. Rubbishing the dialogue (C26).

61. Acting out learned dialogues with others (paraphrasing the sense rather than repeating by rote).

62. Learning and acting a part with others in a skit or original dialogue.

63. *Devinez mon métier:* student mimes a series of actions, others ask yes-no questions until they have guessed what the student does for a living.

With writing

64. Student answers questions in writing after he has listened to a story or conversation.

65. Student writes down what he has learned from another student's oral report.

66. Cloze test on content of what has been heard (W28).

Intermediate level (I)

A. IDENTIFICATION (I)

1. Aural discrimination of small sound distinctions which change meaning of sentences.

2. Recognition of characteristics of familiar level of speech with elisions, *e caduc,* syllables omitted (e.g., *tu n'es pas bête* as /tepabɛt/) through listening to authentic informal speech on tapes, disks, or film sound tracks.

With visual

3. Aural recognition of French pronunciation of names of foreign personalities and places (supplied on scrambled lists).

4. Aural recognition of French/English cognates from scrambled lists.

With action

5. Recognition of aural indicators of tense: *Aujourd'hui ou demain* (C51)—tapping for future tenses, miming present tenses.

With writing

6. Demonstrating recognition of French equivalents of contemporary, international scientific, technical, political, and social vocabularies by writing these down.

B. IDENTIFICATION AND SELECTION WITHOUT RETENTION (I)

7. Listening to complete reading of story studied in sections.

8. Listening to dramatization of story read.

9. Listening to the acting out of scenes from play read.

10. Listening to disk or tape of reading by French professional of short story, poem, or extracts from novel.

11. Listening to a version in SAAD's before listening to a more complicated version (see C52–53). No questions asked.

12. Listening to teacher or other student telling amusing incident which happened on the way to school or at school.

13. Listening to a news item told by teacher or another student.

14. Listening to teacher or another student give background information for news item.

15. Listening to teacher or another student give background information for reading or for a class or group project.

16. Following the line of discussion in a group conversation.

17. Listening to French songs.

With visual

18. Listening to a presentation of slides of some aspect of France, French history, or the arts.

19. Watching and listening to a documentary film on some aspect of France or French life.

20. Watching and listening to a final showing of a scholastic film, with background of contemporary French culture, which has already been studied in class.

21. Listening to a story as one is reading it silently, to improve fluent reading techniques.

With action

22. Following directions for classroom organization.

C. IDENTIFICATION AND GUIDED SELECTION WITH SHORT-TERM RETENTION (I)

23. Selecting from aural choices completions for sentences heard.

24. Listening to oral compositions of other students.

25. Listening to skits and spontaneous role-playing of other students.

26. Students discuss news beforehand; then listen to newscasts to find answers to certain questions raised.

27. Students listen to exchange tapes and correspondence tapes.

28. *Qu'est-ce que je décris?* (guessing object described by fellow student). Alternatives: *Où suis-je? Qui est-ce?*

With visual

29. Student is provided with multiple-choice or true/false questions beforehand, then checks answers as he listens, or immediately afterwards.

30. Student chooses among written completions for sentences given orally.

31. Student practices reading aloud with tape model: student reads segment, listens to model reading, then rereads segment.

32. Students watch films of which they have previously studied sound track or synopsis.

33. Students watch films in which they are looking for specific cultural details, certain interactions of characters, or particular developments of the story.

With action

34. Following instructions for making something.

With speaking

35. Providing oral sentence completions at end of longer and longer sequences.

36. Student is asked questions aurally beforehand, hears passage, hears aural questions again, and gives oral answers.

37. Student gives spontaneous responses on Situation Tapes (C33).

38. *Corrigez-moi* (C47): noting inappropriate words in story given orally and suggesting appropriate replacements.

39. *Vingt et une questions:* group asking of eliminative yes-no questions to discover name of famous person selected for the game. Alternatives: *Identification, Animal-minéral-végétal.*

40. *Ni oui, ni non:* group elimination game where students are asked all kinds of questions which they may answer in any way they can, so long as they never use *oui* or *non*.

41. Oral spelling bees (*concours d'orthographe*).

42. Taking part in Lipson-type puzzle exercises.

43. Fulfilling the supportive role of the listener (*Ah bon? ... Ah oui? ...*).

With writing

44. Written spelling bees.

45. Spot comprehension: students are given incomplete statements about the content of what they will hear; after listening, they fill in the blanks with the missing details, expressed in short phrases.

46. Dictation: gradually increasing length of segment to be retained.

47. Taking dictations containing information on cultural matters discussed: e.g., famous sayings of leading historical figures, famous anecdotes every French child knows (e.g., Jeanne d'Arc recognizing Charles VII; the Vase of Soissons).

48. Taking from dictation notes on the lives and achievements of historical figures, painters, musicians.

D. IDENTIFICATION, SELECTION, AND LONG-TERM RETENTION (I)

49. Listening without a script to readings of plays studied.

50. Listening to a part of a play for which students will develop impromptu continuations later.

51. Listening to episodes of a mystery serial.[39]

With speaking

52. Answering aural questions asked after a long listening passage.

53. Group conversations and discussions on an assigned topic.

54. Preliminary discussion for preparation of oral compositions.

55. Questions and discussion after listening to other students' oral compositions.

56. Participating in spontaneous skits and role-playing.

57. After listening, answering questions asked in SAAD's (see C52–53).

58. Listening to a passage, then giving the gist in SAAD's.

59. Listening to a mystery without hearing the conclusion; then discussing possible explanations.

60. Taking map journeys (C14).

61. *Le Coupable* (discovering crime of which one is accused and defending oneself).

62. Participating in simulated telephone conversations or authentic telephone conversations with monolingual, or presumed monolingual, French speakers.

63. Interviewing visiting French native speaker to find out who he is, what he does, what he thinks, and so on.

64. *Pas de secrets:* discovering the secret a fellow student is concealing (can be pet peeves, career plans, weekend plans, etc.).

65. *Qui dit la vérité?* Three students pretend to be the person whose unusual experiences are recounted at the beginning; other students try to find out, by questioning, who is the real Monsieur Un Tel (Madame Une Telle).

66. *Charades:* see *Categories of Language Use* 10 in Chapter 2, p. 52.

67. *General Knowledge Quizzes (Concours des savants):* students can choose such categories as French history, institutions, contemporary life, current events, language, literature, art, music, sport, exploration, famous French men and women.

68. *Contrôlez le narrateur* (C43–44) as a test of cultural information.

69. Listening to and discussing exchange and correspondence tapes.

70. Taking part in general conversation at French clubs, French tables, French camps, French festivals, during summer abroad programs.

With writing

71. Listening to a passage and then writing the gist in SAAD's (see C52–53).

72. Listening to a mystery which stops before the conclusion, then writing an explanation.

73. Listening to a segment of dialogue, then writing a composition which gives it a context and a conclusion.

Advanced level (A)

A. IDENTIFICATION (A)

1. Aural discrimination of features of rapid spoken style,[40] regional accents, levels of language, through listening to authentic tapes, films, radio broadcasts, plays.

With writing

2. Transcribing and retranscribing tapes of unedited authentic speech until student has recorded it all (to learn, through personal observation, characteristics of unedited speech and tune ear to understand it).[41] Student plays back any sections of the tape as often as he wishes.

B. IDENTIFICATION AND SELECTION WITHOUT RETENTION (A)

3. Listening to a sequal to a passage read.
4. Listening to recordings of plays and poems already studied.
5. Listening to scenes from other plays by the same playwright.
6. Listening to other poems by the same poet.
7. Listening to debates and panel discussions by fellow-students.
8. Listening to French newscasts for personal information and pleasure.
9. Listening to commercials recorded from French short-wave broadcasts or mock commercials prepared by fellow-students.
10. Listening to recordings of French *chansonniers*.
11. Continuing tape correspondence with French friend.

C. IDENTIFICATION AND GUIDED SELECTION WITH SHORT-TERM RETENTION (A)

12. Listening to student presentation of mock radio program, call-in program, or TV talk show.

With visual

13. Watching French films.
14. Listening to student presentation of fashion parade.

With speaking

15. Listening to lecturettes by other students on aspects of French civilization, culture, or literature and asking questions.
16. Listening to an aural text and recording answers to questions on the text.
17. Group conversations with visiting native speakers.
18. Micro-texts: see *Categories of Language Use* 9 in Chapter 2, p. 51.

With writing

19. Students practice taking notes on classroom lecturettes, first with an outline of points to be covered, then without guidance.

20. Dictation: students are expected to listen to and retain whole sentences before writing.

D. IDENTIFICATION, SELECTION, AND LONG-TERM RETENTION (A)

21. Listening to lectures by visiting French speakers on aspects of contemporary French life.

22. Watching performances of French plays by visiting actors.

23. Watching performances of French plays by school French club or on the invitation of other schools.

24. Listening to recordings of group conversations of French speakers discussing subjects of interest.

25. Listening to readings of plays not studied previously.

With visual

26. Extracting different lines of thought from a listening passage: listening with one set of printed questions, then listening again with a different set of questions.

27. Visiting French art show and listening to commentary in French.

With action

28. Seeking information from documentaries, tapes, and records for group projects or class discussions.

29. Listening to lengthy instructions for a task one has to perform.

30. Learning French cooking from oral instructions.

31. Visiting a French restaurant, discussing menu with French-speaking waiter, and eating a French meal in company with other French-speaking students.

32. Making preparations for a French festival with a French exchange student, or teacher, who explains what to do in French.

33. Activities at French club, French camp, or during study abroad tour.

With speaking

34. As much of the lesson as possible is conducted in French.

35. Listening to a passage and recording oral answers to questions about it.

36. Listening to recordings of plays, poems, and speeches and discussing them afterwards.

37. Learning French songs from recordings.

38. Learning a part for a play from a professional recording.

39. Group conversations and discussions on cultural subjects which students have researched, films they have seen, or books and journals they have read.

40. Discussion of newscasts from France.

41. Asking questions at lectures by visiting French speakers or exchange students.

42. Talking on telephone with French native speakers, seeking information for projects or for reporting back to class.

43. Interviewing visiting, or local, French speakers or exchange students to find out information on French life, institutions, and attitudes, for group project on contemporary French culture.

44. Watching French film and being able to discuss afterwards questions which require aural comprehension, rather than kinesic or visual interpretation.

45. Engaging in debates and discussions on controversial subjects.

46. Showing French-speaking visitors around school or town.

47. Listening to a story which members of the class will dramatize spontaneously later.

48. Listening to tapes of radio discussions with French authors and civic leaders, or speeches by political figures, and discussing these in the context of contemporary French life.

49. Listening to newscasts in order to act as daily or weekly reporter for the class.

50. Taking part in such competitions as Intermediate activities 61, 64, 65, and 67.

51. *Reconstitution de texte.*[42] As a preliminary study of the differences between spoken and literary language, leading later to *explication de texte* or *commentaire d'un texte littéraire,* students listen to a poem or short literary extract and, with the help of systematic questioning from the teacher, reconstruct it orally.

With writing

52. Taking dictations containing information related to cultural subjects being researched.

53. While listening to a speech, lecture, or taped discussion, students take notes for use with a group project.

54. Listening to a speech, lecture, or taped discussion and writing afterwards a summary of main points for use with a group project.

55. *Reconstitution de texte.* After having done 51, students reconstruct the text in writing, individually or as a group, and then compare their version with the original as an exercise in stylistics.

56. As an ambitious project for a class in which listening comprehension is a major objective, or as an independent study project: students listen to French broadcasts to draw out information on cultural differences. They write up the results of their research in French. (Much can be learned from the types of news reported and what this conveys about French interests and preoccupations; the types of goods advertised on French-speaking commercial stations and the way they are advertised; the kinds of interviews conducted, and with whom; the types of music played on different stations; the subject matter of comedy hours, situation comedies, and *chansonniers,* and the types of questions asked by listeners.)

4
Oral practice
for the learning of grammar

Deductive or inductive?

At some stage students must learn the grammar of the language. This learning may be approached *deductively* (in which case the student is given a grammatical rule with examples before he practices the use of a particular structure) or *inductively* (the student sees a number of examples of the rule in operation in discourse, practices its use, and then evolves a rule with the help of the teacher; or he sees a number of examples, evolves a rule from these examples with the help of his teacher, and then practices using the structure). In either of these approaches, there is a phase wherein the student practices the use of grammatical structures and applies the various facets of grammatical rules in possible sentences. This subject is discussed in greater depth in Chapter 8.

Oral exercises

In many classrooms, the greater part of grammatical practice has always been in writing. Here, we are concerned with the contribution that can be made by oral practice exercises of many kinds. In this chapter, we shall:

1. examine types of exercises traditionally found in textbooks and see which ones are suitable for or can be adopted to oral practice;

2. study examples of more recently developed drills and exercises and discuss their features;

105

3. categorize, exemplify, and discuss six types of oral practice exercises (repetition, substitution, conversion, sentence modification, response, and translation exercises).

Traditional types of exercises

To make the discussion of different exercises comparable we will base them on the contraction of the definite article after *de* (the use of *du, de la, de l', des*). There are various structural uses of the contraction of the definite article after *de*.

1. It is used for the possessor (*le manteau du professeur*).

2. It is used to show relations in conjunction with prepositions (*il est près du musée*).

3. It forms the partitive article (*il boit du café*).

4. It can mark the indirect object of some verbs (*il parle du président*).

5. It is used to show direction in such sentences as *il vient du musée.*[1]

The first decision to be made is: with which use will the student begin his practice or will he learn all at once? (This decision is usually made for the teacher by the textbook writer, but the type of approach adopted by the author should influence the teacher in his selection of a textbook.)

Sometimes the contraction with *à*, in its directional use (*il va à la gare, il va au musée*), is taught first, because this structure parallels its English equivalent in concept and largely in expression, and is therefore not difficult for English-speaking students. It can also be practiced situationally (*Jean va au tableau, Marie va à la porte, le facteur arrive à l'école*) which brings more reality to oral practice. The directional expressions *il vient du musée* and *il vient de la gare* are analogic in form and use to *il va au musée* and *il va à la gare,* so the learning of the first structure facilitates the learning of the second. For the following comparative study of the treatment of the contracted article with *de* we have chosen examples of the possessive use.

1. GRAMMAR-TRANSLATION TYPE EXERCISES

If we examine older textbooks we find that many of them introduce the students to the possessive use of *de* through paradigms illustrating a grammatical rule. To practice the forms learned from the paradigm, the students are given sentences to translate.

Illustrative of this common practice are the following examples adapted from a book published in 1869.[2] Here we see, almost in caricature, some of the undesirable features of grammatical statements and exercises which, unfortunately, are still found in many textbooks.

G1 *Rules and paradigm*

Contraction of the article, etc.

1. The article *le,* with the preposition *de* preceding, must be contracted into *du,* when it comes before a word in the *masculine* singular, commencing with a consonant or an *h* aspirated.

du frère, *of the brother;*
du héros, *of the hero;* . . .
du chemin, *of the way.*

2. Before *feminine* words, and before masculine words commencing with a vowel, or an *h* mute, the article *le* is not blended with the preposition.

de la dame, f. *of the lady;*
de l'argent, m. *of the money;* . . .
de l'honneur, m. *of the honor.*

3. In French, the name of the possessor follows the name of the object possessed.

La maison du médecin, *The physician's house;*
L'arbre du jardin, *The tree of the garden;* . . .

4. The name of the material of which an object is composed follows always the name of the object; the two words being connected by the preposition *de* (*d'* before a vowel or an *h* mute) . . .

La robe de soie, *the silk dress;*
La montre d'or, *the gold watch.*

To practice the forms learned from the paradigm, the students are given exercises like the following:

G2 Exercise A: Translate into English—

a. Avez-vous la montre d'or?
b. Oui, madame; j'ai la montre d'or et le chapeau de soie.
c. Monsieur, avez-vous le livre du tailleur?
d. Non, monsieur; j'ai le livre du médecin.
e. Le cordonnier a le chapeau de soie du tailleur.
f. La dame a le soulier de satin de la sœur du boulanger.

G3 Exercise B: Translate into French—

a. Have we the horse's hay?
b. You have the horse's oats.
c. Have you the cloth shoe of the physician's sister?
d. No, madam; I have the lady's silk dress.

Commentary

1. *Illogical sequence of rules.* In G1, surely rule 3 should precede 1 and 2? 4 must come under *etc.,* since it does not involve contraction of the article.

2. *Use of fragments as examples.* None of the examples under G1.1–2 would normally be found in isolation, and *de l'honneur* is hardly the most common of segments, even in context.

3. *Translation of short sentences* has its uses (see G45–53), but only when the sentences are ones the students might conceivably use. Even in the nineteenth century "Have you the cloth shoe of the physician's sister?" would have been of limited usefulness. *Avez-vous la montre d'or?* is not a very demanding translation item here, since *la montre d'or* has already been translated as an example of the rule in G1.4. One wonders what is the value of including it twice in the exercise.

4. Exercises G2 and G3 give the appearance of providing the question-answer sequence of conversation. Yet closer examination reveals *improbable responses* as in G3 a–b and c–d. Modern exercises, even when carefully constructed from the point of view of grammatical practice, often show the same disregard for probability and authenticity. As a result, students quickly develop the attitude that French is an artificial classroom game which is irrelevant to real life and best forgotten as fast as possible, with other school nonsense.

One modern text, of which Ionesco is co-author,[3] deliberately employs whimsically absurd sentences on the principle that learning a foreign language in a classroom is essentially artificial, that it is role-playing or acting out. The co-authors believe that, at college level, this artificiality can be brought into service by exaggerating it, thus making material for memorization memorable. Consequently, in this text, sentences like *le professeur est dans la poche du gilet de la montre* come as no surprise.

5. There is no *systematic practice* first of one aspect of the structure and then of the next (e.g., practice of *de la (sœur)* as distinct from *du (médecin)* and *de l'(enfant),* and these as contrasted with *de (soie).*

Instead we have *tests* like "Have you the cloth shoe of the physician's sister?" which require abstract comprehension of the grammar, rather than the ability to produce this grammatical feature in active language use.

6. Exercises like these are clearly designed to *develop skill in reading by translating.* They may be, and often are, translated orally in class, but provide no opportunity for the student to develop his ability to use French for normal communication.

7. The student is trained to *think from French to English and English to French* from the beginning and to seek one-to-one equivalence even if it is necessary to distort the English expression to do so, e.g., *l'arbre du jardin* / the tree of the garden.

8. This whole unit is *teacher, or textbook, directed.* There is no place for student discovery or creativeness, for enjoyment, or even for mild interest.

Some elementary textbooks ask students to perform operations like the following:

G4 Put *du, de la, de l',* or *des* in front of all the words in the vocabulary list at the beginning of the lesson.

Commentary

This is a mechanical, mindless chore, since most vocabulary lists give words with either the definite article in front of them or *m.* or *f.* after them. For learning to take place, students need exercises which provoke thought.

2. FILL-IN-THE-BLANK EXERCISES

These exercises are found in textbooks which profess to teach aural-oral skills as well as in texts oriented to written practice in grammar. They are discussed here because they are often used for oral practice in the classroom. (As written exercises they are examined in detail in Chapter 8.)

G5 Replace the English words in parentheses by the correct French form (*du, de la, de l',* or *des*):

a. Quelle est la date (of the) victoire d'Austerlitz?
b. La porte (of the) magasin est fermée.
c. La sœur (of the) ingénieur a visité le chantier.

Commentary

1. In most cases the student *jots down the French replacement in isolation* in his exercise book. As a result he does not read, let alone hear or say, a complete French sentence. The mixture of French and English encourages the student to think of French as disguised English, and language learning as essentially translation.

2. *Items are quite unconnected* and contain complications of unfamiliar vocabulary and concepts which encourage the student to close his mind to all else but the blank to be filled.

3. When the exercise is completed orally, the student usually gives only the French equivalent for the section in English. For this, he does not even have to understand the sentence; he needs to recognize only the gender and number of the word following the blank. Then the exercise can be completed rather like a crossword puzzle. Since the student is "learning the rules" in isolation, it is unlikely that there will be any high degree of transfer to a spontaneous utterance, without further practice of a different nature.

G6 Include in the sentence the words in parentheses, making any necessary changes:

a. Le mouchoir est dans la poche (de le) professeur.
b. Le tableau est sur le mur (de la) salle de classe.
c. L'image est dans le livre (de le) élève.
d. Les manteaux (de les) garçons sont dans le couloir.

Commentary

1. This exercise avoids the use of English but, even more than the preceding exercise, encourages students to find "answers" for segments. In this case, the student needs only to check to see if the word following the section in parentheses begins with a vowel. If it does not, the words in the parentheses supply all the necessary information.

2. Students are confronted with *incorrect French forms (de le, de les)* which may be impressed on their minds more than the correct form, especially if they read out what is printed thinking it is the correct form.

3. They are also encouraged to think of *de le* first and then transform it to *du,* instead of learning *du* directly as a French form of expression and practicing it frequently in context.

4. Vocabulary in this case is connected with things in the classroom.

The same task can be more effectively accomplished by a rapid oral exercise in which students are asked questions like: Q: *Où est l'image?* (R: *Dans le livre du professeur*); Q: *Où est le tableau?* (R: *Sur le mur de la salle de classe*); or Q: *Qu'est-ce qui est dans le couloir?* (R: *Les manteaux des élèves*). The teacher should make clear that all answers must contain a *de* phrase. This exercise can also be conducted with carefully selected pictures. (See also G12.)

G7 Fill in the blanks in the following sentences with the correct form of *de* + the definite article.

a. Montrez-moi la photo _____ enfant.
b. Donnez-moi les livres _____ professeur.
c. Passez-moi la liste _____ mots.

Commentary

1. Here, the student *must reflect more* than in G6, where gender and number are supplied.

2. The student *does not see incorrect forms* in print.

3. He may still *not see complete sentences* in French since all the information he needs to complete the sentence correctly is supplied by the final segment.

4. This exercise is first of all a *visual* task (blanks cannot be spoken by the teacher). If the answers are read aloud in their full context, students at least articulate a complete French sentence. Otherwise, they rush through, rapidly "filling in the blanks."

5. Items again are disparate and *uninteresting*. The imperative has been used presumably because students learned it recently. This fact could have been exploited more efficiently, allowing some place for student innovation, by devising a rapid oral exercise in which students ask each other to do various things, using extended phrases with *de* (e.g., *Montrez-moi la photo de l'église*).

3. REPLACEMENT EXERCISES

G8 Replace the underlined word by the noun indicated, making any necessary changes.

a. Le professeur ferme le livre du *garçon*. (jeune fille)
b. Avez-vous vu les gants du *professeur?* (élève)
c. Ne cassez pas les jouets des *enfants*. (petites filles)

Commentary

1. The student sees or hears a *complete French sentence* and responds in a complete French sentence.

2. The exercise can be given orally. This is actually close to the substitution drill technique of G9. However, because of the continual changes in struct.ral formation and lexical content in successive sentences, it would be difficult to hold the sentences in the memory while making substitutions orally. For this reason, it is *essentially an exercise for written practice.* In the next section we shall see how by observing certain restrictions it could be transformed into an oral exercise.

More recently developed oral practice exercises
1. PATTERN OR STRUCTURE DRILL EXERCISES

These types of exercises are found in most contemporary textbooks and on language laboratory tapes. They are designed for rapid oral practice in which more items are completed per minute than in written practice. Some teachers mistakenly use them for written practice, thus giving students a boring, tedious chore.

Pattern drill exercises are useful for demonstrating structural variations and familiarizing students with their use. They serve an *introductory function* and are useful only as a preliminary to practice in using the new structural variations in some natural interchange, or for consolidation of the use of certain structures when students seem in doubt.

When pattern drills are used, it is important that students understand the rationale of the variations they are performing. Sometimes a grammatical feature has been encountered in listening or reading material or in a dialogue. Its functioning has been experienced, or explained, and a rapid drill is conducted to familiarize the students with the feature in use in various contexts. Sometimes a demonstration pattern drill introduces the grammatical feature, which is then explained, before being practiced again in a drill sequence which requires thought.

Intensive practice exercises or drills are useful for learning such formal characteristics of French as verb endings (not tense use), word order in statements and questions, negation, the use of object pronouns before and after the verb, and so on. They can be of many types, as we shall see in this chapter.

Teaching series

G9   Repeat the model sentence you hear. In successive sentences replace the last word by the cue words given, making any necessary changes. You will then hear the correct sentence. Repeat it if you have made a mistake. (The modeled correction and the repetition of the correct response will be given here only for the first item, as a demonstration of the technique.)

a.
MODEL SENTENCE	C'est la sœur de Georges.
CUE	Marie.
RESPONSE BY STUDENT	C'est la sœur de Marie.
CORRECT RESPONSE CONFIRMED	C'est la sœur de Marie.
REPETITION BY STUDENT OF CORRECT RESPONSE (IF DESIRED)	C'est la sœur de Marie.
FURTHER CUES	Jacqueline, Pierre, Monsieur Dupont, Madame Lebrun

b. C'est le nom du professeur.
   (directeur, concierge, garçon, père . . .)

c. C'est le nom de la directrice.
   (jeune fille, mère, voisine . . .)

d. C'est la maison de l'élève.
   (étudiant, ingénieur, étudiante, hôtelier, Américain, Américaine . . .)

e. C'est le bruit des chevaux.
   (chiens, vaches, ânes, poules, garçons . . .)

f. C'est le bruit des enfants.
   (ânes, oiseaux, autos, avions . . .)

g. C'est la photo de la ferme.
   (Georges, élève, directeur, chevaux, classe, hôpital, animaux, petits enfants . . .)

Commentary

1. This is called a *four-phase drill*. When the student does not repeat the correct answer after the model, it is referred to as a *three-phase drill*. The fourth phase is useful for the student who has made a mistake. The third phase (confirmation of correct response) is usually included on a laboratory tape, but it can become irritating in class when students are giving correct responses smartly. It should be used only when needed.

2. In this exercise there is a *fixed increment*, that is, a segment which is repeated in each utterance in a series. Here it is *c'est*, which makes the use of many different nouns with possessive phrases possible. The fixed

increment reduces the memory load for the student and allows him to concentrate on the minimal change he is being asked to make. It is usually retained during *six to eight items,* especially when a new structure is being learned.

3. The sentences are *short,* thus lightening the memory load.

4. The *lexical content is restricted* to vocabulary with which the student is familiar so that he can concentrate on the structural rule he is applying.

5. Each sentence the student utters is one which could possibly appear in conversation.

6. There is *no ambiguity in the exercise.* The instructions are clear and each item is so composed that only one response will be correct. This makes it possible for the acceptability of the response to be confirmed by a correct response modeled by the teacher or the voice on the tape.

7. Since this is an oral exercise, both (e) and (f) are necessary. In (e) we are using the form /de/ as in /deʃjɛ̃/, and in (f) we are using /dez/ as in /dezɑ̃fɑ̃/. This distinction would not appear in a written exercise.

8. (g) is the *testing phase* of the drill. It ranges over the six possibilities in eight (or more) items. Through it the teacher can tell whether the students need further practice of specific variations of the feature they have been learning.

9. Note the peculiar problems of (g) for an oral drill of this type in French. Words like *élèves, jeunes filles,* and *professeurs* are ambiguous as cues since the singular and plural are pronounced alike. *Petits enfants* is not ambiguous because of the obligatory *liaison. Chevaux* and *animaux* are unambiguous. Context helps the student decide, as in *C'est le nom du directeur.* (In (e) and (f) the problem is not the same since the pattern is plural and the students expect the cues to follow the pattern.)

10. It will depend on the age and maturity of the students and the intensiveness of the course whether this series is taught gradually over a period of days or weeks or taught in one lesson.

11. Since words are grouped according to gender and number, the operation of the drill can become mechanical and cease to be useful because students are no longer concentrating on the grammatical point at issue. It should not be continued beyond the point where students have acquired familiarity with the forms.

Patterned response

The drill in G9 would be *less monotonous* and the students would be participating in a more realistic way if the response were not a simple repetition but required an answer form.

G10 a. Practice with the model (students repeat sentences demonstrating the structural model):

Martin? C'est le professeur, alors?
Non, ce n'est pas *le nom du professeur.*

b. The drill continues, following the same pattern:

CUE	Robert? C'est le directeur, alors?
RESPONSE	Non, ce n'est pas *le nom du directeur.*
(Confirmation)	

CUE	Leroux? C'est le médecin, alors?
RESPONSE	Non, ce n'est pas *le nom du médecin.*
(Confirmation)	

CUE	Girard? C'est la directrice, alors?
RESPONSE	Non, ce n'est pas *le nom de la directrice.*
(Confirmation)	

Chain drill

A *final practice* at the end of this series can be a chain drill on the following pattern: each student in turn invents his own contribution and produces a cue for his neighbor. Students should be encouraged at this stage to be as original as they can within the limitations of the pattern.

G11

STUDENT A TO STUDENT B	Martin? C'est le nom du directeur?
STUDENT B	Non, c'est le nom de la concierge.
(TO STUDENT C)	Jacqueline? C'est le nom de la jeune fille?
STUDENT C	Oui, c'est le nom de la jeune fille.
(TO STUDENT D)	Tu entends le bruit des animaux?
STUDENT D	Oui, c'est le bruit des chiens . . .

This chain drill can be a *team game,* each team gaining a point for each correct link in the chain (with a limit on the time for reflection to keep the game moving). The chain passes to the other team each time an error is made or a student fails to respond within the time allowed.

Patterned response in a situational context

A drill of this type is more interesting and has more reality if it is given a *situational* context.

G12 Context can be provided by the use of objects, pictures, or actions and the learning of a few simple cognates (*la surface, l'intérieur, l'extérieur, l'image, la photo, l'ensemble*). The drill is conducted first in choral fashion with students describing things pointed out by the teacher. Then the drill moves to individual response, with students pointing things out to each other (*c'est l'intérieur de la boîte; c'est la surface du mur*).

Finally a *game* develops.

1. Team points are awarded for correct answers to the question *Qu'est-ce que c'est?* Students understand that the answer must contain a possessive or *de* phrase; they respond with such expressions as *c'est le crayon du professeur* or *c'est la surface de la table*.

2. Alternatively, students gain points for correct descriptions of the actions of the teacher or other students. The teacher, or student, asks: *Qu'est-ce que je fais?* Students reply: *Vous touchez la surface du mur, vous regardez l'image des animaux,* and so on.

With a little practice and some choral responses at the beginning, a game of this type can proceed as smartly as an oral drill. Swift response can be elicited by pausing a short time for one student to reply, then moving to another if the student is still hesitating.

Successful completion of an oral drill does not guarantee that the student will use the correct form in *autonomous production*. The student must try to express himself outside of a framework which forces him to produce certain answers.

G13 The lesson may conclude with the students asking each other questions: *Dans ta chambre, quelle est la couleur des murs? Quelle est la photo qui est dans le bureau du directeur?* Alternatively, they may play a game such as *Je pense à quelque chose . . . Qu'est-ce que c'est?* Students guess: *C'est la montre de Robert, c'est la photo du président . . .* until they find the right answer.

Suggestions for encouraging autonomous production are given in Chapter 2.

* Try to write a series of drills to teach and test the *contraction of the article* after *à,* or the use of the *partitive article* (which is more complicated). Think of *situational contexts* in which these could be practiced and *games* which would produce the same types of responses as a drill. Then see if the types of games you have invented work smoothly by trying them out on other students.

2. SUBSTITUTION OR VARIATION TABLES

Oral drilling can also be performed with the use of variation or substitution tables[4] such as the following.

G14 Qui est-ce?

C'est	la sœur	de la	concierge
	le frère	de l'	élève
	la mère	du	voisin
	la tante	des	garçons
	le cousin	des	jeunes filles

Commentary

1. This is a *mixed drill* and presumes some prior learning of the specific structural items either in dialogues, reading material, oral work in the classroom, or earlier more restricted drills on the different facets of the contracted article with *de*. It serves a useful purpose in drawing together in a systematic way what has already been learned. (See also W1–3.)

2. The drill may be conducted with the complete table in front of the students in an initial *learning phase*. The teacher points to various items on a chart to elicit different combinations from the students, or the students respond to oral cues while looking at their books. In the second or *testing phase*, the students close their books and work from a chart where items have been jumbled and column 3 omitted.

G15 C'est

C'est	le frère		garçons
	la tante		voisin
	la sœur		jeunes filles
	le cousin		élève
	la mère		concierge

Finally, students move on to practice with items not on the original chart, and here suggestions from G12 for *applications in situational contexts* will apply.

3. If the items, as is usually the case, are related to dialogue or reading material already studied, the variations may be taught without books or chart by using *flashcards or pictures* of characters familiar to the students. After considerable practice in this purely aural-oral fashion, students will then look at the chart in their books.

4. As with G9, this practice with variation tables is preliminary learning of grammatical structures. It must be accompanied by more extensive, and more spontaneous, applications of the variations in some form of *personal interchange* between students and teachers. (See G13.)

Limitations of oral exercises for French

Remember that not all grammatical problems in French can be practiced through oral exercises. Spoken French does not signal distinctions in the same way as written French. For instance, the third person singular and the third person plural of the present tense of regular -*er* type verbs beginning with a consonant are not distinguished in any way in spoken French—singular /parl/, plural /parl/—although in writing the distinction is clear: singular *parle,* plural *parlent.* When this type of verb begins with a vowel, the third person plural of the present tense is signalled by an infix /z/ (compare singular /ilekut/, plural /ilzekut/); but there is still no distinction in the verb itself. Similarly, the singular noun *livre* /livr/ and the plural noun *livres* /livr/ are the same in speech, as are most singular and plural forms of adjectives, particularly those which occur after the noun: *vert* /vɛr/, *verts* /vɛr/; *verte* /vɛrt/, vertes /vɛrt/. We hear singular-plural distinctions determined by context for adjectives preceding the noun, whether of the /grɑ̃, grɑ̃t, grɑ̃d, grɑ̃z, grɑ̃dz/ type or the /bo, bɛl, boz/ type, but these occur only when the noun following them begins with a vowel. In *beau jardin* /bo/ and *beaux jardins* /bo/, or *belle femme* /bɛl/ and *belles femmes* /bɛl/, there is no distinction made in speech. Oral exercises on these features should focus on the other spoken signals of singularity and plurality, e.g., the oppositions /lə/le/, /la/le/, /œ̃/de/, /yn/de/, leaving the graphic differences to be taught through written exercises.

The agreement of the past participle is largely a written phenomenon in the same sense. Oral exercises may be employed as preliminary activities, to familiarize the students with some of the rules of this agreement, by keeping to the use of such past participles as *fait* /fɛ/, *faite* /fɛt/, and *pris* /pri/, *prise* /priz/, which distinguish the masculine singular from the feminine singular, without distinguishing singular from plural.

✳ For your future guidance, begin making a list of aspects of French grammar which cannot be practiced adequately through oral drills, and another list of those which cannot be practiced adequately through written drills, e.g., the /grɑ̃, grɑ̃t, grɑ̃d, grɑ̃z, grɑ̃dz/ phenomenon.

Six groups of oral exercises

For each type of exercise in this section a brief description with an example will be given, some comments will be made on common faults to be avoided in constructing such exercises, and some French structural features for which this type of oral exercise would be useful will be listed.

Oral exercises fall into six groups: repetition, substitution, conversion, sentence modification, response, and translation drills.

1. REPETITION OR PRESENTATION DRILLS

In simple repetition drills, the instructor gives a model sentence containing a particular structure or form to be manipulated and the students repeat the sentence with correct intonation and stress. Repetition drills are not, in one sense, a special category of exercises which will be used for practicing certain types of structure; they represent, rather, a commonly used technique for familiarizing the student with the *specific structure,* with the *paradigm,* or with the *procedure for the practice.* For this reason they are sometimes called *presentation drills.* They are useful as *introductory material,* but it must be remembered that from mere repetition, no matter how prolonged, the student will learn little except the requirements of the drill.

G16   MODEL   Où est le cinéma?   Oh, je le vois.
       STUDENT Où est le cinéma?   Oh, je le vois.

       MODEL   Où est la gare?   Oh, je la vois.
       STUDENT Où est la gare?   Oh, je la vois.

       MODEL   Où sont les magasins?   Oh, je les vois.
       STUDENT Où sont les magasins?   Oh, je les vois.

Commentary

1. This example highlights one of the defects of many repetition drills: their unreality and lack of application to the students' situation. Unless the students are looking at a picture showing the buildings in a town, G16 could become completely mechanical,[5] with students attending only to the cue words *le, la,* or *les.* In this case, the structure could just as easily be presented with nonsense words: *Où est le papalin? Oh, je le vois,* a procedure which the students might actually find more amusing and which might focus their attention on the cues in the drill.

2. If students are to use in other situations the object pronouns being demonstrated, they should be concentrating on the meaning of what they are saying. Some reality can be introduced by referring to objects the students can see and having them point to them as they respond: *Où est le placard? Oh, je le vois.*

2. SUBSTITUTION DRILLS

Commonly used types are simple substitution, double substitution, correlative substitution, and multiple substitution drills.

a. *Simple substitution drills* have been demonstrated in G9.

b. *Double substitution drills* are similar to simple substitutions in that the student has no other operation to perform apart from substitution of a new segment in the place of an existing segment, but they require the student to be more alert because they continually change the wording (and, therefore, the meaning) without changing the structure. They are *still mechanical,* however, because each segment is usually signalled in such a way that it can be substituted in the correct slot without the student necessarily understanding its meaning.

G17   MODEL SENTENCE   Si je le trouve / je vous le donnerai.
                      CUE   *Si vous le voulez*
                 RESPONSE   *Si vous le voulez* / je vous le donnerai.
                      CUE   *il écrira la lettre*
                 RESPONSE   Si vous le voulez / *il écrira la lettre.*
                      CUE   *Si je le lui demande*
                 RESPONSE   *Si je le lui demande* / il écrira la lettre
                      CUE   *il partira*
                 RESPONSE   Si je le lui demande / *il partira.*

Commentary

1. The pattern of activity the student learns is "substitute in alternate slots, retaining the new segment for two responses (as in the sequence: *AB, CB, CD, ED, EF . . .*)."

2. If the instructor makes clear what elements are being manipulated (in this case "present tense in the *si* clause: future tense in the principal clause"), the student will find this type of substitution useful for familiarizing himself with the correct tense form for the correct slot in the utterance. He will, however, need a more demanding type of activity later, such as an innovative *chain drill* (G11), a *game,* or a *structured interchange* (where he invents conditional statements himself), if the teacher is to be sure that he can really use the pattern in communication.

c. In *correlative substitution drills* each substitution requires a correlative change to be made elsewhere in the model sentence (See G9 g).

G18   MODEL SENTENCE   *Moi, je* ne le *comprends* pas.
                      CUE   *Vous . . .*
                 RESPONSE   *Vous, vous* ne le *comprenez* pas.

CUE *Marie et Jeanne . . .*
RESPONSE *Marie et Jeanne, elles* ne le *comprennent* pas.

This type of drill is useful for learning such things as tense inflections, possessive forms, reflexive pronouns, irregular verbs, the inflection of the verb after relative pronouns, the agreement of the adjective in gender with the noun, and certain sequences of tenses in related clauses. It is less useful, in a language like French, for plural agreements of the adjective, since these are not signalled in speech. For example, in the sequence:

G19   MODEL un petit mouton blanc.
                CUE *des*
         RESPONSE *des* petits moutons blancs,

the correlative change in the adjectives and the noun is a written phenomenon only. An oral substitution of this type would be a simple substitution for familiarizing English-speaking students with the fact that spoken French (as a general rule) signals the plural through changes in the article, rather than the noun or adjective.

Correlative substitution can be made *more realistic* by designing the cue with a natural-sounding tag which elicits a response that completes a conversational interchange.

G20   CUE Je prends du café chaque matin. *Et Jacques?*
         RESPONSE *Jacques prend* du café chaque matin aussi.
              CUE Je prends du sucre dans mon café. *Et vous deux?*
         RESPONSE *Nous prenons* du sucre dans notre café aussi.

This type of tag can also be used to elicit changes in masculine and feminine adjective forms:

G21   CUE Ce monsieur est vieux. Et la dame?
         RESPONSE La dame est vieille aussi.
              CUE Cette voiture est neuve. Et le vélo?
         RESPONSE Le vélo est neuf aussi.

d. *Multiple substitution drills* are a *testing device* to see whether the student can continue to make a grammatical adjustment he has learned while he is distracted by other preoccupations—in this case, thinking of the changing meaning of successive sentences so as to make substitutions in different slots. In order to make the substitutions in the appropriate slots, students have to think of the meaning of the whole sentence, which changes in focus with each substitution. For this reason, students need to be very alert to perform this exercise successfully.

After study and practice of the partitive article the following multiple substitution drill could be used:

G22 MODEL SENTENCE J'achète des pommes au marché.
                 CUE *Pierre*
            RESPONSE *Pierre* achète des pommes au marché.
                 CUE *viande*
            RESPONSE Pierre achète *de la viande* au marché.
                 CUE *vend*
            RESPONSE Pierre *vend* de la viande au marché.
                 CUE *poisson*
            RESPONSE Pierre vend *du poisson* au marché.
                 CUE *au supermarché*
            RESPONSE Pierre vend du poisson *au supermarché.*
                 CUE *pas*
            RESPONSE Pierre *ne* vend *pas de* poisson au supermarché.

The last response requiring two correlative changes provides a challenge for an enthusiastic class which enjoys showing how much it has learned.

3. CONVERSION DRILLS

The term *transformation* has long been applied to the types of exercises in which affirmative sentences are changed into negative sentences, statements are changed into questions, simple declarations are converted into emphatic declarations, active voice is converted into passive voice, or a present tense statement is changed into a past tense statement. Such exercises have been the staple of foreign-language classes for many years. Some of these processes happen to parallel what are known as "transformations" in transformational-generative grammar (e.g., negativization, passivization, and the interrogative transformation), and others do not; but when they do, this is more a coincidence than a derivative relationship. The term "transformation" is, therefore, misleading to some people because of a presumed connection with transformational-generative grammar. For this reason, the term "conversion drill" will be used for exercises in changing sentence type, combining two sentences into one, moving from one mood or tense to another, changing word class (e.g., replacing nouns by pronouns), substituting phrases for clauses or clauses for phrases (e.g., adverbial phrases for adverbial clauses, infinitive phrases for clauses), or substituting single words for phrases or phrases for single words (e.g., adverbs for adverbial phrases, adjectives for adjectival phrases).

These are conversions rather than substitutions in that they require the use of a different form (frequently with a correlative change), a change in word order, the introduction of new elements, or even considerable restructuring of the utterance. They are useful for developing flexibility in the selection of formal structures for the expression of personal meaning.

a. *General conversion drills*

In our discussion of the construction of common types of conversion drills and the weaknesses to be avoided, we will use examples based on the asking of *questions*. Interrogative forms are among the most frequently used in the language, and practice with them can easily be given a *situational context* and a *personal application*.

G23 Change the following statements into questions, using inversion whenever possible.

CUES   a. Nous sommes assis dans la salle de classe.
       b. Je suis une jeune fille.
       c. Les livres sont dans le placard.
       d. Je prends le petit déjeuner à huit heures.
       e. L'actrice et son mari sont au Canada.
       f. Jeannette et moi, nous sommes au cinéma.

Commentary

1. This traditional type of elementary conversion exercise *over-emphasizes the inversion form* of interrogation. A sentence like *les livres sont dans le placard* with its informal classroom content would most realistically be converted into *Est-ce que les livres sont dans le placard?* or *Les livres sont dans le placard?* (with rising intonation). These last two forms of interrogation are the easiest for the student to acquire and he can use them immediately without the frustrations imposed by selecting the appropriate form of the pronoun and remembering the *-t-* infix, where it is required.

2. When (a), (b), and (d) are converted into questions they produce utterances which have close to zero probability of occurrence, yet such sentences can still be found in books in use at the present time. For (b) and (d), it is obvious that examples were sought to contrast possible inversion with *je* and unacceptable inversion with *je*. A better example for

(b) would have been *je suis le chef de l'équipe aujourd'hui* and for (d) *j'écris les mots correctement,* both of which would produce probable questions of use to the students.

3. Statement (f) also results in an absurd question. Even with a probable theme for conversion into a question such as *Jeannette et moi, nous sommes trop exigeants,* a Frenchman would be more likely to say *Est-ce que nous sommes trop exigeants, Jeannette et moi?* or simply *Nous sommes trop exigeants, Jeannette et moi?* both of which involve a transposition of elements into the position of stress[6] which the writer of this exercise was clearly not seeking to elicit.

4. Statement (e) illustrates a common tendency for exercises of this type to range over any and all topics, and into any vocabulary area, with no meaningful coherence. This may not appear to be a grave fault, but it deepens the impression of many students that language study is mere manipulation of words and has no reality or relevance.

In these six sentences the student is *tested* for his knowledge of five aspects of the interrogation rules. The exercise should, therefore, come after a *series of learning exercises,* in which the student encounters the various aspects of the conversion and practices them step by step. Each exercise in such a series will consist of six or more sentences, with familiar vocabulary, which will produce after conversion questions formed on the same pattern and semantically related, as in the following:

G24 Convert the following statements into questions according to the model:

REPEAT   Pierre a une voiture neuve.

           Est-ce que Pierre a une voiture neuve?

CUES   a. Vous avez une voiture neuve.

          b. La voiture est rouge.

          c. Les étudiants roulent vite dans cette ville.

          d. Ils arrêtent la voiture trop brusquement . . .

A *complete series on yes-no question formation* would include a set eliciting questions in statement form with rising intonation, a set requiring interrogation with *est-ce que,* a set with inversion of pronouns, a set with the inversion and non-inversion of *je,* a set mixing *je* with other pronouns, a set with double pronoun subjects, a set of questions with noun subjects using *est-ce que,* the same set with noun subjects requiring inversion (these sets could even be divided into masculine and feminine subsets and singular and plural subsets), a set with double noun subjects, and a set with mixed noun and pronoun subjects. Some review drills would be interpolated. Some study of all of these aspects, although not necessarily all at once, would normally precede a mixed exercise of the G23 type. At some stage also, students will learn to use the tags *n'est-ce pas* and *oui/non (Tu viens, non?)*. Differentiation of the responses *oui* and *si* can also be usefully learned while practicing affirmative and negative question forms.

The great *advantage of oral exercises* is that so much more practice can be accomplished in the time available, thus allowing for step-by-step progression through a series of rules. The practice sets will normally be spread over several lessons. The amount of subdivision within these sets and the number of sets presented at any one time will depend on the level of instruction, the maturity of the students, and the intensiveness of the course. For elementary classes, the forms necessary for simple communication will suffice. For more mature students, discussion of the various possibilities can reduce the necessity to proceed by one-feature-at-a-time drills.

Earlier, examples were given of statements which after conversion produced improbable questions (see G23). This problem of *appropriateness of items after conversion* must be kept constantly in mind.

A recent textbook contains the following item for conversion. Write in the *passé simple: tu t'es assis*. If this phrase appeared in a modern novel, it would be either in conversation and therefore in the *passé composé,* or in informal narrative of a personal character and also most probably in the *passé composé*. Rare would be the context in which one would expect to find it in the *passé simple (tu t'assis)*. Such a conversion is a useless learning activity for the student as well as being misleading. Students should be taught early the contemporary trends in the use of the past tenses.

The same comment applies to certain forms of the subjunctive. Another contemporary textbook requires students to put *nous nous trompâmes* in the pluperfect subjunctive. Yet the same textbook informs students that the use of the pluperfect subjunctive has been limited to first person singular and third person singular and plural in written texts for a century and a half.

Before selecting a textbook the teacher should look through it carefully to see that the French it elicits from the students is probable, useful, and contemporary.

Situational and personal application. Another set of grammatical rules commonly practiced through conversion drills is the series determining the form, position, and order of pronouns which occur as direct and indirect objects of the verb. Most textbooks resort here to the replace-

ment in sentences of nouns by pronouns: Paul donne *les livres* à *son père*
becomes Paul *les lui* donne, and Donnez *les livres* à *votre frère* is
rewritten as Donnez-*les lui.*

Conversion exercises like the following are also used.

G25 For each negative sentence you hear give the affirmative form:

    a.   Paul, ne les lui donne pas.
    b.   Je ne leur parle pas.
    c.   Ne nous le dites pas . . .

The question of the form and position in the sentence of pronoun
objects is very complicated. Apart from the examples above of their
position and order in affirmative and negative statements and commands,
there are the further problems of certain verbs which require *de* or *à*
before the object and have two ways of substituting for the noun, depending on whether the object is animate or inanimate (je parle du *départ de
mon père:* j'*en* parle; and je parle de *mon père:* je parle *de lui;* je pense à
mes vacances: j'*y* pense and je pense à *mon père:* je pense à *lui*). The
series of exercises necessary for assimilating these rules thoroughly would
be very extensive. Once again, the series can be shortened by judicious
explanations of grammatical functioning. Those conversion drills which
are retained can be made more vivid by associating structure with action.
Students may be asked to respond to instructions by making statements
of their own invention, as in a normal conversational interchange, along
the following lines:

G26 (I)   Ne donnez pas ce livre à Pierre. Je ne le lui donne pas.
Donnez-le-lui maintenant. Je le lui ai déjà donné.
Jeannette, parlez-nous de votre cousin en Afrique. Mais je vous ai déjà
    parlé de lui la semaine dernière.
Pensez à votre devoir de ce soir. J'y ai déjà pensé.

Commentary

1. If students prepare ahead of time they can come to class with instructions to give each other which will require quick-wittedness in responding
and cause quite a lot of amusement for the class.

2. A *mixed practice* of this type presumes preliminary sequential learning, but it is very effective in providing for *review of a complicated set
of rules.* Conducted orally, without hesitation, it enables the student to
absorb the rhythm of the sequences. This is an aid to memory which is

quite lost if the student constantly writes out his responses—editing and re-editing his first attempts as he "puts the objects in the right place" in a conscious, artificial way.

b. *Combinations*

Combinations are a form of conversion drill which has also been used for many years. It involves a process which reflects certain features of transformational grammatical analysis and can be very illuminating in differentiating some aspects of the rules. For instance, students often have difficulty in understanding the different uses of *qui/que* and *ce qui/ce que*. If we examine the sentence

J'ai lu le livre que mon frère a emprunté,

we find it combines two underlying sentences:

J'ai lu le livre,
Mon frère a emprunté le livre.

Asking students to combine these two underlying sentences by using a relative pronoun involves moving from a deeper level of structure to surface structure. The relative pronoun *que,* in the example above, replaces one occurrence of the element found in both sentences (*le livre*), the final choice of form (*qui* or *que*) depending on the function the relative pronoun performs in the expanded sentence (object of *emprunté*).

On the other hand, the combining of two underlying sentences such as

Je crois *A,*
Tu me dis *A,*

(where *A* refers to something not explicitly stated in either sentence) requires a choice from the set *ce qui/ce que,* to form the sentence

Je crois ce que tu me dis.

(Contrast with these the pair

Je crois l'histoire,
Tu m'as raconté l'histoire,

which combine as
Je crois l'histoire que tu m'as racontée.)

The following oral exercises, G27–28, require more active construction of sentences with relative pronouns than the traditional fill-in-the-blank exercise of the type:

Voilà le professeur _____ j'ai rencontré à Lyon.

G27 Combine the following pairs of sentences, using *qui* or *que* as required. In each case make the first sentence the main clause.

  a. Voilà le professeur. J'ai rencontré le professeur à Lyon.
  b. Voilà le crayon. Le crayon est tombé de la table.
  c. Voilà le canot. J'ai acheté le canot.

G28 Combine the following pairs of sentences, using *ce qui* or *ce que* as required:

  a. Le professeur a corrigé A. Jacqueline avait écrit A.
     RESPONSE Le professeur a corrigé ce que Jacqueline avait écrit.

  b. Il m'a montré A. A était dans le tiroir.
     RESPONSE Il m'a montré ce qui était dans le tiroir.

These sets of exercises would be expanded with sets using *dont* and *ce dont,* as well as *lequel* and its combined forms, and interspersed with mixed drills reviewing the various uses of the relative pronoun.

The procedure of combining sentences to form one utterance can also be used for creating dependent phrases beginning with present or past participles (*il est arrivé à la gare/il s'est assis sur un banc—Arrivé à la gare, il s'est assis sur un banc*), or with prepositions such as *avant de* and *après*. It is also useful for situations which require a special sequence of tenses in successive clauses, e.g., conditional statements and complex sentences with dependent subjunctives. (Where one clause will be subordinate to another, it must be clear to the student which of the two sentences to be combined will be the main clause and which the dependent clause.)

c. *Restatement*

Restatement is another useful kind of conversion drill.

G29 One frequently used type of *directed dialogue* is a restatement exercise. (See also C24 c.)

         CUE Dites à Georges que vous vous appelez Louis.
    RESPONSE Georges, je m'appelle Louis.
         CUE Demandez à Pierre où il va.
    RESPONSE Pierre, où vas-tu?
         CUE Dites-lui de vous attendre.
    RESPONSE Attends-moi.

A series of this type is usually based on a dialogue which has been learned, but all kinds of restatements can be invented to practice different grammatical features. A realistic note is added if one student pretends to be giving directions to a third party by telephone, while a second student tells him what to say.

G30 A *running commentary* by one student on what another student or the teacher is saying softly gives practice in restatement of direct speech in indirect speech form.

> (I) STUDENT A Je viens d'arriver mais je vais partir tout de suite.
> STUDENT B Elle a dit qu'elle venait d'arriver mais qu'elle allait partir tout de suite.
> STUDENT A Pourquoi me regardes-tu comme ça?
> STUDENT B Elle m'a demandé pourquoi je la regardais comme ça.

Another type of restatement (sometimes called a *contraction*) consists of replacing a clause with a phrase, or a phrase with a single word, while retaining the basic meaning.

G31 Restate each of the following sentences, replacing the adverbial clause with an adverbial phrase of similar meaning.

> a. *Dès qu'il arrive,* invitez-le chez moi.
> RESPONSE *Dès son arrivée,* invitez-le chez moi.
> b. *Avant qu'elle parte,* je lui dirai la vérité.
> RESPONSE *Avant son départ,* je lui dirai la vérité.

G32 In each of the following sentences, replace the descriptive clause with an adjective of equivalent meaning. (This exercise can be used to practice the position of adjectives which convey different meanings when used before and after the noun.)

> a. L'église *qui est ancienne* a été restaurée.
> RESPONSE L'église *ancienne* a été restaurée.
> b. L'église *qui servait autrefois au culte* a été restaurée.
> RESPONSE L'*ancienne* église a été restaurée.
> c. L'homme *qui est pauvre* n'a pas d'argent.
> RESPONSE L'homme *pauvre* n'a pas d'argent.
> d. Cet homme *que je plains* n'a pas d'argent.
> RESPONSE Ce *pauvre* homme n'a pas d'argent.

✱ List for yourself other areas of French grammar for which some form of restatement would be a suitable exercise and try to think of ways in which this restatement can be incorporated into a natural communication activity.

4. SENTENCE MODIFICATIONS

Sentence modification exercises are of three kinds: expansions, deletions, and completions.

a. *Expansions*

Expansions serve two purposes. Type A requires strictly grammatical manipulation and is useful for learning such things as the position of adverbs. It can be teacher or student directed. Type B is more spontaneous; it gives students the opportunity to create new and original sentences from a basic sentence, often in an atmosphere of competition.[7] Students should be encouraged to spice the exercise with humorous items.

Type A expansions. There are in French three groups of adverbs each of which has a different pattern of positional occurrence.

Group 1: Adverbs like *toujours, encore, déjà, parfois, souvent* follow that part of the verb which varies with changes in time relationships. Compare: *Il oublie toujours, il a toujours oublié, il a toujours été aimé.*

Group 2: Adverbs which set out precisely when an action took place like *hier, demain,* adverbs of place like *partout, là, ailleurs,* and adverbial expressions like *en voiture, à la fin de la journée,* usually come at the end of the complete verbal group. Compare: il nous a évité *hier,* il a été assassiné *dans la rue,* il l'a caché *ailleurs.*

Group 3: Adverbs of quantity like *trop, beaucoup,* adverbs of manner like *rigoureusement,* and the frequently used adverbs *bien* and *mal* vary in position, appearing after the auxiliary or at the end of the verbal group depending on whether it is the meaning of the past participle or the meaning of the adverb which is stressed. Compare: il l'a rigoureusement *rejeté;* il l'a rejeté *rigoureusement;* il a beaucoup *travaillé;* il a travaillé *beaucoup.*

This complex set of rules can be practiced very effectively in an oral expansion of Type A:

G33 (I)

MODEL SENTENCE   Il a travaillé.

CUE   beaucoup

RESPONSE   Il a beaucoup travaillé.

Il a travaillé beaucoup.   } both acceptable

CUE toujours
RESPONSE Il a toujours beaucoup travaillé. $\Big\}$
Il a toujours travaillé beaucoup. $\Big\}$ both acceptable

CUE après dîner
RESPONSE Il a toujours beaucoup travaillé
après dîner. $\Bigg\}$ both acceptable
Il a toujours travaillé beaucoup
après dîner.

Many other grammatical features can be practiced in a Type A expansion:

G34 Insert in the sentences you hear the expressions supplied in the cues, making any necessary changes:

a. BASIC SENTENCE Il a de l'argent.
  CUE Beaucoup?
  RESPONSE Il a beaucoup d'argent.
  CUE Pas?
  RESPONSE Il n'a pas beaucoup d'argent.

b. BASIC SENTENCE Il a acheté un mouchoir.
  CUE Grand?
  RESPONSE Il a acheté un grand mouchoir.
  CUE De soie?
  RESPONSE Il a acheté un grand mouchoir de soie.
  CUE Blanche?
  RESPONSE Il a acheté un grand mouchoir de soie blanche.

Type B expansions provide students with the opportunity to create new sentences from a basic frame by expanding the frame as they wish, as often as they wish. In this type of practice no two students would produce exactly the same answer.

G35 CUE L'homme traverse la rue.
STUDENT A Le vieil homme qui boite traverse la rue lentement.
STUDENT B L'homme qui est pressé traverse la rue principale sans faire attention à la circulation.

A Type B expansion may be conducted as a *chaining activity,* with each student in succession adding a new element to the sentence until a limit seems to have been reached. At that stage, a new chain begins with another simple sentence.

b. *Deletions*

Flexibility in manipulating structures can be developed by reversing processes.

Type A deletions, which are the reverse of Type A expansions, provide further variety in practice.

G36 Delete the negative elements in the following sentences:

CUE Il n'a pas de café.
RESPONSE Il a du café.
CUE Il n'aime pas le café.
RESPONSE Il aime le café.
CUE Il ne prend jamais de café.
RESPONSE Il prend du café.

Type B deletions serve a less useful purpose than Type B expansions. Expansions require the student to decide at which point in the sentence to insert additional information of his own choosing. Deletions of extra information usually require only formal changes, as practiced in Type A deletions. For this reason deletions are not creative.

c. *Completions*

In completions, part of the sentence is given as a cue and the student finishes the sentence either with a semantically constant segment in which some syntactic or morphological change must be made according to the cue (Type A_1), with a suitable segment which is to some extent semantically governed by the cue (Type A_2), or with a segment of his own invention (Type B).

Type A_1 completions.

G37 (I) In the following exercise you will hear the model sentence: *Je suis content qu'il m'ait écrit.* Throughout the exercise, you will retain the same concluding notion, varying the segment from subjunctive to indicative as the introductory segment changes.

MODEL SENTENCE Je suis content qu'il m'ait écrit.
CUE Je regrette . . .
RESPONSE Je regrette qu'il m'ait écrit.
CUE Il paraît . . .
RESPONSE Il paraît qu'il m'a écrit.

> CUE Croyez-vous . . .
> RESPONSE Croyez-vous qu'il m'ait écrit . . .

Type A₂ completions.

G38 (I) In the following exercise you will hear the model sentence: *Il me rend mon stylo parce qu'il préfère le sien.* Throughout the exercise you will retain a concluding segment similar in meaning to *parce qu'il préfère le sien,* but as the introductory segment varies you will vary the person referred to in the concluding segment.

> MODEL SENTENCE Il me rend mon stylo *parce qu'il préfère le sien.*
> CUE Je vous rends votre gomme . . .
> RESPONSE Je vous rends votre gomme *parce que je préfère la mienne.*
> CUE Nous lui rendons ses crayons . . .
> RESPONSE Nous lui rendons ses crayons *parce que nous préférons les nôtres.*

Commentary

With an exercise involving a correlative change of this type, it is usually advisable for the student to repeat two, or even three, items with the instructor at the beginning in order to be sure of the kind of manipulation required.

A Type A₂ completion is very useful for *vocabulary learning:*

G39 Complete the following statements with the appropriate occupational term, according to the model:

> MODEL Celui qui conduit le taxi, *c'est le chauffeur.*
> CUE Celui qui distribue le courrier . . .
> RESPONSE Celui qui distribue le courrier, *c'est le facteur.*
> CUE Celui qui vend les billets à la gare . . .
> RESPONSE Celui qui vend les billets à la gare, *c'est l'employé.*

Type B completions. A Type B completion allows the student to make his personal semantic contribution within a syntactically fixed framework. It is useful for practicing such things as the governance of infinitives with *à, de,* and zero links, the use of the subjunctive, and the sequence of tenses where the dependent clause is in the subjunctive.

G40 (1) Invent a completion containing an infinitive construction for each sentence you hear, according to the following model: Je vous défends ... Je vous défends *de marcher sur la pelouse.*

>   CUE   Je vous prie ...
> RESPONSE   Je vous prie *de me rendre mes affaires.*
>   CUE   Il réussit ...
> RESPONSE   Il réussit à me faire changer d'avis.

Commentary

In a Type A₁ completion on governance of infinitives the concluding segment would remain the same throughout the exercise, except for the change of link: Je vous défends/*de lui parler;* Je vous prie/*de lui parler;* Il réussit/*à lui parler.* An exercise of Type A₁ may precede the Type B exercise above in order to familiarize the student with the required structures, or to refresh his memory. All practice should, however, move toward Type B exercises where the student supplies something of his own invention, and then beyond Type B to creative practice, like that described in Chapter 2 under *Autonomous Interaction,* p. 45.

✳ Look for other areas of grammar for which sentence modifications would be useful and try to think of original ways of presenting them which draw close to the real purposes of communication.

5. RESPONSE DRILLS

All oral exercises may, in one sense, be called response drills. In the particular type to which we are referring here, *question-answer* or *answer-question* procedures are used, or students learn to make appropriate conventional responses (*rejoinders*) to other people's utterances.

a. *Question-answer practice*

Ability to ask questions with ease and to recognize question forms effortlessly, so that one can reply appropriately, is of the essence of communication. It has always been a basic classroom activity. Unfortunately, much question-answer material is very stilted, questions being asked for the sake of the form, without attention to their real interest to the student. The structure of the question form itself can be practiced through conversion exercises; question-answer practice is useful for such things as forms and uses of tenses, various kinds of pronouns, and forms of emphasis (*tours présentatifs,* e.g., *Ce n'est pas lui qui me l'a dit;* and *phrases segmentées,* e.g., *Ce livre-là, est-ce que vous l'avez emprunté?*). It is most frequently associated with a picture, slide, or film, reading material, some project or activity, or a game. It can, however, be carefully structured for language-learning purposes. Since the form of an appropriate answer is nearly always a reflection of the question, the teacher can elicit the forms and uses he wants by skillful construction of his questions. In the following series, for instance, successive questions elicit the use of different tenses from the student, yet the communicative interaction develops naturally.

G41 (I) The students have been reading about or viewing a film of the adventures of a group of young people in Paris.

Q. Pourquoi ne sont-ils pas rentrés à l'heure convenue?
A. Ils ne sont pas rentrés parce qu'il faisait si beau ce soir-là.

Q. Est-ce que vous rentrez souvent tard le soir?
A. Non, je préfère rentrer tôt parce que j'aime les repas chauds.

Q. Mais quand vous serez en vacances au mois de juin, vous rentrerez peut-être plus tard de temps en temps?
A. Oui, c'est possible. Je ferai sans doute beaucoup de natation pendant l'été.

Q. Qu'est-ce que vous feriez si votre mère refusait de vous préparer des repas à cause de vos rentrées tardives?
A. Je lui demanderais de l'argent pour m'acheter des hot-dogs.

Commentary

The development of this type of interchange is not predictable, but the alert questioner can keep on switching the conversation to a different time perspective. The same type of approach can be developed at the elementary level through discussion of an action picture.

Many *situations* can be created in the classroom for the asking of questions and the obtaining of answers.

G42 With a simulated telephone link, all kinds of situations can be invented which elicit questions and answers from students.

1. Student A calls student B on the phone. Student B asks questions until he is able to identify the person calling and his purpose.

2. Student C calls student D to get some information from him. Student D has a French brochure, menu, or a collection of advertisements from which he gives the information requested.

b. *Answer-question practice*

Frequently the teacher asks all the questions, yet in a foreign-language situation it is more commonly the language learner, or foreign visitor, who needs to be able to ask questions with ease. Certainly, in a natural conversation, each participant passes freely from the role of interlocutor to that of respondent. Answer-question practice occurs when the teacher, or some student, has the answer and the others must find out what it is. This type of exercise takes place naturally and interestingly in such games as *Vingt et une questions, Animal-minéral-végétal,* and *Identification.*

G43 In *Vingt et une questions* one person (A) thinks of someone or something. By asking eliminating questions to which A may reply only *Oui* or *Non,* the players narrow the field of possibilities until they are able to guess the person or object in question. Only twenty-one questions may be asked before the game is lost.

Animal-minéral-végétal is similar except that the first eliminations are in these three categories and the number of questions is not limited.

In *Identification,* A thinks of a person and an object typically associated with this person. Forms of questions will be more varied than in the first two games because A may give information, although he tries to do this as ambiguously as possible. When the students have guessed the person, they must guess the object associated with this person (e.g., the school janitor and his keys; Jeanne d'Arc and her sheep).

c. *Rejoinders*

In every language there are conventional ways of responding to the utterances of others which ease social relations and make continued communication less effortful: ways of agreeing, disagreeing, expressing pleasure, astonishment, surprise, displeasure, or disgust, ways of responding to another person's monologue so that one appears to be participating, and ways of acknowledging replies to one's questions. These common responses are frequently not taught in any systematic way to foreigners, with the result that the latter often offend, either by not contributing as they should to an interchange or by contributing too forcefully or pedantically. Some rejoinders will be learned incidentally because the teacher will use them frequently; others can be practiced in an oral exercise from time to time.

G44 (I) Listen to the following sentences and respond to each with an appropriate exclamation or rejoinder:

CUE Ah, ça alors! Je me suis cassé une dent!
RESPONSE *Quel dommage!*

CUE Tu me retrouves à deux heures devant le cinéma?
RESPONSE *D'accord.*

CUE Je ne veux plus revoir Jacques. Heureusement, il m'est impossible de sortir ce soir.
RESPONSE *Tant mieux.*

Commentary

This mixed exercise is, of course, a review and presumes preliminary learning of appropriate rejoinders, either through a series of exercises on particular rejoinders or through the teacher's continual use of them in class. Rejoinders learned artificially, out of context, are easily forgotten. Students should be encouraged to intersperse them liberally through their communication activities.

* Begin keeping a list of frequently used French rejoinders so that you can employ them yourself in class and teach them to your students. Your list will certainly include such expressions as *(C'est) dommage* and *quel dommage, d'accord, vraiment? en effet! sans blague! dites donc, bien sûr, de rien, je vous en prie, ça ne fait rien, ce n'est pas la peine . . . , pas de chance, comment? pardon, tant pis, tant pis pour lui, tant mieux,* and *formidable, ça!*

6. TRANSLATION DRILLS

Translation exercises have slipped into disfavor in recent years. This is not because translation itself is reprehensible. In fact, it is a natural process with many practical uses. Unfortunately, for many teachers it became an end, rather than a means of improving the student's control of the structure of the language. As a result, many translation exercises became tortuous puzzles. (Try translating a sentence like: Didn't you wish the old woman had died before she knew about it?) The question of translation, and how it can be used most effectively, is discussed in depth in Chapter 9.

The habit of translating everything one hears or says (or reads or writes) can become a hindrance to fluency. Many students do not realize that it is possible to learn to comprehend and think in the foreign language directly; hence the need for procedures which encourage and develop this ability. For these reasons translation drills, if used at all, should be used sparingly, and then only for linguistic features which it is difficult to practice entirely in French.

Oral translation drills differ from the older types of translation exercises in several ways:

1. Since the native language serves solely as a stimulus for the production of authentic French utterances, only natural idiomatic utterances that the student could conceivably use in communication are introduced:

G45 *He went home early.* Il est rentré de bonne heure.

2. Stimulus sentences are *short,* centering exclusively on the grammatical feature being practiced:

G46 *I saw him.* Je l'ai vu.
I didn't see him. Je ne l'ai pas vu.

3. Stimulus sentences remain within a *familiar vocabulary range* so that the student's attention is not distracted from the grammatical feature being practiced.

4. Translation drills do not encourage students to look for one-to-one equivalences between English and French by distorting the English, as in the following example from a grammar-translation type textbook:

G47 *What did you let fall?*
Qu'avez-vous laissé tomber?

Instead they require students to produce a French utterance which is *semantically equivalent* to the English stimulus.

G48 *Do you like it?* Est-ce qu'il vous plaît?

In this way, they encourage students to think in French. They are particularly useful for practicing distinctively French idioms:

G49 *It's no use my saying anything to him; he never listens.*
J'ai beau lui parler; il ne m'écoute jamais.
Don't be mad at me. Ne m'en veux pas.

5. Although stimulus sentences are short, they are not fragments, but *complete utterances* providing a context which indicates usage. Instead of being asked to translate: *he came, she went, they left,* students are presented with more likely utterances, such as:

G50 *He left yesterday.* Il est parti hier.
She went to the post office. Elle est allée au bureau de poste.

6. As with other oral drills, translation drills provide practice of one grammatical feature consistently through six or seven items before the drill moves on to a related feature, or to a further complication of the same feature.

G51 Set of stimulus sentences for practicing the *passé composé* with *être* or *avoir* as auxiliary

Dites en français:
a. He came in.
b. She went out.
c. She walked quickly.
d. He went upstairs immediately.
e. He came down later.
f. She left early.
g. She ran fast.
h. She arrived late.

Commentary

This is a mixed practice exercise, to be conducted after other practices which have been limited to one aspect of this complex feature. Here, the student is expected to decide rapidly to which category the different verbs belong, as he would have to do in communication. (As a written exercise, it would require also careful consideration of past participle agreements.) See also W62.

7. After several drills developing familiarity with a certain feature, a mixed drill may be given (as in G9).
8. Translation drills provide a stimulus for quick production of verb forms for particular tenses as in G52 (but not for the use of these tenses, which is more complicated), and for irregular verb forms as in G53:

G52 *He'll arrive tomorrow.* Il arrivera demain.
They'll arrive tomorrow. Ils arriveront demain . . .

G53 *He takes it.* Il le prend.
He took it. Il l'a pris.
He'll take it. Il le prendra.
We used to take it. Nous le prenions . . .

It would be difficult to change G53 into a substitution drill, or even a conversion drill, yet such rapid checking of knowledge of irregular forms is useful and necessary.

9. Translation drills are *useful for quick review*—for refreshing students' memories and pinpointing persistent inaccuracies. Conducted orally, at a brisk pace, they do not give the students time to pore over the French equivalents and edit them, as they do with written exercises.

Simultaneous interpretation

When some grammatical features are well learned, oral translation drills for review may be placed in a more realistic setting by giving individual students the opportunity to act as French simultaneous interpreters for the poor monolingual English-speaking teacher or a fellow student. With classroom-laboratory facilities, an authentic simultaneous interpreting situation can be staged. The passage for interpretation will be carefully prepared by the teacher so that it is possible for the student to interpret successfully. (It can also be designed to elicit certain features, for instance, specific tenses.) Other students will be asked to comment on the success of the interpreting and have the opportunity to improve on it. This type of activity is also suitable for recording in the language laboratory.

* Form small groups of students interested in different types of oral exercises.

1. Find examples of the selected type of oral exercise in textbooks, workbooks, or laboratory manuals, and discuss whether or not they are well constructed.

2. Try writing an exercise of this type for a structural feature for which it is appropriate.

3. Try your exercise out on the class to see if it is effective.

4. Take some poorly constructed oral exercises of this type, rewrite them in a more effective form, and then try them out on other students.

5
Teaching the sound system

In order to follow the discussion in this section, the reader needs to be familiar with certain commonly used terms. The sounds we make are *phones*. Although the number of phones that can be produced by any individual speaker is practically unlimited, only certain sounds are recognized by the speakers and hearers of a particular language as conveying meaning. The smallest unit of significant or meaningful sound has been called a *phoneme*. A phoneme is actually an abstraction rather than a concrete description of a specific sound. Any particular phoneme comprises a group or *class* of sounds that are phonetically similar but whose articulations vary according to their position relative to the other sounds which precede or follow them. The environmentally conditioned variants of any particular sound occurring in complementary distribution are *allophones*. "In complementary distribution" means that these sound variants are regularly found in certain environments where they do not contrast with each other, e.g., variant A may occur perhaps only in medial position between vowels, whereas variant B always occurs in initial or final position.

In *articulatory phonetics,* we study the positions of the organs of speech, e.g., the tongue, lips, or vocal cords, in the production of different sounds. These articulatory descriptions are intended to help us to form unfamiliar sounds. In speech, however, the organs are in continual motion, so that

141

sounds may vary slightly as they are produced in association with other sounds or are given differing degrees of stress. This variation must remain within a certain band of tolerance if it is not to hinder comprehension (that is, if the phonetic variants are still to be recognizable to a listener familiar with that language as manifestations of the same phoneme).

The concepts mentioned above are useful for the teacher in understanding and defining problem areas which speakers of one language encounter when attempting to learn another. For example, the French /l/ is phonemic, as shown by the fact that *un gros lot* and *un gros mot* have different meanings which are signalled only by the change of the element /l/ to /m/; in English /l/ is also phonemic, as witness *it's a lot, it's a pot*. The phoneme /l/ in English, however, has two allophones, the *clear l* [1] and the *dark (velarized)* [ɫ], which occur in different environments ([1] before vowels and /j/, and [ɫ] after vowels) and are, therefore, in complementary distribution. Since these varying sounds always appear in certain environments they may be termed allophones of the phoneme /l/. (They are not merely accidental or dialectal variants, because they do not alternate with each other in the same position but have each a clearly defined distribution.)

The recognition of the phoneme is basically a psychological process which results from experience with a particular language. Many English speakers do not notice the difference between [1] and [ɫ] in their own language, because these sounds are non-distinctive in English, that is, they do not clearly differentiate one word from another. Students need to be made aware of differences to which they are not accustomed but which may be phonemic in a new language; otherwise, they may unwittingly transfer their English speech habits to the new language. Naturally teachers of French need to be very familiar with the significant differences between the French and English sound systems if they are to help their students acquire a pronunciation acceptable and comprehensible to a native speaker.

In *generative phonology*,[2] sound systems are described in terms not of phonemes but of *distinctive features*. These features are *binary*, that is, either present $(+)$ or absent $(-)$, which enables the phonologist to represent the phonological system of a language by a feature matrix. Features are described in terms which may be *articulatory* (taking into account such things as place and manner of articulation), *acoustic* (referring to information detectable by technical instruments), or *perceptual* (e.g., syllables or stress). Generative phonologists are attempting to establish a set of *universal* distinctive features which may be used to characterize the sounds of all languages. To the generative phonologist the pronunciation of a word is a surface representation resulting from the application of transformational rules to an abstract underlying form. This approach has brought to light some interesting relationships between surface sound realizations and traditional spelling systems.

Languages change: how many phonemes are there in modern French?

Martinet stated in 1960 that there were 34 phonemes in his own dialect of French. "Mais parmi les sujets parisiens nés depuis 1940," he observed, "un système de 31 phonèmes n'est pas rare."[3] Martinet attributed this reduction to three tendencies in modern Parisian French (normal non-formal speech):

1. The distinction between /œ̃/ and /ɛ̃/ is no longer maintained; many speakers pronounce *lundi* as /lɛ̃di/, *emprunter* as /ɑ̃prɛ̃te/, *les yeux bruns* as /lezjøbrɛ̃/. Since /ɛ̃/ is never realized as [œ̃] in words traditionally pronounced with [ɛ̃], such as *pain* and *main,* this eliminates the phoneme /œ̃/ from the inventory of these speakers; the contrast [ɛ̃] versus [œ̃] no longer signals a difference in meaning and is therefore no longer functional. [œ̃] cannot be considered an allophone of the phoneme /ɛ̃/, however, since it is not in complementary distribution with [ɛ̃]. (The infrequently used *brin,* as in *brin d'herbe,* will not be confused with *brun* since they occur in different grammatical environments.)

2. Martinet also discovered that "66 Parisiens nés avant 1920, réunis par le hasard, ont tous deux voyelles distinctes dans *patte* et *pâte;* parmi quelques centaines de Parisiennes nées après 1940, plus de 60% ont, dans ces deux mots, une même voyelle /a/."[4] In this case one phoneme /ɑ/ is apparently disappearing from the speech of many Parisians.

3. The status of /e/ and /ɛ/ has been and is still changing. Martinet (1960) observed that these two phonemes were tending to become allophones of an archiphoneme /E/,[5] that is, in complementary distribution, with /e/ occurring in open syllables as in *maison* /mezɔ̃/, *blé* /ble/, and /ɛ/ occurring in closed syllables as in *bêtement* /bɛtmɑ̃/, *belle* /bɛl/. Delattre (1965) noted that "/ɛ/ occurs finally in the dialect of nearly one-third of northern French speakers, mainly in words of the types *prêt* [prɛ] and *j'allais* [ʒalɛ] . . . . in the unaffected speech of the most cultivated class, [pre], [ʒale] is not only the pronunciation of all southern speakers but also that of a majority of northern French speakers."[6] Léon (1972), however, found that a sample of 31 working-class Parisian boys maintained a stable distinction between final /e/ and /ɛ/. These subjects pronounced with /e/ words ending in *-é, -er,* or *-ez* (*beauté, raser, rasez*) and with /ɛ/ words spelled with *-ai* (*quai, gai,* even *prendrai*) and, in most cases, *-et* as well (*billet, ticket*).[7] There is obviously considerable flux in this regard, depending on age, socioeconomic status, and regional influences. On the other hand, it seems generally agreed, in recent research, that the /e/ɛ/ distinction has disappeared in unstressed syllables,

where an "e moyen" is the usual realization.[8] Harvey suggests a *règle simplifiée*, which is certainly sufficient at the elementary level:

   a. voyelle inaccentuée: ad libitum
   b. accentuée plus consonne prononcée: [ɛ]
   c. accentuée en finale absolue: [e].[9]

We may note further that there is also controversy as to the independent status of the *e muet*, as in donne-l*e* or parce qu*e*, since many French native speakers equate it with /ø/ and some with /œ/.[10] As Valdman et al. have observed, "the letter *e* sometimes represents no sound whatsoever, and at other times it represents either the vowel /œ/ or the vowel /ø/, between which French speakers make no distinction. This alternation between no sound and /œ/ or /ø/ is commonly called *mute e*. It must be remembered that mute *e* is not a sound feature but a type of grammatical behavior."[11]

Valdman (1972) suggests that the teacher use a simplified pedagogical norm in fluctuating situations such as these, that is, "an approximation to the actual speech behavior of French speakers which will nonetheless permit the foreign learner to communicate effectively within the context of the natural and meaningful use of language."[12] Certainly, teachers should not insist on fine distinctions not made by the average French speaker. At a more advanced stage, students may be taught a more fastidious pronunciation for reading poetry or prose aloud or for more formal speech.

Languages contrast: major differences between the French and English phonological systems

Delattre has said of French and English: "Ces deux langues sœurs, si rapprochées quant au vocabulaire depuis Guillaume le Conquérant, contrastent . . . dans tout le domaine phonétique. Elles occupent dans le tableau des langues du monde les deux extrémités phonétiques."[13]

Speaking of the English vowel system Delattre states:[14]

Comparatively, English vowels are predominantly low, back, unrounded,[15] with a strong tendency to center the short and unstressed (except when very low). Duration contributes to vowel distinctions. All English vowels are more or less diphthongized. Most characteristic series: the somewhat back-unrounded /u, ʊ, ɜ, ʌ/.

. . . Comparatively, French vowels are predominantly high, fronted, rounded, and extreme (except when low). The /i, e, y, ø, u, o/ are nearly cardinal. The open/close difference in the mid-vowels is very pronounced. Duration is negligible in vowel distinction. There is no diphthongization. Most characteristic series: the front-rounded /y, ø, œ/ and the nasals /ɛ̃, œ̃, ɑ̃, ɔ̃/.

For English speakers, then, cultivating a forward position of the tongue and a strong rounding of the lips to which they are not accustomed, and producing vowels which are not diphthongized and do not vary noticeably in duration will pose particular problems.

It is lack of realization of basic contrastive differences such as these which results in a marked "foreign accent" as the student tries to make a few new sounds and fit them into his native-language phonological system. The teacher will not explain these differences to his students in scientific terms, except to an interested adult group, but he will need to understand them himself if he is to help his students form correct French sounds. Slight distinctions in sound which can hinder comprehension of a message are made by movements of the tongue and other organs in the teacher's mouth and throat which the students cannot normally see. Consequently, merely making French sounds which are different from English sounds and urging students to imitate these, without giving some indication as to how they can be produced, may not be sufficient to ensure accurate production by the students. This is the case particularly when a specific sound does not exist in English, as with /y/ and the French /r/, or when the French sound varies in some significant way from a familiar English sound, as does the French /l/.

Articulatory descriptions and empirical recommendations

Articulatory descriptions for the production of a particular sound, using terms like those in the previous section, are useful for the preparation of the teacher. They make clear to young teachers what they themselves have been doing, perhaps intuitively rather than consciously, in the pronunciation of French. They highlight the types of articulatory difficulties English speakers may be expected to encounter. The teacher does not usually give such descriptions to the students at the introductory stage (although they may be helpful for remedial work and of interest to older students or to students learning a third language). Instead, from their knowledge of the articulatory data,[16] teachers develop empirical recommendations to help their students produce sounds they do not seem to acquire easily by imitation.[17] (This subject is discussed in more detail below under *Phonétique Corrective*, p. 159.)

TEACHING A FRENCH *r*

We may take as an example of a sound which often proves difficult for speakers of English the French standard /r/, sometimes called the Parisian *r,* which may also be transcribed /R/. In teaching students to produce this /r/, we begin by considering the *r* of the student's native language.

Prator's advice for the production of an American *r* is as follows:

S1 "Pronounce the vowel /a/. As you do so, curve the tip of your tongue up and slide the sides of the tongue backward along the tooth ridge, and you should have no difficulty in producing a perfect American /r/." [18]

Armstrong describes the production of the British English fricative *r*, usually transcribed /ɹ/, as follows:

"1. The tip of the tongue is raised to the back part of the teeth-ridge.
"2. The passage is narrowed at that point, but not sufficiently to cause much friction.
"3. The sound is voiced." [19]

Next we consider the formation of the standard French *r*. Peyrollaz and Bara de Tovar describe its production as follows:

S2 "Le [r] *parisien* est prononcé en laissant la pointe de la langue reposer derrière les dents inférieures, tandis que le dos de la langue s'élève contre le palais. L'air, en passant, frotte contre la langue et le palais et produit le [r]. Son point d'articulation peut varier légèrement suivant la voyelle qui l'accompagne." [20]

From these three descriptions it seems clear that the first step for an English speaker learning to pronounce a French *r* is to keep the tip of the tongue down behind the lower teeth. This prevents him from making either kind of English *r* described above and forces him to use other organs in the production of the French *r*. This simple, essential fact is rarely explained to the student. With the tip of the tongue accounted for, the student may then proceed as recommended by Harvey:

S3 "Commencer avec /ɑ:/ de *father*. Demander aux élèves de soulever un peu le dos de la langue en maintenant le bout de la langue contre les dents inférieures. Le résultat devrait être un /R/. Faire faire l'exercice /ɑ : R ɑ : R ɑ :/." [21]

Other ways of teaching a French *r* have been suggested, but in all cases the tongue must be kept behind the lower teeth, with tip lowered to give the tongue the convex fronted shape required for the French *r*.

S4 The student may begin, for instance, with [g] as in *go* (the [g] in *get* will not suffice as it brings the tongue further forward). [g] forces the student to raise the back of the tongue as required for the French *r* and also to bring his vocal cords into a position for voicing (the French *r* being also voiced). As he attempts to say [gr] without moving the tip of his tongue, he forces air through the narrow passage above the tongue, producing a slightly fricative sound. He must then learn to make this sound without the preceding [g].

In neither S3 nor S4 is any articulatory description given to the students but the correct articulatory positions are induced through the production of familiar movements which lead to the unfamiliar movement desired. These are, then, empirical recommendations.

✳ From your knowledge of English and French articulatory movements, work out in similar fashion empirical recommendations for inducing students to make correct /y/ and /l/ sounds.

Teaching French sounds as a system

Teachers often concentrate on correct articulatory production of those distinctive French sounds which do not exist in English (the so-called "difficult" sounds), while allowing students to produce English near-equivalents for the rest. Unfortunately, incorrectly articulated consonants affect the production of vowels just as incorrect vowel production affects the contiguous consonants.

EFFECT OF INCORRECT PRODUCTION OF FINAL *l*

Many students do not realize that in English they are using two *l*'s: the so-called *clear l*, as in *leaf* and *lack*, which is different from the so-called *dark l* of *bull, fell,* or *table.* The *l* used in initial positions in English is not very different from the French *l.* In English the initial *l* is produced by the tip of the tongue touching the tooth ridge, whereas in French the *l* used in all positions is produced with the tip of the tongue down against the upper (sometimes lower) teeth. This new position should be practiced. When, however, the student unwittingly uses an English *dark l* in final position in French he distorts and tends to dipthongize vowels like /ε/ in *elle* /εl/, and /i/ in *pile* /pil/ because the general tongue position for the English *final l* is close to the position of /ʊ/ as in *pull.* The efforts the teacher has made to teach students to pronounce correctly /ε/ and /i/ are thus negated by failure to teach the correct pronunciation of /l/.

CONSONANT ANTICIPATION

In English there is a tendency to anticipate the position of the consonant in articulating preceding vowels. This tendency is particularly marked for the English-speaking student since 60 per cent of English syllables are closed syllables (that is, syllables ending in a consonant). By contrast, only 24 per cent of French syllables are closed.[22] The English-speaking student must learn to pronounce French with open syllables, for the most part, even across word boundaries:

e.g., il a quitté son appartement cet après-midi.
/ i la ki te sɔ̃ na par tə mɑ̃ se ta prɛ mi di /

When articulating closed syllables he must guard against consonant anticipation. Should he anticipate the consonant following a nasal vowel in a closed syllable he may unwittingly insert a nasal consonant, *m* or *n*, between the vowel and the final consonant. If the final consonant is a *b* or *p*, he will tend to insert an *m*, pronouncing *tombe* as /tɔ̃mb/ instead of /tɔ̃:b/. The point of articulation for *m* and for *b* or *p* is identical, the difference between the nasal and non-nasal consonants being that the velum, or movable part of the soft palate, is in its lowered position for *m*, allowing the air to pass through the nasal cavity, whereas it is raised for *b* and *p*, thus preventing the air from passing through the nasal cavity. When the student anticipates the position of *b* (*p*) while articulating the nasal /ɔ̃/, (that is, while the velum is lowered), the student produces *m* while passing from /ɔ̃/ to /b/ or /p/. Compare the pronunciation of *rampe* as /rɑ̃mp/ instead of /rɑ̃:p/. A similar error results if *d* or *t* are anticipated after a nasal vowel, resulting in an anticipatory *n,* as in *ronde* pronounced /rɔ̃nd/ instead of /rɔ̃:d/, or *pente* pronounced /pɑ̃nt/ instead of /pɑ̃:t/.

The same error of consonant anticipation can, of course, occur when a nasal vowel in an open syllable is followed by an initial *b, p, d,* or *t* in the next syllable as in:

tomber pronounced /tɔ̃m be/ instead of /tɔ̃ be/;
sympathique pronounced /sɛ̃m pa tik/ instead of /sɛ̃ pa tik/;
Vendôme pronounced /vɑ̃n dom/ instead of /vɑ̃ dom/;
santé pronounced /sɑ̃n te/ instead of /sɑ̃ te/.

Consonant anticipation is particularly marked when English speakers try to pronounce non-nasal vowels followed by nasal consonants in closed syllables. Thus *Jeanne* /ʒan/ may be incorrectly pronounced /ʒɑ̃n/, and *bonne* /bɔn/ mispronounced as /bɔ̃n/.

✱ The above discussion of the differences between the English and French sound systems is illustrative only and by no means exhaustive. Be sure you are aware of and able to help students with other problems, such as the unaspirated *p* and *t*; the elusive difference between English and French semi-vowels as in onion/*oignon;* bilious and *il y a,* or million and *million,* and English Louis versus *Louis* and *lui;* the difference in articulation of final consonants as in port/*porte;* ball/*balle;* tip/*type;* the assimilation of voiced and unvoiced consonants; differences in stress; and patterns of intonation.[23]

Aural discrimination

Students confronted with strange sounds will at first tend to perceive them as variants of the categories of sounds with which they are familiar in their native language. If this continues, it will, of course, affect comprehension, but it will also hinder the development of a near-native pronunciation. The student who is not aware of the existence of certain distinctions of sounds is unlikely to produce these correctly, except by chance on random occasions. When he is able to "hear" the differences, that is, discriminate between sounds aurally, he can work toward perfecting these distinctions in his own production.

French sounds which have no counterpart in English will at first be difficult for speakers of English to distinguish. They will tend not to perceive the difference between *la rue* /lary/ and *la roue* /laru/, or between *dessus* /dsy/ and *dessous* /dsu/. In fact, inexperienced English-speaking students are likely to identify both /y/ and /u/ as variants of the English phoneme /u/, as in the word *too,* which is a sound similar to, but not identical with, the French /u/ of *roue.* If they do hear a difference, they may associate the French /y/ of *rue* with the English /i/ of *feet.*

English speakers often have difficulty also in hearing the difference between the nasals /ɔ̃/ and /ɑ̃/, since neither occurs in English. To the naive English speaker, /ɔ̃/ and /ɑ̃/ may sound at first like variants of the vowel sound of English *song* with consonant anticipation. Yet the distinction of these nasals is important for comprehension in French, as witness such minimal pairs as *long* /lɔ̃/ and *lent* /lɑ̃/; *ton* /tɔ̃/ and *temps* /tɑ̃/; *don* /dɔ̃/ and *dent* /dɑ̃/.

French sounds for which there are *apparently similar sounds in English* may pose problems as great, or even greater, than those for which there are no corresponding sounds in English. Students will tend to hear the French /i/ of *mite* as the English /i/ of *meat* or, in unstressed position, as English /I/, particularly in cognates like *histoire* /istwar/ and *finissent* /finis/ which will tend to be heard, and later reproduced, with the English /I/ of *history* and *finish.*

Similarly, the French /ʒ/ will often be perceived as English /dʒ/ (which occurs as the initial and final affricate in *judge*), even though /ʒ/ does occur in English, but only in non-initial position as in *pleasure.* Likewise, the semi-vowel /ɥ/ as in *lui* /lɥi/ will usually be perceived as the already known English /w/, which is similar, but not identical, to the French /w/ of *Louis* /lwi/.

Exercises may be designed to help students discriminate sounds which are causing them difficulty, once the kind of problem involved has been identified. Particular French sounds should be differentiated both from closely related French sounds and from English sounds that may be interfering with the student's perception.

Just how much difficulty a particular English-speaking student may have in distinguishing one sound of French from others depends on a number of factors, such as his individual sensitivity to distinctions of sound, the pronunciation of the teacher, and how carefully the student happens to be listening on that day. As a rule, the students are first taught to discriminate a problem sound from a similar sound in French, or from an interfering sound in English. If the students' inability to distinguish the sound persists because of confusions with other sounds, then the number of discrimination exercises is increased to cope with this complexity. Problem areas in French which involve one or more discriminations are illustrated in examples S5–9. In the diagrams accompanying these examples, the sounds to be discriminated are connected by arrows. The various discriminations involved in each example are numbered.

1. A simple French-English discrimination.

S5 (1)   Fr. /t/⟵⟶Eng. /t/
                (1)

The student learns to discriminate between the French unaspirated *t* and the English aspirated *t*.

2. Distinguishing a French sound which does not exist in English from two interfering English sounds.

S6

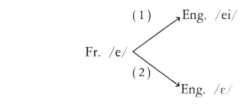

The student learns to discriminate the French /e/ of *été* from the English /ei/ of *say* and also from the English /ɛ/ of *set*.

3. Distinguishing two French sounds which do not exist in English from an English sound to which the student tends to assimilate them.

S7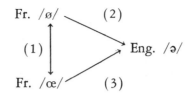

The student learns to discriminate the French /ø/ of *peu* from the French /œ/ of *peur*, and to recognize that both of these differ from the English /ə/ of *but* (or Brit. Eng. *bird*).

4. Distinguishing one French sound from three interfering English sounds.

S8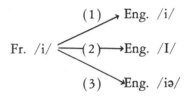

The student learns to discriminate the French /i/ of *cite, ville, village*, from the English /i/ of *seat*, the English /I/ of *sit, village*, and the English /iə/ of *seal* and *veal*.

5. Distinguishing two French sounds from each other and each of these from certain interfering English sounds.

S9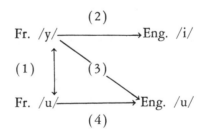

The student learns to discriminate the French /y/ as in *but* from English /i/ as in *beat* and from English /u/ as in *boot*, as well as discriminating French /u/ as in *sous* from English /u/ as in *sue*. He must also learn to distinguish French /y/ as in *rue* from French /u/ as in *roue*.

* Show diagrammatically the discrimination problems an English speaker can encounter in learning to distinguish *sol* and *sôle*, stressed *treize* and *traité; pain, pan,* and *panne.*

These exercises are necessary only when discrimination problems become evident. Often they serve remedial purposes. Which types of exercises and how many are used at the one time and how these are interspersed with production exercises will vary according to the needs of a particular group of students at a particular time. Usually, after some aural discrimination exercises, students will be encouraged to produce the sounds themselves to demonstrate what they have observed. If confusions are still evident, more aural discrimination exercises may be tried.

The sounds /ɔ̃/ and /ɑ̃/, which are easily confused by English speakers, will be used for demonstration purposes in the following examples. These sounds may be identified and practiced separately, discriminated from each other and from interfering English sounds (like the English sound in *song*), and finally produced in close proximity (as in *un long ban; un enfant content*).

Type 1: Identification of the sound, e.g., /ɔ̃/

The sound will have been encountered in dialogue or conversational narrative, or in oral work in the classroom, in an utterance like: *Bonjour, Pierre,* or *le crayon est long.*

1. The sound in a familiar context.

S10 Listen carefully to these sentences:

a. Bonjour, Pierre.
b. Bonjour, Pierre.
c. Bonjour, monsieur.

2. The sound in single words of consonant + vowel construction.

S11 Listen again to the sound /ɔ̃/ in the following words:

d. bon, long, bonbon

3. The sound in a larger context.

S12 How many times do you hear the sound /ɔ̃/ in the following sentences?

e. Bonjour, Jacques.
f. C'est bon, ce bonbon.
g. Ce crayon est jaune.

Type 2: Minimal pair technique

1. Discrimination between similar sounds in French and English.

S13 Listen to the difference between the French /ɔ̃/ and the English sound /ɔŋ/.

   a. *son* / song
   b. *bon* / bong
   c. *long* / long

   2. Discrimination between similar sounds within the French phonological system.

S14 The sound /ɔ̃/ is not the same as /ɑ̃/. Listen carefully to the differences between the following pairs:

   d. pont / pan
   e. dont / dans
   f. long / lent
   g. bon / ban
   h. C'est long / C'est lent

Type 3: Same-different exercises

Listen carefully to the vowel sounds in these pairs of words and tell me (or: mark on your answer sheet) if the two vowel sounds are the same or different.

   1. French / English

S15 (For ɔ̃/ɔŋ):
a. *bon, bon*	(same)
b. *bon,* bong	(different)
c. song, song	(same)

S16 (For ɑ̃/ɔŋ):
d. wrong, *rang*	(different)
e. *sang, sang*	(same)
f. *gant,* gong	(different)

   2. French / French

S17 (For ɔ̃/ɑ̃):
g. bon, bon	(same)
h. bon, ban	(different)
i. lent, lent	(same)
j. dent, don	(different)

S18   k. C'est long, c'est lent   (different)
        l.   Quelle dent?, quelle dent?   (same)
        m. Quelle dent?, quel don?   (different)

With French/French discriminations it is possible to use larger contexts than single words as long as the only difference in sound is the change of vowel.

Type 4: Differentiation exercises

You will hear three sounds numbered 1, 2, and 3. Write down (or: tell me) the number of the one which is different from the others.

    1. French / English

S19 (For ɔ̃/ɔŋ):   a. 1. *bon*   2. *bon*   3. bong   (3)
                           b. 1. song   2. *son*   3. song   (2)

S20 (For ɑ̃/ɔŋ):   c. 1. *tant*   2. *tant*   3. tong   (3)
                           d. 1. dong   2. *dent*   3. dong   (2)

    2. French / French

S21 (For ɑ̃/ɔ̃):   e. 1. lent   2. long   3. long   (1)
                        f. 1. Quel don?   2. Quel don?   3. Quelle dent? (3)

S22 *Variation*

In the following groups of words, one does not have the same vowel sound as the others. Make a check mark for each word as you hear it, crossing the one which has a different vowel sound from the others:

g. temps, champ, *pont*, lent, dent
h. il tombe, il monte, *il chante*, il compte, il songe

Type 5: Rhyming exercise (combining aural discrimination and production)

S23 Listen to the following word and give me as many words as you can think of which rhyme with it:

TEACHER tant
STUDENTS Jean, gant, dent; bon, pont, enfant, évident.

✱ Construct items similar to those in Types 2, 3, and 4 of this section to help students discriminate:

    1. French /y/ from French /u/, and both of these from English /u/;
    2. French /ɥ/ from French /w/, and both of these from English /w/.

Production

INTRODUCTION OF THE FRENCH SOUND SYSTEM

Should the learning of a language begin with a series of lessons on the sound system? This is the approach of some textbooks. Usually, when this is done, little attention is paid to the usefulness of the words in which the sounds are produced or whether they will be used in classwork in the early lessons. In a quick check of several such textbooks the following words were found for practice: *béguin, bine, dague, goupil, huche, jeun, jeûne, larron, lippe, meute, ouate, pâtre,* none of which appears in the *français fondamental premier degré et second degré,*[24] one of which does not appear in the *Petit Larousse* (the most frequently used dictionary in the schools), and three of which do not appear in the *Dictionnaire du français contemporain* (Larousse). This approach may be acceptable for highly motivated adult learners to whom the rationale of the teaching has been explained, but it is unwise for elementary, junior high school, or senior high school classes. It can become boring, and its relevance is not understood by the students, who are anxious to be able to say something practical in French.

In the early lessons, the students can be introduced to the whole array of French sounds which they try to repeat after the teacher, before being drilled carefully in particular problems of pronunciation. Sentences like the following are frequently the first the student learns: *Bonjour, Pierre. Comment vas-tu?* /bɔ̃ʒuːr *pjɛːr/ kɔmɑ̃vaty/.[25]

These five words contain sixteen different sounds, of which only one, /r/, is repeated and only three, /k, m, v/, pose no difficulties for English speakers. A normal reply: *Très bien, merci. Et toi?* /trɛbjɛ̃ mɛrsi etwa/ introduces five more, making a total of twenty-one distinct sounds. This shows the impracticability of trying to keep early material within the limits of a certain number of sounds if natural, usable utterances are to be learned. Sentences such as *Elle danse lentement en pensant aux chants de son enfance* which are artificially constructed to introduce only one or two sounds at a time may have some place in laboratory drill, particularly of a remedial nature, but their utility is limited in developing conversational interchange. Tongue-twisters like *Didon dîna, dit-on, du dos d'un dodu dindon,* for practicing the undervoiced French *d,* may be used for relaxation in the classroom and to focus attention on a particular problem. Repetition of such concentrated conglomerations of one sound gives some practice in the correct articulation of the sound. This, of itself, does not ensure equally successful transfer to utterances where the sound is more sparsely distributed. The sound will need to be practiced in many contexts if it is to reappear correctly articulated in spontaneous utterances.

Language learning usually begins either with the simple dialogue, useful expressions for classroom interchange, or a conversational narrative in the textbook. As the student listens to the teacher or model, his ear becomes attuned to the overall system of sounds of the language and its characteristic rhythm (*groupes rythmiques*), stress (*accent*), and intonation or melodic patterns (*mélodie de la phrase*). *Approximations to correct pronunciation* are sought in everything the student reproduces, without insistence on perfection at every point since this is too discouraging for the students at this early stage.

Problem sounds are singled out at intervals in the first few weeks and practiced, with attention to acceptable and comprehensible production.

1. The teacher begins with *short phrases* from current work, then, if necessary, isolates *specific words,* gives practice in *a specific sound,* returns to the practice of *words* and then to *the complete phrase,* moving, e.g., from *c'est sa mère* to *sa mère,* to *mère* and, if absolutely necessary, to /ɛ/, then rebuilding to *mère, sa mère,* and finally *c'est sa mère.*

Students may be asked to produce the sound in isolation a few times if they are having trouble with it, but not for long. Most sounds are rarely heard in isolation, and students must become accustomed to the slight variations which occur when sounds are made in association with other sounds.

2. Where possible, the sound is practiced first in *stressed* position (*accentué*), then in *semi-stressed* position (*demi-accentué*), and finally in *unstressed* position (*inaccentué*), with the students being trained to retain in unstressed position the full quality of the French sound as a counteraction to their English language habits.

S24 Où vas-*tu?* (accentué: end of utterance)

Où vas-*tu* ce matin? (demi-accentué: end of *groupe rythmique* within utterance)

Tu vas bien. (inaccentué: within *groupe rythmique*)

Est-ce qu'il a f*i*n*i?* (inaccentué/accentué)
Il a f*i*n*i* hier. (inaccentué/demi-accentué)
Il f*i*n*i*ra bientôt. (inaccentué/inaccentué)

3. When the teacher senses that students would profit from intensive practice in specific pronunciation problems, the training should move from *identification* of the sound (associated with aural discrimination of similar sounds, where necessary, as in S6–19), to *imitative production.* When imitative production is well advanced, the practice moves to *guided non-imitative production* (where the exercise is so structured that the student is induced to produce the sound without first hearing the model). The

goal must be *autonomous production* of the correct sound in non-structured contexts.

During intensive training in the production of a certain sound, it is helpful for the student to hear a correct model after he has produced the sound himself. He needs to be sensitized to the differences between his own production and the desired pronunciation if he is to improve in unsupervised practice. Where his own production has been faulty he should correct it immediately, while he still retains the auditory image of the model. (The four-phase format of G9 is often employed for this reason.)

STAGES OF INTENSIVE PRACTICE

1. Identification. Student listens.

S25 MODEL Dans la rue... la rue... dans la rue... la rue... la rue... dans la rue.

2. Imitative production (stressed position).

S26 MODEL Dans la rue. STUDENT: Dans la rue. MODEL: Dans la rue.
Student repeats after the model to correct his production or confirm it.

A similar four-phase format continues while the student imitates *la rue, rue, la rue, dans la rue,* thus practicing the sound in reduced contexts and then producing it once more in the larger context.

The practice moves on to such expressions as:

S27 C'est ma rue; Oui, c'est ma rue. (stressed position);
Quelle rue est-ce? Dans quelle rue est-ce? (semistressed position);
J'habite rue Martin; J'habite rue du Parc. (unstressed position).

3. Guided non-imitative production.

S28 TEACHER Dans quelle rue habitez-vous?
STUDENT J'habite rue Martin. (inaccentué)

TEACHER Rue du Parc? Est-ce votre rue?
STUDENT Non, ce n'est pas ma rue. (accentué)

TEACHER Demandez à Jean dans quelle rue il habite.
STUDENT Jean, dans quelle rue habites-tu? (*rue:* demi-accentué; *tu:* accentué)

4. Autonomous production.

S29 An interchange takes place between students, with the students themselves selecting the way they will ask the questions or answer them.

Où habites-tu?
J'habite rue de la Gare.

Dans quelle rue habites-tu?
Dans une rue loin d'ici.

Dans quelle rue est l'école?
Dans la rue qui mème au Jardin des Plantes.

Où est la gare?
Dans la rue de la Gare.

Rue Martin, est-ce ta rue?
Non, ce n'est pas ma rue.

Où habite Jacques?
Dans la même rue que moi (or) Je ne sais pas.

If the interchange is truly autonomous, students will occasionally produce sentences which do not contain the sound being practiced.

In the early lessons it is not only particular sounds which are practiced, but also smooth production of *élision, liaison,* and *enchaînement.* (Make sure you are familiar with contemporary usage in these areas.)[26]

WHAT DEGREE OF PERFECTION SHOULD BE EXPECTED IN THE EARLY STAGES?

Practice should concentrate on errors of pronunciation which would hinder comprehension, e.g., /semaru/ for *c'est ma rue,* and errors which force students into other errors (like those discussed above under *Teaching French Sounds as a System*). The teacher will need to return again and again, in an unobtrusive fashion, to certain persistent faults which are crucial to comprehension or acceptability, while continuing to improve the overall standard of pronunciation.

Phonétique corrective: *remedial training*

A distinction must be drawn between the types of exercises suitable in the very early stages, when the student knows only a little of the foreign language, and appropriate exercises for remedial training at a later stage (*phonétique corrective*). At first, emphasis is laid on phonemic distinctions which hinder comprehension. Later, advanced students often need intensive practice in the production of certain problem sounds or sequences of sounds to correct a "foreign accent."

Remedial work at an advanced level usually takes the form of a *systematic review of the French sound system.* At this stage, students have a wide-ranging vocabulary and considerable knowledge of grammatical structure. After a certain number of retraining drills (see S35–38), exercises can be used which exploit the students' knowledge of the language, eliciting from them the sounds being reviewed while they are concentrating on grammatical conversions and manipulations (see S39).

REMEDIAL PRODUCTION EXERCISES

Exercises of this type are usually constructed on a contrastive basis, highlighting problems of interference from English sounds which are close to the French sounds being practiced and from other French sounds which to an English ear appear similar to the particular sound to be produced (see S5–9). The remedial exercises in production may be preceded by *aural identification exercises* in which the sound is used in short utterances which are meaningful.

1. Remedial production exercises are frequently preceded by *articulatory instructions* for the correct production of the sound, with warnings about English habits which interfere with correct articulation. These are sometimes accompanied by photographs or diagrams showing the recommended position of the speech organs. (Articulatory information, can, of course, be supplied without the use of technical terms. In the instructions below, *dental, alveolar,* and *aspirated* can be omitted and the explanations of these terms used instead.)

S30 *Articulatory instructions for the production of a French* /t/

French /t/ is *dental,* that is, it is produced with the tip of the tongue down and the tongue pressed against the upper teeth, whereas English /t/ is *alveolar,* that is, is is produced with the tip of the tongue raised and touching the gums or tooth ridge. French /t/ is *unaspirated,* whereas English /t/ is usually *aspirated* (that is, when it is articulated a puff of air is emitted) except when it follows English /s/ as in s*t*op.

These articulatory instructions are often accompanied by *empirical recommendations* for achieving the correct articulation or for testing whether the sound is being correctly produced.

S31 *Empirical recommendations: French /t/—English /t/*

Hold a piece of paper (or a lighted match) in front of your mouth as you say English *t*op and notice how the paper (or flame) is blown by the puff of air emitted with the /t/. Now say *s*top and observe that the paper (or flame) does not move very much at all. This is because the English /t/ is aspirated in initial position and unaspirated after /s/. Try to say s...top, s...top, s...top without aspirating the *t*; now try to say s...top with your tongue against your upper teeth with the tip down and no aspiration. You will now have made a French /t/.

S32 *Articulatory instructions for the production of a vowel: French /y/*

French /y/ is a high, front, rounded vowel. The tongue is arched high in the front of the mouth, but not quite so high or so far forward as for /i/, and the lips are rounded. The vowel is tense and not diphthongized, that is, it does not have the glide of English /u/ or /iu/.

S33 *Empirical recommendations: French /y/*

Some books recommend that the student put his mouth into a correct position for whistling and then try to say /i/ without unrounding his lips. (The whistling position moves the tongue into the high, front position with tongue firmly against the lower teeth which is essential for the production of /y/. It also requires tense muscular control.) If students do not know how to whistle they may be told to round their lips firmly and thrust them forward while pressing the tongue tip against the lower teeth.

Other books recommend taking the mouth position for French /i/ with lips stretched as for a wide smile and then, without moving the tongue, rounding the lips and saying /y/. Rapidly moving from /i/ to /y/ to /i/ to /y/ makes the student conscious of the tenseness of these two vowels and the similar tongue position. If the tongue or lips are relaxed in the switch from /i/ to /y/ the student will tend to produce English /u/ which has an element of glide in it.

Note: Students may be able to produce an acceptable /y/ in isolation but fail to do so when it follows a consonant. This is because they are not aware of the characteristic *vowel anticipation* in French, which means that the mouth must have already taken the rounded or unrounded position of the vowel when articulating the preceding consonant. Contrast *fit* with unrounded lips for /f/, and *fut* with rounded lips for /f/. For this reason it is essential to practice French vowels with preceding consonants.

(This contrasts with the characteristic consonant anticipation of English which, if transferred to French, tends to diphthongization of vowels as the mouth position changes in mid-vowel.)

2. Production exercises *should not begin with the sound in isolation.* This is useful only when articulatory movements are being practiced. No French sound occurs normally in isolation, except in a few exclamations and tags, e.g., *ah! oh! hein?* The various relationships into which a sound enters modify it slightly, and it is these natural sequences which must be learned. Production exercises begin, then, with the *sound in single words or short phrases* which demonstrate the various environments in which it can occur. For instance a consonant may be practiced in initial, medial, and final positions and in association with certain other consonants; a vowel may be practiced in stressed, semi-stressed, and unstressed position and after or preceding certain consonants. This is the stage of *imitative production.* The words in which the sounds are practiced should be words which students can use, rather than nonsense words.

S34 *Relationships in which the consonant /t/ may occur*

    a. tu, thé, tôt, teint, très, tiers (*initial* in various relationships)
    b. hôtel, quitter, estimer, acheter, entrer (*medial* in various relationships)
    c. toute, peinte, sotte, forte, poste (*final* after various vowels and consonants)
    d. style, sténo, statue, strict (in *initial consonant clusters*)
    e. juste, titre, maître, frustre (in *final consonant clusters*)

S35 *The vowel /o/ in various positions*

    a. le tableau; j'en ai trop (accentué)
    b. il faut le faire; le morceau qui manque (demi-accentué)
    c. la beauté; mauvais; Daudet (inaccentué)

    The above examples also provide practice in pronouncing /o/ after various consonants and consonant clusters.

3. The sound is then practiced in short sentences, also in various environments and intonation patterns. This is still imitative production.

S36 *The consonant /t/ in short sentences in various environments*

    a. Tu t'es coupé.
    b. Elle est prête.

    c. Tentez la chance.
    d. Fermez la porte.
    e. Est-ce ta fête?
    f. Combien de fautes?
    g. Que tu es bête!
    h. Tais-toi donc!

    4. Remedial exercises often *practice two similar sounds at the same time* in order to highlight auditory and kinesthetic differences, since it is oppositions and contrasts within the sound system which make a language meaningful.

S37 *Vowel contrasts* are demonstrated in such pairs as:

    a. il l'a sali: il la salue;
    b. il l'a sali: il l'a salé;
    c. il lut: il loue.

S38 *Difference in voicing* distinguishes the meaning of the following pairs:

    a. le thé: le dé;
    b. il aura pu: il aura bu.

    5. Exercises are next introduced which, through some form of grammatical manipulation, force the student to *produce the sound unmodeled.* This is guided non-imitative production.

S39 *Vowel production*

    a. A change of *je dois* from present tense to *passé composé* forces the student to produce the sound /y/ in *j'ai dû,* while concentrating on the grammatical manipulation he is asked to perform.
    b. A change from the singular form *il prend* to the plural form *ils prennent* forces the student to produce /ɛ/ in a stressed closed syllable.

    6. The sound is then practiced in *longer utterances,* in mixed environments, or in sections of discourse. In this way the effects of proximity to other sounds in characteristic sequences and the influence of intonation, stress, *liaison, élision,* and *enchaînement* are more fully experienced. This practice need not be purely repetitive and imitative. It can take the form of a question-answer series, so designed as to induce the student to produce certain sounds.

S40 *The vowel* /œ/

a. A quelle h*eu*re commencent les premiers cours?
   A n*eu*f h*eu*res.

b. Est-ce qu'il y a un profess*eur* dans le laboratoire en ce moment?
   Oui, il y a un profess*eur* ici. (Non, il n'y a pas de profess*eur* ici.)

c. Avez-vous des frères et des so*eu*rs?
   J'ai trois frères mais je n'ai pas de so*eu*rs.

In application practice of this type, there is no need to concoct sentences loaded with a particular sound, like: N'avez-vous pas p*eu*r de faire des err*eu*rs sans profess*eur*? Such artificiality makes the student over-conscious of what the exercise demands of him and the resulting production is no real indication of what he will produce autonomously.

7. Sounds may finally be practiced *in a formal context* such as the reading of *poetry or literary prose,* since much of the language in earlier exercises will have been informal. It is important that students learn the differences between the formal and informal styles of spoken French.

If a passage is read after a model this is merely imitative production. If it is later read by the student alone, this is guided non-imitative production.

8. There is a place for some *anticipation practice.* The student reads each section first before hearing it read by a model. He then has the opportunity to reread this section and continue reading the next section before again hearing the model. This can be done as spaced reading on tape, provided that the natural pauses between word groupings are as obvious as in the following passage of simple conversation.

S41 /ɔ̃ — ɑ̃/ *contrasts*

STUDENT Vous avez mis c*om*bien de te*m*ps?
   MODEL Vous avez mis combien de temps?
STUDENT Vous avez mis combien de temps? dem*an*da Monsieur Laur*en*t.
   MODEL ... demanda Monsieur Laurent.
STUDENT ... demanda Monsieur Laurent. *On*ze heures tr*en*te minutes, les
   arrêts n*on* c*om*pris.
   MODEL Onze heures trente minutes, les arrêts non compris.
STUDENT Onze heures trente minutes, les arrêts non compris. C'est ce que
   je c*om*pte aussi.
   MODEL C'est ce que je compte aussi.

9. The goal of this type of remedial practice is for the student to demonstrate control of the sound he has been practicing when he is engaged in autonomous production in conversation.

✱ *Questions to discuss* in class or with other teachers.
    1. Should remedial production exercises be conducted with book open or with book closed? (What has been your own experience?)
    2. Why do you think nursery and counting rhymes (*comptines*) like S42 are often used for pronunciation practice?

S42 Il est midi.
    Qui vous l'a dit?
    C'est la souris.
    Où est-elle?
    Dans la chapelle.
    Que fait-elle?
    De la dentelle.
    Pour qui?
    Pour ces demoiselles.
    Combien les vend-elle?
    Trois quarts de sel.[27]

3. How would you help a student correct the following faults? Aspiration of /p/; pronouncing *tu* the same as *tout;* pronouncing *garçon* as though the last syllable rhymed with *enfant;* giving strong stress, as in English, to a syllable which is not the last, e.g., nous *arrīvons.*
    4. Which do you consider the most useful for practicing sounds: poems or prose extracts? Why?

✱ *Find some short poems* which would be useful for practicing certain types of sounds. They must be attractive and simple in content, with vocabulary and structures appropriate for the level at which you propose to use them. A certain amount of repetition of lines, or segments of lines, will make them more useful, particularly if this involves alliteration of a feature to be practiced or assonance involving vowels requiring special attention. Short lines are an advantage if you wish the poem to be memorized.

STIMULATING INTEREST IN REMEDIAL PRONUNCIATION PRACTICE

If students need corrective training but have become bored with the usual sound production exercises, this remedial work can be associated with the study of the *International Phonetic Alphabet* (I.P.A.) as applied to

French. As students concentrate on learning which sounds are represented by which symbols and as they endeavor to write down dictated passages in phonetic symbols, they become more sensitive to fine distinctions of sound. The reading aloud of passages in phonetic symbols can be a useful remedial production exercise. The transcribing of passages in I.P.A. into normal written French draws the students' attention to the relationships between the French sound and spelling systems (a study for which the term *orthoépie* is used). These new intellectual interests often stimulate motivation to improve pronunciation where "more pronunciation exercises" would fail.

Similarly the organization of a poetry recitation competition, the production of some short one-act plays by different groups for a festival or an inter-school social gathering, or the exchange of letter-tapes with French correspondents will make students conscious of the need to improve their pronunciation and intonation.

MONITORING ONE'S OWN PRODUCTION

When working with tapes on their own, students have difficulty in detecting their errors of pronunciation. Aural discrimination exercises help the student refine his ability to perceive distinctions.

To make them more conscious of these distinctions in their own production, students may be asked to read on to tape a series of aural discrimination exercises of Types 3 and 4 (S15–21) and then, later, to use this recording as an exercise, comparing their final discrimination decisions with the original script from which they recorded the exercise.

Students can be encouraged to evaluate their progress in perfecting their pronunciation by marking their weaknesses and their successes on a *pronunciation checklist* (S43).

1. When *working with tapes,* students should keep the checklist beside them as a guide to the features of the French sound system to which they should be attentive.

2. If the practice session is monitored, students should mark on the checklist the weaknesses in pronunciation which the monitor has drawn to their attention, so that they may concentrate on improving their production of these features.

3. The monitor should keep a cumulative record on a pronunciation checklist for each student, so that at each session he may refresh his memory of the weaknesses he has already drawn to the attention of the particular student to whom he is listening. In this way he will be able to emphasize some faults at one session and others at another, thus making maximum use of the short time at his disposal.

4. If pronunciation tapes are checked from time to time by the teacher,

comments may be entered on a duplicate pronunciation checklist for the student's consideration when recording.

S43 *Sample Pronunciation Checklist*

Features for Attention	Estimate of Quality (E, A, or U)*	Monitor's Comments or Personal Notes on Progress
General Features		
1. Predominantly forward position of tongue and lips.		
2. Tense muscular control.		
3. Vigorous lip movement (firm rounding, unrounding, opening).		
4. Division of syllables.		
5. Stress: equal syllable stress with increased stress at end of *groupe rythmique* and end of utterance.		
Vowels		
6. Purity of vowels (no diphthongization).		
7. Purity and distinctiveness of nasals (no consonant anticipation).		
8. /e/ɛ/ distinction (particularly in semi-stressed and stressed position).		
9. /ə/† caduc.		
10. /i/		
11. /ɔ/o/		
12. /u/y/		
13. /ø/œ/		
Consonants		
14. /l/		
15. /p; b/‡		
16. /t; d/		
17. /r/		

Features for Attention	Estimate of Quality (E, A, or U)*	Monitor's Comments or Personal Notes on Progress
18. Semi-vowel /j/: /aj; εj; ij; uj; œj/ and /jɛ̃; sjɔ̃/ etc.		
19. Semi-vowels /ɥ/w/		
20. Articulation of final consonants.		
Intonation		
21. Short statement.		
22. Long statement.		
23. Yes-no question.		
24. Information question.		
25. Exclamations and interjections.		
General Fluency		
26. *Elisions.*		
27. *Liaisons.*		
28. *Enchaînement.*		
29. Grouping of words (*groupes de souffle* and *groupes rythmiques*).[28]		

* E = Excellent (near-native); A = Acceptable (but not yet perfect); U = Unacceptable (needs attention).

† / between sounds indicates that these sounds should not be confused in pronunciation e.g., /u/y/.

‡ ; indicates grouping because of similarity of articulation, e.g., /p; b/.

✱ Use this checklist to evaluate a recording of your own speech in French. You will have to ask another student, a fellow teacher, or your instructor to evaluate points 1, 2, and 3 for you by watching you. Later, discuss in class how the list can be improved. Is it too long for practical use? Could certain categories be evaluated together?

✱ Sometimes teachers (and students) use, for initial or final evaluation of pronunciation, a recording of a passage such as the following which was specially written to include most of the features in the sample checklist.[29] Try to evaluate a recording by one of your fellow students of this passage.

S44 *Evaluation Passage*

Study the following passage carefully for three minutes to see that you understand the development of the dialogue but do not make any marks on the paper. Read the passage clearly and expressively into the microphone with your tape recorder set at Record. Do not read the names Michèle and Philippe.

Le bureau de poste

MICHÈLE   Cela t'ennuie de demander un renseignement à cet agent de police en haut de l'escalier?

PHILIPPE   Du tout . . . Pardon, monsieur, est-ce qu'il y a un bureau de poste près d'ici?

L'AGENT   Mais oui, monsieur, là-bas, tout droit, à cent pas.

PHILIPPE   Merci, monsieur . . . Eh bien, ce n'est pas bien loin. On peut y aller à pied, hein?

MICHÈLE   Allons-y.

PHILIPPE   Qu'il fait beau! Toute la ville est ensoleillée aujourd'hui, et les arbres sont couverts de feuilles.

MICHÈLE   Oui, Paris est beau au mois de mai.

PHILIPPE   Dis donc, combien de timbres veux-tu acheter?

MICHÈLE   Huit.

PHILIPPE   Mais tu as écrit au moins vingt-cinq lettres, j'en suis sûr.

MICHÈLE   Tu exagères, Philippe. Il ne faut pas exagérer. C'est un vilain défaut.

PHILIPPE   Eh bien, si tu achètes seulement huit timbres pour tant de lettres, ton pire ennemi ne pourrait pas dire que tu gaspilles ton argent.

II
THE WRITTEN WORD

6
Reading I:
purposes and procedures

Most students learning French expect to be able to read the language sooner or later. Their personal desires and expectations vary from wanting to be able to read a novel by Camus or a scientific journal to being able to read a menu, a tourist brochure, or advertisements in the Paris *métro*. Fortunately, reading is a completely individual activity, and students in the same course may be reading at very different levels of difficulty in French, just as they do in English.

To be able to read in French in the sense of extracting meaning from a graphic script is not an aim in itself. The student's aim is to be able to extract something specific—something of interest to him—and this must be kept in mind from the beginning. Many a French textbook in days gone by started the student reading with such inanities as:

R 1 Je suis un élève. Je suis dans la salle de classe. Le professeur est devant la classe. Il commence la leçon. Il ouvre le livre. J'ouvre le livre aussi. Le livre est vert. C'est un livre de français.

Reading activities should, from the beginning, be directed toward *natural uses of reading*. We read normally:

1. because we want information for some purpose or are curious about some topic;

2. because we need instructions in order to perform some task for our

work or for our daily life (we want to know how an appliance works, we are interested in a new recipe, we have forms to fill in);

3. because we want to act a play, play a new game, do a puzzle, or carry out some other activity which is pleasant and amusing;

4. because we want to keep in touch with friends by correspondence or understand business letters;

5. because we want to know when or where something will take place or what is available (we consult timetables, programs, announcements, and menus, or we read advertisements);

6. because we want to know what is happening or has happened (we read newspapers, magazines, reports);

7. because we seek enjoyment or excitement (we read novels of all kinds, short stories, poems, words of songs).

Activities for developing reading skill should exploit these natural desires and impulses, preferably by supplying something which cannot be readily obtained in the native language: something which is interesting, amusing, exciting, useful, or leads to pleasurable activity.

R2 A quick check of one commonly used textbook reveals as reading material:

Long *dialogues,* introduced by a few narrative sentences, which are stilted, dull, and too obviously contrived to illustrate particular points of grammar to be taught in that unit (e.g., agreement of many adjectives; question forms of various types; the future tense; comparisons). These dialogues are strained to include an unrealistic number of items of vocabulary related to one particular theme (animals, or eating utensils, or parts of the body).

Lengthy *prose passages* about France, packed with geographical detail which cannot be absorbed in such density and is therefore tedious.

Long, detailed *descriptions* of people, the small actions they perform from day to day, and the places where they live and work, with no unusual, exciting, or amusing happenings to relieve the monotony.

The most expressive sentences in this book, from the student's point of view, are:

Et lui, qu'est-ce qu'il fait? Il s'ennuie!

✳ Look at the reading material in several elementary and intermediate textbooks and class this material according to the normal uses of reading. Mark in each case whether it is interesting in content, amusing, exciting, useful, or promotes some activity.

There are various ways of approaching the teaching of reading. The approach will be selected according to the objectives of the students. Teachers now realize that students must be attracted to the learning of a foreign language by the assurance that they will be able to attain the kind of competence they themselves are interested in, rather than being "put through the mill" according to someone else's preconceptions of the ideal foreign-language course.

Five possible objectives for a reading course are: reading for information; reading of informal material; fluent, direct reading of all kinds of material; literary analysis; and translation of texts.

A. *Reading for information*

Some students may wish to learn merely *to extract certain kinds of information from French texts* (scientific, historical, political, philosophic, economic, sociological). They wish only to learn to *decipher,* to break the code sufficiently for their purposes. Courses of this type appeal particularly to students in the senior years of high school (especially those who are anxious to acquire some knowledge of a third language), and they fulfill the needs of some undergraduate and graduate students.

Courses (and materials) can be designed to teach the students to extract information from texts with only a recognition knowledge of basic grammatical relations[1] and of the commonly used function words (determiners, prepositions, conjunctions, common adverbs, interrogative and negation words)—words which commonly emerge among the first two hundred words in frequency lists. The students can then achieve their purpose with the help of specialized dictionaries of terms used in their particular fields of interest. Students can be taught to guess audaciously at the content. They then discuss the reasons for their guesses and reasons for the inaccuracy of some of these guesses.[2] From the beginning students read texts of interest to them, carefully selected to provide a gradation of difficulty. In a course of this type the students do not want, nor expect, to learn fine points of pronunciation or aural-oral or writing skills, nor do they want to learn to read directly and fluently in the foreign language for pleasure. They gain their pleasure from their ability to draw the information they want from the text rapidly, without attention to style.

These students need the following skills:

1. *Complete control in recognition of points of grammar which impede comprehension of written French.*

R3 One such problem area is the *qui/que* distinction.

The unwary student equates in meaning the two sentences:

Le commerçant qu'avait trompé le négociant en vins.
Le commerçant qui avait trompé le négociant en vins.

✳ List five other points of *recognition grammar* which could cause problems for the English-speaking reader.

2. *Knowledge of word formation* which will help them to recognize the functions and nuances of meaning of words derived from the same radical.

R 4 They should be able to separate *prefixes and suffixes* from the radical and recognize the part of speech indicated by the suffix.

commencer, recommencer
lever, relever
porter, apporter, emporter
jardin, jardinet
fille, fillette
mont, montagne, montagneux, montagnard, monticule
pauvre, appauvrir, appauvrissement, pauvreté, pauvrement, pauvresse
riche, enrichir, enrichissement, richesse, richement, richard, richissime
cent, centaine; vingt, vingtaine
beau, beauté; bon, bonté; sain, santé
rouge, rougir, rougeâtre, rougeur, rougeole
brun, brunir, brunâtre, brunissement, brunette

R 5 They should be able to extract meaning from compound forms like the following.

ouvre-boîte, tire-bouchon, porte-avions
station-service, wagon-restaurant
avant-poste, avant-propos
sourd-muet

* Make up some word games which would develop sensitivity to word families, e.g., competitions in listing derivatives, in constructing as many words as possible from letters supplied, in extending radicals with affixes to make new words.

3. *Practice in recognizing French-English cognate radicals.* Since many of these cognates are learned words in English, because they are derived from Latin rather than Germanic roots, we often over-estimate the student's ability to recognize them. The area of meaning they cover and the way they are used in the two languages, that is, their distribution, often do not exactly coincide, which creates a further difficulty.

R 6 *Il est très célèbre.* "Celebrated" in English in the sense of "famous" is always used with a noun: "a celebrated opera singer." We would not expect in English, "He is very celebrated."

R7 *Il veut se perfectionner en français.* In English we do not have a verb "to perfection." With the radical "perfect" smothered by the suffixes *-ion* and *-er* on one side and the *se,* which does not correspond with anything in the English version, on the other, the inexperienced student is likely to seek the help of his dictionary.

R8 *L'Écriture sainte.* The student who has no knowledge of the relationship between English *s* and French *es/é-consonant*—(cf. *esprit, état*) will look on *Écriture* as a new word, despite his knowledge of *écrit.* He will associate *sainte* with English "saint" rather than "holy" and will look in his dictionary, where he will find "Holy Scripture."

Many French/English cognates are disguised by historical change, but some of these disguises are systematic enough to be useful to the reader.

R9 a. Fr. *e + t* or *é + c* or *es + consonant* often equal Eng. *s-* or *es-* or *ex-;* as in:

étendard,	*standard*
étrange,	*strange*
étrangler,	*strangle*
écarlate,	*scarlet*
établir,	*establish*
étend,	*extends*

b. French *gu-* sometimes equals English *w-.*

guerre,	*war*
guerrier,	*warrior*
Guillaume,	*William*
guêpe,	*wasp* (note ˆ often = *s* in the English cognate: cf. forêt, mât)

c. Fr. *ch-* sometimes equals Eng. *c-.*

château,	*castle*
chat,	*cat*
chameau,	*camel* (*-eau* often = *-el*, cf. French *beau/bel*)

✳ Share notes within the class on other regular features of French/English cognates and disguised cognates that you have observed or can discover.

4. *Recognition knowledge of the most frequent "faux amis"* (that is, cognates whose meanings have diverged in the two languages). Students

should begin a self-constructed cumulative list of *faux amis* which should contain for each item a short sentence illustrating its use.

R 10 *Faux amis:*

Fr. avertissement = Eng. warning
Avant l'explosion ils n'ont pas entendu l'avertissement.

Fr. annonce = Eng. advertisement
J'aime lire les petites annonces dans les journaux.

Fr. avis = Eng. opinion, also Eng. notice/notification
Fr. conseil = Eng. advice.
Fr. conseiller = Eng. to advise.
Il m'a donné son avis mais il a refusé de me conseiller.

✱ Add to this list by sharing with others in your class the *faux amis* which have caused you trouble.

WHAT DO WE DO ON THE FIRST DAY?

As with all teaching, the way the students are oriented toward the course at the beginning can be crucial to their progress. In a course where students are reading for information they should be *given confidence* from the first lesson that they will be able to read French without difficulty in a very short time. Because of the many cognates in French and English this is possible very early with carefully selected texts. The teacher should *explain to the students the techniques* that will be employed to extract meaning from the text and impress on them that they must acquire rapidly a *recognition knowledge of basic grammar* and an automatic recognition knowledge of *common relational words,* like prepositions, conjunctions, adverbs, and pronouns, so that these no longer impede their extraction of meaning. They must also learn thoroughly the *most frequently used nouns and verbs* so that these can provide a framework for guessing the meaning of new words from the context. Very early, they must begin a *personal list of words* which often cause them to pause as well as of specialized vocabulary of interest to them (their *vocabulaire disponible,* which will be discussed later in this chapter).

A PLAN FOR THE FIRST LESSON

1. Begin with all the French words you and your students can think of which are commonly used in English:

R 11 restaurant, foyer, café, carte blanche, cadre, entrée, ballet, petite, mêlée, rendez-vous, venue . . .

As you write each word on the chalkboard, pronounce it in French and ask students to repeat it after you. The length of the list will impress the students with the number of French words they already know.

2. Have a short discussion on the history of the English language with its intertwined Anglo-Saxon (Germanic) and Norman-French (Latin) origins (and many subsequent borrowings). Show how we tend to use the two strands in parallel:

R12 *Informal* Germanic strand: start; leave; end.
Formal Latin-derived strand: commence; depart; terminate.

3. Ask the students to think of as many English parallels of this type as they can. Write these on the chalkboard with their French equivalents and use them as a further incidental introduction to French pronunciation.

R13
East	Orient	*Orient*
reward	recompense	*récompense*
land	nation	*nation*
ghost	phantom	*fantôme*
smell	perfume	*parfum*
stink	odor	*odeur*
feed	nourish	*nourrit (nourissent)*
new	novel	*nouvelle*

By this time students should begin to see that differences in spelling are a thin disguise for cognates.

4. Give them sentences to read based on cognates, like:

R14 La nation mérite notre respect.
Le président termine la discussion.

Design these sentences so that you can point out incidentally simple French function words like: *le, la, les; un, une, des; à; de; dans, pour* (*le pour et le contre* is a useful expression here to highlight the meaning of the definite article).

5. Give some further sentences which show that determiners and verbs vary more in form in French than in English, and that this helps to make the meaning clear:

R15 The sheep in the park: how many are there?
Le mouton dans le parc; les moutons dans le parc.
The French expression tells you twice it is plural, so you cannot miss it.

— *les moutons blancs dans le parc.* (Remember *carte blanche?*)
Here the French expression tells you three times it is plural so only a very
inattentive person could miss it.

6. At this point, the position of the adjective may be discussed, using
as examples well-known English expressions and place names:

R16 (les moutons blancs)
Carte Blanche, Terre Haute, Eau Claire, Baton Rouge, bête noire
In this context Grosse Pointe would need explaining.

7. Students may volunteer such place names as Des Moines and Des
Plaines. These contributions should be followed up by linking them with
the earlier discussion of *des* in 4.

8. The first lesson should end with a group deciphering of a short
passage with a great number of cognates, so that the students can leave
the class "knowing how to read French already."

A passage like the following would be suitable:

R17 Pour beaucoup d'Américains la France se divise en quatre parties: le gai
Paris, la Côte d'Azur, les châteaux de la Loire, et le Mont-Saint-Michel.
Ses habitants possèdent tous la joie de vivre. Cette joie de vivre consiste à
tout faire avec passion, avec frénésie: leurs conversations sont naturellement brillantes. . . . Même frénésie dans le domaine de la galanterie et
de la séduction où les Français sont les maîtres incontestés. . . . Quand la
télévision, la presse ou une certaine littérature décrivent avec beaucoup de
détails des scandales français, on conclut . . . que la France est une nation
inférieure. . . . L'anti-slogan *Air France Air Chance* est un exemple carac-
téristique de l'attitude de l'Américain.[3]

9. As preparation for the next lesson, ask the students to make a list
of expressions, slogans, trade names, hotel names, quotations, inscriptions,
and proper names in common use which are borrowed from French. Use
these in the second lesson for pronunciation practice and further incidental
teaching.

ACTIVITIES IN THE READING FOR INFORMATION CLASS

As soon as students have acquired some skill in extracting information
from a French text they may begin to work in small interest groups, in
pairs, or individually, according to temperament, as a supplement to large-
group guidance on aspects of written French. Gradually, large-group

activity is reduced to those occasions when students feel the need for further help in specific areas. Students begin seeking out the types of reading materials in which they are most interested. The task of the teacher is then to be available to help with language problems, to draw the attention of the students to interesting chapters in books or articles in contemporary foreign-language magazines, and to discuss with them what they have been reading.

Every possibility for encouraging autonomous activity should be explored. One such avenue is the preparation of group projects centered around special interests. Students in the project group may fan out in exploratory reading for a certain period in order to report back and establish a list of what is worthwhile reading for all members of the group. Alternatively, students may assign each other specific articles or sections of books on which the readers will report back to the group for a sharing of the information gathered.

Eventually, students should become interested in seeking out information in the foreign language to enhance research projects in other subjects and thus develop the habit of using their newly developed skill purposefully.

B. Reading of informal material

Some students, more interested in French for interpersonal communication, may want only to be able to *read correspondence, notices, newspaper headings, and advertisements.* For these a course emphasizing listening and speaking will be complemented with practice in reading informal French materials and in writing informally, with some study of the clichés of officialese and popular journalism. These students will be satisfied, for instance, with the present tense (*je parle*) and the *passé composé* (*j'ai parlé*), and the parallel informal forms of the subjunctive (*je parle, j'aie parlé*), ignoring the *passé simple* (*je parlai*) and the imperfect and pluperfect subjunctive (*je parlasse, j'eusse parlé*), and the *passé antérieur* (*j'eus parlé*) among other literary forms. They will use more freely the immediate future (*je vais parler*) than the more distant future (*je parlerai*), although the latter will be useful at times. They will feel at home with the formulas for the immediate past (*je viens de manger*) and action in progress (*je suis en train d'écrire*). They will be more familiar with: *Est-ce que ses parents sont partis?* than: *Ses parents sont-ils partis?* In other words they will read French written in the informal style they use in speech, rather than in a formal literary style. Their reading will thus reinforce their speech patterns.

The earlier stages of reading development described later in this chapter will prepare this group for their objectives.

C. Fluent, direct reading of all kinds of material

Students who want to learn to use French flexibly in all modalities, who hope to be able to pick up a novel, a biography, a newspaper, or a magazine (light or serious) and read the contents fluently for pleasure, as well as being able to communicate orally and in writing, will require a course which provides balanced development of all language skills. It is to this group that the six stages of reading development described in this chapter and the next apply. This is the group which aims at attaining the stage of reading directly in French without mental translation and without constant recourse to a dictionary.

D. Literary analysis

Some of Group C will wish to develop also the skill of in-depth analysis of literary material, which requires considerable refinement in perception of nuances and choices in language. For this they require special training.

Teachers interested particularly in the preparation of this group are referred to:

L'Enseignement de la littérature française aux étrangers, FM, No. 77 (décembre, 1970); "The Times and Places for Literature," F. André Paquette et al., in *Foreign Languages: Reading, Literature, Requirements,* ed. T. E. Bird (*NEC,* 1967), pp. 51–102; *The Teaching of Foreign Literatures,* theme of *MLJ* 56,5 (1972), and M. Benamou, *Pour une nouvelle pédagogie du texte littéraire* (Paris: Hachette/Larousse, 1971).

E. Translation

Other students may want to *translate French texts* accurately into English. This is an art which requires a sophisticated knowledge of English as well as French. A course with finesse of translation as its objective will concentrate on fine distinctions of syntax and vocabulary and contrastive aspects of sentence and paragraph formation. The perfecting of pronunciation, fluency in oral communication, and composition in French will not be emphasized. Translation for scientific and industrial purposes requires a more than superficial acquaintanceship with many fields and much experience with the many dictionaries available for the specialized vocabularies of medicine, physics, engineering, chemistry, electronics, business, and so on. Translation of literary works requires a sensitivity to nuances and subtleties of meaning, speech registers, and levels of style in French and a perceptive awareness of the flexibility and potentialities of the English language. Such a course can be engrossing for those with a special fascination for language, but tedious and frustrating for any who are not in the course of their own volition. Translation is discussed more fully in Chapter 9.

Each of these five objectives is, of course, legitimate. In designing or selecting reading materials and learning activities, the teacher needs to keep clearly in mind the specific purpose toward which the course, or a particular student's interests, are directed.

The remainder of this chapter will concentrate on the needs of Group C (which covers in its earlier stages the needs of Group B, and from which Group D and some of Group E will later emerge). Some of what is said about this program for progressive development of reading skill can be adapted also to certain aspects of courses for Group A. The teacher of the latter course will extrapolate what seems to him to be appropriate.

Lexical, structural (or grammatical), and social-cultural meaning

The reader must learn to extract from the graphic script three levels of meaning: lexical meaning (the semantic implications of the words and expressions), structural or grammatical meaning (which is expressed at times by semantically empty function words, but also by interrelationships among words, or parts of words), and social-cultural meaning (the evaluative dimension which French people give to words and groups of words because of their common experiences with language in their culture). When we consult a dictionary we find an *approximation of lexical meaning,* usually in the form of a paraphrase. Where a synonym is given, this frequently has a non-matching distribution of meaning, e.g., for *lâche* the synonym *peureux* may be given; yet all who are *peureux* are not necessarily *lâche,* which is a denigratory term. A study of grammar rules and experience with language in action help us to apprehend *structural meaning.* It is *social-cultural meaning* which is most difficult for a foreigner to penetrate. This is meaning which springs from shared experiences, values, and attitudes. When this type of meaning is not taken into account, or when the student interprets a French text according to his own cultural experiences, distortions and misapprehensions result. Living among French people for a long period will give a teacher or student an insight into this aspect of meaning, but the average student will need at first to depend on footnotes and his teacher's explanations. As his vicarious experience of French life and attitudes increases through much reading, he will come to a deeper understanding of the full meaning of a text.[4]

R18 In the following passage the personal style of living in a small apartment in some close-knit *quartier* of a city or small town and the impersonality of life in a modern housing complex are contrasted in a way which is immediately comprehensible to anyone who has experienced life in a contemporary urban society.

Le citadin fatigué, lorsqu'il a passé le coin de sa rue et aperçoit la carotte lumineuse de son bureau de tabac familier, à dix mètres de sa porte, dit un petit bonsoir à l'épicier, et désigne sa fenêtre au camarade qu'il ramène pour le dîner: "C'est là chez moi."

Mais l'habitant des grands ensembles, bloc huit, escalier quatorze, onzième étage, porte dix-neuf, ne voit pas en rentrant de boutiquiers sur le pas de leur porte à qui dire bonsoir, n'a pas *d'amitiés au café du coin,* et n'éprouve pas l'envie de dire: "C'est là chez moi" en désignant la vingt-septième et la vingt-huitième fenêtre de la rangée numéro onze, sur l'immense façade, là-haut, à trente mètres.[5]

The expression *amitiés au café du coin,* on the other hand, can be comprehended fully only by a person familiar with French social life.

Café has a *lexical meaning.* The *Petit Larousse* gives the meaning as "lieu public où l'on prend du café et d'autres boissons." This has been translated in the widely used Harrap's *Standard French and English Dictionary as* "café (always licensed to sell alcoholic drinks)." To a person from a country other than France, neither the *Larousse* nor the Harrap rendering conveys the full connotational meaning of *café du coin.* They may even convey quite a different connotational meaning in countries where the public consumption of alcoholic drinks is generally restricted to licensed bars. The Frenchman reading this phrase sees a small room with a counter at one end, behind which are ranged all kinds of alcoholic drinks as well as the all-important coffee maker. Scattered about are a few small tables neatly covered with colorful cloths where the local people gather for social discussion, arguments, or games of cards or dominoes over a glass of wine or beer or Pernod, depending on the region. Here one can order cognac or *tilleul* (an infusion of linden-tree leaves which is considered soothing to the nerves), or coffee with or without *croissants* or *brioches.* This is the workingman's club, where he comes after his day's work for an *apéritif* (*apéro*), or in the evening or over the weekend for social intercourse over his favorite glass. Here he argues about sport (*le football* or *le cyclisme*), politics, or the decisions of the *syndicat.* He knows the *patron,* he knows the *serveuse* (often a member of the family), and he knows *Madame* who usually takes care of the *caisse.* A person living in an *H.L.M.* (*Habitation à Loyer Modéré*) or a *Z.U.P.* (*Zone d'Urbanisation Prioritaire*), the widespread housing projects, misses the intimacy of the *café du coin* and the company of fellow *habitués* of long standing. The *social-cultural meaning* of *amitiés au café du coin* can be understood only by a student who has learned something of the way of life of the average Frenchman (*le Français moyen*).

Structural meaning:

R 19 ... et n'éprouve pas l'envie *de* dire: "C'est là chez moi" *en* désignant la vingt-septième et la vingt-huitième fenêtre de la rangée numéro onze....

In this sentence, neither *de* nor *en* can be assigned a precise lexical meaning, yet they are essential if the sentence is to be understood; they show structural relationships between parts of the sentence and may therefore be said to have *structural* or *grammatical meaning*.

Word counts and frequency lists

Several lists of the most frequently used words in the French language have been published. The two word counts most often used in the editing of texts for students are G. E. Vander Beke, *French Word List* (1929) and *Le Français fondamental, premier et deuxième degré,* established by a Commission of the French Ministère de l'Education Nationale in the 1950's under the direction of G. Gougenheim and P. Rivenc.[6]

Vander Beke's list (VB) was established from a corpus of over a million running words in eighty-five excerpts from representative school reading materials of the twenties, that is, from written texts.[7] The list contains 6,136 words (if we include the sixty-nine very common words listed separately).[8] The words are set out in order of frequency of occurrence across the eighty-five texts, that is, by range. *Quelque* occurs, for instance, in all eighty-five texts, being found 1,232 times, and therefore heads the list with *non,* also found in eighty-five texts but only 854 times.[9] The words in the Vander Beke list are very useful for students learning to read texts found in traditional school reading materials, because the list was drawn up from such materials. It was used for establishing levels of difficulty in many readers published in the thirties and forties.

Le Français fondamental (FF) was established from a corpus of 312,135 words of spoken text (recorded conversations of 275 persons of different sexes, ages, occupations, and social classes from different regions of France). Of the 7,995 different words in the corpus only the 1,063 words which appeared twenty or more times were retained for *le français fondamental premier degré.* This list is intended to represent a *basic* French vocabulary. Examination of the list developed from the corpus revealed, however, a paucity of nouns. Inevitably, the noun we use, or replace with a pronoun, or assume our listener is thinking about, is very much dependent on the situational context of our conversation (physical and mental). The first list was, therefore, supplemented with nouns associated with "centers of interest." These words were elicited from 904 French schoolchildren in widely distributed areas. The resulting final list of the *premier degré* contains 1,475 words, and there are approximately 1,500 more in the *deuxième degré*. The lists of the *premier degré* are available in G. Gougenheim, P. Rivenc, et al., *L'Elaboration du français fondamental (1ᵉʳ degré)*. Those of the *premier* and *deuxième degré*, together with some useful words from the Vander Beke count which did not appear in *Le Français fondamental,* are listed in G. Gougenheim, *Dictionnaire fondamental de la langue française: Nouvelle édition revue et augmentée* (Paris: Didier, 1958). This helpful dictionary for schools contains 3,500 of the most frequently used words in the French language and limits the vocabulary used in its definitions of their meaning to these 3,500 words.

Obviously 3,500 words is insufficient for fluent reading of all kinds of texts. Gougenheim et al. distinguish between *le vocabulaire fréquent* and *le vocabulaire disponible*. They maintain that "même en dehors des statistiques de fréquence, la distinction de ces deux vocabulaires est extrêmement nette. Seul le vocabulaire disponible suscite notre intérêt, le vocabulaire de fréquence, si utile qu'il soit, ne nous retenant pas."[10]

R20 As an example of this distinction, on reading the sentence: *Mon petit frère, qui a disparu derrière un arbre, me répond "J'ai trouvé une araignée,"* a student is more likely to be interested in the word *araignée* (which does not appear in either Vander Beke or the Gougenheim dictionary) than in words such as *mon* (FF 74), *un* (FF 14), or *répond* (FF 396). *Mon, un, répond* belong to the *vocabulaire de fréquence, araignée* would be added to the student's *vocabulaire disponible,* that is, *available to him* when in a situation where spiders are relevant.

Knowledge of a basic vocabulary will ensure that a student knows the most widely used words, which provide the framework of any sentence, revealing to him a set of relationships that will serve as a basis for "intelligent guessing" or "inferencing" when he encounters unfamiliar content words. (R24 demonstrates this process.) Each student will need, then, to build his own *personal vocabulary* (his *vocabulaire disponible*) from his reading, and for this he should be encouraged to keep an individual notebook in which he copies words he wishes to remember, setting them out in short sentences demonstrating their use in context.

How an unfamiliar text appears to a student

In the following discussion, a slightly adapted version of some paragraphs from the first pages of "Les Bœufs" by Marcel Aymé[11] will be used for demonstration. The full text is given at the end of this section (R25). Readers should refrain from referring to it until they have worked through this section, in order to get the feeling their students may have on being confronted with this text for the first time.

R21 Text from "Les Bœufs" as it would appear to a student knowing only the first 200 words of *le français fondamental premier degré* (FF), based on spoken language. On the right are shown additions and deletions to be made to the text if the student has learned the first 200 words of the Vander Beke *French Word Book* (VB). Numbers refer to the order of blanks in the line. Words in italics are among the first 200 words of FF, but occur here in tense forms which the student would not yet have encountered.

A la ____ des ____, (Delphine) *eut* le ____
d'____ et (Marinette) le ____ d'____. Dans
son ____, le ____ dit:
— Mes ____ enfants, l'____ est une bonne
chose et ____ qui n'en ont pas sont bien à ____.   (1) add *ceux*
(Delphine) et (Marinette) trouvaient qu'il
était vraiment très bien, ce ____. Même, elles   omit *vraiment*
étaient ____ de n'avoir pas sous la ____ ____   (2) add *main*
de ____ ____ à qui faire comprendre les ____
de l'____.
— Dire que nous avons deux mois de ____,
deux mois qui *pourraient* être si ____ ____. Mais   omit *mois*
____? Il n'y a ____.   (2) add *personne*
Dans l'____ de leurs ____, il y avait deux ____
de la même ____ et du même ____, l'un était
____, l'autre ____. (Marinette) alla ____ au
____ ____, et lui dit en lui ____ le ____:
— ____, est-ce que tu ne veux pas ____ à
____?
____, le grand ____ ____ ne ____ pas. Il   (4) add *répondit*
croyait que c'était pour ____.

R22 Text from "Les Bœufs" as it would appear to a student knowing only the first 200 words of FF and VB and recognizing certain cognates. Notes on cognates appear in the correspondingly numbered sections of the commentary following the passage.

A la distribution des prix[1], (Delphine) *eut* le prix d'excellence et (Marinette) le prix d'honneur. Dans son discours[2], le _____ dit:

— Mes _____ enfants, l'instruction est une bonne chose et ceux qui n'en ont pas sont bien à _____.

(Delphine) et (Marinette) trouvaient qu'il était vraiment très bien, ce discours. Même, elles étaient _____ de n'avoir pas sous la main _____ de _____ ignorant à qui faire comprendre les _____ de l'instruction.

— Dire que nous avons deux mois de _____, deux mois qui *pourraient* être si _____ employés[3]. Mais _____? Il n'y a personne.

Dans l'_____ de leurs parents, il y avait deux _____ de la même _____ et du même âge[4], l'un était _____, l'autre _____. (Marinette) alla _____ au _____ _____, et lui dit en lui caress*ant*[5] le front[6]:

— _____, est-ce que tu ne veux pas _____ à _____?

_____, le grand _____ _____ ne répondit pas. Il croyait que c'était pour _____.

Commentary

1. *Prix:* would not be recognized by all students as a cognate of "prize," but readers are helped by *distribution* and *excellence.*

2. *Discours:* it is doubtful whether all students would recognize this as a cognate of "discourse" (not a common word) and then move to the more usual word "speech." The word *dit* helps.

3. *Employés:* unless students are already familiar with the past participle form ending in *-é(s),* they may still hesitate about this word, since the cognate "employed" is not usually associated in English with "months"; furthermore the blank preceding *"employés"* makes the structural development unclear.

4. *Âge:* some inexperienced students will be disconcerted by the circumflex accent and hesitate to identify this word with "age." If the title has been translated for the students they will know that this phrase refers to two bullocks. This could help with the identification of *âge.*

5. Unless students are familiar with the present participle *-ant* ending and have been taught how to find the radical (or stem) of a verb, they will not necessarily realize that this is a cognate of "caressing."

6. *Front:* this is a *faux ami,* since it means "forehead" not "front."

However, the sense is clear even if the student interprets the word here as "front."

R23 This passage shows how the text from "Les Bœufs" would look if the 200 most frequent words from FF and VB were omitted.

_____ _____ distribution _____prix, Delphine _____ _____ prix _____ excellence _____ Marinette _____ prix _____ honneur. _____ _____ discours, _____ sous-préfet _____:

— _____ chers_____, _____ instruction _____ _____ _____ _____ _____ _____ _____ _____ _____ _____ _____ _____ plaindre.

Delphine _____ Marinette _____ _____ _____ _____ _____ _____ _____, _____ discours. _____, _____ _____ ennuyées _____ _____ _____ _____ _____ _____ _____ quelqu'un _____ tout à fait ignorant _____ _____ _____ _____ _____ bienfaits _____ _____ instruction.

— _____ _____ _____ _____ _____ _____ _____ _____ vacances, _____ _____ _____ _____ _____ _____ utilement employés. _____ quoi? _____ _____ _____ _____ _____.

_____ _____ étable _____ _____ parents, _____ _____ _____ _____ bœufs _____ _____ _____ taille _____ _____ _____ âge, _____ _____ _____ roux, _____ _____ blanc. Marinette _____ d'abord _____ bœuf roux, _____ _____ _____ _____ _____ caressant _____ front:

— Bœuf, _____ _____ _____ _____ _____ _____ apprendre _____ lire?

D'abord, _____ _____ bœuf roux _____ _____ _____. _____ _____ _____ _____ _____ _____ rire.

Commentary

Here we have a clear demonstration of the indispensability to meaning of function words (like *de, à, pour, le, ne, en,*); common verbs (*avoir, être*); adverbs (*bien, si*); prepositions and conjunctions (*sous, que*), and pronouns (*il, elles, lui*).

R24 This passage shows how the text from "Les Bœufs" would look to a student knowing the 750 most frequent words of FF and VB. The obvious cognates not in the first 750 words are given in parentheses. (In the right margin are indicated words not included in the first 750 words of VB, which is based on written language.)

À la (distribution) des prix, (Delphine) eut le prix d'(excellence) et (Marinette) le prix d'(honneur). Dans son (discours?), le ____[1] dit:

— Mes chers enfants, l'(instruction) est une bonne chose et ceux qui n'en ont pas sont bien à ____[2].

(Delphine) et (Marinette) trouvaient qu'il était vraiment très bien, ce (discours). Même, elles étaient ____[3] de n'avoir pas sous la main quelqu'un de tout à fait (ignorant) à qui faire   omit *tout à fait*
comprendre les ____[4] de l'(instruction).

— Dire que nous avons deux mois de vacances,   omit *vacances*
deux mois qui pourraient être si ____[5] employés.   omit *employés*
Mais quoi? Il n'y a personne.

Dans l'____[6] de leurs parents, il y avait deux   omit *parents*
____[7] de la même ____[8] et du même âge, l'un était ____[9], l'autre blanc. Marinette alla d'abord au ____ ____, et lui dit en lui (caressant) le (front):   add *front*

— ____, est-ce que tu ne veux pas apprendre à lire?

D'abord, le grand ____ ____ ne répondit pas. Il croyait que c'était pour rire.

Commentary

Once the reader is familiar with the function words and common verbs, adverbs, pronouns, prepositions, and conjunctions and has a recognition knowledge of some basic vocabulary, he can usually work out the meaning of most of the remaining words in a passage by intelligent guesswork or inferencing. We will presume that the title "Les Bœufs" has been explained (by translation or by a visual representation). This disposes of 7 (specialized vocabulary). Inferences will be indicated with an asterisk.

1. Someone is speaking at a prize distribution (*dit*). He is probably a person with some official position; it is immaterial to the development of the story what that position is: *some important person. (If the student has not recognized "discours" as a cognate, he now infers that this important person made this statement in his *speech at the prize distribution.)

2. Since instruction or education is a good thing those who don't have it are *unfortunate (*bien à plaindre:* "to be pitied").

3. The contrast between the statement about instruction being good and there being no one ignorant at hand to help implies that the girls were *disappointed, *unhappy (*ennuyées:* "vexed").

4. An ignorant person does not realize the _____ of instruction, since it seems that the girls would like to make such a person understand these. Since instruction is a good thing (the girls agreed with what was said in the speech) and the unknown word breaks up into *bien/faits* (*bien* implies good), we may infer *the good things instruction brings (*bienfaits:* "benefits, advantages").

5. _____*ment:* adverb ending, usually *-ly*. The girls want to help, or be of use to, someone. They have two months of holidays which could be _____ly employed: *fruitfully, *usefully (*utilement:* "usefully").

6. There are two bullocks in some place, probably *a barn or *cowshed. (If the student has learned the conversion Fr. *é* + cons. = Eng. *s* + cons. of R8, he will have transformed *étable* to "stable" and will infer: *place where animals are kept.)

8. The two bullocks are of the same age and _____ (not color, because we are immediately told they are of different colors). In what ways do we compare two bullocks: age, color, *size?* Probably they are similar in *size (*taille:* "size").

9. Bullocks are usually white or reddish brown or a mixture of the two. Since one animal is white, the other must be *reddish brown (*roux*).

Students should be taught to reason in this way about the probable meaning of words with which they are not familiar, instead of rushing to look in a dictionary.

R25 Complete adapted text from "Les Bœufs" (M. Aymé). Parentheses indicate additions and suspension points indicate deletions from the original text.

(A la distribution des prix,) Delphine eut le prix d'excellence et Marinette le prix d'honneur.... (Dans son discours,) le sous-préfet... (dit):

— Mes chers enfants, ... l'instruction est une bonne chose et ceux qui n'en ont pas sont bien à plaindre....

...Delphine et Marinette...trouvaient qu'il était vraiment très bien, ce discours. Même, elles étaient ennuyées de n'avoir pas sous la main quelqu'un de tout à fait ignorant à qui faire comprendre les bienfaits de l'instruction....

— Dire que nous avons deux mois de vacances, deux mois qui ·pour-
raient être si utilement employés. Mais quoi? Il n'y a personne.

Dans l'étable de leurs parents, il y avait deux bœufs de la même taille
et du même âge, l'un (était)... roux, l'autre blanc. ... Marinette alla
d'abord au bœuf roux et lui dit en lui caressant le front:

— Bœuf, est-ce que tu ne veux pas apprendre à lire?

D'abord le grand bœuf roux ne répondit pas. Il croyait que c'était pour
rire.

Six stages of reading development

To help the student develop progressively his ability to read more and
more fluently and independently materials of increasing difficulty and
complexity, six stages of reading development are recommended. Materials
in French of an appropriate level of difficulty for each stage are presented
and discussed, and suitable activities are suggested for reinforcing the
developing reading skill and for ensuring a clear grasp of the meaning of
what is read. More detailed discussion will be found in *Teaching Foreign-
Language Skills* (Rivers, 1968), pp. 221–37.

The six stages do not represent six levels of study (in the sense in which
Brooks used this term[12]). Stage One may begin after the first oral presentation of a short dialogue, or after some active learning of simple
actions and statements in the classroom context, or in simulated situations.
Should teacher and class prefer it, Stage One may be postponed to allow
for two or three weeks of entirely oral work. This is often the case with
younger students. As soon as students acquire some familiarity with sound-
symbol correspondences in French and the word order of simple sentences,
they pass from Stage One to Stage Two (reading of recombinations of
familiar material). For a while Stage Two may alternate with Stage One.
A more mature group of students, already adept at native-language reading, may pass rapidly through Stages One and Two and move on to Stage
Three (reading of simple narrative and conversational material which is
not based on work being practiced orally). Some textbooks plunge the
student directly into Stage Three at the beginning, particularly if development of reading skill is the primary objective. Progress through Stages
Three, Four, and Five becomes a largely individual matter as students
outpace one another in ability to read increasingly complicated material.

Stage One: Introduction to reading

The introduction to reading will be very short or longer depending on the
age of the students and the intensive or non-intensive nature of the course.

Students learn to read what they have already learned to say either in short dialogues, in informal classroom conversation, or through the oral presentation of the initial conversational narrative. Questions require only recognition of material in the text.

The major emphasis is on the identification of *sound-symbol correspondences* so that the student perceives in graphic form the meaning with which he has become familiar in oral form.

Reading is an integrated part of language study, not a specialized activity. At this stage:

Reading is linked with listening.

Students learn to segment an oral message[13] (that is, to identify its phrase structure groupings) and then try to recognize these groupings in graphic form.

Reading is linked with speaking.

Students learn to say a few simple things in French and then to recognize the graphic symbols for the oral utterances they have been practicing. The script helps them to remember what they were saying, to see more clearly how it was structured, and to learn it more thoroughly. It also provides further variations of these utterances for them to use orally.

Reading is linked with improvement in pronunciation and intonation.

Students practice correct production of sounds and appropriate phrasing as they learn to associate symbols with sounds.

Reading is linked with writing.

Students consolidate sound-symbol associations through dictation or spot dictation exercises. They confirm this learning by copying out, with correct spelling, sentences they have been learning. They write out sentences associated with pictures and use, as practice in reading, what their fellow students have written. Teacher or students write out instructions which others read and then put into action.

R 26 *Spot Dictation*

Spot dictation enables the teacher to focus the attention of the students on the correct spelling of certain words and on slight differences in the spelling of near-homographs. It is a testing device to encourage the mastery of the spelling system, as contrasted with word recognition. Sometimes students write the words separately, sometimes in blanks on a partial script.

The teacher reads a complete sentence to the class so that the students hear the word in context.

TEACHER Pierre a un camarade qui s'appelle Robert.

The teacher then repeats a particular word or group of words which the students write down.

TEACHER *qui s'appelle* . . . (Students write *qui s'appelle*.)
TEACHER Pierre a un camarade qui s'appelle Robert.

      Robert n'aime pas la musique.

      La musique . . . (students write)

      Robert n'aime pas la musique mais il aime beaucoup les études.

      beaucoup . . .

      Mais il aime beaucoup les études.

      les études . . .

      Il parle bien français.

      français . . .

Reading is linked with the learning of grammar.

Students see in written form what they have been learning orally and consolidate their grasp of grammatical structure.

Reading is linked with learning about language.

Students become conscious of differences in the surface structure of French and English. Students take language universals for granted because they are universals, e.g., the fact that sentences consist of noun phrases and verb phrases. They tend to expect other features to be universals too. Many surface differences are more clearly observable in written language, e.g., the manifestations of gender and number agreements in French.

Reading is linked with learning about the culture of the speakers of the language.

The written script in textbooks should be accompanied by illustrations and photographs which elucidate many aspects of the life and customs of the people and add new meaning to even the simplest of exchanges in the foreign language. Even culturally neutral material (see Rivers, 1968, p. 275) becomes more alive when the student sees how everyday situations vary in other cultures and have a different import. Some time should be spent from the earliest lessons in arousing the students' interest in French life and attitudes. (As reading skill develops and students read more widely, this particular link becomes more and more important.)

RECOGNITION OF SOUND PATTERNS REPRESENTED BY THE GRAPHIC SYMBOLS

The student beginning to read French will find as many as nine different spelling combinations corresponding to the sound /ɛ/.

R27 1. s*ai*ne /sɛn/

      2. la b*ai*e /labɛ/

3. le l*ai*t /ləlɛ/
   il f*ai*t /ilfɛ/
4. la Se*i*ne /lasɛn/
   la re*i*ne /larɛn/
5. le r*e*nne /lərɛn/
   *e*lle /ɛl/
   le s*e*l /ləsɛl/
6. il achète /ilaʃɛt/
7. la t*ê*te /latɛt/
8. le j*e*t /ləʒɛ/
9. le m*e*ts /ləmɛ/

R28 A speaker of English will also find that some words spelled like English words (and even in some cases having a meaning similar to that of their English counterparts) which he has hitherto pronounced in English with an /ɛ/ sound now have a distinctly different pronunciation in French: e.g., *rare* will now be pronounced /rar/; *mare* will now be pronounced /mar/.

R29 On the other hand *-ai-*, which, the English speaker has just learned, is pronounced /ɛ/ in French, will nevertheless be pronounced /a/ in such words as *ail* /aj/, trav*ai*l /travaj/, and *aille* /aj/.

The student will become more conscious of variations of the types described if, instead of merely repeating after the teacher as he reads or is corrected, he also constructs lists from his reading of different combinations of letters which are pronounced the same, and combinations of letters which have several possible pronunciations.

* Compare notes in class on sound-symbol areas which you yourself have found particularly confusing.

MATERIALS FOR STAGE ONE

If a dialogue-learning approach is being used, an early dialogue the student will read after having practiced it orally may resemble the following:

R30 *Unit One: Basic Dialogue Four*[14]
   MME. DUCLOS Tiens! Voilà Véronique et Serge.
   MME. DUPRÉ Véronique est un peu distraite. Et lui, c'est un garçon pas très travailleur.

MME. DUCLOS Ils sont sympathiques, quand même.

MME. DUPRÉ On dit qu'ils sont fiancés.

MME. DUCLOS Mais non. Certainement pas. Ce sont de bons amis, voilà tout.

(Construction of suitable dialogues is discussed in detail in Chapter 1.)

Commentary

1. The subject matter is of interest to high-school students.

2. The utterances are authentic.

3. The speech patterns are typical of informal French (e.g., *phrase segmentée: Et lui, c'est un garçon très travailleur;* use of *on; c'est* + noun phrase; and *voilà*).

4. The sentences are short or break into short semantically and structurally replaceable segments (e.g., *pas très travailleur* and *ils sont fiancés*), thus providing opportunities for variation and recombination practice.

5. Useful exclamations and tag phrases are provided (e.g., *Tiens! Voilà tout; quand même*).

6. Provision is made for the study of basic grammar (*est-sont;* adjective agreement: travailleu*r*, distrait*e*, sympathique*s;* two forms of negation, *non* and *pas; de* bons amis). Note that many of these elements are more clearly marked in written form.

7. With additional vocabulary supplied, this dialogue provides a natural stepping stone to the recombinations for reading practice of Stage Two. The forms provided permit interesting recombinations.

8. Sound-symbol correspondences: every vowel and consonant in French is represented in this passage, except /ʃ/ and /ɲ/. There is ample material for practice in the contrasting French syllabification, the nasal vowel phenomenon, *liaison,* graphic symbols which are not pronounced, and contrasts with English phonic values for certain symbols, e.g., Ser*g*e, travai*ll*eur, *t*ou*t*. Three diacritics are introduced: *accent aigu* and *accent circonflexe* (with contrasting unaccented *e* in certainement), and *cédille,* with a contrast available between *garçons* and *fiancés*.

When dialogues are not used, the first reading material consists of a graphic representation on the chalkboard, in the textbook, on the overhead projector, or on flashcards of the French sentences being learned orally in the classroom context or in simulated situations. (These are often associated with pictures.)

R31 Où est le livre?

Voilà le livre, monsieur.

C'est le livre pour le cours de français, n'est-ce pas? . . .

Marc, avez-vous un ami dans la classe de français?
Oui, j'ai un ami dans la classe de français.

Comment s'appelle-t-il?
Il s'appelle Jacques.[15]

Stage Two: Familiarization

Students read rearrangements and recombination of material they have been learning orally. These recombinations may be situational dialogues, conversations that can be acted out in class, or take the form of interesting narratives.

The recombinations may be written by the students themselves, thus linking writing practice with reading. All material will be written in informal style. Students may write out such things as directions from the school to their home; these may be passed out to the class and other students asked to identify the address. Students may write down things they are presumed to be doing while other students try to identify the time of day or place associated with these actions. Many other realistic activities can be invented which use the vocabulary and structure the students have learned at this particular stage.

MATERIALS FOR STAGE TWO

R32 When dialogues like R30 have been used in Stage One, a *recombination conversation* like the one below[16] may be used for Stage Two. (The previous occurrence of a similar item in the book from which this passage has been taken is indicated by the following symbols: P—preliminary unit; BD—basic dialogue; R—a previous recombination.)

    SIMON Voilà Pierre Mireau qui arrive (BD 3).
    ANTOINE Et Lucie Menot (P). Tiens! Tiens (BD 4)!
    SIMON Tu la connais (P. and BD 1)?
    ANTOINE Mais oui (P). C'est une amie de ma sœur (R and BD 1 and 2).
    SIMON Comment la trouves-tu (BD 2 and 3)?
    ANTOINE Elle n'est certainement pas (P and BD 4) très jolie (BD 2).
    SIMON Et Pierre n'est certainement pas très intelligent (BD 2).
    ANTOINE On dit qu'ils sont fiancés (BD 4).
    SIMON Tant mieux (P).

R33 When classroom conversations like R31 are used, recombination readings like the following[17] are appropriate. (In the book this is taken from, segments which have not been practiced in previous lessons are italicized and glossed in the margin.)

Robert est un camarade de classe. Louise demande à Robert: —As-tu les disques pour le cours de français?

— Oui, répond Robert. Voilà les disques. *Regarde!* C'est de *la musique yé-yé!*   Look!   rock and roll

— *Comment?* De la musique yé-yé pour le   What? cours de français? demande Louise.

— Mais oui, répond Robert. C'est du *rock—en*   rock and roll—in français!

— *Chic alors!* s'exclame Louise. Prête-moi deux   Great! ou trois disques pour le cours de musique? Mon professeur de musique aime beaucoup le rock!

R 34 Sometimes a little whimsy helps. (Every word in the following passage has already appeared in previous work in the textbook or the workbook.)

La Classe[18]

> PHILIPPE Vous allez maintenant faire des phrases avec l'ensemble des mots. Sinon, vous allez avoir une mauvaise note.
>
> JEAN-MARIE Bien, Monsieur, je vais essayer. La table est dans le cahier. Le professeur est dans la poche du gilet de la montre. Le tableau noir écrit sur la craie blanche et la craie efface l'éponge. Le couloir et la cour se trouvent sur le bureau et le stylo se trouve dans la récréation. La craie est au plafond, la fenêtre est sur le plancher. J'ouvre l'élève et la porte s'assoit sur le banc. . . .

It is certain that the student who could read and understand this passage would not be depending on recollection of memorized sentences!

R 35 *Recombinations in narrative form*

As a further step away from dependence on what has been learned in conversational form, the following recombination narrative reintroduces words, phrases, and structures previously learned and practiced, but extends the vocabulary range by the use of cognates (indicated by an asterisk), and creates a completely new and entertaining narrative which is nevertheless conversational in tone.

Il n'y a pas de justice (Unit 7).[19]
J'ai une amie qui s'appelle Régine Vatel. Elle a toujours faim et elle

mange tout le temps. Au petit déjeuner elle mange quatre ou cinq croissants, du pain, du beurre et de la confiture. Elle prend toujours deux bols*
de café au lait. Après la classe* de dix heures, elle a encore faim. Alors
elle mange un sandwich*. A midi elle rentre pour le déjeuner. Mme.
Vatel prépare toujours des hors-d'œuvre, de la viande, deux légumes, de
la salade, du fromage, et des fruits. L'après-midi, Régine achète toujours
du chocolat et le mange en classe quand le professeur* ne la regarde pas.
A cinq heures, quand elle rentre, elle mange du pain et du chocolat, deux
bananes* et une ou deux oranges*. Au dîner, Mme. Vatel prépare encore
un énorme* repas avec de la soupe, de la viande, des légumes, de la
salade, du fromage et un dessert. De neuf heures à dix heures, Régine
travaille ou écoute des disques. A dix heures, dix heures et demie, elle
commence à avoir faim, alors elle va voir ce qu'il y a dans le frigidaire*. . .
Et avec tout ça, elle maigrit!

Moi, je ne prends jamais de petit déjeuner. A midi, je mange de la
viande et un fruit. Au goûter, je prends du thé, c'est tout. Au dîner, je
mange de la soupe et du fromage. Le matin je fais des exercices avec la
radio. Je vais toujours au lycée à pied. Après le lycée je vais à la piscine.
Le soir après le dîner je joue au tennis . . . et je grossis! Il n'y a vraiment
pas de justice!

At Stage Two, students learn to recognize meaningful segments of
thought and read in coherent word groupings. The familiarity of the
structure and of most of the lexical items enables students to relate segments of meaning in what they are reading to what has preceded and to
keep all of this in their immediate memory while processing what follows.
Students are acquiring reading habits basic to fluent direct reading. For
this reason reading practice at this stage is best done in class, where the
teacher can guide the student in techniques, rather than being set as
homework. Questions require answers which force students to recombine
known elements in new combinations.

Stage Three: Acquiring reading techniques

Students read simple narrative and conversational material which develops
an uncomplicated and entertaining theme. They are introduced to written
style and more complicated structure. Vocabulary remains largely in the
area of the known, with some unfamiliar words whose meaning can be
deduced from illustrations, from cognates, or from the context. (See
examples of inferencing in comments on R24.) Reading materials are a
step behind what is currently being learned in order to encourage direct
reading in French, a process which becomes exceedingly difficult when

too many novelties of vocabulary and structure are encountered at the same time.

A recombination narrative like R35 bridges the gap between Stages Two and Three.

MATERIALS FOR STAGE THREE

R36 This passage is accompanied by four amusing sketches which illuminate the meaning of the sentences I have marked with an asterisk. The words marked ° are explained with small sketches or French glosses in the margin.

La journée du Président [20]
Le général de Gaulle a été Président de la République française pendant onze ans. Comment ce grand homme a-t-il passé ses journées? Voici la réponse d'une petite fille française.

Voilà comment j'imagine la journée du général.
—Sept heures: il se lève.* Il est seul parce qu'il dort° seul.
—Huit heures: il a lu les journaux.* On lui apporte son petit déjeuner, comme à l'hôtel.
—Neuf heures: le général prend son bain et écoute la radio.
—Dix heures: il va au concert des ministres°, où il jure° beaucoup. On dit qu'il fait cela seulement quand Mme de Gaulle ne l'entend pas.
—Midi: le général regarde la télévision* avec ses amis et se met en colère° quand c'est stupide.
—Deux heures: le général ne fait rien.
—Trois heures: le général se promène° avec Madame. Quelqu'un répond pour lui au téléphone, une autre personne fait un résumé des journaux, une autre de la radio, une autre des livres.
—Cinq heures: le général mange un petit quelque chose.*
—Six heures: il reçoit le Premier Ministre et lui donne des ordres pendant deux heures. Le général parle. Tout le monde écrit, écoute. On exécute les ordres.
—Huit heures: le général dîne.
—Dix heures: il regarde la télévision.
—Onze heures: il fait sa prière°, après avoir mis son pyjama.

Le dimanche: le général va à la messe°. Après, il ne fait rien. Quelquefois c'est lui qui parle à la télévision. Alors, Mme. de Gaulle le regarde.

Adaptation d'un extrait d'*Idoles, Idoles*
de JEANNE DELAIS

Commentary

1. The passage was written by a native speaker but has been simplified and adapted without destroying its authentic flavor. The language is contemporary.

2. Vocabulary and structures are of the type commonly taught in elementary courses, or else are easily recognizable cognates.

3. Since the original text is supposed to have been written by "une petite fille française," the segments are short and uncomplicated.

4. The extract shows a nice balance between familiar situations in the native culture of the learner and situations in the foreign culture. Because of its central theme it is more suited to high-school or college students, since the humor springs largely from incongruity which would not be recognized fully by students who did not know anything about General de Gaulle.

5. The level of difficulty of the vocabulary is defined: words which do not appear in both the *premier degré* of *le français fondamental* and six widely used elementary textbooks are glossed in the margin on their first appearance.

When fluent reading is considered the primary objective,[21] Stages One and Two are frequently omitted and simple, entertaining narrative and conversational material with much repetition of vocabulary and structures, often profusely illustrated, is used from the beginning. These passages are usually written in such a way that they can be used for dramatic readings or role-playing; in this they resemble the dialogues of Stage One. An example of such material is given below. The meaning of the italicized expressions is made clear in the book by amusing illustrations.

R37 *Chapitre Deux: Voici Mimi*[22]

"Mimi" par-ci.

"Mimi" par-là.

Qui donc est Mimi?

Voilà! C'est *un chat!*

—Oui, monsieur l'artiste, nous regardons Mimi . . . Oui, c'est un chat . . . Merci, monsieur . . . mais où est-il? Est-il dans le jardin?

—Mais non!

—Est-il dans la cuisine?

—Mais non!

—Est-il sous la table?

—Mais non, mais non, mais non!

—Où est-il donc? Donnez des détails, s'il vous plaît, monsieur.
—Regardez . . .
Mimi est sur une chaise . . .
devant une commode . . .
dans la chambre de Zazou.
   —Ecoute-t-il les cris de Chantal, d'Alain, de Madame Bernard?
   —Mais non! Il regarde. Il regarde . . . des poissons! Oui . . . des poissons!
Voici *les trois poissons* de Zazou.
Et où sont les trois poissons de Zazou, demandez-vous?
Mais . . .
       . . . *dans l'eau!*
Et où est l'eau, demandez-vous?
Mais . . . *dans un bocal, sur la commode,* dans la chambre de Zazou.
   Mimi regarde les poissons et les poissons regardent Mimi.
Résumé
   Chantal, Alain, et Madame Bernard cherchent Mimi. Nous regardons Mimi. Mimi regarde les poissons. Les poissons regardent Mimi.
Mystère
   Qui est Zazou?

Commentary

The cultural background in this passage is neutral. The structures to be practiced orally and in writing are introduced in various contexts. In this lesson, the author includes *C'est . . .*; *Qui est . . .?*; plural of definite article and noun; present indicative of *-er* verbs (*elle ouvre* and *ouvrez* are already known); *Est-il?* and the present tense of *être*.

For students who have passed through Stages One and Two, material for reading at Stage Three will be more demanding than the extract just quoted. In the following passage, specially written by a native speaker, new words, beyond the usual vocabulary of classroom texts, are introduced at the rate of about one word in every hundred running words and are glossed in the margin on their first appearance. Easily recognizable cognates are also used and marked with an asterisk to encourage the student to think first before rushing to a dictionary or vocabulary list.
   Details of French life are introduced in a narrative of a young Greek student who meets a French student by chance in Paris and visits various parts of the city with him (thus providing an opportunity for the American

student of French to identify himself in his reading with people of his own age and interests).

R 38 *Promenade à Paris*[23]

J'avais attendu ce voyage à Paris depuis longtemps. Mais maintenant que j'y étais, je ne savais vraiment pas où aller. Je connaissais de nom le Quartier Latin et le Louvre, mais c'était tout. J'ai décidé de commencer par le Quartier Latin. On m'a indiqué un autobus qui y allait. Il est arrivé au bout de quelques minutes. J'ai été content de voir que c'était un vieil autobus avec une plateforme ouverte à l'arrière. C'est là que je me suis installé: on est à l'air et on voit beaucoup mieux que de l'intérieur. Malheureusement il paraît que dans quelques années ils seront tous remplacés par les nouveaux qui sont complètement fermés. Le progrès*! Un homme en uniforme—j'ai appris plus tard qu'on l'appelle le receveur— est venu près de moi et m'a regardé d'un air interrogateur.

—C'est combien? lui ai-je demandé.

—Où est-ce que vous allez?

—Au Quartier Latin.

—Où au Quartier Latin? C'est grand, le Quartier Latin.

—Eh bien, au centre du Quartier Latin... là où il y a tous les étudiants.

—Bon, alors, place Saint-Michel, ça fait trois tickets.[1]

1. Bus routes are divided into sections. For each section of the route traveled, a passenger must pay the *receveur* (bus conductor) one *ticket*. [More recently this system has changed. *Métro* and bus tickets are identical, and bus routes are divided into one- or two-ticket journeys.—W. M. R.]

RECOGNITION OF STRUCTURAL CLUES

For fluent reading, the student must be able to detect rapidly meaningful groups of words, even when their lexical content is not clear to him.

Through Stages Three and Four, students will be learning to detect effortlessly the indicators of word classes (parts of speech), and of persons and tenses of the verb; the words which introduce phrases (*dans, en, depuis, pendant, avant*...) and clauses (*depuis que, pendant que, avant que, parce que, si*) and the particular modifications of meaning they indicate; the adverbs and adverbial expressions which limit the action in time, place, and manner (*demain, souvent; y, là, quelque part; bien, trop, assez, vigoureusement*...); and the indicators of interrogation (*Qu'est-ce que? Quand? Où? Comment? Pourquoi?*...) and negation (*ne...pas, ne...jamais, ne...rien*...). Questions will be designed to attract the students' attention to these structural clues.

R39 For rapid comprehension, students should be trained to recognize such features as the *-r-* which is always present as an indicator of future time or of some type of hypothetical or unrealized action:

Elle arriv*er*a (contrast: elle arriva);

Elle vien*dr*a bientôt;

Elle s*er*a déjà partie (where this is the speaker's presumption—he has no certain information);

Si je le voyais je le pai*er*ais.

R40 Students should be conscious of the usefulness of *que* as a structural indicator, recognizing rapidly that "Je n'ai mangé que quatre petits gâteaux" means that I have eaten something, whereas "Je n'ai même pas mangé ces quatre petits gâteaux" means that I haven't eaten anything.

R41 They should be conscious of the relationship between two people indicated by the function word *à* (which is not necessarily directional), so that they can trace the second person in an interaction wherever it may be in the sentence:

Il a donné le parapluie à sa femme;

Il a volé le parapluie à son voisin;

J'ai demandé à mon frère la raison de son départ précipité;

J'ai caché les photos que vous aviez prises à mon frère qui les cherchait.

* Discuss other structural clues on which you depend to clarify the meaning of what you are reading.

7
Reading II:
From dependence to independence

Stage Four: Practice

Students now practice their reading skill with a wider range of language. Reading is of two kinds: *intensive,* where reading is linked with further study of grammar and vocabulary, and *extensive,* where the student is on his own, reading for his own purposes or for pleasure. In both cases texts are authentic writings by French authors, but they are carefully selected to be accessible to the student at this stage of his development; that is, difficult or complex style or esoteric vocabulary is avoided. As the student progresses through this practice stage he reads material of increasing complexity with a wider and wider range of vocabulary. The 3,500 words of the Gougenheim dictionary as a recognition vocabulary seems a reasonable limitation. This will, of course, be augmented by cognates and some specialized vocabulary associated with a specific topic.

INTENSIVE READING

This provides material for close study of problem areas.

1. *The systems and subsystems of the language*[1]

English-speaking students always have difficulty understanding the French system for expressing time relationships and particularly the subsystem for expressing action in the past.

R 42 Through reading, the student becomes conscious of the fact that in French what has taken place can be expressed either in *time value* through the *passé composé* (informal expression) and *passé simple* (formal writing), or as an *aspect* (a way of looking at an action or situation as it is taking place).[2]

L'accident a eu lieu le 3 novembre. Elle ne pensait plus à autre chose. Cet incident la préoccupait à un tel point qu'elle voulait se suicider. Enfin son mari a pu la distraire . . .

Commentary

A eu lieu, *a pu* la distraire express time value; these events can be precisely dated. The story moves on: *pensait, préoccupait, voulait* express *aspect;* we look at her predicament, her state of mind, as though we stopped the film for a moment; we live through the situation with her for a short interval before the story continues.

R 43 Compare the variations of aspect and time value in the following:

Je relisais ses livres, je l'écoutais, je l'interrogeais, j'étais si occupée que je ne pensais pas à me demander pourquoi au juste il se plaisait avec moi . . . Quand il m'a prise dans ses bras, une nuit, au milieu des jardins du Carrousel, j'ai dit avec scandale: "Je n'embrasserai qu'un homme que j'aimerai!" Et aussitôt j'ai su que c'était vrai.
                    SIMONE DE BEAUVOIR, *Les Mandarins* (Gallimard, 1954)

R 44 In formal style:

Devant moi, Messaoud parlait. Je voyais bouger ses lèvres, je ne   1
comprenais pas ce qu'il disait, et d'ailleurs cela me paraissait n'avoir aucune   2
véritable importance. Soucieux cependant de le rassurer, de lui montrer   3
que je n'avais rien de grave, j'essayai de me relever, mais pus à peine   4
(le faire). . . . Alors je pensai à Silvia avec une pitié infinie. Je la voyais,   5
je voyais bien son visage sur ce fond d'arbres et de nuages, à présent que   6
je ne bougeais plus. . . . Je pensais: "Pauvre, pauvre Silvia!" tandis qu'on   7
m'essuyait les joues, les lèvres, le menton.   8
                    E. ROBLES, *Le Vésuve* (Le Seuil, 1961)

Commentary

To make students more aware of this important distinction, in the use of past tense forms, they may be asked questions like the following:

1. Discuss the reasons for the use of the *imparfait* in the section: "Devant moi, Messaoud parlait . . . aucune véritable importance" (ll. 1–3) and in the section: "Je la voyais . . . je ne bougeais plus" (ll. 5–7).

2. In l. 4 could *pus* be replaced by *pouvais* and still convey the same effect as in the present text? Give reasons for your answer.

3. Explain the distinction conveyed by the use of *pensai* (in "je *pensai* à Silvia," l. 5) and *pensais* (in "je *pensais:* 'Pauvre, pauvre Silvia,' " l. 7).

Focusing the students' attention on the tense choices of French writers who wish to convey certain effects will make the French way of expressing past action, and specifically the distinctive uses of the *passé composé* (or *passé simple*) and the *imparfait,* appear more rational and meaningful. Many other problems of contrastive French-English usage are also more efficiently studied through the thoughtful analysis of a text than through the study of a rule, illustrated by examples detached from the wider context of interacting rules. Nor is translation of sentences from English to French particularly effective in such areas of contrast just because at these points English does not make a particular distinction in parallel fashion.

✱ Look for passages of French which show clearly the use of the subjunctive mood for expressing a subjective way of looking at the situation (that is, personal opinion) as opposed to an objective view, as in such statements as: *je ne pense pas qu'il soit parti* (some people say so, but I don't believe it), and *je pense qu'il est parti* (his car isn't in the parking lot). Work out questions which would bring a student to an understanding of this distinction. (See also discussion in Chapter 8, pp. 266–67.)

2. *Contrastive problems of meaning*

It is in functioning language that students will begin to assimilate the differences in coverage of semantic space of French words which seem to be equivalent in meaning to certain English words.

R 45 The concept of the English verb "to leave" does not coincide with French *laisser,* nor with French *partir.* Sometimes it would be rendered in French by *quitter, sortir,* or even *ne pas toucher.*

Il a *laissé* le livre sur la table. He *left* the book on the table.
Il a *quitté* la pièce. He *left* the room.
Il vient de *partir.* He's just *left.*
Il est *sorti* pour un instant. He's just *left* the room for a minute.
N'y touchez pas! Leave that alone!

R 46 Similarly, a familiar concept like "to take" becomes a problem for English speakers.

Il a *pris* le livre. He took the book (= picked it up).

Il a *porté* le livre à la bibliothèque. He took the book to the library.

Il a *emporté* mon livre! He took my book!

Il a *emmené* son frère. He took his brother with him (when he left).

Il a *amené* son frère à la réunion. He took his brother to the meeting.

Such uses as these must be encountered in context on many occasions if they are to be used spontaneously.

Students come to appreciate the resources of the French language when they *listen* to the plays, poems, and prose they have studied intensively being acted, recited, or read by French actors and sometimes by the writers themselves.

This is the stage for intellectually challenging ideas and the cultivation of aesthetic values. Material for Stage Four should be selected for the literary, informational, or provocative value of its content, not merely as a language vehicle. Questions should go beyond Who? What? When? Where? How (manner)? and yes-no questions to considerations of implications, that is, Why? If . . . then what? and How (explanation)? questions.[3]

EXTENSIVE READING

This gives the student the opportunity to use his knowledge of the language for his own purposes. It is an individualized or shared activity as the student prefers. With some help from the teacher in selection as he needs it, the student reads for his own pleasure short stories, plays, short novels, newspapers or magazines specially written for schools, or selected articles and advertisements (particularly those profusely illustrated) from French or French Canadian sources. He may read for information about a topic which interests him or prepare a project, a report, or a debate with a friend or a group of friends. He attempts to increase his reading speed; setting timed goals may help him in this. He learns to tolerate a certain vagueness, reading whole sections at a time in order to establish the general meaning, so that he can develop his ability to deduce from semantic and syntactic clues the meaning of unfamiliar words and phrases.

MATERIALS FOR STAGE FOUR

Passages like *Promenade à Paris* (R38) may be read and discussed in class at Stage Three to supplement the steady diet of the intermediate level textbook or used for the *extensive reading* of Stage Four, which should always be at a lower level of difficulty than material for intensive reading.

R 47 A book published in 1930 gives the following passage for "French classes of the elementary stage." (We may hope that "elementary" in that period meant at least "intermediate" in modern terms.) In this passage I have italicized all words, except cognates, not contained in the 3,500 words of the Gougenheim dictionary, that is, FF *premier et deuxième degré,* augmented with extra words from VB.

Le cabinet *sous-directorial* est une pièce spacieuse, haute de plafond, sévère d'aspect, avec ses deux fenêtres garnies de rideaux de *damas* vert, son papier de *tenture* et ses fauteuils de drap du même *ton,* ses *cartonniers* et sa bibliothèque d'*acajou.* Le parquet soigneusement ciré reflète comme un miroir la froide symétrie de ce *mobilier* administratif, et la glace de la cheminée renvoie avec la même correcte fidélité l'image d'une pendule-*borne* de marbre noir, *accostée* de deux lampes de bronze et de deux *flambeaux* dorés. Tournant le dos à la cheminée, le *sous-directeur,* Hubert Boinville, travaille penché sur le large bureau d'*acajou encombré* de dossiers. Il relève sa figure grave et mélancolique, *encadrée* d'une barbe brune où brillent *ça* et là quelques fils gris, et ses yeux noirs aux *paupières* fatiguées laissent tomber un regard indifférent sur la carte que lui tend le digne et *solennel huissier.* Sur ce petit carré de *bristol,* il y a écrit à la main, d'une *écriture vieillotte* et tremblée: "Veuve Blouet".

ANDRÉ THEURIET, *La Saint-Nicolas* (Gautier, 1890)

Commentary

1. This story, reproduced in many textbooks since, appears in identical form in a book printed in 1960 for the equivalent of Stage Four reading.

2. Of the words italicized *damas, ton,* and *encombré* could be considered cognates, but it is unlikely that all students would recognize them as such. *Ecriture* would probably be recognized as a derivative of *écrire* because of the proximity of *écrit.* (Only *bristol* is footnoted in a way which makes its meaning clear.)

3. Presuming that students know all the words in the Gougenheim dictionary (which is not at all certain at this stage), this passage contains 18 new words in 176 running words, a rate of one new word in 10. Scherer recommends a rate of one new word in 35.[4] Scherer also recommends that the new words be spaced evenly, that the new vocabulary be useful, that cognates be signalled in some way, and that new words "be surrounded by contextual clues so that it is possible to infer the meaning."[5]

The reader should look again at the italicized words in the preceding passage in the light of these recommendations.

4. The sentences in the passage are also long and complicated, placing a strain on the memory of the student who is making any attempt at direct reading of the extract.[6]

We may say that this passage was intended for intensive reading and therefore extension of vocabulary and knowledge of structure. The words italicized are hardly likely to be encountered in further reading or in communication (*damas, cartonniers, acajou, flambeaux, huissiers,* and so on). In the following passage, discovered at first glance in a book of French Canadian short stories,[7] there are three words not in Gougenheim in 102 running words (if *asphalte* is considered a cognate). All three (*s'enroule, autoroute,* and *décrochera*) are useful and are easily understood in the context. The passage is certainly much more interesting for Stage Four students than R47.

R48 L'asphalte est d'un noir luisant. Un brouillard s'enroule autour des édifices. Avec impatience, Sebastien s'engage sur l'autoroute tant de fois parcourue. Il regarde l'heure à sa montre. Il appuie sur l'accélérateur. Les pneus crient. Le combat s'engage contre la distance muette. Il se frotte les yeux: trop de nuits blanches! Il devrait se reposer. En arrivant chez lui, il se préparera un grand bol de café noir, il écrira quelques mots à sa mère, ensuite il décrochera le téléphone et dormira toute la fin de semaine. Cette lettre sera pour sa mère la plus belle surprise de sa vie . . .

In case it should be objected that this passage is mainly in the present and future tenses, with fewer structural complexities than R47, I have selected, equally haphazardly, from the same book, a passage[8] with a use of formal tenses similar to that of R47.

R49 La voiture venait de s'arrêter devant un immense bâtiment. Il m'accompagna à l'intérieur. Nous nous retrouvâmes dans une sorte de hall aux murs épais et sévères. Une infirmière arriva aussitôt. Le gendarme lui parla tout bas quelques instants. Elle donna un coup de téléphone et deux minutes plus tard deux colosses arrivaient qui m'escortèrent dans une cellule étroite où je passai le reste de la nuit.

J'avais voulu jouer une dernière fois à mon personnage et maintenant j'en étais pour mes frais. Je me rendais bien compte de ce qui m'arrivait, mais je comptais m'en tirer indemne. Il m'était facile de prouver que c'était une histoire montée. Puisque j'avais affaire à des gens intelligents, ils comprendraient. Ces médecins psychiâtres se devaient de prouver leur bon jugement.

Je fus introduit vers deux heures le lendemain dans le bureau du médecin-chef. La porte refermée, il demanda à l'infirmière de nous laisser seuls. J'intervins.

—Je préférerais qu'elle reste.

—Pourquoi?

—Point de vue esthétique.

Il sourit et l'infirmière quitta la pièce.

Commentary

Here in 187 running words there are 5 words, apart from recognizable cognates, which are not in the Gougenheim dictionary. If we consider *refermer* comprehensible, as a regularly constructed derivative, there are four. *Histoire montée,* as an idiomatic combination, will probably require explanation. At this rate there are at most three new words per 100 running words. It seems one has to search to find a passage as difficult as R47 in completely unadapted material, unless one deliberately looks for nineteenth-century descriptive writing.

✳ Examine some reading passages in textbooks in common use for Stage Four to see how they measure up to the criteria discussed; then find some suitable passages in novels and short stories in the library and share them with your fellow students, before adding them to your personal file.

Stage Five: Expansion

At Stage Five, students can read without becoming discouraged a wide variety of materials in their original form. At most there will have been some judicious editing to eliminate occasional paragraphs of excessively complicated structure and rare vocabulary. Once again the material the student is encouraged to read entirely on his own, his extensive reading, will be more readily accessible in language and content than that which is being studied intensively. Reading is now a technique, not an end, and language is a vehicle and a model. Students are expected to be able to discuss, not only the content, but the implications of what they have been reading.

Material for intensive reading is chosen with a view to developing the student's aesthetic appreciation, imagination, and powers of judgment and discriminative reasoning. Students learn to scan for information, to read with careful attention, and to extract the major ideas and arguments. Attention is paid to matters of style in writing, and students are given some experience in exact translation from French to English to make them more conscious of the choices involved in literary writing and the potentialities of their own language, as well as the French language. Reading is still linked with *listening* (to plays, poems, readings, speeches), with *writing* (of reports, summaries, commentaries, and, for self-selected students, even poetry), and with *speaking* (discussion of ideas, themes, and values). Students seek to penetrate the mind and heart of the French people and compare and contrast their attitudes and aspirations with their own. They continue to read widely on subjects which interest them personally (political, social, scientific, artistic, practical) and prepare presentations in which they share what they have enjoyed with their fellow students.

Teachers need not feel at a loss in providing widely diversified reading for their Stage Five students, since material now being made available by publishers is much more varied than in previous decades.

✱ Examine advertisements in recent journals and publishers' catalogues to see how many areas of interest you can identify in recently published books of readings.

Students at Stage Five still need help with more difficult aspects of French written style. Many students, for instance, never grasp the essential differences between the common logical connectives such as *cependant, pourtant, toutefois, donc, enfin, ensuite, alors,* and *d'ailleurs,* yet words such as these are indispensable for understanding the development of thought and for drawing implications. A situational technique may be used to familiarize students at this level with their meaning.

R 50 A key sentence is selected, such as:

Il n'a pas payé ses dettes.

A situation is described in French and the student is asked to link this key sentence with the idea: tu lui prêtes encore de l'argent, in some such way as: Il n'a pas payé ses dettes, *pourtant* tu lui prêtes encore de l'argent.

Other possibilities are:

Il n'a pas payé ses dettes. Il n'en a pas l'intention.
Il n'a pas payé ses dettes. Il n'en a pas l'intention *d'ailleurs.*
Il n'a pas payé ses dettes. Il est très embarrassé quand il me voit.
Il n'a pas payé ses dettes. Il est *donc* très embarrassé quand il me voit.
Il n'a pas payé ses dettes. Je n'accepte plus de sortir avec lui.
Il n'a pas payé ses dettes. *Alors* je n'accepte plus de sortir avec lui.

Important clue words like these are frequently omitted entirely from the French course, with the result that students continue for years to express themselves in simple sentences, or link sentences only with *et* and *mais* and are incapable of recognizing the signifiance of the logical connectives in modifying the meaning of what they are reading. A careful study should be made of the way an argument is developed in French through a succession of such connectives.

READING WITH WRITING

A class which is reading for information would find practicing these connectives orally very difficult. A written exercise which requires analysis of the logical development and choice among possible connectives may be used instead.

R 51 Write out the following passage as a paragraph, selecting from the logical connectives supplied those which will provide the most natural development of thought.

Je te rends ce livre dont je n'ai essayé de lire que la moitié. Je n'y ai rien compris (alors; d'ailleurs; toutefois). (Pourtant; donc; ainsi) c'est un sujet qui m'intéresse, et j'emprunterais bien encore un livre de la même série. (Enfin; en effet; car) ce n'est pas la première fois que j'ai essayé de me renseigner sur l'opération des ordinateurs. (Puis; par contre; donc) je n'y renonce pas. (Toutefois, d'ailleurs; par conséquent) je n'ai pas l'intention d'y perdre trop de temps.

MATERIALS FOR STAGE FIVE

Some textbooks propose for intensive reading in a general course at this level material like the following:

R 52 *Ballade des Pendus*

Frères humains, qui après nous vivez,
N'ayez les cœurs contre nous endurcis,
Car, si pitié de nous pauvres avez,
Dieu en aura plus tôt de vous merci.
Vous nous voyez ci attachés cinq, six,

Quant de la chair, que trop avons nourrie,
Elle est pieça dévorée et pourrie,
Et nous, les os, devenons cendre et poudre.
De notre mal personne ne s'en rie,
Mais priez Dieu que tous nous veuille absoudre!

Si frères vous clamons, pas n'en devez
Avoir dédain, quoique fûmes occis
Par justice. Toutefois, vous savez
Que tous hommes n'ont pas bon sens assis;
Excusez-nous—puisque sommes transis . . .

                                        F. VILLON

Naturally enough these fifteen lines, even with modernized spelling, require fifteen footnotes. Important, and moving, as the poem is, it is not clear how the average intermediate-level student could do more than decipher it, whereas he would be able to read easily and with enjoyment many poems of Verlaine, Eluard, or Prévert. For a general textbook, then, this poem is unsuitable, whereas it would fascinate Group D which has chosen to specialize in literary analysis.

A poem which has delighted many non-specialized students and made French poetry accessible to them is this section from *Sagesse* (1881) by Verlaine. It. has been reprinted in many textbooks and anthologies for students of French for nearly a hundred years, but poetry is timeless in its appeal to new generations.

R 53 *Le ciel est, par-dessus le toit . . .*

Le ciel est, par-dessus le toit,
    Si bleu, si calme!
Un arbre, par-dessus le toit,
    Berce sa palme.

La cloche dans le ciel qu'on voit
    Doucement tinte.
Un oiseau sur l'arbre qu'on voit
    Chante sa plainte.

Mon Dieu, mon Dieu, la vie est là,
    Simple et tranquille.
Cette paisible rumeur-là
    Vient de la ville.

—Qu'as-tu fait, ô toi que voilà
    Pleurant sans cesse,
Dis, qu'as-tu fait, toi que voilà,
    De ta jeunesse?

This poem, in contrast to R52, is easily understood by all students. Its theme is universal, yet immediate, calling forth an emotional response with little need for explanation.

Many twentieth-century poems are equally accessible to the general student. As an example, we may take the following poem of Paul Eluard.

R 54 *Je ne suis pas seul*

Chargée
De fruits légers aux lèvres
Parée
De mille fleurs variées
Glorieuse
Dans les bras du soleil
Heureuse
D'un oiseau familier
Ravie
D'une goutte de pluie
Plus belle
Que le ciel du matin
Fidèle

Je parle d'un jardin
Je rêve
Mais j'aime justement.

From *Choix de Poèmes*

Again, the theme is universal and appealing to modern students. The poem would be learned by heart with pleasure by many and added to their store of treasured literary memories. In this way poetry becomes a personal experience, not another arduous classroom assignment.

With prose readings similarly, care must be exercised in the selection of materials for Group C. (Group D, as we have noted, is a self-selected group of specialized interests with a declared desire to explore literature.) Some books offer selections like the following where the language is not inaccessible and there are many cognates, but the content is very difficult for the average student of French.

R 55 Car enfin qu'est-ce que l'homme dans la nature? Un néant à l'égard de l'infini, un tout à l'égard du néant, un milieu entre rien et tout. Infiniment éloigné de comprendre les extrêmes, la fin des choses et leur principe sont pour lui invinciblement cachés dans un secret impénétrable, également incapable de voir le néant d'où il est tiré, et l'infini où il est englouti.

Que fera-t-il donc, sinon d'apercevoir quelque apparence du milieu des choses, dans un désespoir éternel de connaître ni leur principe ni leur fin?

Toutes choses sont sorties du néant et portées jusqu'à l'infini. Qui suivra ces étonnantes démarches? L'auteur de ces merveilles les comprend. Tout autre ne le peut faire.   PASCAL, *Pensée 72*

A passion for the chronological presentation of literary masterpieces must be curbed at this stage if students are to become fluent in reading and using contemporary language. If the oral skills are to be kept at a high level, reading material must be such that the students can discuss its content and implications with ease and confidence. This does not mean that the content must be of little literary or philosophical value, as the following extract from Camus' "L'Hôte" demonstrates.

R 56 The story is set in Algeria during its struggle for independence. Daru is an elementary-school teacher in an isolated area who is devoted to helping the local people. He is asked by the gendarme of a nearby town to take to prison an Arab who has killed his cousin and whose life is threatened by his fellow villagers. Daru, who is unwilling to be involved in this act, gives the Arab several opportunities to escape but the Arab does not avail himself of them. Daru gives him food and money and shows him a road to the south where he can find refuge.

Au bout d'un moment, pourtant, il se retourna. L'Arabe était toujours là, au bord de la colline, les bras pendants maintenant, et il regardait l'instituteur. Daru sentit sa gorge se nouer. Mais il jura d'impatience, fit un grand signe, et repartit. Il était déjà loin quand il s'arrêta de nouveau et regarda. Il n'y avait plus personne sur la colline.

Daru hésita. Le soleil était maintenant assez haut dans le ciel et commençait de lui dévorer le front. L'instituteur revint sur ses pas, d'abord un peu incertain, puis avec décision. Quand il parvint à la petite colline, il ruisselait de sueur. Il la gravit à toute allure et s'arrêta, essoufflé, sur le sommet. Les champs de roche, au sud, se dessinaient nettement sur le ciel bleu, mais sur la plaine, à l'est, une buée de chaleur montait déjà. Et dans cette brume légère, Daru, le cœur serré, découvrit l'Arabe qui cheminait lentement sur la route de la prison.

Un peu plus tard, planté devant la fenêtre de la salle de classe, l'instituteur regardait sans la voir la jeune lumière bondir des hauteurs du ciel sur toute la surface du plateau. Derrière lui, sur le tableau noir, entre les méandres des fleuves français s'étalait, tracée à la craie par une main malhabile, l'inscription qu'il venait de lire: "Tu as livré notre frère. Tu paieras." Daru regardait le ciel, le plateau et, au-delà, les terres invisibles qui s'étendaient jusqu'à la mer. Dans ce vaste pays qu'il avait tant aimé, il était seul.   From *L'Exil et le royaume*

Commentary

This story is relevant to the problems of modern societies and would lead to discussion of interest to the students, yet in language it is within the reading scope of Stage Five. Scherer suggests a vocabulary of at least 5,000 words for the last stage before liberated reading.[9] All the words in R56 occur within the 5,000-word limit of VB except *roche* and *craie,* which occur very close to the limit (*rocher* is within the 5,000-word count and *roche* is a very near cognate, *craie* is a common classroom word); *essoufflé* and *buée* (both comprehensible in the context and neither indispensable to the overall meaning); *méandres* (which is an easily recognizable cognate, especially in the context of *fleuves*); and *malhabile* (although *mal* and *habile* both occur well up on the list). There are at most, then, six unfamiliar words in 268 running words and for most students only two.

✳ Look for suitable poems, stories, essays, scenes from plays, and short novels which you think would appeal to Stage Five students and which are accessible in vocabulary range and complexity of structure. (Keep careful notes of bibliographic details and page references.) Share your discoveries with others in your class and add them to your file for future reference.

Stage Six: Autonomy

Students who have reached this stage should be encouraged to develop an independent reading program tailored to their special interests. They should be able to come to the teacher on a personal basis at regular intervals to discuss what they have been reading and share the exhilaration of their discoveries.

Their reading may be in some special area of literature which interests them, or they may be reading widely with the aim of finding out as much as they can about the cultural attitudes or the civilization of the French people. On the other hand, they may have some specialized interest they wish to pursue: a contrastive study of French and American advertising, or of the content of popular magazines; the theories behind modern French architecture; urban problems; or folklore. An independent reading unit becomes more purposeful if it leads to some form of display: a one-man show at a French club festival, an illustrated presentation to interested French classes, an article for the school magazine, or the elaboration of a plan for study abroad in the area of the student's interest. Independent study of this type for advanced students stimulates self-disciplined motivation and is an excellent preparation for autonomous intellectual exploration in later life.

Ordering the reading lesson

The reading lesson is not a quiescent interlude as some teachers seem to think. Because students have learned to associate sound and symbol in their native language, it does not follow that they know how to extract the full meaning from what they see in print. For the teacher the reading lesson or reading assignment has six parts.

1. *Selection* of suitable material at an appropriate level of reading difficulty for this particular group of students; selection of the right amount of material for the time available and for arousing and maintaining interest in the content of the text.

2. *Preparation* by the teacher, who checks on: the necessary background information; words which need explaining (and how best to explain them—by visual, action, French definition or synonym, or translation); structural complications; obscurity of meaning or allusion; and the most effective way to arouse interest in this particular text.

The teacher who has prepared the material ahead of time can often slip some of the unfamiliar vocabulary into class discussions and exercises in a preceding lesson, or can center an oral lesson on a semantic area germane to the reading text, thus not only introducing useful vocabulary but also preparing students unobtrusively for intelligent guessing when they are face to face with the text. A review of certain grammatical features may refresh the students' memory so that comprehension is not impeded by structural complexity.

3. *Introduction* of the material to the students. This introduction may take the form of the provision of background information or some explanation of cultural differences, either directly—visually or orally—or indirectly, during some other activity when the students may have been given the opportunity to find out information which will be useful for a later reading lesson. Sometimes the introduction will take the form of a provocative discussion on a question which is raised in the reading text, with the students then reading more alertly as they find out how the author has viewed the problem or whether the outcome is as they had anticipated. This approach is particularly valuable at Stage Five when a writer is developing difficult concepts or setting out a complicated discussion of ideas. Stimulating the student's own thinking about the central issue or problem helps him to anticipate the probable meaning of unfamiliar vocabulary and to perceive disguised cognates in the matrix of the development of ideas.

4. *Reading.* Throughout this section, and particularly in the discussion of the different stages, many practical suggestions have been given as to ways to approach the actual reading of the passage. These should be exploited on different occasions to ensure that the reading lesson does not

fall into a set pattern. Individualized reading assignments also should be designed with a variety of activities in mind. The cardinal principle for each approach (except for Group E: *Translation*) is that it should encourage students to keep looking ahead for meaning, rather than stopping at each word to seek an exact English equivalent.

5. *Discussion.* It is at this point that the teacher is able to gauge and increase the student's overall comprehension of the passage, not by explaining and restating, but by encouraging the student to go back to the passage and look into it more carefully. Suggestions for improving this part of the lesson are developed in the next section.

6. *Application.* Reading is not an isolated activity. In a language class it should lead to something, and thus be integrated with the improvement of all skills. This idea is developed below in the section *Integrating the Language Skills*, p. 232.

✱ From all the indications scattered throughout this section, draw up three different lesson plans for the reading of R57 below.

Assisting and assessing reading comprehension

The following passage will be used as a basis for demonstration and evaluation of various methods for assisting and assessing the student's comprehension of reading material. In each example, items given are for illustration only and in no case represent a complete set.

R57 *Ma petite chienne Douchka*

Au petit déjeuner, je lui laissais la casserole de lait à lécher. Elle en   1
prenait le bord entre les dents et l'emportait fièrement sur son divan.   2
"Fièrement" était le fait de son air satisfait et du redressement de son cou   3
pour ne pas renverser les quelques gouttes de lait qui restaient au fond.   4
Elle léchait longtemps le fond avec sa langue et je n'avais jamais à nettoyer   5
la casserole quand je la retrouvais abandonnée. Un jour je lui demandai de   6
me la rapporter elle-même: "Rapporte la casserole, Douchka." Il me sem-   7
blait, quand elle me regardait, qu'il n'y avait qu'à lui dire les choses,   8
qu'elle ne pouvait pas ne pas me comprendre et je ne pouvais pas   9
m'empêcher d'essayer. "Rapporte la casserole à la cuisine." Naturellement   10
elle ne comprit pas, mais le fait que je m'adressais visiblement à elle, ce   11
ton aussi, qui n'était que pour elle et qui contenait un ordre, parut la   12
préoccuper. Elle remua la queue, puis s'immobilisa en m'interrogeant du   13
regard. Je répétai ma demande en lui désignant la casserole puis la direc-   14
tion de la cuisine. Elle courut au divan, se remit à lécher la casserole, et,   15

ne trouvant plus rien au fond, revint vers moi avec ses yeux questionneurs. 16
Je lui montrai de nouveau la casserole, j'essayai de la lui remettre entre les 17
dents, elle n'en voulait plus, il n'y avait rien de plus nettoyé que cette 18
casserole. Je ne sais pourquoi je recommençai le lendemain, puis le sur- 19
lendemain, si ce n'est parce que le petit déjeuner est une halte au début 20
du jour et que je m'arrange pour ne jamais le prendre précipitamment. 21
Ainsi une fois, au moins une fois, j'allais me donner le temps de lui 22
enseigner quelque chose.   C. AUDRY, *Derrière la baignoire,* 23
                                            with some vocabulary adaptation.

Commentary

All the words in this passage are in the Gougenheim dictionary except
lécher, which can be inferred from the context. (*Dresser, immobile, question,* and *lendemain* are in Gougenheim, so *re/dresse/ment, immobil/iser,
question/neur,* and *sur/lendemain* should not pose problems.)

1. *Content questions,* that is, Who? What? When? Where? How (manner)? and yes-no questions, are most appropriate at Stage Three.

R 58   a. Quand la maîtresse laissait-elle la casserole de lait pour sa chienne
Douchka?
   Elle laissait la casserole de lait pour sa chienne Douchka au petit
déjeuner.
   b. Où Douchka emportait-elle la casserole?
   Douchka emportait la casserole sur son divan.
   c. Qu'est-ce que sa maîtresse a demandé à Douchka la première fois?
   Elle a demandé à Douchka: "Rapporte la casserole à la cuisine."

Commentary

Questions of this type are too simple for Stages Four and Five. Answers
to the questions can be copied directly from the text with a little infusion
of words from the question itself. They do not necessarily require comprehension of the text; once the student has identified the place in the text
where the answer can be found he responds to structural clues—*quand?
à...au petit déjeuner; Où? sur....sur son divan; demandé: "Rapporte...."*

2. *Implication questions,* that is, Why? If...then what? and How
(explanation)? questions, should be asked at Stages Four and Five.

R 59   a. Pourquoi la maîtresse croyait-elle pouvoir enseigner quelque chose à Douchka?

Parce que quand Douchka regardait sa maîtresse elle avait l'air de comprendre ce qu'on lui disait (ou autrement: elle avait l'air intelligent).

b. Comment sa maîtresse a-t-elle su que Douchka n'avait pas compris l'ordre de rapporter la casserole à la cuisine?

Sa maîtresse a su que Douchka n'avait pas compris l'ordre parce qu'elle s'est remise à lécher la casserole (ou: parce qu'elle n'a pas fait ce que sa maîtresse lui avait demandé; ou alternativement: parce qu'elle a regardé sa maîtresse avec des yeux questionneurs).

Commentary

Question (a) requires the student to answer from lines 7–10 a question based on lines 22–23. Question (b) is based on line 11 and requires an answer from a whole section of the text (lines 11–16). Some teachers insist that students copy out, or repeat, the relevant part of the question and thus always answer with a complete sentence. If the aim is to evaluate degree of reading comprehension, this is really busy work at this point and can become laborious for the student, with no particular gain in skill. The student who has not done so should not be penalized. Note that with questions of this type there will be a number of possible answers, depending on the way the student chooses to express the idea.

The problem arises: If one is evaluating reading comprehension, should one require skill in composition, written or oral, at the same time? If the student has demonstrated quite clearly that he has understood the passage by giving the right facts in answer to the questions, should he be penalized for writing or phrasing his answers in incorrect French, since this has nothing to do with reading comprehension? At Stage Five one should expect students to be able to express themselves in simple correct French. For some students at Stage Four, and certainly at Stage Three, it may be better to try other methods of eliciting information gained from reading. If the method outlined is used because students are seeking to attain a high level in all skills, a form of dual credit will be adopted: allowing some credit for comprehension and some for the way the answer is formulated.

3. *Multiple-choice questions* are frequently used.

a. At Stage Three, *sentence completions* requiring only discrimination among several short alternative phrases may be used. The choices are usu-

ally set out in written form; if they are given orally, they also test listening
comprehension and auditory memory.

R 60 Choose a completion for each of the following sentences according to the
information given in the text you have just read:

Au petit déjeuner Douchka avait l'habitude de
A. renverser la casserole de lait;
B. cacher la casserole;
C. nettoyer la casserole;
D. rapporter la casserole à la cuisine . . .

Commentary

The choices are designed so that the correct answer (C) is quite clear to
the student who understood the text. (A), (B), and (D) pick up expressions in the text which may attract students who did not understand completely. (A) points to line 4: *renverser les quelques gouttes de lait.*
(B) could attract a student who carelessly read *sur son divan* as *sous son
divan.* (D) could attract a student who did not understand the passage
very well at all but who sees in line 10: *Rapporte la casserole à la cuisine.*
Multiple-choice selections must always be designed so that they reflect
some element in the text which may have been misunderstood, but the
correct version should never reproduce word for word some sentence in
the text. The choices should also be plausible completions—in this case
(A), (B), (C), and (D) all describe the kinds of things dogs do. There
must be no ambiguity in the choices which would cause an intelligent
student to hesitate between possibilities. If students are warned in advance,
there can occasionally be more than one correct choice in a set.

Variation: Sometimes single-word completions are used.

R 61 Douchka _____ toujours la casserole de lait.

A. rapportait
B. renversait
C. nettoyait
D. laissait tomber

Commentary

With single-word completions, once again, it is important that the correct
completion does not parallel a sentence the student can identify in the

text without understanding its meaning. Since the purpose of this exercise is to assess comprehension of the passage, it is important that the choices contain words whose meanings the students may be expected to know.

b. At Stages Four and Five, multiple-choice sets will consist of *longer statements* which the student must be able to comprehend as well as the original text.

R 62 Quand Douchka n'a pas compris l'ordre,

A. sa maîtresse lui a donné une nouvelle casserole de lait;
B. sa maîtresse a tenté de lui faire reprendre la casserole;
C. sa maîtresse a arraché la casserole d'entre ses dents;
D. elle a cherché la casserole mais elle n'a pu la trouver.

Commentary

Once again, each of the choices is plausible in the context. (A) draws attention to line 17 ("je lui montrai *de nouveau* la casserole"), (B) is correct, (C) points to lines 17–18 ("j'essayai de la lui remettre entre les dents") where the correct answer lies, but puts a wrong interpretation on this sentence, and (D) is for students who did not understand the passage but who can see *trouver* in line 16 ("ne *trouvant* plus rien au fond").

Variation: In an expository text, one sentence important in the comprehension of the development of ideas may be chosen and students asked to select a correct paraphrase for the idea in the sentence from several alternatives.

DIGRESSION

In "How to Pass Multiple-Choice Tests when you Don't Know the Answers," Hoffman[10] sets out for ambitious but indolent students a few rules based on common faults of multiple-choice tests. Below are seven which are applicable to reading comprehension tests.
1. With five alternatives the correct answer tends to be the third, with four alternatives the second or third.
2. An alternative which is much longer or shorter than the others tends to be the correct answer.
3. With a sentence to complete: if the alternative when added to the stem does not make a grammatical sequence, that alternative is not the correct item. (In French, when the stem ends in a vowel an alternative which begins with a vowel when all the others begin with a consonant will

not be the correct choice, e.g.: La voisine d'Elisabeth savait *que:* (A) sa mère n'était pas venue (B) son mari était sorti (C) *elle* était sortie (D) personne n'était sorti.)

4. Look for clues in other questions.

5. If two alternatives are exactly the same except for one word, one of them is usually the correct answer.

6. "None of the above" is usually wrong.

7. Find out before the test if there is a penalty for guessing the wrong answer.

∗ Apply these rules to some tests you have constructed to see if a wily student could have "guessed" his way to an A.

4. *True-false–don't know checks.* True-false checks are useful as a quick assessment of reading comprehension, particularly for extensive-reading assignments. If students are given two points for a correct answer, lose a point for an incorrect answer, but do not lose a point for answering Don't Know, they will be less likely to make wild guesses and the score will more truly reflect their comprehension of the passage.

R 63 Read the following statements and check whether each is T (True) or F (False) according to the information in the passage you have just read. If you are not sure circle D (Don't Know). (If the instructions are written in French the terms *Vrai, Faux,* and *Indécis* will be used.)

1. T F D Sa maîtresse ne laissait jamais de lait dans la casserole pour Douchka.

2. T F D Sa maîtresse avait peur que Douchka ne renverse la casserole de lait.

3. T F D Douchka aimait cacher la casserole sous le divan.

4. T F D Douchka savait bien que sa maîtresse voulait lui faire comprendre quelque chose.

Commentary

As with multiple-choice items, all statements must be plausible in the context and must be based on possible misunderstanding of specific phrases in the text. Care must be taken not to develop a pattern of correct responses, e.g., TFTFTF, or TFFTTFFTT. There is no need for an equal number of T's and F's: students are quick to discover that this is usually the case and will adjust their answers accordingly. Correct statements should not be so phrased that they repeat exactly the words of the text. True-False questions provide a good opportunity to test the student's attention to structural clues, e.g., "Douchka *ne* comprenait *que* le ton de la voix de sa maîtresse."

5. *Questions in French requiring answers in English.* We have discussed the particular problem of reading comprehension questions requiring written or spoken answers in French. Some teachers avoid this problem by asking questions in French to which the students respond in English. This makes it impossible for a student to frame a response using words from the question or the text without knowing their meaning. It also requires comprehension of the questions, which are in French.

R 64 Est-ce que Douchka a compris ce que sa maîtresse lui a dit? Justifiez votre réponse.

No, Douchka didn't understand what her mistress said. She knew her mistress was speaking to her and wanted her to do something, but she didn't know what it was because, instead of taking the pan to the kitchen, she tried to lick it clean again.

Commentary

Many students who have understood the text perfectly would have trouble saying all this in correct French. This method enables the teacher to dig more deeply into the student's comprehension of what he has read. If this approach is used, questions should not move methodically through the text so that the student can pinpoint the particular sentences in which the answers can probably be found, but should require the student to think about and interpret the content of large sections of the text.

6. *Questions in English to be answered in English* are not advisable. The questions in English often solve problems of vocabulary and structure for some of the students, and the very sequence of the English questions sometimes supplies a kind of *résumé* of the meaning. *Questions in English to be answered in French* would be pointless. Students capable of answering the questions in French would also be capable of understanding the questions in French, and once again the questions would supply the students with clues to the meaning of many sections of the text.

7. *Anticipatory Questions.* With a difficult text, the student may be supplied with questions before he begins to read. These questions are

designed to lead the reader to seek for certain information which will make the passage clearer to him. Anticipatory questions are more appropriate for expository and informational passages than for a narrative like R57. However, questions like the following would make the student look carefully at the text.

R65 1. Comment Douchka s'occupait-elle chaque matin au petit déjeuner?
2. Est-ce que sa maîtresse croyait vraiment que Douchka comprendrait si elle lui donnait des ordres?

8. *Résumé with key words omitted.* After the student has read the text and put it away, he may be supplied with a *résumé* in French of the content, with certain words omitted. He then shows by the way he completes the *résumé* how well he understood the text and how much attention he paid to the vocabulary.

R66 L'auteur de ce livre avait une petite _____, qui s'appelait Douchka. Douchka aimait _____ la casserole de lait au petit _____. Elle l'emportait _____ment sur son _____. Un jour sa maîtresse décida de lui _____ quelque chose. Elle lui adressa un _____: "_____ la casserole à la _____."

9. *Assessing overall comprehension.* Depending on the content of the passage, students may be asked to do such things as:
a. supply in French a suitable title for a film of the story and subtitles for the main sections into which it could be divided;
b. make a chart of the relationships of the persons in the story;
c. sketch (or describe) a suitable stage setting for a dramatization of the scene;
d. draw a map showing the various areas in which the action took place;
e. write a brief day-to-day diary of the hero's adventures;
f. outline the plot under the headings: presentation of characters, development, climax, dénouement (or unraveling of the complications).

10. *Assessing comprehension of expository reading.* (Exercises of the types below would be suitable for R67.)
a. Give the passage a suitable title. (In this case no title would be supplied with the text.)
b. For each paragraph, give the main gist in one sentence, then set down the important details related to the central idea, showing clearly their relationships in the development of this idea.
Exercises (a) and (b) would be given and completed in English for

Group A who are reading for information, but in French for Groups C and D.)

c. Below are four sentences for each paragraph in the text. Select from the four choices in each case the one which best sums up the central idea of that paragraph. (Choices are given in French.)

d. Rearrange the following statements to form a simplified but consecutive account of the development of ideas in the passage you have just read. (The student is presented with a jumbled set of paraphrases of statements made in the text. The statements are in French, but are so worded as not to be identifiable by simple matching with the text.)

e. For Group A: In which paragraphs are the following ideas discussed? (Paraphrased summaries of the ideas in the passage are given in French, care being taken to see that they are so expressed that they cannot be matched from the text without being fully understood. To give practice in reading rapidly to extract the main ideas, the student is set a time limit within which to complete the exercise.)

✱ Below is a reading passage suitable for Stage Four or Stage Five. Develop some questions of the different types which have just been described and discuss in class their effectiveness.

R 67 *La Fatigue en milieu scolaire*[11]

L'enfant français commence sa journée scolaire fatigué... Le réveil provoqué crée un traumatisme, le petit déjeuner est souvent négligé, les trajets jusqu'à l'école ou au lycée—longue marche à la campagne, entassement dans les transports publics en ville—sont déjà épuisants.

Les classes durent trop longtemps, si l'on tient compte de la "capacité normale d'attention" d'un enfant, les coupures entre les classes sont insuffisantes et les cours de récréation sont trop petites.

Les enseignements sont mal répartis. Une matière importante ne devrait être enseignée ni en quatrième heure le matin (la faculté d'attention tend alors à s'éteindre) ni en première heure l'après-midi (où se situe la phase gastrique de la digestion de repas absorbés le plus souvent dans de mauvaises conditions). Après le déjeuner une heure devrait être consacrée à des jeux tranquilles et les classes d'après-midi sont en général trop chargées en matières intellectuelles.

Pour travailler chez lui le soir, l'enfant n'a souvent qu'un coin de table; il est sans protection contre le tapage ambiant (frères ou sœurs plus jeunes, conversations d'adultes et surtout radio et télévision). Il se couche tard... pour des raisons qui n'ont rien de pédagogique, et donc il se lève fatigué. La boucle est bouclée. D'après un rapport dans LE FIGARO

Building and maintaining an adequate vocabulary (Stages **Four** and **Five**)

Moulton gives foreign-language students three practical recommendations for acquiring vocabulary: "First, never 'look a word up' until you have read the whole context in which it occurs—at least an entire sentence. . . . Second, don't be afraid of making 'intelligent guesses.'. . . Third, make a special list of your 'nuisance words'—the ones you find yourself looking up over and over again. Put them down on paper and memorize them."[12] These recommendations may well be passed on to students as an essential form of personal discipline. Going beyond this, however, the teacher may develop exercises to help the student "increase his word power" in French through focusing on form, focusing on meaning, expanding by association, and recirculating the vocabulary he has acquired.

FOCUSING ON FORM

Often students are not given guidelines for multiplying the vocabulary they already know through recognition of related forms.

Many are not familiar with simple facts about the French language such as those exemplified in R4 and R5.

They have never been taught to recognize the many *nouns formed from the masculine or feminine forms of the past participles of verbs.*

R68 recevoir   le reçu
     faire   le fait
     écrire   l'écrit
     arriver   l'arrivée
     sortir   la sortie
     venir   la venue
     tenir   la tenue
     prendre   la prise
     mettre   la mise (cf. mise en train)
     conduire   la conduite

They do not know how to discover the meanings of *words prefixed by common prepositions or adverbs* with which they are familiar.

R69 contre   contredire
     pour   le pourboire
     sous   un sous-entendu
               un souterrain
     sur   surchargé
               surimposé

bien   le bien-être
        bienvenu
mal   un malentendu

Recognition of common *changes due to phonetic environment* will help them to see *in-/im-/il-/ir-* as the same negative prefix, and *co-/con-/com-* as variations of the familiar English prefix of "co-worker," "compatriot."

R70 incapable, inconnu
impossible, imbuvable
illisible, illimité
irréel, irremplaçable

copropriétaire, cohéritier
concitoyen, conjoint (= époux, épouse)
compatriote, combattre

* Think of words which can be deciphered through recognition of *re-/ré/ra-/* as meaning "again" or "back" and *dé-/dés-* as indicating the opposite meaning to that of the radical (or the lack of something).

Common *suffixes* also give clues to the meanings of seemingly "new" words.

R71 *-eter, -iller, -oter* diminish the action of well-known verbs:

voler (to fly)   voleter (to flutter)
mordre (to bite)   mordiller (to nibble)
pleurer (to weep)   pleurnicher (to snivel)

Teachers who are not familiar themselves with these formal indications of meaning variation will find much of interest in Chapter 3 of *Le Vocabulaire français,* in J.-C. Chevalier et al., *Grammaire Larousse du français contemporain* (Paris: Larousse, 1964).

Exercises

1. Students may be asked to give nouns corresponding to adjectives (*rouge, la rougeur*), adjectives corresponding to nouns (*la pauvreté, pauvre*), verbs corresponding to nouns (*fin, finir*), adverbs corresponding to adjectives (*heureux, heureusement*), verbs corresponding to adjectives (*libre, libérer*), and so on.

2. Students may be asked to change the meaning of sentences by the addition of a prefix to a word italicized (son arrivée m'a rendu *heureux;*

son arrivée m'a rendu *malheureux*) or to complete sentences with a word
with a different suffix (Ce n'est pas tout à fait rouge. C'est plutôt rouge-
âtre).

FOCUSING ON MEANING

Valuable practice in vocabulary building is provided when students are
asked to do exercises like the following:

1. To supply paraphrases or definitions for words in the text they have
just read (il se promène, il fait une promenade);

2. to identify from multiple-choice items the correct paraphrases or
definitions for certain words in the text (in R56: *lécher* = [A] *manger*,
[B] *jouer avec*, [C] *passer la langue sur*, [D] *emporter*).

3. To find words in the text to match paraphrases or definitions supplied (in R56: Find the words in the text which mean [A] *passer la
langue dessus*, [B] *deux jours après*).

4. To complete sentences, based on the text, with certain words on
which they will need to focus their attention. These sentences should not
reproduce the original text exactly and should usually require the student
to reuse the vocabulary in a different form, e.g., in a different person,
number, or tense.

R72 Complete the following sentences with words from the text you have just
read (R57).

a. Quand un chien est fier de pouvoir porter quelque chose, il _____
le cou.

b. Pour nettoyer la casserole entièrement Douchka devait en lécher le

_____.

c. Douchka ne comprenait pas ce que sa maîtresse lui disait mais elle
savait bien qu'elle _____ à elle.

5. *Exercises may be unrelated to a known text,* e.g., students discover
for themselves, through dictionary search, synonyms and antonyms (*sage,
bien élevé; bon, mauvais*). They may compete to see who can find the
largest number of synonyms and antonyms in a given period of time.
Learning to enjoy a purposeful search for information in dictionaries and
grammars is an important preparation for autonomous progress. (See also
W68–75.)

6. Students complete an unfamiliar text in a plausible way by supplying
for each blank a word carefully selected from multiple-choice alternatives.
This type of exercise can be developed with simple texts or more complex
texts, serving as an amusing and challenging exercise right through to the
advanced level.

R73 Il y a des (livres, jours, dîners) qui commencent comme tous les (autres, bouquins, repas) et qui soudain prennent un tour (normal, étrange, drôle). Ce (matin, soir, mois)-là je m'étais (endormi, dépêché, réveillé) tôt, comme d'(ailleurs, autres, habitude).

Commentary

A passage such as this teaches the student to pay attention to distinctions of meaning, but it is also an exercise in reading comprehension. The student should write out his completed version as a coherent paragraph, rather than merely circling choices. In this way he can read his version through to see that it makes sense and then read it aloud to his fellow students. With a little ingenuity, passages can be designed to have several possible final versions, and students can be encouraged to reconstitute the several possibilities. Advanced students may like to prepare such passages for the other students to complete. (A teacher or student who does not feel confident in constructing a passage in French himself can easily adapt paragraphs from books or magazines.)

✻ Find in various composition and reading texts other types of exercises which focus on meaning distinctions and discuss their effectiveness.

EXPANDING BY ASSOCIATION

We tend to recall words through meaningful associational bonds, and words tend to appear in texts in collocations, that is, in relation to centers of interest or semantic areas (*pain* is likely to appear in a text in which *boulanger* appears; *pneu, panne,* and *voiture* are very likely to occur together). It is for this reason that learning vocabulary in context is much more valuable than learning isolated words.

Exercises

Many possibilities suggest themselves, and each teacher can think of his own once he understands the necessity for developing chains of associations and for expanding nuclei. Many of these exercises can take the form of games or team competitions which can be directed by the students themselves. Three come immediately to mind.

R74 What action do you associate with the following objects? Follow the pattern:

Le pain? On le mange.

In each case give as many alternatives as you can find. The team gains
points for every alternative its team members can discover.

Les fleurs?   On les regarde.
               On les cueille.
               On les plante.

Le livre?   On le lit.
               On l'ouvre.
               On le ferme . . .

R75 As each object is named, give the French word for a person you associate
with it. You must answer in three seconds.

papier?   étudiant
craie?   professeur
essence?   garagiste
lettre?   facteur

Alternatively: As each person, animal, or object is named, give the French
word for a place you associate with it. You must answer in three seconds.

boulanger?   boulangerie
confiture?   épicerie/cuisine
bœuf?   étable/ferme/marché

R76 Intelligence-test series can be adapted as follows. This exercise can be used
from elementary to advanced levels and, again, students may be encouraged to make up further exercises themselves.

   In the following lists underline the word which does not seem to belong
with the others in the series:

bleu, rouge, froid, vert
arbre, fleur, pierre, herbe
chaleur, froid, fraîcheur, honneur (This item can be answered in two ways:
by form or by semantic area.)

RECIRCULATING VOCABULARY ACQUIRED

Students learn new words with every passage they read. Often they forget
them rapidly because they do not encounter them again for a long while.
All kinds of games and exercises can be introduced to enliven the class
while giving students the opportunity to retrieve words they have learned
in the past and recirculate them through their conscious minds. In this

way the ease with which these words can be retrieved, when required, is increased. The following suggestions will bring to mind other possibilities. They are arranged in approximate order of difficulty.

R77 From the parallel lists of words given select pairs which have a natural association:

mer   pain
boulanger encre
stylo   vague . . . .

Students working in teams may make their own parallel lists to try out on members of the other teams.

R78 Begin with the words *un arbre* (or . . .) and write down rapidly any ten French words which come to your mind. Write whichever word you think of. Do not try to develop a logical series. (With each word, include some form of the definite or indefinite article.)

The lists, when completed, may be read aloud for amusement. Series may come out like the following:

un arbre, une fleur, le parfum, la dame, une robe, un tailleur, un magasin, la rue, l'agent de police, la prison.

un arbre, un oiseau, un nid, un œuf, le petit déjeuner, le matin, l'école, la salle de classe, un livre, la bibliothèque.

R79 *Semantic areas.* Write down as many words as you can think of which have a natural association with *l'arbre* (or . . .). Points will be given to the team having the largest number of different words. (Include some form of the definite or indefinite article with each word.)

l'arbre, la pelouse, l'herbe, le jardin, des fleurs, les branches, le nid . . .

Or: Write down all the words you know which have a similar meaning to *la maison*. (Include some form of the definite or indefinite article with each.)

la maison, la villa, le château, le palais, l'appartement, l'immeuble . . .

R80 Make as many words as you can from the letters in "C'est un arbre." No letter may be used more times than it appears in the sentence. Accents may be added.

ce, est, un, arbre, te, tas, tes, très, brun, rare, seau, bras . . .

R 81 Write down all the idiomatic expressions you can think of which contain the word *coup* (or . . .) and make up a sentence to show the use of each:

coup de pied　　coup de foudre
tout à coup　　　tout d'un coup
coup d'état . . . .

R 82 List any five words on the chalkboard and ask students to make up a brief story incorporating all five, e.g.: or, épinards, douane, grippe, montagne.

R 83 *Mots Croisés.* Simple crossword puzzles may be constructed by the students as exercises, then tried out on their fellow students. These provide practice in recalling words from their definitions or by association. Students may use definitions they find in monolingual dictionaries, thus giving them a purposeful familiarity with such dictionaries. One source of French crosswords in published form is: *Le Français par les mots croisés* (Hachette).

Scrabble sets geared to the letter frequencies of particular languages are also available.

Vocabulary enrichment and retrieval should be woven into the lesson fabric or the learning packet as an important and purposeful activity, not dredged up to fill in time on the day when the teacher and the class are suffering from end-of-the-week fatigue. By encouraging the students to play with words, the teacher can help to increase their interest in words in relation to concepts and in association with other words, and to refine their appreciation for nuances of meaning.

* Think of further ideas for vocabulary expansion and retrieval and develop these into possible classroom or individual activities.

Integrating the language skills at Stages Three to Five
READING AND WRITING

Students may be asked a series of questions which, when answered in sequence, develop a summary or *résumé* of the material read. They may write an ending to a story or play of which they have read part or develop a different ending from the one in the book. They may write letters which one character in the story might have written to others. Completed compositions may be passed around, with the writer's consent, to be read by other students. Students may create their own stories on similar themes to those they have been reading. They may write *saynètes* based on some parts of the narrative which will be acted in class or at the French club. Comprehension of extensive reading undertaken on an individualized basis will often be demonstrated in activities of this kind.

After reading a play, students may write the story as it might appear in a theater program, adding short descriptions of the characters. Should opportunity arise to act parts of the play before other classes, the best synopsis will be printed in a program for distribution.

Further suggestions for integrating reading and writing will be found in Chapter 9.

READING AND LISTENING COMPREHENSION

Students may listen to a story, play, poem, or speech by a famous person and then read it, or they may read first and then listen to a worthwhile reading or dramatic presentation of what they have read. The aural element adds vividness and life to the reading unit. Students may take turns listening to tapes of news broadcasts from a French-speaking source (France, Belgium, Switzerland, French-speaking Canada, Haiti), and then write summaries of the news which will be posted for other students to read, thus integrating listening, writing, and reading in a purposeful activity. Before listening to a French play, students may read a synopsis of the action. In this way they are better prepared to comprehend because they have some expectations to help them project meaning.

In some ways the processes of fluent, direct reading for meaning appear to parallel the processes of listening comprehension. We recognize in a quick, impressionistic way meaningful syntactic units, interrelating those we have selected and are holding in our memory with what follows, then rapidly revising expectations when these are not supported by the later segments we identify. Practice in direct reading of a text which is readily accessible to the student at his level of knowledge, while listening to a taped model reading it in meaningful and expressive segments, can help the student develop useful habits of anticipation and syntactic identification in both of these skills. Later he can practice rapid reading of a text to which he has already listened without a script.[13] (For further suggestions, see Chapter 3.)

READING AND SPEAKING

Students should be provided with frequent opportunities to give in French the gist of what they have been reading. They may be encouraged to prepare their own questions to ask of others in the class. When small groups are engaged in similar extensive reading projects they should discuss together what they have discovered. Students reading individually may share what they have been reading with others. Some of the material read will serve as a basis for oral presentations of projects; some will be dramatized in the original form or through extempore role-playing; and some will provide ammunition for discussions and debates. Many other ideas can be gleaned from Chapter 2.

READING AND PURPOSEFUL ACTIVITY

At all levels students should be encouraged to do research reading in an area which interests them in order to find the information necessary to carry out some activity. A few indications are outlined below, but at Stages Three through Five students should be expected to propose their own.

1. Students read advertisements for a particular type of product in magazines in order to prepare a commercial for a class television or radio show.

2. Students find out information about a popular French singer in order to introduce a session of records of his songs.

3. Students read a play carefully in order to design a stage setting for a class performance or play-reading.

4. Students seek out information on events, people, costumes, or social customs at a particular period in French history in order to produce a pageant for some historical anniversary.

5. Students study tourist brochures, guide books, geography, history, and art books in order to give an illustrated lecture or slide commentary on some part of France.

6. Students read through French cookbooks in order to prepare some French dishes for a French club festivity.

7. Students undertake tasks set out by the teacher or another student in the form of detailed instructions which lead to the collecting or making of something which can later be brought back as proof of the completion of the task.

At Stage Three, the well-known Scavenger Hunt (*Course au trésor*) can be adapted to the French class. Students work in pairs to find and bring to the class next day a series of strange objects which are described in French on instruction cards. They win points for their team for each object they find.

R 84 One list might be: une lampe de poche sans piles, deux œufs durs, une feuille de papier pliée en trois, un timbre chinois, un cheveu blanc, une pièce d'argent canadienne, un ouvre-boîte, une annonce pour un apparte-ment meublé, la carte météorologique d'hier, la coquille d'un escargot.

While students are looking for these things they read and reread the list so that the words become impressed on their minds. Then, when showing the objects in class, they must state what each one is and how they came to acquire it.

Improving reading speed

The reading speed of different students varies considerably in their native language. The teacher must, therefore, expect considerable variation in the reading of the foreign language. To become fluent readers the students must acquire the skill of reading whole word groups and whole sentences in French and of holding material in their memory over larger and larger sections as they move on with the developing thought.

1. At Stages Two and Three an overhead projector can be used to encourage continuity of reading. The text is moved slowly upward on the roll, so that the slower reader is encouraged to keep his eyes moving forward while the faster reader is not impeded, as would be the case if only one line were shown at a time. This is the process frequently used in films or on television where there is a long introduction to, or explanation of, the story. This procedure will be associated with silent reading for information, rather than reading aloud, since the aim is to help each student to improve his own reading rate.

2. At Stages Three and Four, students may be timed in reading a certain number of pages to a pre-established comprehension criterion level. Mere pace without adequate comprehension is pointless. Since this is an individual endeavor, students should be encouraged to improve their own rate rather than compete with others in number of pages read.

3. As an encouragement to practice *scanning,* which is a very useful reading skill, students may be given questions to which they are to find as many answers as possible in a given time.

4. Students will increase their reading speed in a natural way if they have set themselves the clearly defined goal of reading in a stated period of time a certain amount of material selected by themselves because of the interest of the subject matter.

8
Writing and written exercises I: the nuts and bolts

What is writing?

The Soviet psychologist Vygotsky draws our attention to the fact that all the higher functions of human consciousness, that is, those which involve more than mere physical skill, are characterized by *awareness, abstraction, and control.*[1] Learning to say /u/ by a process of successive approximations in imitation of a model may be relatively easy. Learning to say /u/ in response to various graphic combinations in a script and in a variety of graphic contexts is already more complicated. It demands the recognition of abstract representations and their conversion from a visual to a phonic form, before the skill acquired in the simpler act can come into operation in the new situation. In short, it requires awareness of the relevance of the graphic symbol, recognition of what it stands for in the phonic medium, as well as control of the production of the sound. Similar abstract processes are in operation when one writes *ou* in response to the sound /u/.

That a graphic representation of sound combinations is an abstraction with an arbitrary relationship to that which it represents is frequently overlooked. Convention alone makes the relationship between sound and written symbol predictable. The abstract quality of a written communication is intensified by:

   1. its *complete detachment from expressive features,* such as facial or

body movement, pitch and tone of voice, hesitations or speed of delivery, and emotional indicators such as heightened facial color or variations in breathing;

2. its *lack of material context:* surroundings, feedback from interlocutors, relevant movement (hence the attraction of the comic book for modern readers);

3. its *displacement in time:* a written communication may be read as soon as it is written (like a note slipped to a companion) or months, years, or centuries later. It is interesting that we often do not understand a note we ourselves wrote when we find it years later.

The operation of writing, unlike speaking, must be performed as it were in a void, in response to a personal internal stimulus. Consequently, the writer must compensate for the absence of external contextual elements by the deliberate inclusion and elaboration of explanatory details which the speaker would omit.

For reasons such as these, Vygotsky suggests that the comparative difficulty for the child in acquiring facility in speech and in writing approximates that of learning arithmetic and algebra. All children learn to speak and express themselves effectively in speech at about the same age, even though some by personality and temperament may be more articulate than others. On the other hand, many people never learn to express themselves freely in writing. Even with careful instruction, there is a considerable lag between the achievement of an expressive level in speech in one's native language and a similar level of expressiveness in writing—a gap which, for many, widens as their education or life experience progresses. Certainly, many learn quite quickly to "write things down," if these are not too complicated, but this is the least demanding aspect of writing. Many who know how to "write things down" in their native language avoid expressing themselves in writing almost completely, even in personal letters. To write so that one is really communicating a message, isolated in place and time, is an art which requires consciously directed effort and deliberate choice in language. The old saying, "If you can say it, you can write it," is simplistic in its concept of the communicative aspect of writing. On the other hand, "He talks like a book" emphasizes the elaborations and comprehensive explanations of written messages which are quite unnecessary in face-to-face communication.

WRITING AND OTHER LANGUAGE ACTIVITIES

We must not be surprised, then, that a high level of written expression is so difficult to attain in a foreign language. It cannot be achieved by chance, as a kind of by-product of other language activities, although it draws on what has been learned in these areas. Good writing implies a

knowledge of the conventions of the written code (the "good manners" of
the medium); to be effective, it needs the precision and nuances which
derive from a thorough understanding of the syntactic and lexical choices
the language offers; to be interesting, it requires the ability to vary structures and patterns for rhetorical effect. So good writing will not develop
merely from practice exercises in grammar and vocabulary choice. Experience in speaking freely seems to facilitate early writing, which often
parallels what one would say. For the development of a writing style, however, much acquaintance with the practical output of native writers in all
kinds of expressive styles is essential. Familiarity with the great variety of
expression to which the language lends itself gives the neophyte writer an
intuitive feel for an authentic turn of phrase which he can acquire in no
other way.

Included in this chapter are activities which associate writing with
experiences in listening, speaking, and reading. (Further suggestions are
to be found in Chapters 3 and 7.)

WHAT ARE WE TEACHING WHEN WE TEACH "WRITING"?

As with oral communication, we can classify writing activities as either
skill-getting or *skill-using* (see model C1), with the same need for bridging activities which resemble the desired communicative activity to facilitate transfer from one to the other. *Interaction through the written message* is the goal: what is written should be a purposeful communication,
on the practical or imaginative level, expressed in such a way that it is
comprehensible to another person. Otherwise, we are dealing with hermetic
or esoteric writing of purely personal value which can be set down in any
idiosyncratic code.

Skill-getting, for oral or written communication, is based on knowledge
of the way the language operates (*cognition*). Many grammatical rules
are the same for speech and writing (e.g., the agreement of subject and
verb in certain conventional ways: *nous allons,* /nuzalɔ̃/; the position and
form of the relative pronoun: *qui* for the subject of the relative clause,
que for the direct object, both appearing invariably at the beginning of the
clause, in close proximity to the expression for which they are acting as a
substitute). Other rules vary according to the degree of formality of the
spoken or written communication (e.g., formal writing: "Son oncle est
très riche"; informal speech: "Il est archi-millionnaire, son oncle!").[2] Note
that a personal letter may retain many of the features of informal chat,
whereas a scholarly lecture given on a formal occasion adheres in the main
to the same rules as a written paper or scientific report. In an orally
oriented course, early writing will consist of the writing down of what

one would say, moving further away from oral forms as knowledge of the rules of written language advances.

Learning the rules and conventions of written language is reinforced by writing out examples and applying the rules in new contexts, thus developing *awareness of the abstraction and control of its graphic manifestation*. For written language, this activity parallels the oral-practice exercises which help students develop flexibility in structuring their oral expression. Writing things out helps with the organization of material to be held in memory and clarifies rules at points of uncertainty. It gives concrete expression to abstract notions. All of this is, however, merely preliminary activity which is pointless unless it is serving some clearly understood purpose of meaningful communication.

Considerable disappointment and frustration will be avoided if the nature and purpose of any particular writing task are clearly understood by student and teacher alike. In this chapter and the next, we will discuss writing under four heads. These do not represent sequential stages but, rather, constantly interwoven activities. They are:

I. *Writing down:* learning the conventions of the code.

II. *Writing in the language:* learning the potential of the code (we shall include here grammatical exercises and the study of samples of written language to develop awareness of its characteristics).

III. *Production:* practicing the construction of fluent, expressive sentences and paragraphs.

IV. *Expressive writing or composition:* using the code for purposeful communication.

Finally, *translation* will be discussed at some length as a separate activity.

I. Writing down

Activities of this type, although apparently simple, contribute to awareness. The student either copies or reproduces without the copy in front of him. To do this accurately, he must focus his attention on the conventions of writing: spelling; capitalization; punctuation; agreements for person, number, or gender which may not be discernible in spoken language (e.g., *ils travaillent;* /iltravaj/ or, in familiar speech, /itravaj/); diacritical marks (accents, cedillas, apostrophes, diaereses); number conventions (W6); abbreviations (*c.-à-d., p. ex.*); indicators of direct discourse and quotation (*tiret, guillemets*), and so on.

This activity prepares for eventual expressive writing. It is, however, useful in itself. Language users need to be able to interpret and copy down printed schedules, timetables, records, details of projects, charts, formulas, prices, recipes, new words and phrases they wish to remember. They should be capable of writing down accurately and comprehensibly oral arrangements and instructions for themselves and others. As students studying in the language they may need to copy accurately diagrams, details of experiments, quotations from literary works.

COPYING

1. (E) Students are given dittoed sheets with simple *outline illustrations,* or stick figures, suggesting the lines of a dialogue or parts of a narrative they have been studying. They transcribe from the text sentences which are appropriate to each sketch.

2. (E) Each student copies a line of dialogue and passes it to his neighbor, who copies out an appropriate response. This operates like a *chain* dialogue (C25), with students selecting utterances and appropriate responses from any material they have studied.

3. (E) Students copy the initial part of an utterance and pass it on to their neighbors for a *completion,* or students choose and copy completions for parts of utterances supplied on a dittoed sheet, trying to make as many different sentences as they can with each opening phrase.

4. (E) Students make new sentences by copying segments from *substitution tables.* This activity familiarizes the students with the logical segmentation of sentences into subject, verb, object, and adverbial extensions.

W1 (E) Make six different sentences by selecting one segment from each column in the following table:

Jean-Paul	montre	Janine	devant le restaurant
Le concierge	regarde	le chat	dans la rue
La jeune fille	cherche	l'agent de police	derrière la maison
Le professeur	trouve	le petit garçon	en face de l'école

Note: If pronoun subjects of different persons and numbers are used, it is advisable to keep subject and verb in the one column to accustom elementary-level students to the correct combination of pronoun subject and verb ending:

W2 (E)

Nous cherchons	la mère de Georges	devant le cinéma
Ils trouvent	l'agent de police	en face de l'école
Je remarque	le chat	dans la rue

Developing sentences from a substitution table becomes a more thought-ful process when only some subject items can be appropriately used with some of the verb items, some of the objects, and so on. Aupècle[3] gives the following example of a *table de combinaison:*

W3 (E)

Un									
avion		passé			l'enfant				vu
chat	est	entré			Sami		as		entendu
camion			mais		elle	ne l'	a	pas	regardé
oiseau		miaulé			les enfants		ont		remarqué
chien	a	aboyé			tu				aperçu
rat					Paulette				

New tables of this type can be developed as a writing exercise by groups of students for use by other students, thus moving into the second activity, writing in the language.

5. (E) Students copy from the chalkboard a simple poem they have been learning orally. An old friend like La Fontaine's "La Grenouille qui se veut faire aussi grosse que le bœuf," with its segments of interpolated speech, is a useful copying exercise. Its use of the *passé simple* can be explained as a feature of literary language and should not worry the stu-dents unduly, since poetry is often unusual in any language. Its presence alerts them early to the fact that formal written language in French has distinctive characteristics.

✻ Find for your personal file some suitable short poems for elementary classes. Share these with other members of the class and discuss their appropriateness.

REPRODUCTION

Copying activities 1, 2, and 3 may also be reproduction exercises, with students writing the utterances, or completing them, from memory.

6. (E) *Scrambled sentences* are sometimes used as a stimulus to the reproduction of a dialogue or narrative. This technique forces students to think of the meaning of what they are reproducing. Credit should be given for ingenuity in working out novel but possible recombinations.

7. (E) Students write down from *dictation* utterances they have learned or recombinations of familiar segments, or they may concentrate on the spelling of more difficult words in *spot dictation* (see R26).

(E and I) The spot dictation may focus on subjects and verbs (tense endings, irregularities, past participle agreements), or on noun and adjective agreements.

8. (I and A) *Dictation of unfamiliar material* as an exercise in auditory recognition and accurate reproduction has been a standard classroom technique for centuries. The passage to be dictated should normally have some thematic relationship to something already read or discussed. It can often provide supplementary material worth keeping on some subject of cultural interest. The standard procedure is described below. There are also several possible variations which are useful language-learning aids.

a. *Standard procedure.* The material is read in its entirety at a normal, but unhurried, pace. It is then dictated in meaningful, undistorted segments, each segment being read twice. After students have looked over what they have written, corrected obvious mistakes, and tentatively filled in gaps according to semantic or grammatical expectations, the passage is read again at a normal pace to enable students to check on doubtful segments. After opportunity for a final check, students correct their own versions from a model. If one student has written his dictation at one side of the chalkboard, or for projection on the overhead projector, the correction process is facilitated: students suggest corrections and the teacher is able to comment on errors probably committed by other students as well or answer questions about problem segments. Each dictation should be regarded as an opportunity for learning, not as a test. For this reason, immediate correction is desirable, before students have forgotten which segments they found difficult and why they solved the problems as they did. Since it is difficult for students to detect all the errors in their own work, they should exchange papers for a final check by a classmate.

b. *Variations.*

i. (E) *Students are encouraged to repeat the segment* to themselves before writing it. This forces them to make identification decisions before they begin writing and strengthens their memory of what they have heard.

ii. (E and I) If interpreting the aural signal and writing the message down accurately is a valuable exercise, there is no reason why students should be limited to an arbitrary number of repetitions of the segments. The dictation may be taped and *students encouraged to keep playing the passage over* until they have been able to take down the complete message.

iii. (E and I) Students are asked to *hold longer and longer segments in their immediate memory* before beginning to write. In this way they are not working with echoic memory, but are forced to process the segments, that is interpret them and situate them syntactically in the structure of the sentence, before reproducing them. Dictation then becomes more challenging and more meaningful.

iv. (I) *The speed of the dictation is gradually increased* as students become more adept at making the various morphological adjustments, particularly those which are not apparent in the spoken signal.

v. (I and A) *The repetition of segments is eliminated* and students are expected to listen carefully, retain the segment they have heard only once, and write it down without expecting further help. This forces students to concentrate on the message and the semantic and syntactic expectations it arouses.

vi. (A) Finally, students should be able to *take down a dictated letter or report,* with their own set of abbreviations, and write it out, or type it up correctly, as they might be expected to do in a business situation. This activity can be practiced individually with tapes.

FOCUSING ON SPELLING AND ACCENTS

1. (E and I) This goes beyond the initial stages. The teacher can focus the students' attention on spelling conventions by asking them to work out for themselves, from reading passages or dialogues they have studied, *probable rules of spelling* like the following:

W4 /k/ is spelled *c* before *a, o,* or *u: casser, comment, cube.*
It may also be spelled *qu* as in *qui, que, musique.*

/s/ is spelled *s: sac, seau, si, sot, sucre.*
It may also be spelled *c* before *e, i* as in *cette, ici.*
Before *a, o, u,* it may be *ç: ça, garçon, reçu.*
Between vowels it may be *-ss-,* as in *glisser.*
Note: *-s-* between vowels is /z/ as in *poser, oser.*

This is a suitable small-group activity. It can be undertaken whenever particular spelling problems emerge in dictation or writing practice.

2. (E and I) Students are frequently bothered unnecessarily by *indecision about which accent to use* in writing familiar words. To relieve this uncertainty they may be given a research project to find out from printed texts regularities in the positional occurrence of the various accents. Through personal observation they will easily discover facts like the following:

W5 1. Acute or grave?

a. Acute accents occur only on *e*'s: *était.*
b. Grave accents are found on *e*'s mainly: *père, mère.*
They are found on *a* and *u* in a few common words: *à, çà et là, où.*

c. When the accented *e* is the first letter of a word, the accent is acute: *étendu, étui.* (The only exception to this rule, *ère,* is too infrequent to cause problems. In any case, it conforms to rule (e).)

d. When the accented *e* is the last letter of the word (or is followed only by a mute *e*) the accent is acute: *beauté, arrivée.*

e. A grave accent occurs when an *e* is followed by a *consonant* + *e* in the last syllable of a word or in a monosyllable: *première, remède, ébène, père.*

2. What about the circumflex?

a. Circumflex accents are found on all vowels: *mât, bête, boîte, tôt, dû.*

b. A circumflex accent occurs in a number of cognates which would approximate English words of similar meaning if an *s* were inserted after the vowel with the circumflex: *hôtel,* hostel; *hôpital,* hospital; *forêt,* forest.

When students have discovered that the positions in which the different accents occur follow regular patterns, they find them easier to remember. (I and A) This project may be continued to discover pronunciation rules reflected by accents.

Note: Correct use of the different accents should not be so emphasized that it becomes an important element in the grading or evaluation of writing. Many educated Frenchmen use an acute accent instead of a grave from time to time, or even consistently reverse the direction of these accents as a personal idiosyncrasy (e.g., *èté*); others use signs of their own devising (e.g., *ētait* or *ĕtait*). Emphasis should be placed where it belongs—on fluent, idiomatic writing comprehensible to a native speaker, not on incidental graphic features.

LEARNING NUMBER CONVENTIONS

Misunderstandings can result from the use of English numerical conventions in French writing.

W6 (E) Students should be familiar with such differences as the indicators for decimals and for thousands, e.g., English 21.5 = French 21,5; English 3,365,820 = French 3.365.820; with abbreviations like 3,65 m and 11.000 km, N° 2, 1° and 2°, 1ᵉʳ and 2ᵉ, and 4⁻CV; and with ways of writing times (15 h.45) and dates (31.12.75). It is also useful for students to learn the handwritten forms for French numbers, particularly 1 and 7 .

These special features can be practiced in projects such as *describing a trip from Paris to Chamonix,* in which the student studies timetables, route maps, and area maps and gives full details of times of departure and arrival, distances traveled, and heights of surrounding mountains. Prices of rooms and meals can be found in Michelin guides or information sheets obtained by writing to the Syndicat d'Initiative in towns on the way and in Chamonix itself.

PROOFREADING

It is a commonly held opinion that students should not be shown incorrect French because they will learn the errors in the text and these misapprehensions will be difficult to eradicate. This assumption does not seem to have been scientifically tested. It is clear that young teachers improve in their control of the syntax and spelling of the language as they teach it, yet they see a great deal of incorrect French in the process. The difference, in the latter case, is that these young teachers are looking for errors and check facts in grammars or dictionaries whenever they are uncertain about correctness of usage or form in the exercises they are grading. This attitude of alertness to erroneous forms, and pleasure in finding the facts when in doubt, needs to be developed in students so that they will take an interest in proofreading their own work before submitting it for checking or grading by the teacher. It can be cultivated by an occasional problem-solving competition along the following lines.

W7 (E and I) *Préparons le texte final*

1. The teacher takes a text of a level comprehensible to the students and types it out, double- or triple-spaced, with a certain number of spelling errors (*fautes d'orthographe*) of the type the students themselves tend to make (e.g., *beacoup, recontrer*), some incorrectly placed accents (e.g., *mére, chât*), a few typing slips (*fautes de frappe*) which do not change pronunciation (e.g., *vous arrivé* or *il est aller*), and some other typing slips which constitute morphological or syntactic inaccuracies in written language (e.g., *les livres vert, la premier occasion, les erreurs que j'ai trouvé*).

2. The students work in pairs or small groups to prepare a perfect text for the final typing. Each group has a different text, a pencil of a distinctive color, and a group symbol which they put beside each correction they make. Students may check in dictionaries, grammars, or their textbooks.

3. Points will be awarded for every correction made and deducted not only for errors not detected but also for miscorrections.

4. After a time, corrected texts are passed on to the next group for rechecking. Groups gain further points for discovering miscorrections and undetected errors in the texts from other groups, but they lose points for wrongly challenging another group's corrections. (In this second round, it is essential that groups remember to put their group symbol beside their corrections and recorrections.)

5. Final results in points for each group will usually have to be deferred till the next day, to allow the teacher time to sort out the different corrections and challenges. The perfected texts, with corrections still visible, are then retyped on dittoes by those students who are learning business skills. The final text is then used for some class or individualized activity.

6. When the next composition is due, students are given some class time to proofread each other's work and write suggested improvements in colored pencil.

✱ The regular *relationships between many noun endings and the gender* of the noun are frequently not made clear to students, yet they can provide a considerable shortcut to the mastery of this troublesome feature. It is also reassuring to students to know that the gender of a new noun is not completely unpredictable.

Make notes for your teaching file on these regularities, with lists of words of high frequency in each of the categories and the common exceptions.[4] Work out an interesting activity students could undertake to discover many of these regularities for themselves (e.g., *-eur* f., abstract qualities: *chaleur, blancheur, laideur, grosseur, profondeur,* with exceptions *bonheur, malheur, honneur; -eur* m., agents: *acheter—acheteur, parler—parleur* as in *beau parleur; porter—porteur; conduire—conducteur; chauffeur, acteur,* etc.).

II. Writing in the language

Writing down words from a French dictionary inserted into native-language patterns in native-language word order is not "writing in the language."

W8 Aussi j'ai été à voir deux ou trois spectacles. Tout le monde me semblait à savoir que faire.

Commentary

This extract from a student's composition about her experiences during Freshman Orientation Week at college is clearly *Frenglish* (English structure dressed in French lexicon)—a form of fractured French which may, or may not, be comprehensible to a Frenchman, depending on his patience and imagination, or his knowledge of English. Our students will want to go beyond this stage. Unless they can eventually write so that their meaning is immediately comprehensible to a French reader, they are wasting a great deal of precious time on this demanding activity.

To acquire an adequate foundation for autonomous writing, the student studies the potential for diversity of meaning of the French syntactic system. He seeks to understand how it works (*cognition* in model C1) and essays the expression of a variety of meanings in written exercises (thus learning *production* through the *construction* of fluent, idiomatic sentences). This controlled micro-practice, like limbering-up exercises, is useful for developing the linguistic flexibility needed to communicate specific meanings.

PRESENTING THE GRAMMAR: COGNITION AND ABSTRACTION

Students must not only understand the grammatical concepts they encounter, but also appreciate how each, like a link in a coat of chain mail, interrelates with all the others in one fabric—the French language system. They may practice a concept in isolation, e.g., the immediate future, *il va partir,* becoming familiar with its form and primary function. No concept, however, is fully assimilated until it can be used, or its specific meaning recognized, in a matrix of other grammatical concepts (e.g., *il va partir parce qu'il vient de finir son travail* as contrasted with *il partira quand il aura fini son travail*). The student must be able to select, with conscious differentiation of meaning, what he needs from this matrix (e.g., whether *il va partir, il partira, il part tout à l'heure,* or *il est sur le point de partir* is the most appropriate).

1. The teacher, or more usually the textbook writer, decides, for example, that the students should now learn the future tense (or negation or the relative pronoun). This decision is an arbitrary one, and the next lesson is designed accordingly. The forms of the future tense are set out in a paradigm, and the way it is used is explained and demonstrated in some example sentences. Students are then asked to write out the future tense forms of some verbs and to use them in written (or oral) exercises or translation sentences.

This is the standard *deductive approach.*[5] It highlights aspects of the grammar extracted from the matrix. The new forms being learned then need to be incorporated into reading or oral activities, where their relationships with other aspects of the grammar may be observed; otherwise, the students will tend to think of them as separate "rules" rather than elements in an interacting system. This deductive approach is incorporated, in a non-arbitrary fashion, as part of 3 below.

2. The student may encounter a new aspect of the grammar in a matrix of language and become curious about its function. This is the initial stage of *inductive learning.*

a. The student may hear a form which is unfamiliar to him as he is listening to oral French. He may look puzzled or ask about it. In response, the teacher explains that this is a way of expressing future action and discusses its use. Opportunity is then provided for the student to hear other examples of the use of this future form in further oral work.

b. The future form may be encountered in reading material. Its function may be inferred from the context and then discussed in relation to other expressions of time relations. The forms and use of the future tense are then practiced orally in other contexts or in written exercises.

3. The student may need an expression of futurity for something he wishes to say or write. He asks for the form he needs. The teacher tells him briefly how to create future tenses from known verbs and explains the difference between expressions for the immediate and for a more distant, less certain, future. The teacher then encourages the student to use other future forms in what he is trying to say or write. This is a *deductive approach in response to a felt need.*

Each of these approaches has its use for specific age-groups or for particular aspects of the language. The deductive approach is most useful for mature, well-motivated students with some knowledge of the language who are anxious to understand the more complicated aspects of the grammatical system; students who have already learned one foreign language and are interested in the way this language deals with certain grammatical relationships; and adult students in intensive courses who have reasons for wishing to understand how the language works as fast as possible. The inductive approach is very appropriate for young language learners who have not yet developed fully their ability to think in abstractions[6] and who enjoy learning through active application; students who can take time to assimilate the language through use; and those studying the language in an environment where they hear it all around them. Most classroom teachers use a mixture of inductive and deductive approaches according to the type of student with whom they are dealing and the degree of complication of the problem being presented.

What about grammatical terminology?

Grammatical terminology has long been the bugbear of foreign-language teachers. Even switching from traditional terms to those used by any of the several competing systems of contemporary grammatical study does not seem to solve the problem. Students learn new terms and a schematic apparatus readily enough without coming to grips with the concepts they represent.

Ultimately, foreign-language teachers must take the responsibility themselves for teaching the student as much, or as little, abstract grammar as seems to be needed by each particular group for the specific language they are learning. Teachers must feel free to adapt or invent terminology which they find helps their students grasp the concepts and use the language effectively. In French, for instance, it is often more useful in the early stages to talk about *le* and *la* words and the ramifications of their behavior, rather than about masculine and feminine nouns. The latter concept, in its French form, seems extraordinary to the average English-speaking student and causes him to hesitate about such usages as *Pierre parle à* sa *sœur* and *il est* sa *victime*. The concept of *le* and *la* words, augmented by *les* words, carries the student from definite articles to indefinite articles (*un, une,* and *des* words), possessive adjectives (*mon, ma, mes* words), and demonstrative adjectives (*ce, cette, ces* words, with *cet* paralleling *l'* for demonstratives, as *mon* does for possessives). The same concept helps elucidate adjective agreements and the agreement of the past participle (*Cette petite fenêtre, qui l'a ouverte?*). Each teacher should experiment with his own non-traditional ways of talking about grammar and continue with those that work.

How do written exercises for learning grammatical concepts differ from oral practice?

1. Oral exercises provide the opportunity for many more examples of the rule to be practiced, immediately corrected, and repracticed in a given time.

2. When exercises are practiced orally, the observant teacher can judge more accurately when to skip some exercises which performance indicates are not needed, and when to add further exercises to ensure assimilation of the rule.

3. Oral exercises can be used to prepare students for written exercises by allowing opportunity for questions and comment on obvious areas of misunderstanding and a rapid repracticing of the point at issue.

4. Written exercises provide useful reinforcement of what has been practiced orally; they help to build in concepts through the abstract process of thinking out the written forms.

5. Written exercises have an individual diagnostic function, revealing what sections of the work have not been thoroughly assimilated by a particular student and where their application in wider contexts is not fully understood. It is in written exercises that one focuses the student's atten-

tion on specific problems, rather than in expressive writing where the student is attempting to do a number of things at the same time.

6. Because they allow time for editing and re-editing, written exercises are less likely than oral exercises to reflect slips due to inattention or momentary distraction, and are often better indicators of genuine misunderstanding of the functioning of the system.

7. Certain aspects of the language are best practiced in writing because they are more fully expressed in the written code, e.g., agreement of adjectives and past participles and certain verb inflections for person or tense.

8. It is easier for the student to submit in writing several possible versions, in which he can show how one rule parallels, interacts with, or contrasts with other rules.

9. Written exercises allow time for consulting references (dictionaries, grammars, or the textbook) and can, therefore, take on problem-solving characteristics.

10. Written exercises allow students with physical or emotional aural difficulties, or with slow response reactions, to demonstrate what they know through a medium in which they feel more relaxed.

COGNITIVE EXERCISES

Whether the grammar has been presented deductively or inductively, a time comes when the students need to try for themselves whether they can use the various parts of it in novel contexts to express specific meanings. Through cognitive exercises they explore its possibilities and become more conscious of the constraints it imposes. They also clarify for themselves their individual areas of vagueness and miscomprehension.

Several very commonly used types of exercises may be termed cognitive, in the sense that they require of the student an abstract comprehension of the workings of the grammatical system. It is not surprising, therefore, that in form some of them resemble various well-known tests for estimating intelligence and ability to undertake abstract learning tasks. Success in these types of exercises does not necessarily mean that the student will be able to think of the appropriate rule at the appropriate moment when he is composing sentences himself. Nevertheless, it is a step on the way, since this basic knowledge is indispensable for effective language use. Students must, however, clearly understand that such exercises mark only a beginning—a foundation on which to build the all-important structure of personal meaning.

Under this heading we will consider multiple-choice exercises, fill-in-the-blank and completion exercises, the cloze procedure, and exercises in living language for the inductive exploration of particular problems of grammar. Conversions, restatements, expansions, and combinations will be considered under *Production*.

Some of these types of exercises are also dealt with in Chapter 4 and occasional reference will be made to the discussion in that section. Most of these exercises are also commonly used as *tests*.

Multiple-choice exercises

A *typical multiple-choice grammar exercise* will look like the following:

W9 (E or I) Circle in the margin the letter corresponding to the correct form to complete the following sentences when

A = le   D = du
B = des   E = les
C = de   F = no extra word

1. J'ai lu très peu ⎯⎯ livres cette semaine.	A	B	C	D	E	F
2. Mon petit frère n'aime pas ⎯⎯ lapins.	A	B	C	D	E	F
3. Ses parents ne comprennent pas ⎯⎯ français.	A	B	C	D	E	F
4. Il ne fait pas ⎯⎯ soleil aujourd'hui.	A	B	C	D	E	F
5. Ils font toujours ⎯⎯ bruit en sortant.	A	B	C	D	E	F
6. Chaque année il a ⎯⎯ très bons étudiants.	A	B	C	D	E	F
7. La plupart ⎯⎯ restaurateurs sont d'origine grecque.	A	B	C	D	E	F
8. Il y a tant ⎯⎯ problèmes dans toutes les grandes villes.	A	B	C	D	E	F

Commentary

1. This exercise forces the student to think over carefully the various aspects of the interrelated rules for the use of the definite and indefinite articles in specific grammatical and semantic contexts. He must understand the whole sentence and the implications of each part to be able to select successfully.

2. The number of choices is too great for a student to succeed through guessing, except by a fluke. The fluke probability is also reduced by the fact that the student thinks he knows at least some of the items and so is not depending on pure guesswork for the complete exercise.

3. If a separate computer answer-sheet is used, the exercise may be machine-scored as a test. The answer format of W9 can be rapidly checked with an easily constructed punched-stencil key (with holes punched to mark the positions of the correct answers).

4. The W9 format provides a useful mechanism for students in individualized programs to check their mastery of certain concepts and their readiness to move on.

5. It is easy to construct from a basic model several equivalent versions of an exercise of this type by changing the lexical items, and thus the semantic context, while retaining the grammatical context. The following three items are equivalent in grammatical difficulty and test the same rule:

W10   a. J'ai lu très peu _____ livres cette semaine.
        b. Elle a trouvé très peu _____ fromage dans le frigidaire.
        c. On met très peu _____ beurre dans ce gâteau.

From the point of view of knowledge of the rule, the following items are also equivalent:

    d. Ma petite sœur a déjà beaucoup _____ jouets.
    e. Je n'ai pas fait le marché aujourd'hui, mais j'ai assez _____ camembert quand même.

Note, however, that (e) contains expressions and vocabulary of a level of difficulty above the level of the grammatical item sought. *Quand même* is advanced level, or at least intermediate; *camembert* is a culturally linked noun which may disconcert an elementary-level student—the only one who would normally be working through exercises on *de* after expressions of quantity.

6. It is essential in this type of exercise or test that each of the items be unambiguous. Students should not have to hesitate over possible inter-pretations while they try to decide what the instructor had in mind.

W11   a. Je n'ai pas _____ lapins.
        b. Je n'ai pas de lapins.
        c. Je n'ai pas les lapins.
    Both (b) and (c) are possible French sentences in the appropriate context. Clearly the constructor of item (a) had the particular problems of the partitive after a negation in mind and, therefore, expected (b). With more context, as in W12, the correct choice is clear.

W12   a. Je peux vous offrir des cochons d'Inde, mais je n'ai pas _____ lapins.
        b. Je n'ai pas _____ lapins à vous vendre.

This multiple-choice format can be used for a number of aspects of grammar, even the *use of tenses:*

W13 (I) Read the following sentences carefully. Circle in the margin the letter corresponding to the tense and mood of the verb that you would use to complete the sentence when

A = present indicative
B = conditional indicative
C = future indicative
D = present subjunctive

1. Elle m'avait dit deux fois qu'elle me _____ cette   A B C D
(payer)
semaine.
2. Je regrette qu'elle _____ en vacances le mois pro-   A B C D
(partir)
chain.
3. Si tu ne peux pas le faire toi-même, je le _____   A B C D
(faire)
pour toi.
4. Je te raconte cette histoire pour que tu _____   A B C D
(savoir)
la vérité.
5. Ces jours-ci, ils _____ toujours tard le dimanche.   A B C D
(se lever)
6. Elles _____ trop de bruit en ce moment, n'est-ce pas?   A B C D
(faire)
7. Il faut que vous _____ ce travail avant trois heures.   A B C D
(finir)
8. S'il parlait espagnol, il _____ une belle situation.   A B C D
(avoir)

Commentary

1. This is clearly a review exercise since it requires comparative knowledge of the use of three tenses in two different moods.

2. The exercise tests knowledge of the functioning of the language system, not ability to produce the forms required. As it is constructed, it is useful as an objectively corrected test of cognitive assimilation of the rules. When using W13 as an exercise, students would, of course, also fill in the appropriate forms of the verbs in the blanks.

3. In constructing items to test ability to select correct tenses, sufficient indicators of time relationships must be given to make the appropriate choice clear. In most of the above examples, tenses and moods required in the blanks are either syntactically constrained by other tenses in associated clauses (as in 8: *S'il parlait espagnol, il aurait une belle situation*), semantically and temporally constrained by a superordinate verb (as in 2:

Je regrette qu'elle parte en vacances), or clearly indicated by an adverbial phrase of time (as in 6: *Elles font trop de bruit en ce moment, n'est-ce pas?*).

4. Other factors which have been kept in mind in constructing the items are:

a. that the sentences should be of a type that the students might encounter or wish to use;

b. that the vocabulary and general construction of the sentence should be of a level that the students can easily comprehend, so that they are not distracted from the real task of deciding on tense and mood.

The same format can be used for practice in *distinguishing among expressions* whose precise usage is often confusing.

W 14 (I) Circle in the margin the letter corresponding to the most appropriate completion for the following sentences when

A = se lève   D = s'assied
B = est debout   E = est assis
C = reste debout   F = reste assis

1. Dans l'autobus il n'aime pas voyager assis. Il   A B C D E F
_____ même quand il y a des places libres.
2. Où est Yves? Il _____ là-bas dans le fauteuil.   A B C D E F
3. Ce jeune garçon devrait offrir sa place à ce vieil-   A B C D E F
lard. Le pauvre homme _____ depuis une demi-
heure et il semble fatigué.
4. Toute la classe _____ spontanément pour applau-   A B C D E F
dir quand le champion de boxe entre dans leur
salle de classe.
5. Parce qu'il se sent fatigué tout d'un coup, il   A B C D E F
_____ sur un banc libre.

Commentary

In this example, the number of items is not equal to the number of choices. This is one way to avoid selection by pure elimination procedures. Another way is to write the items so that some of the choices are appropriate for more than one item.

The novice multiple-choice item constructor should not be misled by the final product into underestimating the difficulty of constructing unambiguous, useful test items in this format. The first step is to make a careful list of exactly which items it is desirable to include. After the test has been constructed and carefully scanned for ambiguities, inappropriate vocabulary, unintentional comprehension difficulty or obscurity, stilted expressions, unlikely meanings (e.g., *Je ne porte jamais _____ vêtements*), and a regular pattern order of correct choices (e.g., A B C A B C),[7] it should be passed on to another person to be read and checked for these weaknesses. Even an experienced test constructor is sometimes temporarily blinded by the knowledge of his intentions.

A similar format may be used for testing the students' understanding of the *meanings of words*.

W15 (E or I) Circle in the margin the letter corresponding to the phrase which correctly completes the sentence:

1. Dans une charcuterie on vend   A   B   C   D
   A. des crabes.
   B. des côtelettes de veau.
   C. du jambon.
   D. des fruits.

2. Un camembert est   A   B   C   D
   A. un pain.
   B. un fromage.
   C. un légume.
   D. un poisson.

3. Dans une boulangerie on peut acheter   A   B   C   D
   A. une baguette.
   B. du coton blanc.
   C. des petits suisses.
   D. une livre de beurre.

Commentary

1. Items 1 and 3 are based on traditional, but still existing, French shopping patterns. (Teachers will keep up, through reading and visits, with the changes taking place in France as elsewhere, e.g., the rapid spread of *supermarchés*.)

2. These items would not be given to students out of the blue. The exercise is obviously based on material in the students' textbook.

3. This type of exercise can be fun to make up and groups of students may be asked to construct exercises for other groups of students. Another format, which is not suitable for a test because of the fifty-fifty chances it provides, but which is very amusing to construct and to answer, is as follows:

W16 (I) Some of the following statements are sensible and some are ridiculous. Circle in the margin
    A: if the sentence is sensible,
    B: if the sentence is ridiculous.

1. Le rez-de-chaussée est un magasin où on vend des chaussures. A B
2. Le pâtissier vend des pattes. A B
3. Un quotidien est un journal qui paraît tous les jours. A B
4. Un rhume est une boisson alcoolisée. A B
5. Le menuisier est un homme qui travaille le bois. A B
6. Un robinet est un petit oiseau qu'on voit souvent dans le jardin. A B

The multiple-choice format can be used also to test appreciation of *appropriate rejoinders, responses, or comments* as in the following:

W17 (E) Circle in the margin the letter corresponding to the most appropriate response to the following questions:

1. Avez-vous la monnaie d'un dollar?   A B C D
    A. Un dollar vaut à peu près cinq francs français.
    B. De rien, monsieur.
    C. Bien, monsieur.
    D. Je crois que oui . . .

Alternatively, the student may be asked to select the appropriate response in a particular situation.

W18 (E) Circle in the margin the letter corresponding to the appropriate response in the situation described.

1. Vous rencontrez dans la rue le directeur du lycée où A B C D
    vous êtes élève. Vous lui dites:
    A. Bonjour, monsieur. Comment allez-vous?
    B. Salut, monsieur.
    C. Bonjour, monsieur. Ça va?
    D. Tiens, tu te promènes aussi?

✻ Construct a multiple-choice test for the forms of the relative pronoun or
the uses of *c'est* and *il est*. Try the test out on other members of the class.
Discuss the strengths and weaknesses of the various tests constructed by
the class members.

Fill-in-the-blank exercises

Some weaknesses of this format have already been discussed in Chapter 4,
particularly the type of construction which makes these exercises mechanical busywork. To earn a place as a cognitive exercise, the fill-in-the-blank
activity must demand of the student *understanding of the complete sentence and careful thought.* W13 meets this criterion as a fill-in-the-blank
exercise when each verb has to be written in with the correct form for
the tense and mood selected. The purpose of W13 can also be achieved
in the format of W19.

W19 (E or I) Read the following sentences carefully and write in the blank
the most appropriate past tense form of the verb in the margin.

se coucher 1. Puisque j'étais fatigué hier soir, je _____ de bonne heure.

acheter 2. La semaine dernière mon père _____ une auto pour ma
mère.

attendre 3. Marie _____ l'autobus quand je suis arrivé.

trouver 4. Quand il a vu les églises florentines, il les _____
magnifiques.

travailler 5. Je lui ai dit que je/j'_____ dans cette usine depuis deux
ans.

croire 6. Avant de vous rencontrer, je/j'_____ que vous étiez plus
jeune.

Commentary

1. In this exercise, the students must first look carefully at all indicators
of time relationships in each sentence. Then, having selected an appropriate tense, they must make decisions about this particular verb: Is it
regular? If so, which type? Has it any peculiarities? What kinds of agreements are required?

2. If items are written in, the exercise cannot be mechanically scored.

3. Each item should be allotted at least two points so that credit may be
given to the student who chooses the correct tense, even if he makes some
mistake in the spelling of the verb. (The student's choice here is between
the *passé composé* and the *imparfait* since all the sentences are conversational in tone.)

4. Students may be asked to write out the whole sentence. This depends on whether W19 is used as a practice exercise in writing or as part of a test with a large number of items to be covered in a restricted amount of time. If students do write out the whole item, points should not be deducted for slips in copying other parts of the sentence when the fill-in item is correct. If the copying is careless throughout, a penalty of two or three points may be deducted from the total for this specific fault.

5. Note that in sentence 4, *les églises* was used rather than *l'église* to avoid the use of *l'* before the blank, which would have indicated to the student that the *passé composé* was expected. Using *la* before the blank would lead, for many students, to the awkward completion *il la (a trouvée) magnifique*. The problem would then arise as to whether to deduct a point from the student who had written the correct verb form but had not elided the *a,* when this could be sheer inadvertence, rather than ignorance. Depending on the level of study of the student, one would expect the agreement of the past participle to be correctly made as a matter of course, or one would allot three points to this item.

At the intermediate and advanced levels fill-in-the-blank exercises can become very demanding as in a *mixed, overall structure test* with no guides to the blanks:

W20 (I and A) Complete the following sentences appropriately as indicated by the clues in the sentences.

1. Ta mère ne s'en _____ jamais doutée si tu ne le lui avais rien dit.
2. Il s'intéresse _____ sciences naturelles, n'est-ce pas?
3. Je ne comprends pas _____ vous venez de me raconter.
4. Choisis entre ces deux paires de chaussures _____ qui te va le mieux.
5. Bien qu'elle _____ dix ans de plus que son amie, elles s'entendent très bien.
6. Jean-Claude a caché _____ son père ce qu'il avait pris dans l'atelier.
7. Je suis sûr qu'il _____ du brouillard demain.
8. Ils ont réussi enfin _____ s'en libérer.

The fill-in-the-blank format is also useful for *testing irregular verb forms in context.*

W21 (I and A)

Write in the margin the correct forms of the verbs on the left, as indicated by the clues in the sentences.

1. devoir   En effet, ce livre n'est pas à lui! Il _____ se   1. _____
            tromper.

2. vouloir   Je/j'_____ tellement le voir dès qu'il sortira   2. _____
            de prison.

3. pouvoir   Expliquez-le-leur, pour qu'ils _____ com-   3. _____
            prendre.

4. s'asseoir   Il termina son discours et _____ brusque-   4. _____
            ment.

Commentary

1. In a complete exercise more items would be given for each verb.

2. The format with blank in the right-hand margin provides for rapid correction of the test, since all the answers are in one column. As a class exercise, it would be preferable for students to write in the blanks within the sentences so that they could read over the complete sentence as they checked the appropriateness of their choice of tense and mood.

3. A set of such exercises, with alternative versions, covering all the common irregular verbs is useful in an individualized program. Students can then check regularly their control of this troublesome area.

The fill-in-the-blank exercise may take the form of a *connected passage* of prose. This is a common way of giving practice in, or testing, choice between the *passé simple* (or *passé composé*) and the *imparfait*.

W22 (A) Write out the following passage, putting each verb into either the *passé simple* or the *imparfait* as would be most appropriate in a literary passage of vivid description. Underline each verb in your answer.

Encore quatre ou cinq kilomètres, se _____-il, remuant ses orteils
                          (dire)

blessés dans ses chaussures boueuses. Mais il _____ sans force ni volonté.
                                       (être)

Il _____ du regard un endroit paisible pour s'allonger et dormir.
  (convoiter)

Il _____ soudain l'oreille. Il lui _____ entendre quelqu'un
   (tendre)   (sembler)

ramper sur le ventre autour d'un arbre démesurément agrandi. Ce ne/n'_____
                                                             (être)

rien. L'oiseau de nuit se/s'_____ tu. Silence et sommeil. Il _____ sa
                      (être)   (allumer)

lampe électrique, _____ sa carte. Il ne se _____ pas. Belle-
                    (consulter)   (tromper)
ville, dernier village suisse avant la frontière, se _____ bien à quatre
                                                       (trouver)
kilomètres. A la sortie du bois, sans doute, _____-il tristement. Il
                                              (penser)
faut continuer à avancer. Il _____ un coup d'œil sur sa montre. Il
                              (jeter)
_____ deux heures du matin.
  (être)
                              Adapted from G. GOVY, *Le Moissonneur d'épines*
                                                        (Table Ronde, 1955)

Clearly, this format is also useful for other areas of grammar, e.g., the recurrent problem of which preposition to use after different verbs when they are followed by an infinitive. This is a more natural way to practice this feature than by writing out lists of *à* and *de* verbs.

W23 (E or I) Complete the following passage by inserting *à* or *de* or leaving a blank, as required by the context.

J'ai demandé à mon patron _____ ne pas fumer dans le bureau. Il a insisté qu'il ne pouvait pas _____ se passer de ses cigarettes, mais enfin j'ai réussi _____ le convaincre . . .

Uses for fill-in-the-blank exercises are limited only by the imagination of the instructor, as witness the following miscellany:

W24 (E or I) With English translation stimulus.

(what)   1. _____ vous voulez savoir?
(that)   2. Je connais une boutique _____ ne ferme pas le dimanche.
(that)   3. Il ne devrait pas vendre le transistor _____ son père lui a
            offert.

Commentary

The indications in English are unnecessary for any of these items. In item 1, the use of *savoir* precludes the possibility of anything but *qu'est-ce que;* to make this more obvious to the student more context could be supplied, e.g., *Vous cherchez des renseignements?* _____ *vous voulez savoir?*

W25 (E or I) With French paraphrase as stimulus.

Ce soir-là Jean _____ aller au cinéma.
(Jean avait envie d'aller au cinéma.)

Commentary

Presumably *voulait* is sought. With this type of exercise care must be taken to see that the paraphrase is not in less familiar language than the item sought. Here also *avait envie* could distract the student into thinking that *avait voulu* was expected, especially as this would make a possible sentence.

W26 (I) With grammatical indications given.

> Jeanne et Marie _____ de direction.
> (se tromper, plus-que-parfait)

Commentary

This would be a more cognitive type of exercise if a suitable context were given for the item rather than the precise tense reference (see W13, W19, and W20). In this example, only the form for the tense is being tested, not the use. Both would be tested in:

> Jeanne et Marie m'ont téléphoné pour dire qu'elles _____
>
>   (se tromper)
>
> de direction en quittant la station de métro.

W27 (E or I) With information given in associated sentences to show what is required.

> 1. Yvonne est bonne violoniste. Françoise ne joue pas très bien.
>   Yvonne est _____ violoniste que Françoise.
> 2. Marc est grand. Jacques n'est pas très grand.
>   Jacques est _____ grand _____ Marc.

The cloze procedure

If we combine the idea of W20 with the sequential format of W22, we arrive at the cloze procedure. Strictly speaking, the cloze procedure, as developed for native speakers, was a test of reading comprehension. It consisted of giving the student a passage to complete in which every nth word was deleted. In one passage it could be every fifth word, in another every tenth word, or whatever the examiner chose. This will immediately recall the discussion in Chapter 3 of Cherry's uncertainties of a spoken message and Schlesinger's semantic-syntactic decoding. In a cloze test, the native speaker projects expectations about the development of the message. The foreign-language learner has also to think carefully about grammatical detail. For the foreign-language learner, then, the blanks need not be kept rigidly to a set pattern. The cloze procedure provides an interesting and thought-provoking exercise which trains the student to look carefully at all structural clues and to range around within a semantic field for related concepts. It is good preparation for careful reading and a useful overall written test.

W28

(E) Roger et Monique sont _____ Lyon depuis quelques heures. Ils _____ d'arriver de Paris. Ils ne _____ pas venus en train mais _____ voiture. Malheureusement, en _____ ils se sont trouvés _____ panne. Un _____ avait crevé. Puisqu'il n'y _____ pas de téléphone tout _____, ils sont _____ en ville à pied. Quelle _____ enfin! . . .

Commentary

1. Any completion which makes sense in the context and fits into the grammatical structure is acceptable. Passages can be constructed which are more ambiguous than W28, thus allowing more scope for student ingenuity. (See also W47.)

2. (I and A) After a reading passage has been studied intensively, the students may do a cloze test on it to see how much of the vocabulary and grammatical structure they have retained.

✻ Prepare a cloze test from one of the passages in Chapters 6 or 7.

✻ Look at fill-in-the-blank exercises in various textbooks and suggest ways to make them more intellectually stimulating.

Beyond the elementary level

Inductive learning need not be limited to a few early lessons of patterned oral practice of the type discussed in Chapter 4. At the intermediate and advanced levels, the students' curiosity can be channeled into discovering for themselves quite complicated sets of rules which they tend to remember better because they themselves have worked them out.

The Rosetta procedure[8]

(I) The rules for the *agreement of the past participle* in French are not difficult to discover inductively from manifestations in written script.

The students express curiosity about differences they have observed in past participles and hazard guesses as to the rules governing these divergencies. The teacher then gives them the following sets of sentences to study and asks that they develop from them coherent, mutually exclusive rules which will explain each participal form.

W29   1. Tiens, Michel, je croyais que tu connaissais mon frère. Tu l'as vu ce matin. Tu lui as même parlé. Il est monté dans le même ascenseur que toi. C'est ce garçon qui s'est cogné contre la portière en entrant. Tu as remarqué peut-être qu'il boite? Il s'est cassé la jambe l'année dernière en faisant du ski. En descendant la montagne, il s'est trompé de direction. La piste qu'il a prise l'a jeté dans des buissons cachés sous la neige. Quels ennuis ça lui a causés!

2. Tiens, Micheline, je croyais que tu connaissais ma sœur. Tu l'as vue ce matin. Tu lui as même parlé. Elle est montée dans le même ascenseur que toi. C'est cette fille qui s'est cognée contre la portière en entrant. Tu as remarqué peut-être qu'elle boite? Elle s'est cassé la jambe l'année dernière en faisant du ski. En descendant la montagne, elle s'est trompée de direction. La piste qu'elle a prise l'a jetée dans des buissons cachés sous la neige. Quels ennuis ça lui a causés!

Learning from living language

Even at the advanced level, English-speaking students find the subtleties of the use of the modal auxiliary *devoir* difficult to grasp. Instead of telling students all over again, with demonstration sentences, about its use to indicate probability or supposition, intention or expectation, constraint or necessity, or moral obligation, the teacher may give advanced students extracts of living language in which the context clarifies the nuance supplied by *devoir*. Through an exercise of this type, the students focus on the variable semantic contribution of this auxiliary and the formal indications of its role (that is, the tense in which it appears).

W30 (A) Examine the following extracts carefully, and identify the *nuance of meaning* of *devoir* in each. Does it indicate a probable or supposed situation, an intention or arrangement, a constraint or necessity for the person concerned, or a moral obligation? Note the *tense used* in each case. From your answers, work out which tenses of *devoir* are used to convey particular meanings. Do any tenses of *devoir* seem to be ambiguous, that is, capable of bearing two different meanings?

1. Il a prononcé ces derniers mots d'une voix si sombre que *j'ai dû pâlir* . . . car il m'a versé un second verre de genièvre et nous avons parlé d'autre chose.   (Bernanos)
2. "On n'est pas en retard? demanda Chevrier au navigateur.
   —Non. En principe, *nous ne devons pas bombarder* avant cinq minutes.

—Tant pis! Pilote, . . . ouvrez les trappes."   (Roy)

3. C'est au Moulin de la Chanson que nous nous sommes retrouvés pour la dernière fois. Je ne le savais pas, alors qu'*elle devait avoir tout décidé* . . .   (Cabanis)

4. Après dîner, il est plus de dix heures, elle s'installe sur la terrasse avec une brassée de linge. Sans compter que pour se retirer dans sa chambre, *elle devra traverser* la pièce où j'ai l'intention de dormir, cette présence active, le glissement du fer, la lumière qui donne sur mon lit, tout conspire à éloigner de moi le sommeil . . . (Jouhandeau)

5. Les professeurs peuvent enseigner toutes les doctrines qu'ils voudront, ils auront droit à une attention polie; au moment de l'examen les candidats leur diront *ce qui doit leur faire* plaisir . . .   (Sartre)

6. *Le marxisme devait être* conquérant: il ne l'est pas. . . . Il *devait provoquer* un immense mouvement économique, sociologique, et philosophique. . . . *Il devait* à lui seul *être* la raison historique et la culture de notre temps: il ne l'est pas.   (Sartre)

7. —Ecoute, reprit-elle: *Alissa doit venir* demain matin arranger avec moi l'arbre de Noël, je verrai bien vite de quoi il retourne.   (Gide)

8. Le Noir était là depuis peut-être deux heures et Zulma arriva. *Elle avait dû marcher* exactement dans ses traces. "Comment as-tu fait pour trouver?" dit-il.   (Giono)

9. Malgré sa fierté, *M. le maire a dû faire* bien des démarches auprès du vieux Sorel, paysan dur et entêté; *il a dû lui compter* de beaux louis d'or pour obtenir qu'il transportât son usine ailleurs.   (Stendhal)

10. J'ai eu tort de ne pas m'occuper davantage de mon corps. Peut-être n'aurais-je pas d'asthme. . . . *J'aurais dû* au moins *faire* un peu de gymnastique suédoise tous les matins.   (Blondel)

Commentary

1. These examples are not sufficient to cover all aspects of this complex subject, but they provide enough material to alert students to the complications of meaning of *devoir,* to stimulate their curiosity to identify the nuances of *devoir* in what they are reading, and to help them to use it in a more versatile fashion in speech.

2. There is enough material in W30 to draw together the following information. (I have supplied in parentheses what is still missing.)[9]

Probability or supposition: présent, *ce qui doit,* 5
                              passé composé, *j'ai dû,* 1 (or

passé simple, *je dus*)
imparfait, *elle devait*, 3
plus-que-parfait, *elle avait dû*, 8

Intention, expectation, arrangement:	présent, *Alissa doit*, 7 *nous ne devons pas*, 2 imparfait, *il devait*, 6
Constraint or necessity:	(présent, *je dois*) passé composé, *il a dû*, 9 (or passé simple, *je dus*) (plus-que-parfait, *j'avais dû*) futur, *elle devra*, 4.
Moral obligation:	(présent, *je dois*) (conditionnel, *je devrais*) conditionnel-passé, *j'aurais dû*, 10.

(I and A) The *imparfait* continues to be a particular problem for successive groups of English-speaking language-learners. They have great difficulty in using it correctly in association with the *passé simple* or *passé composé*. Many scholars consider that the *imparfait* shows an *aspect*[10] of the action, rather than the time value we associate with a tense. This notion of aspect is unfamiliar to most of our students. Consider the following example.

W 31 Quand Jean-Pierre, exténué, porta la main à ses yeux et voulut s'adosser contre un arbre, Marc le considéra d'un air dédaigneux, et disparut. Hervé bégaya des mots sans suite comme pour le soutenir, puis il partit à son tour. Ses jambes *se soulevaient* avec peine, il *trébuchait* sur les souches et sur les cailloux. . . . La forêt *se resserrait* autour de Jean-Pierre, il *avançait* à pas hésitants, les bras tendus comme un aveugle.

Adapted from M. SCHNEIDER, *Le Tombeau d'Arminius*
(Albin Michel, 1961)

Commentary

This short passage demonstrates what a deductive explanation of the use of the *imparfait* rarely makes clear to students—the way in which the *imparfait* brings the reader into the action as though he were there, observing the details as in a picture. Traditional explanations such as "the *passé simple* is used for a series of actions in the past, the *imparfait* for an action seen as having no beginning and no end," simply do not explain a passage like this one, where in the first half we have a series of actions in the *passé simple* and in the second half a series of actions in the *imparfait*. The actions in the first half, however, pass before our eyes in rapid succession; in the second half, we watch a man in pain, every action verb adding to the picture and deepening its emotional impact, so that our thoughts are completely focused on his suffering at that moment in time.

Only through living language can we really assimilate differences like these which are fundamental to the effective use and understanding of French. (See also R42–44.)

Teachers who wish to retain and improve upon the level of French they attained on graduating will seek opportunities to visit France and French-speaking countries. Meanwhile, they will read widely and constantly in French for pleasure. Material of the type used in W30 and W31 can be collected by teachers from their own reading of newspapers, magazines, plays, novels, or books of general information.

✱ Find other material of this type to clarify the uses of the tenses in contemporary written French. Remember that there must be sufficient context in each item to establish the particular meaning conveyed by the use of one tense, or aspect, rather than another.

Deductive learning also has its place at the advanced level. Because of the subtlety of the distinction and the paucity of comparable examples in any one text, it would be very time-consuming, for instance, to try to work out inductively the way the subjunctive mode[11] is used in French to convey a subjective assessment of the situation, as opposed to the objective observation of fact of the indicative.

In a particular context, the writer may have chosen to express his opinion, and to make it clear that this is his opinion, by using the subjunctive, whereas he might very well have used the indicative in an identical sequence of lexical items had he wished to convey a different impression. For instance, (a) *il semble que vous vous êtes trompé* and (b) *il semble que vous vous trompiez* could occur in similar contexts without any clear contextual clues as to why the author selected one rather than the other. Yet the intention of the author in selecting (a) rather than (b) would be basic to the interpretation of the text.

For these reasons, the particular problems of the subjunctive would normally be explained deductively, with demonstrations in passages of living language of the various ways in which it is used. Students would then be encouraged to explain why an author had used a subjunctive whenever an interesting example was encountered in texts for intensive study. They would also be expected to have a reason for using a subjunctive in their own writing.

* Begin a collection of suitable extracts for the advanced level demonstrating interesting uses of *negation forms* and share them with other members of the class.

GRAMMAR AND WRITING SKILL

However grammatical concepts are introduced and demonstrated, it is essential that the students' activity be directed as soon as possible to *the concept in use.* Understanding the operation of the grammar, observing its functioning, or practicing the effective use of it in exercises will not ensure that the student can use it efficiently in writing.

Experiments in the writing of English by native speakers have shown specifically that the formal study of grammar and of grammatical terminology does not improve skill in writing.[12] Native speakers who can control the grammar of their language in speech and have been taught in elementary and secondary school how it operates still write ungrammatical and incomplete sentences. Formal grammar is an abstract study. After foreign-language students have been shown how the various parts of the language system operate, they seem to benefit more from discussion of the types of errors they are making in their writing in relation to what they were trying to say, with opportunity provided to correct their errors in context, than from a second (third, fourth, fifth?) exposition of the workings of the French pronoun system.[13] In this way they focus on the details they partly know or do not know, rather than having their attention dispersed over a wider area of abstract concepts.

9
Writing and written exercises II: flexibility and expression

III. Production: Flexibility measures

Cognitive exercises of the types described, despite their usefulness in clarifying grammatical concepts, do not require students to construct their own sentences to express their personal meaning, nor to develop their ideas in logical and coherent paragraphs within a larger discourse. "Knowing about" is not "knowing how." *Practice is needed in actual sequential writing.* Having learned about the various parts of the machine, and parts of parts, and how these synchronize in action, the student needs to set the machine in motion with the different parts active in weaving the intricate pattern of meaning. Here guidance is helpful in learning which parts will operate together to form new patterns. Student aptitudes vary widely in writing. Some need considerable help in developing a smooth and effective operation; others seem intuitively to take off and create interesting patterns of their own. The teacher needs to distinguish these types early and *individualize writing activities* so that each benefits to the maximum, according to his preferred style of activity.

Although writing within a framework and expressive writing will now be discussed in sequence, it must be emphasized that opportunities for expressive writing should be provided as soon as possible. Even the elementary-level student should have opportunities to experiment with the potential for expression of his rudimentary knowledge of the language. Students should not, however, be left to sink or swim in such a difficult area. Most students need some guided practice in using new combinations and exploring possibilities of expression, if they are to go beyond simple, uncomplicated sentences; they need resources other than Frenglish when they wish to express more sophisticated ideas in the new medium.

Expressive writing experiments with all the possibilities of syntax and lexicon. If there is to be transfer from guided practice in using this potential, then the practice itself must be recognizably purposeful and applicable.

This section will concentrate on measures for developing flexibility in the construction of sentences and paragraphs within the shelter of a framework.

CONVERSIONS AND RESTATEMENTS

The problems of single-sentence conversions have been discussed at length in Chapter 4. Since they are to be found in any textbook, examples of all the different kinds will not be given here. Some will be examined in detail to show ways in which they can be made to serve the ultimate purpose of developing ability to write clearly, comprehensibly, and expressively.

Conversions are cognitive exercises in that they require the student to think through the rules and select the ones applicable to the particular case under consideration. Two of the commonest types are the following.

W32 (E) Rewrite the following sentences in the feminine, making all necessary adjustments.

1. Mon frère aîné est parti en vacances avec son cousin breton.
   (Expected conversion: Ma sœur aînée est partie en vacances avec sa cousine bretonne.)

W33 (E) Answer the following questions according to the indication given, replacing the italicized words with appropriate pronouns.

1. Est-ce que *votre frère* a choisi *la cravate verte?*
   Oui . . .
   (Expected conversion: Oui, il l'a choisie.)
2. Est-ce que *Jacqueline* a acheté *la montre?*
   Non . . .
   (Expected conversion: Non, elle ne l'a pas achetée.)

Students may learn to complete exercises like W32 and W33 accurately, without there being any necessary transfer of what has been learned to expressive writing. Some items of this type may be useful for familiarizing students with the mechanics of these operations, but, as soon as the students seem to have grasped the idea, they should be given a more interesting and imaginative task like W34, which requires of them the same types of operations in a simulated, possible situation. (After completing the writing, they may act out the short scene they have created.)

W34 (E or I)

1. Vous venez d'acheter un transistor en ville, mais malheureusement il ne marche pas bien. Vous retournez voir le commerçant pour lui en demander un autre en échange. Le commerçant ne croit pas que vous l'avez acheté chez lui, et vous vous disputez là-dessus. Ecrivez le dialogue qui en résulte.

This subject should elicit sentences like the following:

CLIENT Bonjour, monsieur. Je rapporte le transistor que j'ai acheté chez vous la semaine dernière. Malheureusement, il ne marche pas bien du tout.

COMMERÇANT Mais ce transistor, vous ne l'avez pas acheté ici. Je ne vends pas cette marque-là. Je ne peux pas le remplacer. Il faut le rapporter au magasin où vous l'avez acheté.

CLIENT Mais si, monsieur, je l'ai acheté ici. Voilà la facture . . .

2. Vous avez acheté chez une commerçante une chaîne stéréo qui ne marche pas bien. Même situation: la commerçante maintient qu'elle ne vous a jamais vendu une chaîne stéréo de cette marque-là. Ecrivez le dialogue qui s'ensuit.

Possible dialogue:

CLIENT Bonjour, madame. Je rapporte la chaînee stéréo que j'ai achetée ici jeudi dernier. Elle est belle, mais malheureusement elle ne marche pas bien du tout.

COMMERÇANTE Mais cette chaîne stéréo, vous ne l'avez pas achetée chez moi . . .

✱ Take from a textbook an exercise for converting conditional clauses from one tense to another (e.g., *Si je le vois, je lui donnerai ce rapport* for conversion into *Si je le voyais, je lui donnerais ce rapport* or *Si je l'avais vu, je lui aurais donné ce rapport*) and work out a more imaginative exercise which would elicit these types of conversions in a creative framework.

A conversion becomes a *restatement* when it retains the general form of the original, but the changes made are more than mere switches from tense to tense, gender to gender, or sentence type to sentence type. W35 below is a conversion and W36 a restatement using the same basic material.

W35 (I) Selon Daninos,[1] un lord anglais imposait Dix Commandements à son chauffeur. En voici plusieurs:

—Avoir une tenue impeccable et réglementaire.
—La casquette doit être posée droit sur le crâne.
—Ne jamais fumer dans la voiture . . .

Ecrivez ces commandements en forme de discours direct au futur, comme dans la phrase: "vous conduirez toujours doucement."

W36 (I) Dans *Snobissimo,* Daninos énumère les Dix Commandements qu'un lord anglais imposait à son chauffeur. En voici sept:

—Avoir une tenue impeccable et réglementaire: complet bleu, gants marron, souliers noirs;
—La casquette doit être posée droit sur le crâne . . .
—Ne jamais fumer dans la voiture;
—S'y tenir, à l'arrêt, comme une statue;
—Avoir le respect du radiateur en observant le comportement plus haut décrit;[2]
—Ralentir pour laisser passer les piétons;
—Ralentir jusqu'à l'arrêt total pour le passage d'une nurse, en lui faisant obligeamment signe de passer . . .

Vous êtes une vieille dame qui voyait passer tous les jours Sir Henry dans sa Rolls. En racontant vos souvenirs de jeunesse, vous faites des observations sur la tenue de son chauffeur.

The restatement comes closer to *composition or expressive writing,* when W36 is followed by W37.

W37 (I) Rédigez sur le même modèle Dix Commandements pour un conducteur d'autocar touristique ou pour une ouvreuse dans un théâtre.

SENTENCE MODIFICATION

Flexibility in writing means being able to make a sentence say what you want it to say and to say it vividly, humorously, poignantly, obliquely, or succinctly.

W 38 The simple notion *je veux vous accompagner* can be expressed with all kinds of nuances:

Je vous accompagnerai avec le plus grand plaisir.
Bien sûr que je vous accompagnerai.
Je t'accompagne, va!
Je vous accompagnerais volontiers, mais malheureusement . . .
Je voudrais bien vous accompagner, mais malheureusement . . .
Ce n'est pas que ne je voudrais pas vous accompagner, mais . . .

PRACTICE IN TYPES OF SENTENCES

Students should learn early to try to express similar ideas in different forms from various points of view. One amusing way to do this is to take a particular situation and ask the students to express the reactions of a number of people to it.

W 39 (E or I) Un jeune médecin qui vient de quitter l'hôpital traverse en courant la rue étroite qui est encombrée des voitures de l'heure de pointe. Cette action hardie suscite des émotions de tous les côtés. Proposez quelques observations selon les indications.

Un agent de police (question)
Un enfant à sa maman (question, observation)
Un conducteur d'autobus (exclamation)
La femme du médecin (exclamation, question)
Un piéton à l'agent de police (question)
Un jeune homme à motocyclette (exclamation)
Une vieille dame à l'enfant (question négative)
Un commerçant à la porte de son magasin (observation)

Since what is written is intended to be read, students may copy down the comments in W39 as one side of a dialogue, exchange papers with other students, and complete the dialogues for acting out.
One side of the dialogue might read:

W 40 Agent de police: Qui est cet homme qui traverse la rue là-bas?

. . . .

Enfant à sa maman: On peut traverser, maman? Cet homme-là le fait.

. . . .

Conducteur d'autobus: Tiens, regarde cet idiot-là! Il est fou!

. . . .

La femme du médecin: Pierre, reviens! Tu veux te suicider?

. . . .

Piéton à l'agent de police: Et moi, je peux traverser aussi? . . .

Combinations

If students are to write well they must be shaken out of the shelter of the simple sentence and the compound sentence with *et* and *mais*. One way of eliciting complex sentences from students has been the combination exercise.

W 41 (E) Combine the following pairs of sentences into one by using relative pronouns.

1. Je suis allé chez un artiste italien.
   Il avait sept enfants.
      (Expected combination: Je suis allé chez un artiste italien qui avait sept enfants.)
2. Ma tante a préparé le déjeuner.
   J'ai mangé le déjeuner.
      (Expected combination: J'ai mangé le déjeuner que ma tante a préparé.)

or (E) Combine the following sets of sentences into one sentence without using *et* or *mais*.

3. Voilà un agent de police.
   Il arrête les voitures.
   Il laisse passer une vieille dame.
      (Expected combination: Voilà un agent de police qui arrête les voitures pour laisser passer une vieille dame.)

Too many of these become busywork exercises. After a few examples, the students know what is expected of them and their energies are taken up with "completing the set."

A more interesting approach which challenges the students' ingenuity is as follows.

W 42 (E) Students are asked to think of simple sentences—any simple sentences. These are written on the chalkboard in the order in which they are supplied. Students are then given time, singly, in pairs, or in groups, to combine these sentences in any way they like to make a sensible paragraph. No simple sentences may be used and only one *et* and one *mais* for joining clauses are permissible in each paragraph. Adverbs, adjectives, and a few phrases may be added to improve the narrative.

Below is an example of how the procedure might work.

Sentences provided by students:

L'homme quitte la maison.
Le boulanger vend du pain.
Le chat chasse une souris.
Le chien aboie.
La mère gronde l'enfant.
L'enfant laisse tomber ses jouets.
Le Père Noël embrasse les enfants.

Possible paragraph:

Le boulanger vend du pain pendant la journée, mais le soir, habillé en Père Noël, il quitte la maison pour aller embrasser les enfants dans le supermarché. Soudain, un chien aboie devant le supermarché, parce qu'il voit un chat qui chasse une souris. Un enfant qui court à la porte pour voir passer le chat laisse tomber ses jouets. Naturellement sa mère le gronde, même devant le Père Noël.

Contractions

Writing in French can be made more concise and succinct if certain clauses are reduced to phrases (*avant qu'elle parte—avant son départ; parce qu'ils ont faim—à cause de leur faim*) and some phrases reduced to single words (*celui qui conduisait le taxi—le chauffeur du taxi; la personne qui a commis le crime—le coupable*). Instead of giving students a series of disconnected sentences to contract in specific ways, the teacher may provide a complete passage and ask students to use their ingenuity to reduce its length by at least a third.

Expansions

Students should have many opportunities to expand simple statements by using all the variations they have been learning—to flex their writing muscles as it were. Most textbooks provide a number of expansion exercises, but these are usually very dull affairs. Sometimes, a list of adjectives is set down beside a series of simple sentences and students are asked to insert before or after the nouns appropriate adjectives from the list. In other cases, the student is given a series of adverbs or adverbial phrases and asked to expand a set of simple sentences by inserting these at the appropriate places. Students may complete these exercises dutifully, but it is doubtful whether they thereby improve their ability to write in the language, since they contribute nothing of their own to the task. Much of the cognitive learning involved in these tasks can be accomplished as effectively or at least more briskly in the types of oral exercises described in Chapter 4.

Even if staid exercises like those described above appear in an imposed textbook, teachers should be prepared to think up more imaginative ways of presenting the same material. Writing assignments should be interesting, amusing, or useful—never boring or trivial.

Below are some suggestions for creative approaches to the same problems.

Expanding with adjectives. Students can be handed part of a passage like C58 and asked to help the police identify the skyjacker.

W 43 (E or I) Une femme s'est emparée d'un avion d'Air France effectuant la liaison Paris–Nice. Sous la menace de ses armes, elle a obligé le pilote à mettre le cap sur Marseille. Juste avant la descente à Marseille elle a disparu de l'avion. On croit qu'elle a sauté en parachute au-dessus d'un champ en dehors de la ville. La police la recherche.

Après leur débarquement à Marseille les passagers ont été interrogés par la police qui voulait composer un portrait de la pirate de l'air. Malheureusement les descriptions offertes par les passagers ne s'accordaient guère.

Ecrivez quatre descriptions différentes de cette personne. Employez autant d'adjectifs et de locutions adjectives que possible pour aider la police dans sa tache.

Expanding with adverbs.

W 44 (E or I) Votre voisine chante très fort quand elle prend son bain le matin, mais ça ne plaît pas à tout le monde. A chacun son goût. Ecrivez les observations sur ce phénomène faites par les personnes suivantes. (Prenez comme base: "elle chante" et montrez les différences de points de vue par des adverbes et des locutions adverbiales indiquant où, quand, comment, pourquoi.)

1. Le mari de votre voisine parle à son patron.
2. Son fils parle à son copain.
3. Vous parlez à votre coiffeur (coiffeuse).
4. L'employée de maison parle à son amie.
5. Le facteur parle à sa femme.

Possible answer 5: La dame du quinze rue Richelieu chante si fort le matin que je l'entends très distinctement de l'extérieur. Elle chante faux, d'ailleurs!

Expanding frames. Sometimes students are asked to expand what have been called *dehydrated sentences.*

W 45 (E or I) Write out the following outline in the past tense in complete sentences, supplying any words missing and making all necessary changes. Capital letters indicate new sentences and proper names.

Vacances / été / venir / commencer / Matin-là / mère / Marianne / la / réveiller / bonne heure / Falloir / se dépêcher / parce que / rapide / devoir / partir / sept heures / précis / Juste / moment / Marianne / mettre / manteau / elle / entendre / coup de klaxon / dehors / Devoir / être / taxi / crier / mère / Tu / prêt /

W 46 Unraveled, the passage reads as follows:

Les vacances d'été venaient de commencer. Ce matin-là, la mère de Marianne l'a réveillée de bonne heure. Il fallait se dépêcher parce que le rapide devait partir à sept heures précises. Juste au moment où Marianne mettait son manteau, elle a entendu un coup de klaxon dehors. —Ce doit être le taxi, a crié sa mère. Tu es prête?

This format can be useful for testing ability to introduce grammatical features at required points in the sentence, although the same kinds of demands are made by the cloze procedure within a framework which is much closer to normal language. (Cf. W28.)

W 47 _____ vacances _____ été venaient _____ commencer. _____ matin-là, la mère de Marianne l'a _____ de bonne _____. Il _____ se dépêcher parce que le rapide _____ partir à sept heures _____. Juste au _____ où Marianne _____ son manteau, elle a _____ un _____ de klaxon dehors.
    "Ce _____ être le taxi, _____ sa mère. Tu es _____?"

Commentary

A few more grammatical features are supplied for the student in W47 than in W45 and there are several places which allow for more than one possibility, but these are not necessarily undesirable features. In W45, students may become confused by the number of decisions they have to make.

Because of their artificiality, dehydrated sentences can become something of a chore, and therefore counter-productive. A note of reality is added if the dehydrated frame is presented in the form of *news headlines* or *telegrams* for expansion.

Fortunately, there is available in the real world a type of script which resembles the dehydrated sentence but which gives students authentic contact with many aspects of French life, namely, the *petites annonces* in the daily newspapers (*les quotidiens*). One copy of *Le Figaro* will supply the teacher with from three to four thousand items from which to draw, dealing with everything from positions vacant, apartments to let, cars and animals for sale, lost property, or vacation opportunities (even for *le troisième âge*—senior citizens). The less abbreviated classified advertisements supply useful clues for the interpretation of the more abbreviated.

W 48 (I) Write out in full the following advertisements from *Le Figaro* for apartments for sale. Study their location on a map, then write a letter in French to a friend telling her about the advantages of the various apartments and why you decided to buy one rather than the others.

1. 42, r. N-D-de-Lorette. 4p., c., w.-c., bs, ch. cent., 4ᵉ ét. ss asc. Prix 184.000F. Crédit 80%. Vis. ce jour 11-17 heures. BRUN, 336-34-93.

2. 9ᵉ. Gd stud. + pet. chbre. 60m², tt cft, tél. Except., 115.000F. Renseign., 69 rue de Rochechouart. -280-62-81.

3. Mᵒ Plaisance, dans tr. bel imm. prêt à habit., 3 P., cuis., bns, 1ᵉʳ ét., terr., moq., ch., impecc., créd. poss. 15 ans. Vis. s/place tous les jours, de 9h. à 20h., 20 rue Decrès. Ag. s'abst.

At the advanced level, the *petites annonces* can be used as a basis for a practical writing project. Students can learn a great deal from the advertisements for positions vacant.

W 49 Urgt cherchons sécrét. sténodact. expér., bne présent., bne culture génér., min. niv. Bac, pr Sté informatique, connaiss. de l'angl. indispens., Env. c.v. manuscr., photo et sal. souh., Sté Lefebvre, 63 av. Opéra, Paris 1ᵉʳ.

From a number of such listings, the students may make a list of the kinds of qualities and qualifications which seem to be sought (*bonne présentation, niveau d'instruction du Baccalauréat, expérimenté, connaissance de l'anglais parlé et écrit, bonne culture générale,* and so on). They may then list in French the qualifications they feel they possess, select an advertisement, and write an application for the position advertised.

THE IDEA FRAME

Dehydrated sentences and cloze tests control the structures the students will use. Some experienced teachers feel that progress toward expressive writing is more rapid if content rather than structure is controlled.[3] The student, relieved of the complete responsibility for the development of the content, can concentrate his energies on vigorous writing and can experiment with various possibilities for expressing an idea. (In this sense, the *petites annonces* of W48 and W49 can be considered idea frames.)

1. The idea frame may be related to current reading. For instance, the reading passage R49 may be taken as a basis for writing activities. Here we have a young man who has been pretending to be mentally unbalanced and who, despite himself, finds he has been bundled off to a mental institution. The following idea frames can be developed from the passage.

W 50 (I) A questionnaire is developed in such a way that when it is answered consecutively it produces a coherent paragraph:

1. Pourquoi ce jeune homme se trouvait-il dans le bureau d'un psychiâtre?
2. Qui l'avait amené à l'hôpital?
3. Qu'est-ce qui lui était arrivé quand il est entré dans l'hôpital?
4. Quelles étaient ses émotions dans cette situation?
5. Comment espérait-il en sortir?

A set of questions like this provides the student with a developing situation and some essential vocabulary. It should not, however, be the final stage. The student should then be asked to write creatively, thus reusing language material he has just acquired in new ways to express his own ideas.

W 51 (I) Est-ce que notre jeune "malade" a pu se faire libérer? Racontez ce qui aura eu lieu après le départ de l'infirmière, selon le dénouement que vous proposez.

2. Stevick's microtexts can provide useful idea frames (see Chapter 2, p. 51). After a text has been discussed orally, students may be asked to describe a similar situation in which they found themselves, the implications for this particular situation of the arguments in the text, the reasons why they could not agree with the writer of the text, and so on.

3. The land of make-believe. The students as a group invent an imaginary setting as a background for some of their writing activities.

W 52 (E, I, or A) The students *invent a country,* give it a name (*la Lusitanie?*), design its map, describe its history, its economy, its living conditions, and its problems with its neighbors. (If the class is working in small groups, each group has its own country and displays its map prominently on its section of the bulletin board.) From time to time, they write about events which affect *la Lusitanie.*

— La Lusitanie va établir une nouvelle université en province. Expliquez pourquoi la Lusitanie en a besoin. Décrivez le plan qu'on a dressé et les réactions des étudiants de la vieille Université de Lusitanie.

— Une crise en Lusitanie! La Pompidolie vient de lui déclarer la guerre. Ecrivez les bulletins d'informations que transmettent Radio Lusitanie pendant les trois premiers jours.

W 53 (E or I) The students *invent a family* and keep a copy of all the data: number of children and their names, ages, and interests, cousins, aunts, and uncles, where they live, what they do for a living and what they enjoy doing in their leisure, their friends, neighbors, and pets, some of their well-remembered joys and misfortunes, and their hopes and plans for the future. They occasionally tackle problems like the following:

— La tante Lucie qui habite un petit village dans le Midi annonce qu'elle va épouser son voisin, un vieux retraité de 80 ans. Elle a 78 ans. Ecrivez la correspondance qui en résulte (lettres de sa nièce, de son filleul, réponses, etc.).

W 54 (E) For the elementary level, a treasure island (*une île au trésor*) is a fruitful notion. The students themselves will provide plenty of ideas for bringing it into existence and for projects associated with it. If the class is divided into groups, each group may use the same island but have its own theories on where and how the treasure is hidden.[4]

INTEGRATED LANGUAGE ACTIVITIES WITHIN AN IDEA FRAME
Writing with Visual

1. (E or I) *Objects.* Students are shown some object and asked to write a *concise description* which would distinguish it from all other objects, e.g., a pencil, a book, an eraser, or a window. The descriptions are read out in class and other students try to show how the descriptions could apply to other objects. The written description is then further refined to meet these objections.

Variation. (E) An adaptation of *Kim's Game* (*De quoi vous souvenez-vous?*). Students are shown briefly a tray of jumbled objects. Each student may look at the tray for one minute. Students then list as many objects as they can remember with a short descriptive comment, e.g., *un mouchoir bleu avec des fleurs blanches.* Students read out their lists with descriptions and discuss the objects they forgot.

2. (E or I) *Persons.* Students write descriptions of no more than two sentences in length of persons in the class, in school, in the news, on television, or pictured in the textbook. No names are given. The descriptions written by one group are circulated to other groups who try to guess who has been described.

3. (E or I) *Pictures.* Students bring to class pictures selected from magazines or newspapers. Photographs of unexpected situations are useful. These are distributed at random. Students write anecdotes, descriptions, or explanations about the pictures which are then read to the class. Each student may correct his version as he reads it and other students suggest improvements. The student then rewrites his version for grading. Students select by vote the most interesting compositions which will be posted, with the picture, on the bulletin board or reproduced in the class newspaper.

4. (E or I) *Cartoons.* Students working in pairs are given cartoon strips (*bandes dessinées*) without balloons (*ballons*) or captions (*légendes*). Each student writes captions for his series of sketches (*langue écrite*), developing the story line. They then exchange cartoons and write balloon dialogue for the characters in each other's stories (*langue parlée*). Pairs work together in perfecting their cartoons, which are later displayed on the bulletin board for the amusement of the rest of the class. (Note: single-picture cartoons are more difficult since they require witty comments. These may be used at the advanced level.)

5. (I or A) *Films.* Short silent films and documentary sound films may be used to stimulate written composition.

WRITING WITH SPEAKING AND LISTENING

Many activities are listed in C67, under Writing. To these may be added the following:

1. (E or I) The composition is given orally and discussed with other students before being written in its final form. (See *Oral Reports* in Chapter 1.)

2. (E or I) After students have acted out dialogues they have studied, they write, singly or in groups, original dialogues which recombine the material in new situations. They then act their dialogues for the rest of the class.

3. (E or I) Students are given a partial dialogue, that is, with the utterances of one participant but not the other. They make up the other half

of the dialogue so that it fits in with the half supplied. (See also *Situation Tapes* in Chapter 1.) They then act out their different versions. (Originality and whimsicality are encouraged.)

4. (E or I) Activities 1, 2, and 3 in the section *Writing with Visual,* p. 279, may be performed orally.

5. (E or I) *Bavardages.* This is an old party game which makes an amusing writing exercise for groups of eight or less. The eight questions below are typed on a sheet with plenty of space, not only for the written answer but also to allow the paper to be turned back to hide what has been written. Student A answers the first question, turns back the sheet to hide the answer, and passes the sheet to Student B, who does likewise with the second question. The paper is passed on for all eight questions. Each student in the group begins a sheet, so that up to eight sheets can be circulating at once. When the last questions have been answered, the papers are unfolded and the incongruous results are read to the group.

Questions: 1. Qui?
2. a rencontré qui?
3. Où?
4. Qu'est-ce qu'il lui a dit?
5. Qu'est-ce qu'elle lui a répondu?
6. Qu'est-ce qu'ils ont fait?
7. Qu'est-ce qui en a résulté?
8. Et la morale de cette histoire?

6. (I or A) *Une histoire courante.* This is also played in groups. Each person is given a sheet of paper on which is written the opening sentence of a story. He reads what is written and adds a sentence of his own. The papers are then circulated around the group, with each student adding a sentence to each story. The last student in each case writes a concluding sentence and gives the story a title. The complete stories are then read aloud to the group.

7. (I or A) *Qu'en pensez-vous?* Students bring in information on current controversial issues which they present to the class. After class discussion of the data and the problem, students write out their own opinions on the issue, with any supporting information they have been able to find. They then present this viewpoint orally to the class, or to a small group, as a basis for further discussion.

8. (E) Students listen to a story on tape or as told to them by the teacher or an advanced student. They then write the story out in their own words, adding embellishments in keeping with the theme as they wish.

9. (I or A) Students take a story they have been reading, rewrite it in simple French, then tell the story to an elementary class.

10. (I or A) Students interview in French visiting native speakers or French-speaking local residents about their special interests and then

write up the interview for the class newspaper or the bulletin board. If the school newspaper can be persuaded to print the interview in French, this will arouse the curiosity of other students about language study. (If no native speakers are available, a fellow French teacher agrees to be interviewed in French on some hobby or special interest.)

11. (E or I) Students are given a skeleton outline with blanks of a lecture, discussion, interview, story, or play they are to hear on tape. (At the elementary level, the outline may be like C57; at the intermediate level it will omit segments of vital information.) After listening, students either complete the outline or use it as a guide in writing up their own account of what they heard.

12. (I or A) Students listen to interviews with, or speeches by, political leaders, national figures, artists, or writers. They make notes on what they have heard; they complete their notes in group discussion with other listeners; finally, they use the material they have noted in a research project.

13. (I or A) Students complete a written research project on a leading French personality. After this has been presented to the class and discussed, the students listen to a speech by, or interview with, this personality.

14. (I or A) Students watch a French documentary film and use the information in it for a written research project.

15. (E) *Writing with listening at the beginning stage:* Postovsky[5] reports an experiment in which adult students of Russian performed written drills from spoken input, without speaking themselves, for one month of intensive study (six hours per day with additional homework). They heard only native speakers. At that stage, they were superior in morphology and also in pronunciation to the regular audiolingual group. This approach is not necessarily transferable to other age groups and other situations, but it has interesting implications.

Writing with reading

Some suggestions have already been given in the section *Integrating the Language Skills* in Chapter 7. To be able to write well, the student needs to read widely, thus familiarizing himself with the way recognized French writers write. He must, through much experience with written texts, develop his ability to assimilate information directly in French and to think in French, so that his writing acquires the rhythms and associations of the French writer.

1. (E or I) Students rework the linguistic material of a story by rewriting it from the viewpoint of a different character or from the changed perspective of one of the characters when writing in retrospect. R56 may be rewritten from the point of view of the Arab making his way down to the prison or R49 as a reminiscence by the psychiatrist some years later.

2. (I or A) After careful reading of a text, students sum up its main thrust by giving it a title. They then identify the *main topics* and trace *the development of thought* through each paragraph. The processes associated with C52, C53, and C54 may be applied at this point. The students set down the main ideas in a logical sequence in simple active declarative sentences. This skeleton outline is then put away. Another day, the students take the outline and write a text of their own from it. They then compare their text with the original to see what they can learn linguistically from the comparison.

3. (I or A) The appropriate use of *logical connectives* is a problem in writing a foreign language, yet it is essential to the coherent development of ideas. This subject is discussed in Chapter 7, R50 and R51. The procedure in R51 can be applied to full paragraphs and to a reasoned argument of several paragraphs in length.

4. (I or A) An excellent intellectual and linguistic exercise is the *résumé:* the gathering together of the main ideas of the text in succinct summary form. This is a useful art in this busy age. To do this well, the student has to understand the text fully and rethink it in concentrated terms which he expresses in French. Applied to sophisticated texts, this is certainly an advanced-level activity, but it can be practiced with less complicated texts at the intermediate level.

5. (I or A) Writing can be associated with *rapid reading*. Students need to learn to skim through informational material to draw from it the specific facts they require for some definite project. For this, they are given a set of questions beforehand and a specified period of time to find and write down the information from a long article or a chapter of a book.

(E) This approach can be used also with narrative material for *extensive reading,* as soon as students begin to read longer passages for pleasure. It can also serve as a familiarization process before the students study sections of the material in detail.

6. (I or A) Where students are encouraged to read French articles and books of their own choice from an extensive reading library, they should be encouraged to write short *reactions* of a paragraph or two to what they have read. These brief communications should not be stereotyped book reports or summaries of the content, but quite personal, reflecting the concern of the student with some aspect of the reading material, information he gained from it, or imaginative ideas which came to him as he read it. The most interesting of these may, with the writer's permission, be posted on the bulletin board to encourage or discourage other students from choosing the same reading material. (This moves beyond the frame to expressive writing.)

7. (I) Benamou suggests the cloze procedure for introductory courses in *literature* for developing sensitivity to the author's choice of a particular word in preference to other semantic alternatives. He says, "Ce procédé

concerne à la fois la structure et l'écart. Il y a structure quand on peut fermer sans effort un texte incomplet: la pression du contexte seule suffit à remplacer l'élément manquant. Le tout est de comprendre l'organisation structurelle de l'ensemble. Il y a écart lorsque ce n'est pas la fermeture attendue, mais un élément inattendu que l'auteur a choisi à ce point du message. Ici, l'écart entre ce que le lecteur attend et ce que l'auteur a dit fournit une mesure du style." [6]

8. (A) Further sensitivity to literary style can be encouraged at the advanced level by means of attempts to write short passages in imitation of the style and approach of particular authors (*la pastiche*).

9. Further suggestions will be found later in this chapter in *Normal Purposes of Writing,* 3 and 4.

PRACTICE IN STYLES OF WRITING (A)

Arapoff has suggested a format within which students may practice various styles of writing. Taking the content of a simple dialogue, students are encouraged to rewrite it in the form of direct address, narration, paraphrase, summary, factual analysis, assertion, in essay form, as argumentative analysis, with evaluation of the argument, as a critical review which objectively examines the validity of the evidence, and as a term paper. This interesting approach should be studied in the original article, "Writing: A Thinking Process." [7]

Shortening Arapoff's sequence somewhat, the teacher would proceed as follows.

1. Students would be given a short dialogue like W55 as *foundational content.*

W 55 PIERRE Bonjour, Marie.

       MARIE Bonjour, Pierre.

       PIERRE Où vas-tu en ce moment?

       MARIE Je vais à la plage. Viens avec moi.

       PIERRE Mais il va pleuvoir. Regarde ces gros nuages.

       MARIE Impossible. Ça ne peut pas recommencer. Ça fait une semaine qu'il pleut tous les jours!

2. Next, students rewrite W55 as *direct address in a narrative framework.*

W 56 —Bonjour, Marie, dit Pierre en la rencontrant dans la rue.

     —Bonjour, Pierre, répond-elle.

     —Où vas-tu en ce moment? demande-t-il.

     —Je vais à la plage. Viens avec moi, suggère-t-elle.

—Mais, proteste Pierre, en montrant le ciel, il va pleuvoir. Regarde ces gros nuages.

—Impossible, s'écrie Marie. Ça ne peut pas recommencer. Ça fait une semaine qu'il pleut tous les jours!

3. Students then write a paraphrase of W55 in *narrative form.*

W57 En la rencontrant dans la rue, Pierre salue Marie qu'il reconnaît tout de suite. Quand il lui demande où elle va, elle lui dit qu'elle se rend à la plage et l'invite à l'accompagner. Pierre proteste qu'il va pleuvoir et lui montre les gros nuages qui les menacent. Mais Marie refuse de croire qu'il va faire de la pluie parce qu'il n'a cessé de pleuvoir pendant toute la semaine.

4. This is followed by a *résumé,* written very concisely in one or two sentences.

W58 Quand Marie a invité Pierre à l'accompagner à la plage il lui a fait observer qu'il allait pleuvoir, mais elle a refusé de croire que cela pouvait recommencer après une semaine de pluie.

5. Next, the main argument of the passage is set out in the form of an *assertion.*

W59 Pierre et Marie avaient des idées opposées au sujet du temps. Il était pessimiste et elle était optimiste.

6. Finally, this analysis leads to a short *essay* on optimists and pessimists.

W60 Ecrivez une brève dissertation sur le sujet suivant. L'optimiste fait face au pessimiste.

7. The further steps proposed by Arapoff—*argumentative analysis, evaluation of the arguments, critical review* of the essay, and *term paper*—would require a careful study of styles of writing. The complete project would be a very interesting undertaking for a French major, who must learn at some stage to write various kinds of essays, seminar and term papers, and even critical reviews, for literature courses.

IV. Expressive writing or composition

If we wish students to write French spontaneously, we must give them opportunities to acquire confidence in their ability to write. We must, however, expect shavings on the floor in the process. Learning to write is not a natural development like learning to speak. As Arapoff has observed: "Everyone who is a native speaker is not necessarily a 'native writer.' "[8]

Our students will have varying degrees of interest in writing as a form of self-expression, even in their native language. If they are to submit willingly to the discipline of learning to write well in French, they will need to see some *purpose in the writing activity.* In this way writing is differently motivated from speaking, which is an activity in which most people readily and frequently engage every day of their lives. In speaking, a student without much to contribute can often adroitly involve others and support them enough, with his attention and interest, to free himself of the necessity to participate fully. (This support function is a normal form of communicative involvement which the student of a foreign language should also learn to fulfill acceptably.) Faced with a blank page, however, the unimaginative student does not have this alternative.

Personality plays an important role in writing, as it does in speaking. Some feel inhibited as soon as they take pen in hand, although they might have expressed themselves orally without inhibitions. These students need a clearly defined topic, often an opening sentence, or even a framework, to get them started. Just as some are terse in speech, others are incapable of being expansive in writing—they do not waste words and elaborate the obvious. These students find it hard to write a full paragraph, or a complete composition, on something as irrelevant to their preoccupations as "What I did last weekend" or "A day on a farm." We must not forget that there are also some students who are most reluctant to expose their real thoughts on paper, sometimes because, in their experience, teachers have never really cared what they thought. In speech they can be vague, whereas in writing this is rarely acceptable, except in poetry. For them also, writing as a class exercise is unappealing.

For these reasons among others, we cannot expect all of our students to achieve a high standard of expressive writing in our foreign-language class. For many, we will be satisfied if they are able to say what they want or need to say with clarity and precision.

There are students, of course, who enjoy writing, and these will want to write from the beginning. Many of them will have already acquired a style of writing in their native language which has been praised and encouraged. Such students often feel frustrated when they find they cannot express themselves in the foreign language at the same level of sophistication as they do in their native language. In their efforts to do so, they often load their writing with poorly disguised translations of their English thought. The enthusiasm of these students must be encouraged, while they are guided to see that writing well in another language means thinking in the forms of that other language. This does not mean just the adoption of its semantic distinctions and syntactic structures, but also its approach to logic and the development of an idea. Even in writing style, there are culturally acquired differences.[9] A student whose native culture encourages allusive and indirect rhetorical development finds it hard to be explicit, just as one who has learned to express his ideas by building logical step on logical step finds it difficult to indulge in what seem to him digressions from the line of thought. Even students who are natural writers need guidance in adapting to the rhetorical style of a new language.

WHAT WRITING MAY BE CALLED "EXPRESSIVE"?

"Expressive" writing does not necessarily mean imaginative or poetic writing. Not all students have the gift of imagination. Writing is expressive if it says what the student wants it to say in the situation. If writing is to be a natural, self-directed activity, the student must have the choice between writing for practical purposes or creating a work of imagination. Even where guidance is offered—that is, where the student is given a structure and facts on which to base his writing—he should always have the privilege of ignoring what is offered if he can write from his own inner inspiration.

What is needed is writing for the *normal purposes of writing,* not just as a self-contained language exercise. In a diversified foreign-language program,[10] students have the opportunity to concentrate on the use of French for specific purposes: the study of literature, the reading of contemporary informational materials, concentrated aural-oral development, translation or simultaneous interpretation, the learning of special skills through French (e.g., French cooking, French music or art), or the acquiring of certain subject matters taught in French (e.g., French history or political institutions). Clearly, then, what is "expressive" in such cases depends on the student's own goals.

Except in specialized programs, where students learn to write in the language in order to study in the same classes as native speakers, writing should not be a distinctive activity. It should, rather, be a natural ingredient in ongoing activities. Since one writes better in a language on a subject which one has experienced in that language, students more inclined to the practical should have experiences learning in French about practical things, while imaginative topics will spring naturally out of experiences (whether graphic, aural, or visual) with literature of the imagination.

NORMAL PURPOSES OF WRITING

These will be organized in six categories under two main headings: *Practical* (everyday living, social contact, getting and giving information, study purposes) and *Creative* (entertainment, self-expression).

Practical use

  1. *Everyday living.*
  a. *Forms and applications.* Students learn to fill in customs declarations, passport applications, entry permits, identity information, and applications for posts abroad. (The professor who wished to spend his sabbatical doing research at the Pasteur Institute hardly impressed the administration with his command of French when he wrote down his wife's occupation as *femme de ménage,* instead of *sans profession.*) Where there are French-speaking communities nearby, students may go and help monolinguals fill in social security, medical benefit, or welfare claims.

  b. *Arrangements and records.* Students should know how to write notes and notices setting out arrangements for travel, meetings, concerts, dances, weekend camps, or competitions. They should be able to write up short accounts of activities for French club records or for the class or school newspaper.

  c. *Orders and complaints.* Students should know how to order goods and services, and how to protest errors in shipping or billing, shoddy quality of goods, or neglect of services. They should be able to write for hotel rooms, information on study abroad, or subscriptions to newspapers and magazines. They should know the correct formulas for commercial and official correspondence of various kinds.[11] These can all be given a realistic twist by basing them on information in newspapers and tourist pamphlets. Students may write, for instance, to the *Syndicat d'initiative* or the university in the town in which they are interested and request information for friends and relatives, if not for themselves, or for use with a research project.

  2. *Social contact.* Students should learn the correct formulas for congratulations and various greetings, and ways of notifying others of family events or changes of circumstances. They should be encouraged to use this knowledge by sending such greetings and announcements to friends and correspondents, or displaying them on the bulletin board.

  Students should be encouraged to write to correspondents in France and French-speaking areas. Classes should be twinned with classes of a similar level abroad, so that they may exchange projects giving personal, local, and national information, youth trends and customs, ways of spending leisure time, and so on.

  3. *Getting and giving information.* Students gather information for projects, collate it, and report it to others in written form. They prepare comments in writing on controversial articles in newspapers and magazines for later presentation as oral reports or for circulation in the class as a basis for discussion. They may take articles reporting the same event from two French newspapers (or discussing the same topic from two magazines), and write résumés of the content for discussion in class. They

may prepare items of international, national, local, or school news for wall, class, or school newspapers. They may take turns in preparing weekly bulletins of news from French newspapers, or newscasts, for their own class and for distribution to more junior classes. They distribute similarly reviews of French films which are being shown at school or in the local area.

4. *Study purposes.* Students who intend to make French a major study need practice in taking notes of lectures (*conférences*) and of reading material (*lectures*). They should know how the French develop a line of thought. They need to be able to write good summaries (*résumés*), reports (*comptes rendus et rapports*), essays (*dissertations*), and literary analyses (*commentaires d'un texte littéraire*).

Creative expression

5. *Entertainment.* Students write skits, one-act plays, or scripts for their own radio and television programs (which may be taped or shown on closed-circuit television for the entertainment of other classes). They write out program notes for a fashion parade, or captions for a display of students' baby pictures or unidentified photographs of famous people. They write parodies of well-known advertisements or radio and television commercials. They prepare puzzles and mystery stories for other members of the class to solve.

6. *Self-expression.* Students write stories, poems, nonsense rhymes or *comptines,* nursery rhymes, biographical sketches, and autobiographical narratives. They keep personal records of their thoughts and experiences as resources from which to draw material for creative writing. (A good starting point for the inexperienced, or those lacking in confidence, is the writing of a story, poem, or autobiographical incident in the style of an author they have just been reading.)

WRITING AS A CRAFT

Even with motivation to express oneself in written form, coherent, read-able material does not necessarily flow from the pen. Nor is such writing merely a matter of composing carefully constructed grammatical sentences. Lucid writing is only possible when the writer has clarified his own think-ing on the subject and knows how he wishes to present his viewpoint or develop his argument. The idea may be obscure, even esoteric or hermetic, but the writer knows that this is what he wants to say and the reader tries to penetrate his thought. Muddled thinking, however, leaves the reader confused and frustrated.

Arapoff calls the process basic to writing "purposeful selection and organization of experience."[12] If one of the objectives of the French course is ability to write well and expressively in French, then the teacher must guide the student in developing his skills in analyzing his thoughts, shaping them into central and subordinate ideas, and developing a line of thought which carries the reader to the heart of the matter. The French teacher cannot presume that the students already know these things from some other course.

How can we interest students in the process of reflecting on what they really want to say and organizing it before starting to write? This initial stage becomes more attractive as a group experience. The students in the group pool their ideas, break off to gather more information if necessary, discuss various ways of organizing their ideas into a central line of thought, with major topics and subordinate ideas related to these major topics. They decide on a title to express the central theme, a way of introducing the material so that the reader's attention is caught, and the type of conclusion to which they will direct the development of thought. The actual writing is then done in small groups (or individually, if there are students who prefer to work alone). The draft elaboration of the theme is then discussed by the group; the choice of words is refined, and the syntactic structure is tightened up, with transitional elements supplied where these are still lacking. Finally the rhythm and flow of the writing receive special attention, as the completed text is read aloud. The group texts are then dittoed for presentation to and discussion by the class as a whole.

This type of group elaboration of a composition ensures some proof-reading for inaccuracies of spelling and grammar. Valette[13] suggests that the group approach be used also to establish criteria for correcting and assessing the texts prepared by the groups. The students are asked to rank the compositions before them in order of preference. They then "describe which qualities they think characterize a good composition. The class might come up with categories such as: organization, good opening sentence, appropriate use of vocabulary, original imagery, etc." The class then looks over each composition and rates it on a scale decided on by themselves and weighted according to group decision. After the class has perfected its scale in relation to the actual compositions it is considering, this rating scale is adopted by the teacher for grading tests of writing. Valette's procedure has two advantages: the students consider the system fair since they participated in its design and modification, they also understand by what criteria their writing will be graded, and they have guidelines for improving their work in the future.

Some teachers will object that this system cannot ensure that all errors in the texts are corrected. This is true. The question arises: for expressive writing should all inaccuracies and errors be corrected in every composition? Most of us have ourselves experienced the discouragement of staring in horror at a veritable forest of red marks and comments on a piece of writing over which we had toiled in the belief that we were achieving something worthwhile. The place for fastidious correction is at the stage of cognition and production exercises. If students are making serious errors persistently, more practice exercises should be provided at the point of difficulty. When students are writing to express their ideas, corrections should focus on incomprehensibility, inapt word choice, and errors in grammatical form or syntactic structure which mislead the reader. The most serious mistakes must be those which native readers can tolerate the least, rather than those kinds of inaccuracies which native writers themselves commit. Students can be trained to proofread their work for blemishes, as suggested in the previous chapter, but penalizing students for sheer inaccuracy of surface detail at the expressive stage encourages the production of dull, unimaginative, simple sentences, with students taking refuge in the forms they have thoroughly mastered over a long period of study.

With expressive writing, students should learn to check their completed drafts for things other than accents and spelling errors. They should be looking at the way their thought falls naturally into paragraphs and their use of logical connectives and other transitional devices which show the development of thought and cement internal relationships. They should seek ways to eliminate repetitions, tighten the structure through judicious use of complex and compound sentences, and highlight ideas through nuances of word choices and their combinations.

The ever-present danger of anglicisms in structure and lexical choice cannot, of course, be ignored. Students should be sensitized to this problem, which is most likely to arise when they try to express a complex idea in the foreign language. Students should be encouraged to break down a complex idea into a series of simple active affirmative declarative sentences in French which represent the facets of its meaning, and then to rebuild them into a complex or compound sentence which responds to the rules of combination and modification in French as they know them. Francis Bacon said: "Reading maketh a full man, conference a ready man, and writing an exact man."[14] It is when we try to express our meaning in writing that we discover where our ideas are fuzzy or incomplete. Trying to set down the elements of our meaning in simple form pinpoints areas of confusion and uncertainty and forces us to ask ourselves what we are really trying to say. Then, and then only, can we seek the best way to express our ideas in another language.

It cannot be emphasized too strongly that students learn to write well in French by doing all the planning and drafting of their compositions, and discussion of appropriate content, *in French*. The teacher must help the student from the beginning to acquire confidence in writing directly in the foreign language. Where students have done their initial planning and early writing in English and have then translated what they wanted to say into French, the writing is usually stilted and anglicized, lacking the feeling for the language and natural flow and rhythm toward which the student should be aiming. If the flexibility measures recommended earlier in this chapter are adopted, students will have experience, even at the elementary level, in trying to express their own ideas and imaginings in French. Where the writing program is associated with oral language activities of the creative type described in Chapter 2, students begin to think in French and to compose French sentences spontaneously without nervousness or inhibition.

Correcting and evaluating expressive writing

A number of systems for grading expressive writing have been proposed, each of which has merits for particular situations or students with specific aims.

The following guidelines have emerged from the experience of many teachers.

1. One learns to write sequential prose by writing sequential prose. Practice exercises are merely muscle-flexing. What one does correctly in structured practice, one does not necessarily observe when trying to express one's own meaning.

2. It is better to draw a student's attention to a few important faults in his writing at a time and to encourage him to improve these, rather than to confuse him with a multiplicity of detail which he cannot possibly assimilate immediately.

3. The persistent errors of a number of students lead to group discussions and practice. At the intermediate and advanced levels these errors provide a logical framework for a review of grammar based on existential frequency of commission.

4. Students should be encouraged to keep checklists of their own weaknesses, since these, as with errors in spoken language, will vary from individual to individual.

5. Time should be taken in class for students to check their work before submitting it for grading. Editing is a normal part of native-language writing and should be equally normal for foreign-language writing. Research has shown that students "can reduce their grammatical and mechanical errors—including spelling and capitalization—more than half by learning how to correct errors before submitting their papers."[15]

6. Similarly, class time should be given to the perusing and immediate correction of a script in which the errors have been marked, so that the student may ask questions and receive explanations as he needs them.

7. An active correction process is more effective than the passive reading by the student of corrections written in by the instructor.

8. Several active correction processes have been proposed:

a. Errors are merely underlined. Students, alone or in groups, decide in what way their writing was inadequate and make changes.

b. Errors are underlined and marked with a symbol which acts as a guide to the kind of error made (e.g., T = tense, A = agreement, V = lexical choice, etc.).

c. Errors are underlined and given numbers which refer to sections of a brief review of grammar rules to which all students have access.

d. Errors are underlined, with no comments or symbols, but no grade is assigned until the student resubmits a corrected script.

e. Errors are not indicated specifically, but a check mark is placed in the margin opposite the line where the error occurs. The student must identify the actual error himself.

f. Knapp[16] adopts a positive, rather than a negative, approach to grading expressive writing. He establishes a Composition Check-List of items to which students should pay attention in writing compositions. While correcting, he assigns red pluses for all items successfully handled. Students try, from composition to composition, to increase the number of pluses on their individual checklists. Lack of pluses arouses student concern so that they seek help in overcoming specific weaknesses. (Careless mistakes are merely underlined.)

9. Writing in more felicitous expressions can be time-wasting for the teacher unless he makes few such suggestions, discusses these with the students, and encourages them to use the suggested expressions in later writing.

Scoring systems

The subjective nature of grades assigned to written expression has long been criticized. Where one teacher is involved and the students know what that teacher expects, the unreliability of the scoring and ranking is reduced. In allotting a grade, an experienced teacher is considering the interplay of a number of factors. If the number of scripts is not too great, and the teacher is not too tired or harassed, his grading will normally be reasonably consistent.

Inexperienced teachers would, however, do well to consider what qualities they are looking for and to assign grades according to some weighted system until they acquire more confidence. Where more than one corrector is involved with the ranking of one group or of parallel groups, agreement should be reached on the weighting they are assigning to different factors.

The following weighted checklist is proposed for discussion:

W 61 *Weighted assessment scheme for expressive writing in a foreign language*

1. Organization of content (focus, coherence, clarity, originality)

   20 per cent

2. Structure
   a. sentence structure (appropriateness and variety)
   b. morphology (accurate use of paradigms, adjective agreements, forms of pronouns, etc.)
   c. use of verbs (forms, tenses, moods, sequence of tenses, agreements, etc.)   40 per cent
3. Variety and appropriateness of lexical choices   20 per cent
4. Idiomatic flavor (feeling for the language, fluency)   20 per cent

Commentary

1. At the advanced level, there will also be consideration of content in addition to organization of content. Further variation of this checklist will be developed where students have reached the stage of writing in French essays on literary, cultural, or other informational subjects.

2. Students should be aware of the criteria adopted for the assessment of their writing.

Research in native-language writing[17] has shown that for assessment of achievement, two compositions on different subjects written on two separate occasions produce a more reliable evaluation than one composition. It has been found that the performance of good writers varies more than that of poor writers. The fairest procedure is to assess the student according to the grade of the more successful of the two compositions. Apart from the common factor of day-to-day variability in inspiration and energy, the finding seems intuitively transferable to the assessment of foreign-language writing, in that a particular student may find one composition topic unduly cramping from the point of view of content or vocabulary area.

Translation

Translation is both a skill and an art, of considerable practical and esthetic value in the modern world, as it has been down the ages. It provides access for millions to the scientific and technical knowledge, the great thoughts, the artistic achievements, and the societal needs and values of the speakers of many tongues.

In foreign-language teaching, it has been at different periods either an accepted or a controversial element, depending on prevailing objectives and teaching preferences. It was a keystone of the learning and testing process in the grammar-translation approach. Direct-method theorists de-emphasized it as a learning device, excluding it from early instruction as much as possible while admitting it as an art at advanced stages. Audio-lingual textbooks usually printed English translations of the early French dialogues and included translation drills for practice. Translation of continuous passages from the native language into the foreign language was, however, considered an advanced exercise in this approach also.

Unfortunately, much of the discussion between proponents and opponents of translation in foreign-language learning has been at cross-purposes, since the kind of translation and its function in the learning process have not been specified. The following aspects of translation need to be differentiated in such discussion.

1. Translation may be from the foreign language into the native language (*version*) or from the native language to the foreign language (*thème*).

2. Translation may be *oral* or *written*.

3. Translation may be used as a *learning* or a *testing* device or it may be practiced for its intrinsic value as a *practical skill* or a *discriminating art*.

4. Translation may be *simultaneous,* as in oral interpretation, which draws on the interpreter's internalized knowledge of both languages, or carefully *edited* and re-edited after consultation of dictionaries and grammars, as in literary or technical translation.

5. *Oral translation* from the foreign language to the native language may be a classroom technique by which the teacher rapidly clarifies the meaning of an unfamiliar word or phrase in listening or reading exercises. It may be the way the student is required to demonstrate his aural or reading comprehension. It may also, at the advanced level, be a sophisticated activity like oral interpretation. (Since most professional oral interpreters translate only from the foreign language into their native, or dominant, language, this would also be the direction of any classroom practice of this demanding process.) Oral translation from the native to the foreign language may be used for practice or testing of the application of grammatical rules.

6. *Written translation,* as *version,* may be a device to test comprehension of factual detail. On the other hand, as *thème* it may be used to test application of the rules of grammar, as in the translation of sample sen-

tences, specially constructed *thèmes d'imitation,* or passages of English constructed along the lines of W29. Whether as *thème* or *version* it may be an advanced activity to test ability to transfer meaning comprehensively and elegantly from one language code to the other.

In view of these many ways in which the term "translation" is used, it is difficult to take a position for or against its use in the foreign-language class. Rather, one should consider the possible contributions to language learning of each of these activities at various levels and in relation to the objectives of the course.

The main objection to translation as a teaching device has been that it interposes an intermediate process between the concept and the way it is expressed in the foreign language, thus hindering the development of the ability to think directly in the new language. It may be argued that even when students are taught by direct methods, they often mentally interpose this intermediate translation process themselves in the early stages. Such mental translation usually disappears as a superfluous step when students become familiar with the language through continual exposure to it. Teachers will need to decide for themselves which position they will take in this controversy, whether to eschew all translation or use it judiciously for certain purposes. Here we will discuss such judicious use and also opportunities to engage in translation as an activity in its own right at the advanced level.

TRANSLATION AS A TEACHING/LEARNING DEVICE
Translation from the foreign to the native language

This process is useful for clarifying the meaning of certain abstract concepts, some function words and logical connectives, and some idiomatic expressions which context alone does not illuminate. Such translation, if used too frequently, can become a crutch, reducing the amount of effort given to inferencing[18]—a process which is of considerable importance in autonomous language use. Some teachers like to make quick oral checks of comprehension of reading and listening materials by asking for native-language equivalents of certain segments of the messages. In moderation, and in association with other checks of comprehension conducted in the foreign language itself, this procedure can pinpoint and eliminate some areas of vagueness for the student.

In the early stages, some judicious translation of common expressions can familiarize students with different levels of language. Such expressions will normally be presented through situations in which they would be used. Even then, however, it is not always perfectly obvious to the student that different relationships are expressed by the choice, for instance, of *Bonjour, Pierre. Comment vas-tu?* rather than *Salut, Pierre. Ça va?*

Translation from the native to the foreign language

1. *Translation of isolated sentences.* This process as a practice exercise has been brought into disrepute by its excesses. Sentences of improbable or infrequent occurrence, constructed so that they positively bristle with problems, have made language learning an ordeal for many students, without doing more than convincing them of their inadequacies. Such sentences may still be found in many contemporary textbooks.

The process can be useful, however, when a set of short sentences which focus on a particular grammatical feature is used as a stimulus for eliciting formulations in French, as in the following example.

W 62 For practicing the form and order of pronoun objects before the verb.

Dites en français:
1. I give him the book.
2. I give her the book.
3. He gives her the book.
4. He gives me the book.
5. She gives it to me.
6. He gives it to her . . .

Commentary

W62 is a familiarization exercise. Conducted orally, it may be a chaining activity, with students proposing short sentences for each other to translate. It may appropriately be accompanied by action. See also G51.

2. *Thème d'imitation.* This is a specially constructed exercise which is useful for identifying student problems in grammatical and vocabulary usage in written French. The instructor extracts from a passage of French, which has been read and studied, useful features he wishes the student to be able to use. He then prepares for translation into French an English text which requires the use of these features. The student translates the passage without consulting the original on which it is based, and then examines the original to see where he can improve or correct his translation. Group discussion is useful at this stage.

W 63 *Thème d'imitation* based on R38.

Traduisez en français:

Maryse had been looking forward to her trip to Rome for six months, but now that she was there, she didn't really know where to go. She'd heard of St. Peter's Square, but that was all. She was pleased to see that there was a bus which went there. After a few minutes, the bus came along and she found herself a place on the platform at the back . . .

TRANSLATION AS A SPECIALIZED STUDY[19]

Once we go beyond the transposition into French of sentences and sequences of sentences that either parallel what the student has already encountered or test what he is learning at the time, we approach translation as a demanding, often frustrating, study in its own right. Genuine translation involves the exploration of the potential of two languages. It not only involves the student in serious consideration of the expressive possibilities of the foreign language, but also extends his appreciation of the semantic extensions and limitations of his own language, and the implications for meaning of its syntactic options. It is, then, an appropriate undertaking in an advanced course, or even at the intermediate level when a particular group of students is especially interested in attaining competence in it. It may be offered as an advanced option in an individualized or small-group program, or as a specialized course among diversified options.

Translation must be distinguished from the extracting of information from a text. Much information can be gleaned without exact translation, although readers may resort to translation at times to clarify important details. (*See Reading for Information* in Chapter 6, p. 173.)

Translation and meaning

The teacher will want to sensitize students interested in translation to the many facets of meaning with which they will have to deal. This provides an excellent context for familiarizing them with basic concepts of linguistics.

Translation involves careful analysis of the meaning of the source text. Students consider various aspects of the meaning they have extracted and rethink it in terms of the target language so that as little is added and as little is lost as possible. They learn a great deal as they discover that it is not always possible to attain exact equivalence and as they evaluate possible versions to see which most fully captures all the implications of the original. They will find that they need to look beyond single words, segments of sentences, or even complete sentences to whole stretches of discourse as they make their decisions. Much can be thrashed out in group working sessions as they ask themselves some searching questions[20] about the text they wish to translate.

1. What type of writing does the passage represent: descriptive, narrative, conversational, expository, argumentative, polemical, or some other? What are the features of this style in the target language?

2. What is the overall meaning of this passage in its context in a larger discourse? Is it a serious development of ideas or is it satirical? Is it deliberately vague? Is the original inaccurate or fallacious? Is it carelessly put together? (Any of these characteristics, and many others, must be faithfully reproduced.)

3. Is the tone of the passage assured, hesitant, dogmatic, humorous, solemn, neutral, or something else?

4. Is the passage boring, repetitive, exciting, laconic, provocative, mysterious. . . .?

5. Is the general structure such that it can be reproduced in the translation, or would an equivalent in the other language require different sentence division or repositioning of segments, for emphasis or for other reasons?

6. How can the time relationships in the source text be most clearly expressed in the target language? (This is not always a question of which tenses to select.)

7. For which lexical items is the semantic content different from seemingly equivalent lexical items in the target language? Should additional lexical items be introduced to carry the meaning which would otherwise be lost, or can this extra meaning be carried by grammatical morphemes, or by implications from syntactic choices?

W 64 He ate in the dark or by the light through the stove door left ajar. There was still no lamp, no candle. The fixer set a small splinter aside to mark the lost day *and crawled onto his mattress.*[21]

Commentary

The very expressive segment which I have italicized indicates how quite simple expressions may be very difficult to translate succinctly into another language. "He crawled onto his mattress" in English contains the ideas not only of movement, direction, and weariness, but also the most animal level of life to which the fixer has been reduced. "Il s'affaissait sur son matelas" contains the ideas of movement, direction, and weariness, without the feeling of hopelessness of the original.

8. Do superficially equivalent expressions in the original and in the proposed translation have different denotative (referential) meaning or connotative (emotive) meaning? (*Faux amis*[22] fall into these categories.)

9. Are there sociolinguistic or emotional levels of language or specialized fields of knowledge implicit in the text which will need careful attention in the translation?

10. Are there culturally related items in the source text which will need to be rethought in relation to the cultural concepts of the speakers of the target language, or should literal translations be used for these to preserve in the translation the foreign flavor of the original?

11. Are there figurative, rhetorical, or specifically literary aspects of the language of the original which require careful transposition?

12. Are there any idiosyncratic features of the author's style observable in this passage? Are there any mechanisms in the target language which would convey the same impression?

Clearly such a task is formidable for a language learner. If students are not to become discouraged, they will need to be given much practice with translation graded in difficulty, with particular passages selected because they allow the student to focus on specific problems. Students will also derive considerable benefit from pooling ideas in group preparation of a final translation, and from discussion of the efficacy of published translations of passages they themselves have attempted to translate.

W 65 Compare this English translation with the original French passage from *Le Petit Prince* by A. de Saint-Exupéry.[23] Do you think the translator has captured the level of language and tone of the original and reproduced the full meaning?

A. J'ai donc dû choisir un autre métier et j'ai appris à piloter des avions. J'ai volé un peu partout dans le monde. Et la géographie, c'est exact, m'a beaucoup servi. Je savais reconnaître, du premier coup d'œil, la Chine de l'Arizona. C'est très utile, si l'on s'est égaré pendant la nuit.

J'ai ainsi eu, au cours de ma vie, des tas de contacts avec des tas de gens sérieux.

B. So then I chose another profession, and learned to pilot airplanes. I have flown a little over all parts of the world; and it is true that geography has been very useful to me. At a glance I can distinguish China from Arizona. If one gets lost in the night, such knowledge is valuable.

In the course of this life I have had a great many encounters with a great many people concerned with matters of consequence . . .

W 66 Discuss the decisions made by the translator of this passage from Camus' *L'Etranger*.[24] Do you consider them necessary and effective?

A. J'étais assez loin de lui, à une dizaine de mètres. Je devinais son regard par instants, entre ses paupières mi-closes. Mais, le plus souvent, son image dansait devant mes yeux, dans l'air enflammé. Le bruit des vagues était encore plus paresseux, plus étale qu'à midi. C'était le même soleil, la même lumière sur le même sable qui se prolongeait ici.

B. I was some distance off, at least ten yards, and most of the time I saw him as a blurred dark form wobbling in the heat haze. Sometimes, however, I had glimpses of his eyes glowing between the half-closed lids. The sound of the waves was even lazier, feebler, than at noon. But the light hadn't changed; it was pounding as fiercely as ever on the long stretch of sand that ended at the rock.

Version

As with other aspects of the foreign-language course, translation can begin with *useful things which are near at hand.*

1. Students translate French *labels, slogans,* and *advertisements,* trying to produce English versions which ring true to the commercial style to which they are accustomed. This activity can lead to interesting discussions of differences of approach to the consumer.

2. Students translate *instructions* for the use of products for local merchants (car salesmen or hair stylists, for instance) or for relatives, or *cooking recipes* for themselves or friends. Where necessary, they use specialized dictionaries to help them.

3. Students translate interesting sections of *letters from correspondents* to publish in the school newspaper or share with others in the geography or social studies class.

4. Students translate *historical documents,* such as the *Déclaration des droits de l'homme et du citoyen,* for use in their history class; selections from important *political speeches* or *communiqués* (taken from newspapers or news magazines) for a political science or international relations class; *scientific articles* for their science class; or words of *songs* for the school choir.

5. Some students become interested in attempting the translation of passages in all kinds of styles and moods; others try to develop real proficiency in scientific or technical translation in specialized fields.

6. Some students, deeply interested in language and in literature, might work together (or individually) to produce an English *poem* which is a translation of a French poem. (A translation of a poem in poetic form is a new creation.) This would be submitted for publication in the school magazine.

Techniques for version. Early attempts at *version* often result in gibberish (Frenglish).

W 67 Traduisez soigneusement en anglais:

C'est l'année suivante que j'ai eu l'idée de matérialiser mon pays imaginaire. J'ai acheté d'énormes cahiers . . . et je me suis mis à découper dans des prospectus d'agences de voyage des paysages, des villes, des ports que j'ai collés sur les pages de ces cahiers. Je les ai reliés ensuite . . . de manière à former un ensemble . . .

Student translation: It is the following year that I had the idea of materializing my imaginary country. I bought enormous exercise books and put myself to discovering in the prospectuses of agencies of voyages the countries, the villages, the ports that I collected on the pages of these exercise books. I relied on them . . . and managed to put one together.

Commentary

1. Many a student has felt frustrated when this type of translation was rejected. He knew what most of the passage was about and could have answered a comprehension test fairly adequately. This student does not understand what a translation should be like.

2. Many of the weaknesses of this type of response can be corrected by asking students to read their translations aloud. As they read, they become conscious of the odd quality of their English and often correct it as they proceed. Group discussion helps to refine the final version.

3. Group discussion before individual writing of the translation is also helpful in impressing on the student that the passage has a sensible, sequential meaning. Part of the translation may be written on the chalkboard or the overhead projector as the group works it over. The students then complete the translation individually, comparing their versions with each other to decide on the best possible translation.

4. Before considering their translation final, students should ask themselves the following six questions:

a. Have I respected contrasts between French and English structure?

b. Have I fallen for any *faux amis?*

c. Have I used my common sense with time relations?

d. Have I used all the clues in the passage to help me translate unfamiliar words?

e. Have I used the appropriate style and level of language?

f. Is my final translation English or Frenglish?

Thème

We can place translation from the native language into the foreign language in perspective, as a student activity, by asking ourselves the question which has become one of the central preoccupations of this book: To what normal uses can such an activity be put? For *version,* we were able to find many uses. For *thème,* the only one which springs immediately to mind is the translating of school brochures, local area information booklets, or articles from school magazines or newspapers for inclusion in a twinned schools exchange project, or for sending to a French-speaking correspondent who does not know English. Otherwise, it is difficult to think of possible occasions when a student would be called on to perform this task. In writing letters or preparing reports, students should be encouraged to write directly in French, not to translate scripts they have composed in English.

We should consider the production of an acceptable *thème* as a means, not an end—a means for developing sensitivity to the meanings expressed in a stretch of discourse in one's own language and to the different linguistic mechanisms used by the two languages to convey these meanings. Students learn to translate ideas, not words. *Thème* is, therefore, an analytic activity. Through a comparative examination of the syntactic and semantic systems of English and French and the cultural contexts in which they operate, the student attempts to expand his own potential for expression in the French language.

Techniques for thème. 1. If students are to gain the benefits of a comparative study of two language systems, teachers must avoid the types of passages one finds in some textbooks which distort English into near-French to make the translation process "easier" for the student, e.g., "Madeleine burst with joy on seeing the high cliffs. When one sees them before one, one finally has the feeling of having come home."

2. Since *thème* is an intellectual exercise—an active, conscious process of attacking linguistic problems—it is a suitable project for group discussion and preparation before the individual prepares his own draft.

3. Students will begin by analyzing certain basic stylistic factors which will affect the whole translation, e.g., Is the passage informal and conversational in tone so that I should use the associated series of tenses: *passé composé* (*il a parlé*), *passé surcomposé* (*il a eu parlé*), *passé du subjonctif* (*qu'il ait parlé*), rather than the formal literary series: *passé simple* (*il parla*), *passé antérieur* (*il eut parlé*), and *imparfait du subjonctif* (*qu'il parlât*)?

4. Students will learn to use monolingual and bilingual dictionaries and grammars efficiently to verify the appropriateness of their proposed translations.

5. Students will learn to check their own work for basic inaccuracies in writing (incorrect choice of auxiliaries, mistakes in agreement, wrong tense forms, mistakes in spelling and accents). This mechanical task should be the student's own responsibility. (Students may keep checklists of the types of mistakes to which they are prone.) Students may help each other by double-checking each other's work.

6. Group correction and discussion of the translations proposed by the students in relation to the model translation presented by the teacher is more effective than returning individually corrected scripts, since it focuses the student's attention on one thing at a time and gives him several opinions to consider.

7. *Thème* should be a *study of translation techniques*. Several variants may be tried.

a. Students may compare their translations with a professional translation of the same passage, discussing the merits and insufficiencies of the two versions.

b. Students may be given a translation of the passage which was made by a student in another class. They then discuss proposed corrections and improvements to this translation before attempting their own version.

c. Students may discuss the qualities of the translations of the same passage by two professional translators.

d. Students in one group may translate a French passage into English, then pass their translation to another group to translate into French. Subsequent discussion of the original French passage, the English translation, and the re-translation will illuminate many of the problems of conveying every aspect of meaning in a translation and the variety of ways in which a sentence may be interpreted.

EXPLORING THE DICTIONARY

We profess that one of our aims in teaching foreign language is to open up to our students the world of language itself. Part of this world is the wonder of words—their multiplicity, their variety, their elasticity, their chameleon-like quality of changing and merging in different environments. We know that different languages view reality from different perspectives and that many of these cultural differences are reflected in words and in their nuances of meaning. Yet frequently we keep our foreign-language learners impoverished in this area, depriving them of the opportunity to explore another world of words.

For this, the dictionary can be an invaluable friend. Instead of steering our students away from it, we should teach them to use it effectively. We should provide interesting opportunities for them to familiarize themselves with various kinds of dictionaries as aids in their pursuit of personal fluency in speech and writing.

Of course, the dictionary can mislead the neophyte. Until the student has learned how to consult a dictionary, there will be the inevitable crop of "pommes de terre jetons" and "je vais duvet la rue." We must provide the kinds of experiences that will make these aberrations a passing phase.

Quite early, and certainly by the intermediate level, our student should have learned that there are two kinds of dictionaries available to him: the monolingual (the kind to which he is accustomed in his native language) and the bilingual (which he will certainly find in the attic or in the local bookshop if he does not find it in the classroom). Each of these, then, should be accessible to him and he should learn to use them purposefully.

1. *The monolingual dictionary.* For the French student, this will mean the *Petit Larousse* (and, at advanced levels, *Le Petit Robert* and the Larousse *Dictionnaire du français contemporain*).

a. It will be easy to interest the student in the *Petit Larousse* by introducing him to the *Encyclopédie* and maps in the second half and encouraging him to seek quick answers there to many questions which arise in history, geography, art, music, social studies, classical mythology, and literature.

This initial interest can be quickened by a few competitive general knowledge quizzes which draw him into the *Encyclopédie* and related sections, showing him that it is not difficult to extract information there, even though it is in French. (The clues to finding the answers in W68–69 will not appear in the students' quizzes.)

W68 (I) 1. The famous French philosopher, Descartes, built up his philosophy from a basic realization: *Cogito ergo sum.* What does this Latin sentence mean? (The answer is found in the section *Locutions latines et étrangères.*)

2. In what century did Descartes live? (Answer under entry *Descartes.*)

3. We hear a great deal about Louis XIV (*le Roi-Soleil*), Louis XV (who predicted *Après moi, le déluge*), and even Louis XVI, who with his wife Marie-Antoinette was guillotined at the time of the French Revolution. We hear more about the chief adviser of Louis XIII than about the King himself. In fact books have been written and films made about this famous man. Who was he? (Answer under entry *Louis XIII.*)

Note: It may seem that questions like 3 provide a great deal of information which could be broken down to form further questions, but this questionnaire is not intended as a test. Since its purpose is to arouse interest in searching for information in the *Petit Larousse,* the questions should provide interesting reading in themselves. For intermediate and advanced students the questions may very well be written in French, so long as the general appearance of the quiz is not so forbidding as to be self-defeating.

b. Next, the student can be encouraged in spare moments to browse through the first half of the book looking at the *plates.*

W 69 (E or I) 1. The *Marine Française* has many kinds of vessels. What is the French for:

(a) aircraft carrier, (b) helicopter carrier, (c) submarine?

(Answers from the plate: *La Marine Française.*)

2. France is famous for its *champagne,* but also for its *champignons.* One of the most famous, *la truffe,* is used to flavor the famous *pâté de foie gras.* What does a *truffe* look like? (Answer from the plate: *Champignons.*)

3. You think you know the meaning of *la pensée* because you know *je pense.* What other meaning does it have? (Answer from the illustration in the text.)

Very soon, groups of students, or individuals, should be enthusiastic enough to make up their own questions to try out on each other.

c. Next we introduce the student to the *boldface entries* in the main text.

W 70 (E or I) 1. A *fille* is a girl and a *fillette* is a little girl.

What is the French for: a. a little boy, b. a little flower, c. a small house, d. a small garden, e. a little woman?

d. Finally we move to the *small type.*

W 71 (I) 1. *Formidable!* is often heard in familiar speech. What does this exclamation mean?

2. French borrows English words, just as the English language has borrowed words like *petite, chic,* and *chauffeur.* Sometimes these English borrowings are used in ways rather different from their native usage. What is the meaning of: a. faire du footing, b. un boulingrin, c. l'autostop, d. un redingote, e. un appartement haut standing?

e. From this point on, it should be possible to incorporate the consultation of the *Petit Larousse* into as many activities as possible and to direct students to it to find out many things for themselves.

f. Word formation is a fascinating study, already discussed in R4–5 and R68–71. Advanced students should pursue this area further for its intrinsic interest.

W72 (A) From *Le Petit Robert* or the Larousse *Dictionnaire du français contemporain,* comment on the relationships between the pairs of words below. From the dictionary, write down a sentence showing the use of each:

    a. larme   larmoyer
       onde   ondoyer
       poudre   poudroyer . . .

    b. sauter   sautiller
       fendre   fendiller . . .

    c. chanter   chantonner
       mâcher   mâchonner . . .

    d. tousser   toussoter
       chut!   chuchoter . . .

1. *The bilingual (or French-English, English-French) dictionary.* It is this dictionary which every student has tucked away in his desk, usually in a very abbreviated paperback edition, and to which he refers to produce the howlers with which every teacher is familiar.

a. We should help our students by recommending a dependable, reasonably-priced bilingual dictionary which will be used consistently during their studies, so that they will know how to use it when they are on their own.

b. A larger, more comprehensive bilingual dictionary will be available for reference in the classroom and in the library, alongside the monolingual French dictionaries discussed.

c. Students will be given practice exercises in dictionary search so that they become familiar with the various features—pronunciation guides; abbreviations for parts of speech (e.g., n = noun, s = *substantif*); levels of language and usage (e.g., familiar, *populaire, argot* or slang, archaic or obsolete); relationships with other words (i.e., the rubric under which to find derivatives); grammatical indicators (e.g., with dative: *fournir à quelqu'un*); and sample sentences demonstrating general use and inclusion in specifically idiomatic expressions.

d. Finally, and most importantly, students will be trained to check meaning in both parts of the dictionary. The lady who, wishing to compliment a helpful salesgirl, looked up her pocket dictionary and said, *"Vous êtes malade"* could have been saved much embarrassment had she checked the various French entries for "patient" in the French-English section before taking the plunge. Exercises like W73 and W74 are easy to construct and interesting to work out with the help of the dictionary.

W73 (I or A) Find out from a bilingual dictionary how to express in French the expressions italicized in the following sentences:

1. This is *a famous picture* by Rembrandt.
2. He loves *to take pictures.*
3. I love *the pictures of the French countryside* in this book.
4. You're just *the picture of your mother.*
5. She's as *pretty as a picture.*
6. *The pictures of the presidents* are on the stamps.
7. My little sister likes me to "read" to her from *her picture book.*
8. *I can picture him* standing on the beach at Cannes.

W74 (I or A)

1. If you saw the following slogan on a wall in Paris, what would it mean to you: *Chômez le premier mai!*

2. What does this road sign mean: *Stationnement défendu les jours impairs?*

3. A group of soldiers are waiting for orders. The field telephone crackles out the following command: *Il faut faire sauter le pont; que le génie s'en charge tout de suite.* Who will act on this order?

4. What is the difference between *un livre sacré* and *un sacré livre?*

EXPLORING THE GRAMMAR

Students at the advanced level who wish to write well must learn to find answers to their own questions about written French. At this stage they should be given practice in formulating the questions they want answered in such a way that they can find the information they need in a French grammar book, like the *Grammaire Larousse du français contemporain,* Grevisse's *Le Bon Usage,* or Wartburg and Zumthor's *Précis de syntaxe du français contemporain.* For this, they need to know the basic grammatical terms in French so that they can make efficient use of the indexes to these grammars.

If a student wishes to know whether he should write "La symphonie que j'ai entendue jouer," or "La symphonie que j'ai entendu jouer," he will need to know that this is a question of the *accord du participe passé,* and that he will find the answer under either *participe passé—accord,* or *accord—participe passé.*

Learning terms of this type is unexciting, but it can be made more appealing by giving the student interesting problems to solve through personal search in the grammar book. When he feels at home with it, he will enjoy finding his own answers instead of asking other people.

Questions like the following may be proposed. (The indications given here as to how this information might be obtained from the *Grammaire Larousse du français contemporain* would not be given to the students.)

W75 (A)

1. Quand *il a eu chanté,* il est sorti.

Is this tense found in literary or spoken French, or both?

(Answer: The name of the tense is found by looking at the tense tables for the various conjugations, where one finds *passé surcomposé. Passé surcomposé, emplois et valeurs* is then found in the index, which indicates the section where the matter is discussed.)

2. When does one use:

meilleur   *or* plus bon,
pire   *or* plus mauvais,
pis   *or* plus mal,
moindre   *or* plus petit?

(Answer: The student looks for *Comparatif* in the index.)

3. Is it correct to say:
   a. Paris est beau,
   or b. Paris est belle?

(Answer: The student looks in the index for *Genre,* and finds the subheading: *des noms de villes.*)

4. Does modern French make a clear distinction between *voici* and *voilà?* (Answer: The student will find both *voici* and *voilà* in the index of each of the books listed above.)

Students can be asked to propose their own problems, which will be worked into a *search questionnaire.*

Suggested assignments and projects

Communicating (chapters 1–3)

1. Write a situational dialogue suitable for the second month of instruction. Write a critique of the first draft of your dialogue, then rewrite it if necessary. From your final dialogue write a spiral series and a situation tape. (You may find that what you have written needs considerable adaptation for the situation tape. You should try the script for the tape out on several people to see if it is workable.) If you have the facilities available, record your tape in the form in which it would be used by students.

2. Choose a grammatical feature. Write a grammar-demonstration dialogue to display the various facets of this feature. Construct a unit showing how you would exploit this feature in guided oral practice, in student-directed practice, and then in some natural language activity. (Consult also chapter 4.)

3. Design a module for small-group activity which explores some facet of the everyday culture of France, French Canada, or some other francophone country. Include natural communicative activities and some culminating display for sharing the material with the whole class.

4. Take a unit or lesson from a direct method textbook and examine the types of activities proposed. Design a learning packet for individual-

ized instruction or a unit for small-group work using this material. (Remember that individualized instruction does not mean independent study. This distinction is important if communication skills are to be developed.)

5. Design in detail for fourth-year high school, fourth semester of college, or advanced level college an aural-oral communication course based entirely on natural uses of language. Your course should supply ample opportunity for developing facility in listening to all kinds of French and for expressing oneself in different situations and styles of language. (Think of ways of stimulating genuinely self-directed activity by the students. Do not make the course dependent on expensive equipment and aids which you could not realistically expect to be available in the average foreign-language department.)

6. Take two textbooks designed specifically for conversation courses. Analyze and comment on the types of communicative activity they promote, using the following heads as an outline.

Situations. For what situations is practice provided? Are these adequate? useful? culturally illuminating? Could the material be adapted easily to other situations?

Normal uses of language. How do the types of activities proposed relate to the normal communicative categories of chapter 2? What other categories can you establish from this examination?

Strategies of communication. What techniques for expressing personal meaning within a limited knowledge of the language do these texts encourage? What other strategies do learners of a foreign language need to practice? How could these be incorporated into these texts?

7. Design two listening comprehension tests—one multiple-choice and the other based on natural language activities. Discuss for each of the tests the problems involved in assessment of the degree of listening skill and in administration in a practical teaching situation.

8. Design in detail a course for developing facility in listening along with facility in reading. State the level at which the course would be offered and give your reasons for offering it at that level. (See also chapters 6 and 7.)

Oral practice for the learning of grammar (chapter 4)

9. Take six Type A exercises from current textbooks and show how each could be developed as a Type B exercise.

10. Take a unit for grammatical practice from a current textbook, classify the types of exercises proposed, and design further exercises of the types described in chapter 4 which are not already included but which you would consider suitable for practicing this area of grammar.

11. Draft a series of oral exercises for teaching the use of the interrogative pronouns in French. Draw freely from the various types described in chapter 4, passing from teacher demonstration to student-directed application to autonomous student production.

12. Examine critically the oral exercises for the learning of grammar on a set of tapes accompanying a current textbook. What are their best features and their weaknesses? Propose types of exercises which would, in your opinion, make them more interesting and more useful for developing ability to use the language in interaction.

Teaching the sound system (chapter 5)

13. Make a tape of your own reading of the evaluation passage S44. Choose the four most striking weaknesses in your production (see S43) and work out articulatory descriptions, empirical recommendations, and remedial exercises which would help students to correct these same faults.

14. Work out some multiple-choice items to test aural discrimination of /u/y/; /ʃ/ʒ/; /ɔ̃/ɑ̃/; /ɔn/an/; le/lə/ when they occur in context in normal word groups.

15. Make some tapes of your students conversing in French. From an analysis of these tapes, list in descending order of frequency the ten features of French pronunciation and intonation for which you consider they need the most remedial practice. Compare your list with those of other students or teachers and discuss the differences.

Reading (chapters 6 and 7)

16. Take a survey of interests in reading material in the class you are teaching (or in which you are practice teaching). Find suitable materials in French to meet these interests at different stages of reading development. List these (with complete bibliographic information) and explain the reasons for your selection.

17. a. Take a reading passage or story your students have found difficult to read and another they enjoyed but did not consider particularly difficult.

b. Compare the two texts according to: level of difficulty of vocabulary, structural complexity, interest of content, familiarity or unfamiliarity of content, and any other criteria you consider relevant.

c. Ask your students to write down why they found one passage difficult and the other accessible.

d. Compare (b) and (c) and give what seems to you the most reasonable explanation of the students' reactions to the two texts.

18. Undertake a survey of French-language newspapers and magazines available in your area (from France, French Canada, or other francophone areas). Examine various aspects of their content and rate them appropriate in content and language for Stages 4, 5, and 6.

19. The physical aspects of a reading text are important factors in readability. Examine a number of books for reading development in French from the point of view of:
    a. varieties of type (italics, boldface etc.) and length of line;
    b. layout (spacing, headings and subheadings, breaks in the text);
    c. convenience and placing of supplementary helps (glosses, notes etc.);
    d. usefulness and attractiveness of illustrative material;
    e. general appearance of the body of the text;
    f. attractiveness and durability of the cover;
    g. any other physical features which have attracted your attention.

20. Find two textbooks which include the same reading selection. Compare the way the material has been presented and exploited in each (adaptation, if any, of the original text, layout, glosses and supplementary helps, types of questions and exercises, interest and usefulness of these for a particular stage of reading development, integration of reading with other skills).

21. Examine some French children's books and comic books from the point of view of vocabulary level, grammatical complexity, and content. Classify them as possibilities for supplementary reading at specific stages of reading development.

Writing (chapters 8 and 9)

22. On separate occasions within the same week, give your students three tests of one grammatical feature (e.g., form and position of pronoun objects): a multiple-choice test, a cloze test, and a set of stimulus sentences to translate into French. Make graphs of the number of errors made

by the students on each test. Repeat the tests in a different order for another feature and examine these results as well. Give an analysis of what this informal experiment has revealed about the relative difficulty and discriminatory power of the three tests, and the most persistent problems for the students who are learning these features.

23. Examine a textbook for elementary language instruction. What part does writing play in this book? Are the writing activities integrated with the other skills? Are they imaginative and interesting for students of the age to which the book is directed? Are they purposeful? What suggestions can you make to improve their effectiveness?

24. Examine a manual for advanced French composition. Do the types of activities provided leave scope for personal initiative? Are they directed toward normal purposes of writing? What aspects of writing have been ignored? What suggestions would you make for a revised edition of the manual?

25. Examine a book (A) written for instruction in the writing of the native language (English or French). Compare it with a book (B) intended to improve foreign-language writing. What ideas can be gleaned from the study of A for the improvement of B, or vice versa?

Notes

I Communicating

1. The terms "skill-getting" and "skill-using" have been borrowed from Don H. Parker, "When Should I Individualize Instruction?" in Virgil M. Howes, ed., *Individualization of Instruction: A Teaching Strategy* (New York: Macmillan, 1970), p. 176.

2. The rationale for interaction activities of this type is set out in "Talking Off the Tops of Their Heads," in Wilga M. Rivers, *Speaking in Many Tongues* (Rowley, Mass.: Newbury House, 1972a), pp. 20–35.

1. STRUCTURED INTERACTION

1. How this can be done is discussed fully in W. M. Rivers, "From Linguistic Competence to Communicative Competence," in *TQ* 7 (1973), pp. 25–34.

2. In *Le Passe-Muraille* (Paris: Gallimard Livre de Poche, 1943), p. 95.

3. Paris: Gallimard Livre de Poche, 1952, p. 186.

4. All comments in parentheses in the description of the five styles are based on M. Joos, *The Five Clocks* (New York: Harcourt, Brace and World, 1961). For a more detailed analysis of the conversational register from the point of view of Transactional Engineering Analysis, see L. A. Jakobovits and B. Gordon, *The Context of Foreign Language Teaching* (Rowley, Mass.: Newbury House, 1974), Chapter 3.

5. Paris: Gallimard Livre de Poche, 1959, pp. 69–70.

6. John R. Searle, *Speech Acts: An Essay in the Philosophy of Language* (Cambridge, Eng.: Cambridge University Press, 1969), p. 16.

7. Ibid.

8. "Semantics plays a central role in syntax," according to George Lakoff in "On Generative Semantics," in D. D. Steinberg and L. A. Jakobovits, eds., *Semantics* (Cambridge, Eng.: Cambridge University Press, 1971), p. 232, note *a*.

9. Discussed more fully in Wilga M. Rivers, *Teaching Foreign-Language Skills* (Chicago: The University of Chicago Press, 1968), pp. 78–80.

10. Example taken from J. P. Vinay and J. Darbelnet, *Stylistique comparée du français et de l'anglais* (Paris: Didier, 1963), p. 192.

11. C. Gattegno, *Teaching Foreign Languages in Schools: The Silent Way* (Reading, Eng.: Educational Explorers Ltd., 1963). The Silent Way is described in more detail in two articles in *ADFL* 5 (1973–74): C. Dominice, "The Silent Way: A Student Looks at Teaching" (pp. 23–24), and C. Perrault, "The Silent Way: An Experienced User Speaks" (pp. 25–26).

12. Ibid., p. 39.

13. Ibid., p. 21.

14. It is interesting that recently some applied linguists have been advocating beginning an oral approach with the feminine form rather than the masculine form of the adjective because the progression from /vɛrt/ to /vɛr/ and from /blɑʃ/ to /blɑ/ makes for a more comprehensive rule, irregular forms now

being considered regular, in that the final consonant sound is dropped in passing from feminine to masculine

15. Gattegno (1963), p. 40.

16. Ibid., p. 24.

17. The Gouin series is described in detail, with class procedure, in R. Titone, *Teaching Foreign Languages: An Historical Sketch* (Washington, D.C.: Georgetown University Press, 1968), pp. 33–37. A similar approach to the beginning stages was taken by M. D. Berlitz, the founder of the Berlitz schools.

18. From François Gouin, *The Art of Teaching and Studying Languages,* trans. H. Swan and V. Bétis (London: George Philip and Son; New York: Charles Scribner's Sons, 1892), p. 131. This has a contemporary ring. The Berkeley linguist Wallace Chafe considers the verb to be central in semantics. In *Meaning and the Structure of Language* (Chicago: The University of Chicago Press, 1970) he suggests as "a general principle that semantic influence radiates from a verb" (p. 190) and in his work he considers the verb central and the noun peripheral (p. 96).

19. Gouin (1892), p. 162.

20. Ibid., p. 171.

21. The use of the *vous* or *tu* form in this case will depend on the age of the students and the approach the teacher has decided to take to this aspect of the language. Many teachers use *vous* to older students and expect *vouvoiement* in return, while encouraging students to use *tu* to each other. In this way students have regular practice in switching from one to the other.

22. See J. J. Asher, "The Learning Strategy of the Total Physical Response: A Review," *MLJ* 50 (1966), 79–84. Asher claims that the association of action and sound results in longer retention, at least for listening comprehension.

23. Developed by the Institute of Modern Languages in Washington, D.C., and described in John Schumann, "Communication Techniques," *TQ* 6 (1972), 143–46.

24. E. B. de Sauzé's approach is described in *The Cleveland Plan for the Teaching of Modern Languages with Special Reference to French* (Philadelphia: The John C. Winston Company, 1929). Ralph Hester, ed., in *Teaching a Living Language* (New York: Harper and Row, 1970), p. x, claims that the verbal-active method, a "rationalist direct method," derives from de Sauzé. Yvone Lenard dedicated her verbal-active textbook, *Parole et Pensée* (New York: Harper and Row, 1965) to Emile B. de Sauzé, a "maître de l'enseignement."

25. Y. Lenard, "Methods and Materials, Techniques and the Teacher" in Hester, ed. (1970), p. 37.

26. Karl C. Diller, "Linguistic Theories of Language Acquisition," in Hester, ed. (1970), pp. 16–17, 18; and also K. C. Diller, *Generative Grammar, Structural Linguistics, and Language Teaching* (Rowley, Mass.: Newbury House, 1971), pp. 25, 27.

27. Lenard in Hester, ed. (1970), p. 36.

28. Ibid., p. 50.

29. Ibid., p. 55.

30. From Y. Lenard, *Parole et Pensée: Introduction au français d'aujourd'hui,* 2ᵉ éd. (New York: Harper and Row, 1971), p. 341.

31. L. G. Kelly in *25 Centuries of Language Teaching* (Rowley, Mass.: Newbury House, 1969) traces the use of the dialogue in foreign-language teaching back to the *colloquium* of the Middle Ages (p. 120).

32. In a description of direct method techniques in *Méthodologie des langues vivantes* (Paris: Armand Colin, 1921, originally published 1902), C. Schweitzer and E. Simonnot refer to the *scène dialoguée* as *recréative* (pp. 242–43). As well as encouraging creative activity, it is also entertaining (*récréative*).

33. Dialogue No. 7 in Camille Bauer, *La France actuelle,* rev. ed. (Boston: Houghton-Mifflin, 1971), p. 58.

34. There seems to be a misconception among some foreign-language teachers that only learning grammar rules and working deductively and analytically can be called "cognitive." Actually, from the point of view of cognitive psychology, any process which requires students to think, to extract meaning from any symbolic behavior (action, strange utterance, pictorial representation), to work out generalizations from examples or instances (induction), is a cognitive operation. See "The Foreign-Language Teacher and Cognitive Psychology," in Rivers (1972a), pp. 81–83.

35. Earl W. Stevick of the Foreign Service Institute, Washington, D.C., originated the "microwave cycle," which he described in "UHF and Microwaves in Transmitting Language Skills," in E. W. Najam and Carleton T. Hodge, eds., *Language Learning: The Individual and the Process, IJAL* 32, 1, Part 2 (1966), Publication 40 of the Indiana University Research Center in Anthropology, Folklore, and Linguistics, pp. 84–94. In *Adapting and Writing Language Lessons* (Washington, D.C.: Foreign Service Institute, 1971), pp. 310–15, Stevick explains that he developed this device from the question-answer technique of Thomas F. Cummings in *How to Learn a Language* (New York: privately published, 1916), and that he now prefers the term Cummings device. The device has been used with good results in Peace Corps and Foreign Service Institute materials in a variety of languages. Chapter 6 and Appendices P, Q, and R of Stevick (1971) give detailed examples of the device in languages as diverse as English, French, Lao, Bini, Kikuyu, and Ponapean.

36. Stevick (1971), p. 311.

37. Ibid., pp. 312–13.

38. Stevick (1966), p. 92.

39. Stevick (1971), p. 314.

40. Ibid., p. 37.

41. Lenard in Hester, ed. (1970), p. 50, says, "There should be [an oral composition] for every lesson, to be followed the next day by a written one. The oral composition becomes, in fact, the most important exercise of the verbal-active method in building the elements of which fluency is composed: the ability to speak at length, aloud, clearly and confidently, in front of other people, and to use the words and structures that you know freely and correctly in order to say what you mean."

42. Ibid.

43. Ibid., p. 56.

44. Francis A. Cartier reports that a team of programmers under his direction at the Defense Language Institute English Language Branch has developed a series of situational conversations on tape along these lines for individual learning and practice. These tapes seek to elicit certain structures. It was found that students experienced a definite feeling of rapport with the speakers and would work through the tapes several times to try to improve their efforts.

2. AUTONOMOUS INTERACTION

1. Rivers (1968), p. 201.
2. Emma M. Birkmaier, "The Meaning of Creativity in Foreign Language Teaching," *MLJ* 55 (1971), p. 350.
3. Abraham H. Maslow, *Motivation and Personality,* 2nd ed. (New York: Harper and Row, 1970), Chapter 4: "A Theory of Human Motivation" sets out this hierarchy. Its importance in communication in the foreign-language classroom is discussed in Earl W. Stevick, "Before Linguistics and Beneath Method," in Kurt Jankowsky, ed., *Language and International Studies,* Georgetown University Round Table on Languages and Linguistics 1973 (Washington, D.C.: Georgetown University Press, 1973), pp. 99–106.
4. C. B. Paulston and H. R. Selekman, "Interaction Activities in the Foreign Language Classroom or How to Grow a Tulip-Rose," *FLA* 8 (1975), in press.
5. Selekman (1975) tells of the shock and disappointment experienced by one of his students when he discovered that the ostensibly monolingual person to whom he thought he was speaking spoke perfect English.
6. Described fully in Selekman (1975).
7. Alexander Lipson, "Some New Strategies for Teaching Oral Skills," in Robert C. Lugton, ed., *Toward a Cognitive Approach to Second Language Acquisition* (Philadelphia: Center for Curriculum Development, 1971), pp. 231–44.
8. Paulston and Selekman (1975).
9. Lipson (1971), p. 240.
10. Stevick (1971), p. 365–90.
11. Etiemble, *Parlez-vous franglais* (Paris: Gallimard, 1964).
12. P. et T. (Postes et Télécommunications) has now replaced P.T.T. (Postes, Télégraphes et Téléphones).
13. Passage transcribed word for word from a tape of authentic conversation made in Orléans by the Bureau pour l'Enseignement de la Langue et de la Civilisation françaises à l'Etranger (B.E.L.C.), Paris, n.d., for purposes of research into aspects of contemporary spoken French.
14. Stevick (1973), p. 100.
15. Ibid.

3. LISTENING

1. P. T. Rankin, "Listening Ability: Its Importance, Measurement, and Development," *Chicago Schools Journal* 12, pp. 177–79, quoted in D. Spearritt,

Listening Comprehension—A Factorial Analysis (Melbourne: Australian Council for Educational Research, 1962), p. 2.

2. Spearritt (1962), p. 92–93. Spearritt adds, "There is some evidence that performance on listening comprehension tests is related to performance on inductive reasoning, verbal comprehension and certain types of memory tests."

3. R. E. Troike, "Receptive Competence, Productive Competence, and Performance," in J. E. Alatis, ed., *Linguistics and the Teaching of Standard English to Speakers of Other Languages or Dialects,* Report of the Twentieth Annual Round Table Meeting on Linguistics and Language Studies (Washington, D.C.: Georgetown University Press Monograph No. 22, 1970), pp. 63–73.

4. See T. Bever, "The Cognitive Basis for Linguistic Structures," in J. R. Hayes, ed., *Cognition and the Development of Language* (New York: John Wiley and Sons, 1970), and "Linguistic and Psychological Factors in Speech Perception and Their Implications for Teaching Materials," in Rivers (1972a), pp. 94–107.

5. These two levels, the recognition and selection levels, are discussed fully in relation to listening comprehension in Rivers (1968), pp. 142–43.

6. N. Chomsky in *Aspects of the Theory of Syntax* (Cambridge, Mass.: The MIT Press, 1965), p. 9, says that "a generative grammar is not a model for a speaker or a hearer. It attempts to characterize in the most neutral possible terms the knowledge of the language that provides the basis for actual use of language by a speaker-hearer."

7. For some perceptual strategies, see Bever in Hayes, ed. (1970), pp. 287–312.

8. Colin Cherry, *On Human Communication* (New York: John Wiley and Sons, 1957), p. 277.

9. Ibid.

10. B.E.L.C. Index 28 (Sept. 12, 1968), *Délégués syndicaux,* distributed by B.E.L.C., Paris, for research purposes.

11. For a detailed discussion of hearing as a stochastic process, that is, based on expectations, see Charles F. Hockett, "Grammar for the Hearer," in R. Jakobson, ed., *On the Structure of Language and Its Mathematical Aspects* (Providence, R.I.: American Mathematical Society, 1961), pp. 220–36.

12. See G. J. Brault, "Kinesics and the Classroom: Some Typical French Gestures," *FR* 36 (1963), pp. 374–82.

13. Ambiguous sentences in C38 and C39 are based on examples in N. Ruwet, *Introduction à la grammaire générative* (Paris: Plon, 1967) and *Théorie syntaxique et syntaxe du français* (Paris: Editions du Seuil, 1972).

14. The new university system in France and the universities of Paris and the surrounding area are described in R. Ortali, *Entre Nous: Conversation et Culture* (New York: Macmillan, 1972), pp. 28–30.

15. W. von Wartburg and P. Zumthor, *Précis de syntaxe du français contemporain,* 2e éd. (Berne: Francke, 1958), section 411(b), p. 221. Explanations of many nuances of syntax which help with interpretation are easily found in this book because of its detailed index.

16. *France Inter* newscast, September 19, 1973.

17. Most geographical names can be located in the *Petit Larousse*. Proper

names are usually pronounced according to the usual French sound-symbol correspondences, but the teacher should listen to the news broadcast first and prepare the students for idiosyncrasies. Note that most English names ending in *-on* are pronounced /ɔn/ as in /ʒɔnsɔn/ and /niksɔn/.

18. *France Inter* newscast, October 25, 1973.

19. A detailed description of these stages is given in Rivers (1972a), pp. 97–104. See also U. Neisser, *Cognitive Psychology* (New York: Appleton-Century-Crofts, 1967), Chapter 7: Speech Perception.

20. Asher (1966), pp. 79–80.

21. Ibid., pp. 80–82.

22. G. A. Miller's term in "The Magical Number Seven, Plus or Minus Two: Some Limits on Our Capacity for Processing Information," *Psychological Review* 63 (1956), pp. 81–96. Reprinted in G. A. Miller, *The Psychology of Communication: Seven Essays* (New York: Basic Books, 1967).

23. The pros and cons of the backward buildup technique are discussed in detail in Rivers (1968), pp. 171–72.

24. Other structural features which students should learn to recognize rapidly are listed in Rivers (1972a), p. 103.

25. Processes involved in fluent reading are compared with processes of listening in Rivers (1972a), pp. 105–6.

26. From Ortali (1972), p. 44.

27. The information in this paragraph and the quotation are from "Research in Listening Comprehension," by Andrew Wilkinson, *Educational Research* 12 (1970), pp. 140–41.

28. Extracts from Ortali (1972), pp. 238–40.

29. Bever in Hayes, ed. (1970), p. 291.

30. This is basic to the controversy between the transformational-generative grammarians who support the standard theory and the generative semanticists. Chomsky has stated that "there must be, represented in the mind, a fixed system of generative principles that characterize and associate deep and surface structures in some definite way—a grammar, in other words, that is used in some fashion as discourse is produced or interpreted" (*Language and Mind*, 1st ed., 1968, p. 16). According to G. Lakoff, "the theory of generative semantics claims that the linguistic elements used in grammar have an independent natural basis in the human conceptual system.... Generative semantics takes grammar as being based on the independently given natural logical categories, ... and on natural logical classes...." (from "The Arbitrary Basis of Transformational Grammar" in *Language* 48, pp. 77–78).

31. These are basic to Charles Fillmore's Case Grammar. Fillmore adds other functions such as instrument and experiencer.

32. Bever in Hayes, ed. (1970), pp. 286–99. The strategies are described as follows: Strategy A p. 290, Strategy B p. 294, Strategy C p. 296, Strategy D p. 298.

33. In transformational-generative grammar each clause is considered a sentence and assigned the symbol S.

34. I. M. Schlesinger, *Sentence Structure and the Reading Process* (The Hague: Mouton, 1968), pp. 122–41.

35. *France Inter* newscast, October 19, 1973.

36. Prepared by Margaret Denat, University of Melbourne, for the Victorian Universities and Schools Examinations Board, Australia.

37. This chart is a completely revised and expanded version of the one in Rivers (1968), pp. 151–54.

38. Short-term retention, as used in this chart, is not synonymous with short-term memory. Echoic memory is useful for only a few seconds, during which the listener still has recourse to the raw data. Active verbal memory (immediate memory or short-term memory) can hold from five to nine cognitive chunks (e.g., short phrases or groups of digits) created by the listener. This material is then recoded for storage in long-term memory. The expression "short-term retention," as used in this chart, is a pragmatic one, referring to the short interval that elapses before what the student has heard is put to some active use. The student is not expected to hold the material in his memory for use at a later stage, as he is for the long-term retention of Stage D.

39. *Suivez la piste* (Saint Paul, Minn.: EMC Corporation), described as "a detective thriller in French in twenty-five short episodes," is of this type. Based on a BBC television program, it maintains the students' interest by the suspense of the story. The ordinary situations in which the action takes place provide much practice in practical language use (asking someone for help in using a French pay phone, asking the concierge about someone in the building, greeting strangers, telling the time, and so on). More material along these lines would be useful.

40. For examples of standard speech and rapid speech, see Paul Pimsleur, *Le Pont sonore* (Chicago: Rand McNally, 1974).

41. A similar technique is described and discussed by S. Belasco in "C'est la Guerre? or can Cognition and Verbal Behavior Co-exist in Second-Language Learning," in R. C. Lugton, ed. (1971), pp. 223–25. In Belasco's approach. the student is provided from the beginning with a text with visual hints to deviations from standard style of language. Here, at the advanced level, I suggest a purely listening and writing task.

42. The technique of *Reconstitution de texte* is fully described, with examples, in Colette Stourdzé, "De la reconstitution à l'explication de texte," *FM* No. 65 (juin, 1969), pp. 37–47, and in R. Lichet and J-P. Lefebure, "Le texte 'presque reconstitué,'" *FM* No. 74 (juillet-août, 1970), pp. 40–41.

4. ORAL PRACTICE FOR THE LEARNING OF GRAMMAR

1. These are not an exhaustive list of uses of the contracted article, but simply five common uses to which the student is usually introduced in early lessons.

2. Adapted from *A New Method of Learning the French Language: Embracing both the Analytic and Synthetic Modes of Instruction: Being a Plain and Practical Way of Acquiring the Art of Reading, Speaking, and Composing French. On the Plan of Woodbury's Method with German,* by Louis Fasquelle, LL.D. *Revised and Improved.* (New York: Ivison, Phinney, Blakeman and Co., 1869), pp. 33–35. The first edition seems to have appeared in 1850.

3. M. Benamou and E. Ionesco, *Mise en train* (London: Collier-Macmillan, 1969).

4. The use of substitution tables has been traced back to Erasmus in the sixteenth century. See L. Kelly (1969), p. 101. Harold Palmer gives examples of substitution tables and advocates their use in *The Scientific Study and Teaching of Languages* (London: Harrap, 1917).

5. An interesting analysis of drills into mechanical, meaningful, and communication categories is made in C. B. Paulston, "The Sequencing of Structural Pattern Drills," *TQ* 5 (1971), pp. 197–208. The subject is also discussed in "Talking off the Tops of Their Heads," in Rivers (1972a), pp. 20–35.

6. The influence of the position of stress in French is discussed in Chapter 1, C3.

7. The concept of Type A and Type B exercises is developed more fully in W. M. Rivers, "From Linguistic Competence to Communicative Competence," *TQ* 7 (1973). pp. 25–34.

5. TEACHING THE SOUND SYSTEM

1. It is presumed that most trainee teachers and practicing teachers have at some time studied the French sound system. This very sketchy introduction to terminology is included for the benefit of the occasional student to whom it is new. It is customary to use square brackets [k] for phonetic or allophonic representations and slashes /k/ for phonemic representations. Slashes will be used in this chapter, except within specific quotations.

2. For further information on this subject, see S. A. Schane, *Generative Phonology* (Englewood Cliffs, N.J.: Prentice-Hall, 1973) and S. A. Schane, *French Phonology and Morphology* (Cambridge, Mass.: The MIT Press, 1968).

3. A. Martinet, *Eléments de linguistique générale* Nouv. éd. (Paris: Colin, 1970), p. 20. Original edition 1960, p. 25.

4. Ibid., p. 29. Orig. ed., p. 35.

5. Ibid., p. 79. Orig. ed. pp. 72–73. Martinet says that this archiphoneme "ne se scinde nettement en deux phonèmes qu'à la finale du mot, encore que certains sujets essayent parfois de distinguer en parlant le *pêcher* du *péché.*"

6. P. Delattre, *Comparing the Phonetic Features of English, French, German and Spanish* (London: Harrap, 1965), p. 59.

7. P. R. Léon, "Etude de la prononciation du "e" accentué chez un groupe de jeunes Parisiens," in A. Valdman, ed., *Papers in Linguistics and Phonetics to the Memory of Pierre Delattre* (The Hague: Mouton, 1972), pp. 317–27.

8. See A. Malécot, "New Procedures for Descriptive Phonetics," in Valdman, ed. (1972), p. 353.

9. D. Harvey, *Exercices de phonétique corrective pour anglophones* (Paris: B.E.L.C., 1966), p. 82. This is a very useful aid for teachers produced by the Bureau pour l'Enseignement de la Langue et de la Civilisation Françaises à l'Etranger. See also A. Valdman, "The *Loi de Position* as a Pedagogical Norm," in Valdman, ed. (1972), pp. 473–85.

10. See F. M. Jenkins, "The Phonetic Value of Mute-*e*" in *FR* 45 (1971), pp. 82–87.

11. A. Valdman, R. J. Salazar, and M. A. Charbonneaux, *A Drillbook of French Pronunciation,* 2d ed. (New York: Harper and Row. 1970), p. 289.

12. Valdman (1972), p. 481.

13. P. Delattre, "Voyelles diphtonguées et voyelles pures," *FR* 37 (1963), p. 64.

14. Delattre (1965), pp. 55–56.

15. For students who have not completed a course in French phonetics, the terms used by Delattre in this quotation may seem mysterious. Such students should acquire a clear, explanatory text like P. and M. Léon, *Introduction à la phonétique corrective* (Paris: Hachette/Larousse, 1968), as a teaching reference. The expressions *high-low* refer to the highest position of the tongue-hump during articulation and are visually approximated by their position on a vowel triangle or quadrilateral. The higher a vowel the more *fermé* (*close*) it is, and the lower it is the more *ouvert* (*open*) it is. Students should also know the *front-back* (*antérieur-postérieur*) and *rounded-unrounded* (*arrondi-écarté*) distinctions. Instructors are referred to P. and M. Léon (1968), p. 17, and Delattre (1965), p. 47, for further information. They will find useful the comparative charts of the vowel systems of English, French, German, and Spanish in Delattre (1965), pp. 50–51.

16. Teachers will find clearly presented articulatory information, with diagrams and exercises, in M. Léon, *Exercices systématiques de prononciation française,* Fascicule I: *Articulation* (Paris: Hachette/Larousse, 1964). Disks available.

17. Sometimes a student will succeed in making the correct sound in a somewhat different way, but most students will need the teacher's help and will profit from precise instructions.

18. C. H. Prator, Jr., *Manual of American English Pronunciation,* Rev. ed. (New York: Holt, Rinehart and Winston, 1967), p. 83.

19. L. E. Armstrong, *The Phonetics of French* (London: Bell, 1959), p. 110. First published 1932.

20. M. Peyrollaz and M.-L. Bara de Tovar, *Manuel de phonétique et de diction françaises à l'usage des étrangers* (Paris: Larousse, 1954), p. 137.

21. Harvey (1966), Leçon 8, p. 46.

22. Delattre (1965), p. 42. Prospective teachers should refresh their understanding of the differences between French and English syllabification, since these differences have a marked effect on the accent of the foreign speaker. See P. Delattre, *Principes de phonétique française à l'usage des étudiants anglo-américains* (Middlebury, Vt.: Middlebury College, 1951), pp. 18–19 and 39–40, and P. Delattre, *Advanced Training in French Pronunciation* (Middlebury, Vt.: Middlebury College, 1949), pp. 4–5.

23. Stress has been discussed in some detail in chapter 1. *Intonation* is too complicated to deal with here. It should be taught early through imitation of the teacher or tape model. Exercises for a systematic study of intonation are provided in M. Léon (1964), Fascicule 2: *Rythme et intonation.* Disks available.

24. Discussed in Chapter 6.

25. Some phoneticians insert an asterisk to mark proper names. See P. Léon, *Prononciation du français standard* (Paris: Didier, 1966).

26. *Elision, liaison,* and *enchaînement* are discussed fully in Delattre (1951), M. Léon (1964), P. Léon (1965), and R. Politzer, *Teaching French: An Introduction to Applied Linguistics,* 2d ed. (New York: Blaisdell, 1965). Malécot (1972) found in his 1967–68 data, which is representative of "the conversational style of the Parisian 'establishment,'" that liaisons traditionally labeled "optional" were rarely made; many so-called "required" liaisons showed signs of deterioration, particularly among monosyllabic adverbs (*pas / entière-ment, très / efficace, trop / américain*); the *l* of *il* was pronounced before vowels or when *il* was uttered in isolation, but was dropped regularly before consonants, that is, *il va* was pronounced /iva/ (p. 352).

27. Used in A. Valdman et al. (1970), p. 80.

28. These terms are explained in Chapter 1. See also P. Léon (1966), pp. 17–18.

29. Passage written by Margaret E. Davies for evaluation of the pronunciation of incoming French students at Monash University, Victoria, Australia.

II The Written Word
6. READING I: PURPOSES AND PROCEDURES

1. More research is needed to determine which basic grammatical relations in French are essential to enable a person to read French with comprehension.

2. J. McGlathery describes such a course in "A New Program of Substitute and Supplementary German Language Courses," in W. M. Rivers, L. H. Allen, et al., eds., *Changing Patterns in Foreign Language Programs* (Rowley, Mass.: Newbury House, 1972), pp. 248–53.

3. Selected sentences from Bauer (1971), pp. 4–5.

4. Some students are able to reach this stage more rapidly through the experience of living for a time in a French community—unfortunately many are not.

5. Thierry Maulnier, *Le Figaro,* 1er février, 1962. Reprinted in *Les Meilleures Pages du* Figaro, G. F. Courtney, ed. (London: Longmans, 1963).

6. The method of establishing the frequency lists of *Le Français fondamental* is described in G. Gougenheim, P. Rivenc, et al., *L'Elaboration du français fondamental (1er degré)* (Paris: Didier, 1964).

7. Texts of French prose of the nineteenth and twentieth centuries were used. The list is given on pp. 7–9 of G. E. Vander Beke, *French Word Book* (New York: Macmillan, 1929).

8. These sixty-nine words are the most frequent words listed in V. Henmon's *French Word Book Based on a Count of 400,000 Running Words* (Madison, Wis.: Bureau of Educational Research Bulletin, No. 3, 1924). Vander Beke sets them out before beginning his own list. See Vander Beke (1929), p. 17.

9. The sixty-nine words from Henmon include words such as *à, de, comme, dans, en, que,* and various pronouns and common verbs.

10. Gougenheim et al. (1964), p. 146.

11. M. Aymé, "Les Bœufs," from *Les Contes du Chat Perché* in *Contes et Nouvelles* (Paris: Gallimard, 1953), pp. 725–36.

12. N. Brooks, *Language and Language Learning: Theory and Practice*, 2d ed. (New York: Harcourt, Brace & World, 1964), pp. 120–25.

13. I have explained this concept more fully in "Linguistic and Psychological Factors in Speech Perception with their Implications for Teaching Materials," in Rivers (1972a), pp. 94–107.

14. D. Côté, S. Levy, and P. O'Connor, *Ecouter et Parler*, rev. ed. (New York: Holt, Rinehart and Winston, 1968), p. 22.

15. Remunda Cadoux, *Vous et Moi: Invitation au Français, Un* (New York: Macmillan, 1970), pp. 16, 22. This book also uses *dialogues originaux* to supplement classroom *conversations* like these.

16. Côté, Levy, and O'Connor (1968), p. 23.

17. Cadoux (1970), p. 44.

18. Benamou and Ionesco (1969), p. 48.

19. *A-L M French Level One*, 2d ed., Modern Language Staff of Harcourt, Brace, and World (New York: 1969), pp. 132–33.

20. P. Pimsleur, *C'est la vie* (New York: Harcourt, Brace and World, 1970), pp. 3–6.

21. As in the reading method described in Rivers (1968), pp. 22–24.

22. Denis Grayson, *A la page*, Book I (London: Ginn, 1964), pp. 15–16.

23. *French: Reading for Meaning* by the Modern Language Staff of Harcourt, Brace and World (New York: 1966), p. 8.

7. READING II: FROM DEPENDENCE TO INDEPENDENCE

1. I have discussed the matter of systems and subsystems of language in "Contrastive Linguistics in Textbook and Classroom," in Rivers (1972a), pp. 36–44.

2. *Valeur temporelle* and *aspect* are discussed in J.-C. Chevalier et al., *Grammaire Larousse du français contemporain* (Paris: Larousse, 1964), pp. 328–35. *Aspect* is discussed further in Chapter 8, in association with W31.

3. I am distinguishing here between (1) How (manner)? questions like: *Comment est-ce qu'il a ouvert la porte? Il a ouvert la porte avec la clé* (directly quoted from the text), and (2) How (explanation)? questions like: *Comment pouvait-elle savoir que sa voisine n'était pas à la maison? Parce que toutes les fenêtres étaient fermées et que sa voisine les laissait toujours ouvertes* (drawn from several parts of the text).

4. G. A. C. Scherer, "Programming Second Language Reading," in G. Mathieu, ed., *Advances in the Teaching of Modern Languages*, Vol. 2 (London: Pergamon, 1966), p. 113.

5. Ibid., pp. 114–15.

6. Ibid., p. 120.

7. From *"Les Mots qu'il faudrait . . ."* by Roch Carrier, in K. Brearley and R.-B. McBride, eds., *Nouvelles du Québec* (Scarborough, Ont.: Prentice Hall of Canada, 1970), p. 14.

8. From "La Joie dans le bocal" by Adrien Therio, in Brearley and McBride (1970), p. 132.

9. Scherer (1966), p. 123.

10. Stuart Hoffman, quoted in *Glamour,* August 1972, p. 39.

11. Adapted from *L'Elève fatigué* in Courtney (1963).

12. W. G. Moulton, *A Linguistic Guide to Language Learning* (New York: M.L.A., 1966), p. 18.

13. For further discussion along these lines see "Linguistic and Psychological Factors in Speech Perception . . ." in Rivers (1972a), pp. 94–107.

8. WRITING AND WRITTEN EXERCISES I: THE NUTS AND BOLTS

1. L. S. Vygotsky, *Thought and Language,* trans. E. Hanfmann and G. Vakar (Cambridge, Mass.: The MIT Press, 1962), p. 97.

2. Differences between spoken and written language have been discussed in Chapter 1 (C2–6). The subject should be studied in depth in syntax classes for future teachers.

3. M. Aupècle, "La langue française écrite en milieu étranger à l'école primaire," in *FM* No. 99 (1973), p. 26. Even more elaborate combination tables from R. Moody and N. Arapoff are reproduced in C. B. Paulston, "Teaching Writing in the ESOL Classroom: Techniques of Controlled Composition," *TQ* 6 (1972), pp. 43–44, where they are called "correlative substitution exercises."

4. Clearly there are many exceptions to nearly all the categories one might set up in this area. Some are more dependable than others, e.g., *-isme* m.: *le communisme, le fascisme,* etc. One generalization to be avoided is that nouns ending in *e* are feminine: this is not so and the students will cite *le livre* and *le maître* which they know already. On the other hand, *-ée* f. is predictable, e.g., *arriver, l'arrivée; entrer, l'entrée,* and *-té* f. is very useful, e.g., *la beauté, la qualité, la quantité,* etc.

5. Deduction and induction are discussed at the beginning of Chapter 4.

6. According to Piaget's theory of cognitive development, it is not until somewhere between twelve and fifteen years that the average child reaches the stage of "formal operations," where he is able freely to use verbal, symbolic forms of reasoning. See J. S. Bruner, R. R. Olver, et al., *Studies in Cognitive Growth* (New York: John Wiley & Sons, 1966).

7. It is difficult to randomize deliberately the positions of the correct answers in a pattern of A's, B's, and C's. One way of ensuring that one is not subconsciously arranging them in some way is to allot numbers to the letters and then arrange the correct choices according to a set of telephone numbers selected at random from the telephone book. E.g., A = 1; B = 2; C = 3; D = 4; E = 5; F = 6; the phone numbers are 352-1808, 463-7496, 359-1990; the pattern of correct answers for twelve questions will be C E B A D F C D F C E A. The first part of this randomization has been applied to W14.

8. The whimsicality of the extrapolation in this title is admitted. It was by means of comparison with the same inscription in demotic and classical Greek that Champollion was able to decipher the hieroglyphics on the Rosetta Stone.

9. I have given here the most frequent forms of *devoir* that students will encounter. The full complexities of the subject should be studied by the teacher

in an advanced grammar book. Note that the *présent* (*je dois*) is the most ambiguous. It should be remembered that, in modern French, "il faut que je le fasse" is preferred for a constraint and the expression "j'ai tout ce travail *à faire* avant demain" indicates a necessity. Since the *conditionnel* is frequently used in French to attenuate the more direct present tense (as in "je voudrais le voir tout de suite"), "vous devriez le lui rendre sans délai" is the polite way of telling other people what they ought to do. "Je sais bien que je devrais le faire tout de suite" is often followed by *mais* (I know I should do it now but ... I have so much to do at the moment!).

10. For a definition of *aspect,* see Wartburg and Zumthor (1958), section 334, pp. 182–3. See also Chapter 7, note 2.

11. Some modern textbooks prefer to use the term *mode* for the indicative, subjunctive, and imperative, because the older term *mood* has misleading connotations.

12. R. Braddock, R. Lloyd-Jones, and L. Schoer, *Research in Written Composition* (Champaign, Ill.: National Council of Teachers of English, 1963), p. 83.

13. This was the finding also for native English writers in the Buxton Study, reported in Braddock et al., (1963), pp. 58–70.

9. WRITING AND WRITTEN EXERCISES II: FLEXIBILITY AND EXPRESSION

1. The material for W35 and W36 is from P. Daninos, *Snobissimo* (Paris: Hachette, 1964), p. 109.

2. *Avoir le respect du radiateur* alludes to the fact that over a long period the distinctive form of the Rolls radiator, with its emblem, did not change. As a result it could easily be identified as the aristocratic car it was.

3. M. Bracy, "Controlled Writing vs: Free Composition," *TQ* 5 (1971), p. 244.

4. For further suggestions along these lines, see K. Sandburg's "writing laboratories," quoted in Paulston (1972), pp. 57–58.

5. V. Postovsky, "Effects of Delay in Oral Practice at the Beginning of Second Language Learning," dissertation written at the University of California, Berkeley, in 1970, and reported by S. Ervin-Tripp, "Structure and Process in Language Acquisition," in J. E. Alatis, ed., *Bilingualism and Language Contact: Anthropological, Linguistic, Psychological, and Sociological Aspects,* Monograph No. 23 (Washington, D.C.: Georgetown University Press, 1970), p. 340.

6. M. Benamou, *Pour une nouvelle pédagogie du texte littéraire* (Paris: Hachette/Larousse, 1971), pp. 12–13. See also his article, "Propositions pour une pédagogie de la littérature à l'étranger," in *FM* 77 (décembre, 1970), which is a special number entitled *L'Enseignement de la littérature française aux étrangers.* Other useful references for the teaching of literature are: H. Mitterand, "La Stylistique," *FM* 42 (juillet-août, 1966), pp. 13–18; T. E. Bird, ed., *Foreign Languages: Reading, Literature, and Requirements* (1967 *NEC*); and *MLJ* 56 (1972), of which the theme is "The Teaching of Foreign Literatures" (W. Lohnes special ed.).

7. N. Arapoff, "Writing: a Thinking Process," *TQ* 1 (1967), pp. 33–39. Reprinted in H. B. Allen and R. N. Campbell, eds., *Teaching English as a Second Language: A Book of Readings,* 2d Ed. (New York: McGraw-Hill, 1972), pp. 199–207.

8. N. Arapoff, "Discover and Transform: A Method of Teaching Writing to Foreign Students," in *TQ* 3 (1969), p. 298.

9. This subject is discussed in an interesting article by R. B. Kaplan, "Cultural Thought Patterns in Inter-Cultural Education," *LL* 16 (1966), pp. 1–20, reprinted in K. Croft, ed., *Readings on English as a Second Language* (Cambridge, Mass.: Winthrop, 1972).

10. A number of possibilities for diversification are described in W. M. Rivers, L. H. Allen, et al., eds., *Changing Patterns in Foreign Language Programs* (Rowley, Mass.: Newbury House, 1972).

11. Formulas for beginning and ending all kinds of letters, as well as for greetings, invitations, and announcements, are set out in R. Damoiseau, "Code des convenances épistolaires," in *FM* 76 (octobre-novembre, 1970), pp. 33–40.

12. Arapoff (1967) in Allen and Campbell (1972), p. 200.

13. R. M. Valette, "Developing and Evaluating Communication Skills in the Classroom," *TQ* 7 (1973), pp. 417–18.

14. Francis Bacon, *Of Studies* (1598).

15. R. L. Lyman, "A Co-operative Experiment in Junior High School Composition" (1931), quoted in Braddock et al. (1963), p. 35.

16. D. Knapp, "A Focused, Efficient Method to Relate Composition Correction to Teaching Aims," in Allen and Campbell (1972), pp. 213–21.

17. See "The Writer Variable" in Braddock et al. (1963), pp. 6–7, where the research of G. L. Kincaid and C. C. Anderson is reported.

18. For more information on inferencing, see Aaron S. Carton, "Inferencing: A Process in Using and Learning Language," in P. Pimsleur and T. Quinn, eds., *The Psychology of Second Language Learning* (Cambridge, Eng.: Cambridge University Press, 1971), pp. 45–58.

19. Teachers interested in translation should be familiar with books like E. A. Nida, *Toward a Science of Translating* (Leiden: E. J. Brill, 1964) and J-P. Vinay and J. Darbelnet, *Stylistique comparée du français et de l'anglais* (Paris: Didier, 1958). See also W. M. Rivers, "Contrastive Linguistics in Textbook and Classroom," in Rivers (1972a), pp. 36–44.

20. Note that, since these questions apply to both *version* and *thème,* the expression "source text" refers to a text in either French or English, and the "target language" is the one into which the passage is being translated.

21. From B. Malamud, *The Fixer* (New York: Farrar, Straus and Giroux, 1966), p. 215.

22. *Faux amis* are discussed in *Reading for Information* in Chapter 6.

23. A is from *Le Petit Prince* (New York: Reynal and Hitchcock, 1943), p. 8, and B is from *The Little Prince,* translated from the French by Katherine Woods (New York: Harcourt, Brace and World, 1943), p. 8.

24. A is from *L'Etranger* (Paris: Gallimard, 1942), p. 86, and B is from *The Stranger,* translated from the French by Stuart Gilbert (New York: Alfred A. Knopf and Random House, 1946), p. 74.

General bibliography

Alatis, J. E., ed. 1969. *Linguistics and the Teaching of Standard English to Speakers of Other Languages or Dialects.* Georgetown University Round Table on Languages and Linguistics. Washington, D.C.: Georgetown University Press.

———, ed. 1970. *Bilingualism and Language Contact: Anthropological, Linguistic, Psychological, and Sociological Aspects.* Georgetown University Round Table on Languages and Linguistics. Washington, D.C.: Georgetown University Press.

Allen, E. D., and Valette, R. M. 1972. *Modern Language Classroom Techniques: A Handbook.* New York: Harcourt Brace Jovanovich.

Allen, H. B., and Campbell, R. N., eds. 1972. *Teaching English as a Second Language: A Book of Readings.* 2d ed. New York: McGraw-Hill.

Alter, M. P. 1970. *A Modern Case for German.* Philadelphia: American Association of Teachers of German.

Altman, H. B., ed. 1972. *Individualizing the Foreign Language Classroom: Perspectives for Teachers.* Rowley, Mass.: Newbury House.

Altman, H. B., and Politzer, R. L., eds. 1971. *Individualizing Foreign Language Instruction.* Rowley, Mass.: Newbury House.

Arapoff, N. 1967. "Writing: A Thinking Process." *TQ* 1:33–39.

———. 1969. "Discover and Transform: A Method of Teaching Writing to Foreign Students." *TQ* 3:297–304.

Armstrong, L. E. 1959. *The Phonetics of French.* London: Bell. First published 1932.

Asher, J. J. 1966. "The Learning Strategy of the Total Physical Response: A Review." *MLJ* 50:79–84.

Belasco, S. 1970. "C'est la Guerre? or Can Cognition and Verbal Behavior Co-exist in Second-Language Learning?" *MLJ* 54:395–412. Reprinted in Lugton, R. C., ed. (1971), pp. 191–230.

Benamou, M. 1971. *Pour une nouvelle pédagogie du texte littéraire.* Paris: Hachette/Larousse.

Birkmaier, E. M., ed. 1968. *Foreign Language Education: An Overview.* Britannica Review of Foreign Language Education, Vol. 1. Chicago: Encyclopaedia Britannica.

———. 1971. "The Meaning of Creativity in Foreign Language Teaching." *MLJ* 55:345–53.

Bracy, M. 1971. "Controlled Writing vs: Free Composition." *TQ* 5:239–46.

Braddock, R., Lloyd-Jones, R., and Schoer, L. 1963. *Research in Written Composition.* Champaign, Ill.: National Council of Teachers of English.

Brault, G. J. 1963. "Kinesics and the Classroom: Some Typical French Gestures." *FR* 36:374–82.

Brooks, N. 1964. *Language and Language Learning: Theory and Practice.* 2d ed. New York: Harcourt, Brace & World.

Burney, P., and Damoiseau, R. 1969. *La Classe de conversation.* Paris: Hachette.

Chastain, K. 1971. *The Development of Modern Language Skills: Theory to Practice.* Philadelphia: Center for Curriculum Development.

Chevalier, J.-C. et al. 1964. *Grammaire Larousse du français contemporain.* Paris: Larousse.

Crawshaw, B. 1972. *Let's Play Games in French.* Skokie, Ill.: National Textbook Company.

Croft, K., ed. 1972. *Readings on English as a Second Language.* Cambridge, Mass.: Winthrop.

Damoiseau, R. 1970. "Code des convenances épistolaires." *FM* 76:33–40.

Delattre, P. 1949. *Advanced Training in French Pronunciation.* Middlebury, Vt.: Middlebury College.

———. 1951. *Principes de phonétique française à l'usage des étudiants anglo-américains.* Middlebury, Vt.: Middlebury College.

———. 1963. "Voyelles diphtonguées et voyelles pures." *FR* 37:64–76.

———. 1965. *Comparing the Phonetic Features of English, French, German and Spanish.* London: Harrap.

Diller, K. C. 1971. *Generative Grammar, Structural Linguistics, and Language Teaching.* Rowley, Mass.: Newbury House.

Dubois, Jean et al. 1966. *Dictionnaire du français contemporain.* Paris: Larousse.

Dodge, J. W., ed. 1971. *The Case for Foreign Language Study.* New York: Northeast Conference and MLA/ACTFL.

Etiemble. 1964. *Parlez-vous franglais?* Paris: Gallimard.

Fries, C. C. 1945. *Teaching and Learning English as a Foreign Language.* Ann Arbor, Mich.: University of Michigan Press.

Gattegno, C. 1963. *Teaching Foreign Languages in Schools: The Silent Way.* Reading, Eng.: Educational Explorers.

George, H. V. 1972. *Common Errors in Language Learning: Insights from English.* Rowley, Mass.: Newbury House.

Girard, D. 1974. *Les Langues vivantes.* Paris: Larousse.

Gougenheim, G., Rivenc, P., et al. 1964. *L'Elaboration du français fondamental (1er degré).* Paris: Didier.

Gouin, F. 1892. *The Art of Teaching and Studying Languages.* Trans. H. Swan and V. Bétis. London: George Philip and Son; New York: Charles Scribner's Sons.

Grevisse, M. 1964. *Le Bon Usage.* Gembloux: J. Duculot.

Grittner, F. 1969. *Teaching Foreign Languages.* New York: Harper and Row.

————, and LaLeike, F. H. 1973. *Individualized Foreign Language Instruction.* Skokie, Ill.: National Textbook Company.

Harris, D. P. 1969. *Testing English as a Second Language.* New York: McGraw-Hill.

Harvey, D. 1966. *Exercices de phonétique corrective pour anglophones.* Paris: Bureau pour l'Enseignement de la Langue et de la Civilisation françaises à l'Etranger.

Henmon, V. 1924. *French Word Book Based on a Count of 400,000 Running Words.* Madison, Wis.: Bureau of Educational Research Bulletin No. 3.

Hester, R., ed. 1970. *Teaching a Living Language.* New York: Harper and Row.

Howes, V. M., ed. 1970. *Individualization of Instruction: A Teaching Strategy.* New York: Macmillan.

Jakobovits, L. A. 1970. *Foreign Language Learning: A Psycholinguistic Analysis of the Issues.* Rowley, Mass.: Newbury House.

————, and Gordon, B. 1974. *The Context of Foreign Language Teaching.* Rowley, Mass.: Newbury House.

Jankowsky, K., ed. 1973. *Language and International Studies.* Georgetown University Round Table on Languages and Linguistics. Washington, D.C.: Georgetown University Press.

Jespersen, O. 1904. *How to Teach a Foreign Language.* London: George Allen & Unwin. Reissued, 1961.

Jarvis, G. A., ed. 1974. *Responding to New Realities.* ACTFL Review of Foreign Language Education, Vol. 5. Skokie, Ill.: National Textbook Company.

————., ed. 1975. *The Challenge of Communication.* ACTFL Review of Foreign Language Education, Vol. 6. Skokie, Ill.: National Textbook Company.

Kaplan, R. B. 1966. "Cultural Thought Patterns in Inter-Cultural Education." *LL* 16:1–20.

Kelly, L. G. 1969. *25 Centuries of Language Teaching.* Rowley, Mass.: Newbury House.

Knapp, D. 1972. "A Focused, Efficient Method to Relate Composition Correction to Teaching Aims." In Allen, H. B., and Campbell, R. N., eds. (1972), pp. 213–21.

Lambert, W. E., and Tucker, R. 1972. *The Bilingual Education of Children.* Rowley, Mass.: Newbury House.

Lange, D. L., ed. 1970. *Individualization of Instruction.* Britannica Review of Foreign Language Education, Vol. 2. Chicago: Encyclopaedia Britannica.

————, ed. 1971. *Pluralism in Foreign Language Education.* Britannica Review of Foreign Language Education, Vol. 3, Chicago: Encyclopaedia Britannica.

————, and James, C. J., eds. 1972. *Foreign Language Education: A Reappraisal.* ACTFL Review of Foreign Language Education, Vol. 4. Skokie, Ill.: National Textbook Company.

Lenard, Y. 1970. "Methods and Materials, Techniques and the Teacher." In Hester, R., ed. (1970), pp. 33–64.

Léon, M. 1964. *Exercices systématiques de prononciation française.* Fascicule I: *Articulation.* Fascicule II: *Rythme et Intonation.* Paris: Hachette/Larousse.

Léon, P. 1966. *Prononciation du français standard.* Paris: Didier.

Léon, P. and M. 1968. *Introduction à la phonétique corrective.* Paris: Hachette/Larousse.

Logan, G. E. 1973. *Individualized Foreign Language Learning: an Organic Process.* Rowley, Mass.: Newbury House.

Lohnes, W., spec. ed. 1972. *The Teaching of Foreign Literatures* (theme). *MLJ* 56, No. 5.

Love, F. W., and Honig, L. J. 1973. *Options and Perspectives: A Sourcebook of Innovative Foreign Language Programs in Action K-12.* New York: Modern Language Association.

Lugton, R. C., ed. 1971. *Toward a Cognitive Approach to Second Language Acquisition.* Philadelphia: Center for Curriculum Development.

Moskowitz, G. 1970. *The Foreign Language Teacher Interacts.* Rev. ed. Minneapolis: Association for Productive Teaching.

Moulton, W. G. 1966. *A Linguistic Guide to Language Learning.* New York: Modern Language Association.

Nida, E. A. 1964. *Toward a Science of Translating.* Leiden: E. J. Brill.

Northeast Conference (1959): F. D. Eddy, ed. *The Language Learner.* Containing: Modern Foreign Language Learning: Assumptions and Implications; A Six-Year Sequence; Elementary and Junior High School Curricula; Definition of Language Competences Through Testing.

Northeast Conference (1960): G. R. Bishop, ed. *Culture in Language Learning.* Containing: An Anthropological Concept of Culture; Language as Culture; Teaching of Western European Cultures; Teaching of Classical Cultures; Teaching of Slavic Cultures.

Northeast Conference (1961): S. L. Flaxman, ed. *Modern Language Teaching in School and College.* Containing: The Training of Teachers for Secondary Schools; The Preparation of College and University Teachers; The Transition to the Classroom; Coordination between Classroom and Laboratory.

Northeast Conference (1962): W. F. Bottiglia, ed. *Current Issues in Language*

Teaching. Containing: Linguistics and Language Teaching: Programmed Learning; A Survey of FLES Practices; Televised Teaching.

Northeast Conference (1963): W. F. Bottiglia, ed. *Language Learning: The Intermediate Phase*. Containing: The Continuum: Listening and Speaking; Reading for Meaning; Writing as Expression.

Northeast Conference (1964): G. F. Jones, ed. *Foreign Language Teaching: Ideals and Practices*. Containing: Foreign Languages in the Elementary School; Foreign Languages in the Secondary School; Foreign Languages in Colleges and Universities.

Northeast Conference (1965): G. R. Bishop, ed. *Foreign Language Teaching: Challenges to the Profession*. Containing: The Case for Latin; Study Abroad; The Challenge of Bilingualism; From School to College.

Northeast Conference (1966): R. G. Mead, Jr., ed. *Language Teaching: Broader Contexts*. Containing: Research and Language Learning: Content and Crossroads: Wider Uses for Foreign Languages; The Coordination of Foreign-Language Teaching.

Northeast Conference (1967): T. E. Bird, ed. *Foreign Languages: Reading, Literature, and Requirements*. Containing: The Teaching of Reading; The Times and Places for Literature; Trends in FL Requirements and Placement.

Northeast Conference (1968): T. E. Bird, ed. *Foreign Language Learning: Research and Development*. Containing: Innovative FL Programs; The Classroom Revisited; Liberated Expression.

Northeast Conference (1969): M. F. Edgerton, Jr., ed. *Sight and Sound: The Sensible and Sensitive Use of Audio-Visual Aids*. Containing: Non-Projected Visuals; Sound Recordings; Slides and Filmstrips; The Overhead Projector; Motion Pictures; Television; Let Us Build Bridges.

Northeast Conference (1970): J. Tursi, ed. *Foreign Languages and the "New" Student*. Containing: A Relevant Curriculum: An Instrument for Polling Student Opinion; Motivation in FL Learning; FL's for All Children?

Northeast Conference (1971): J. W. Dodge, ed. *Leadership for Continuing Development*. Containing: Professional Responsibilities; Inservice Involvement in the Process of Change; Innovative Trends in FL Teaching; Literature for Advanced FL Students.

Northeast Conference (1972): J. W. Dodge, ed. *Other Words, Other Worlds: Language-in-Culture*. Containing: On Teaching Another Language as Part of Another Culture; Sociocultural Aspects of FL Study; Ancient Greek and Roman Culture; France; Quebec: French Canada; An Approach to Courses in German Culture; Italy and the Italians; Japan: Spirit and Essence; The Soviet Union; Spain; Spanish America: A Study in Diversity.

Northeast Conference (1973): J. W. Dodge, ed. *Sensitivity in the Foreign-Language Classroom*. Containing: Interaction in the FL Class; Teaching Spanish to the Native Spanish Speaker; Individualization of Instruction.

Northeast Conference (1974): J. Tursi, ed. *Toward Student-Centered Foreign-Language Programs*. Containing: The Teacher in the Student-Centered

FL Program; Implementing Student-Centered FL Programs; FL's and the Community.

Northeast Conference (1975): Warren C. Born, ed. *Goals Clarification: Curriculum, Teaching, Testing.*

Oller, J., Jr., and Richards, J., eds. 1973. *Focus on the Learner.* Rowley, Mass.: Newbury House.

Palmer, H. 1917. *The Scientific Study and Teaching of Languages.* London: Harrap.

Paulston, C. B. 1971. "The Sequencing of Structural Pattern Drills." *TQ* 5:197–208.

———. 1972. "Teaching Writing in the ESOL Classroom: Techniques of Controlled Composition." *TQ* 6:33–59.

———, and Selekman, H. R. "Interaction Activities in the Foreign Language Classroom or How to Grow a Tulip-Rose." *FLA* 8, in press.

Peyrollaz, M., and Bara de Tovar, M.-L. 1954. *Manuel de phonétique et de diction françaises à l'usage des étrangers.* Paris: Larousse.

Pillet, R. A. 1974. *Foreign-Language Study: Perspective and Prospect.* Chicago: The University of Chicago Press.

Politzer, R. L. 1965. *Teaching French: An Introduction to Applied Linguistics.* 2d ed. New York: Blaisdell.

Prator, C. H. 1957. *Manual of American English Pronunciation.* Rev. ed. New York: Holt, Rinehart & Winston.

Reichmann, E., ed. *The Teaching of German: Problems and Methods.* Philadelphia; National Carl Schurz Association.

Rivers, W. M. 1964. *The Psychologist and the Foreign-Language Teacher.* Chicago: The University of Chicago Press.

———. 1968. *Teaching Foreign-Language Skills.* Chicago: The University of Chicago Press.

———. 1972a. *Speaking in Many Tongues.* Rowley, Mass.: Newbury House.

———, Allen, L. H., et al., eds. 1972b. *Changing Patterns in Foreign Language Programs.* Rowley, Mass.: Newbury House.

———. 1973a. "From Linguistic Competence to Communicative Competence." *TQ* 7:25–34.

———. 1973b. "Testing and Student Learning." In O'Brien, M. C., ed., *Testing in Second Language Teaching: New Dimensions.* Dublin: Association of Teachers of English as a Second or Other Language and Dublin University Press, pp. 27–36.

———. 1973c. "The Non-Major: Tailoring the Course to Fit the Person—not the Image." In Jankowsky, K., ed., pp. 85–97. Also *ADFL Bulletin 5,* 2:12–18.

———. In press. "Students, Teachers and the Future." *FLA.*

Robert, Paul. 1969. *Dictionnaire alphabétique et analogique de la langue française.* Paris: Société du nouveau Littré. (Called "Le petit Robert.")

Sauzé, E. B. de. 1920. *The Cleveland Plan for the Teaching of Modern Languages with Special Reference to French.* Philadelphia: The John C. Winston Company.

Scherer, G. A. C. 1966. "Programming Second Language Reading." In

Mathieu, G., ed *Advances in the Teaching of Modern Languages*. Vol. 2. London: Pergamon, pp. 108–29.

Schumann, J. 1972. "Communication Techniques." *TQ* 6:143–46.

Schweitzer, C., and Simonnot, E. 1921. *Méthodologie des langues vivantes*. Paris: Armand Colin. Originally published 1902.

Seelye, H. N. 1974. *Teaching Culture: Strategies for Foreign Language Educators*. Skokie, Ill.: National Textbook Company/ACTFL.

Spolsky, B., ed. 1972. *The Language Education of Minority Children*. Rowley, Mass.: Newbury House.

Stack, E. M. 1966. *The Language Laboratory and Modern Language Teaching*. Rev. ed. New York: Oxford University Press.

Stevick, E. W. 1966. "UHF and Microwaves in Transmitting Language Skills." In Najam, E. W. and Hodge, C. T., eds., *Language Learning: The Individual and the Process. IJAL* 32, Part 2. Publication 40 of the Indiana University Research Center in Anthropology, Folklore, and Linguistics.

———. 1971. *Adapting and Writing Language Lessons*. Washington, D.C.: Foreign Service Institute.

———. 1973. "Before Linguistics and Beneath Method." In Jankowsky, K., ed. (1973), pp. 99–106.

Sweet, H. 1899. *The Practical Study of Languages*. London: Dent. Reprinted 1964. London: Oxford University Press.

Titone, R. 1968. *Teaching Foreign Languages: An Historical Sketch*. Washington, D.C.: Georgetown University Press.

Valdman, A. *Introduction to French Phonology and Morphology*. Rowley, Mass.: Newbury House, in press.

Valette, R. M. 1967. *Modern Language Testing: A Handbook*. New York: Harcourt, Brace & World.

———, and Disick, R. S. 1972. *Modern Language Performance Objectives and Individualization: A Handbook*. New York: Harcourt Brace Jovanovich.

———. 1973. "Developing and Evaluating Communication Skills in the Classroom." *TQ* 7:407–24.

Vander Beke, G. E. 1929. *French Word Book*. New York: Macmillan.

Vinay, J. P., and Darbelnet, J. 1963. *Stylistique comparée du français et de l'anglais*. Paris: Didier.

Wartburg, W. von, and Zumthor, P. 1958. *Précis de syntaxe du français contemporain*. 2e édition. Berne: Francke.

West, M. 1941. *Learning to Read a Foreign Language and Other Essays on Language-Teaching*. London: Longmans.

Wilkins, D. A. 1972. *Linguistics in Language Teaching*. Cambridge, Mass.: The MIT Press.

Supplemental bibliography

SOME INTRODUCTORY READINGS IN LINGUISTICS
AND PSYCHOLOGY OF LANGUAGE LEARNING

Bolinger, D. 1968. *Aspects of Language*. New York: Harcourt, Brace & World.

Bruner, J. S., Olver, R. R., et al. 1966. *Studies in Cognitive Growth*. New York: John Wiley & Sons.

Carroll, J. B., and Freedle, R. O., eds. 1972. *Language Comprehension and the Acquisition of Knowledge*. Washington, D.C.: V. H. Winston & Sons.

Chafe, W. 1970. *Meaning and the Structure of Language*. Chicago: The University of Chicago Press.

Cherry, C. 1957. *On Human Communication*. New York: John Wiley & Sons.

Chomsky, N. 1957. *Syntactic Structures*. The Hague: Mouton.

————. 1965. *Aspects of the Theory of Syntax*. Cambridge, Mass.: The MIT Press.

————. 1972. *Language and Mind*. Enlarged Ed. New York: Harcourt Brace Jovanovich. Original ed. 1968.

————. 1972. *Studies on Semantics in Generative Grammar*. The Hague: Mouton.

Csécsy, M. 1968. *De la linguistique à la pédagogie: le verbe français*. Paris: Hachette/Larousse.

Dubois, J. 1965. *Grammaire structurale du français: nom et pronom*. Paris: Larousse.

————. 1967. *Grammaire structurale du français: le verbe*. Paris: Larousse.

————. 1969. *Grammaire structurale du français: la phrase et les transforma-
    tions*. Paris: Larousse.

————, and Dubois-Charlier, F. 1970. *Eléments de linguistique française:
    syntaxe*. Paris: Larousse.

Elgin, S. H. 1973. *What Is Linguistics?* Englewood Cliffs, N.J.: Prentice-Hall.

Ervin-Tripp, S. M. 1973. *Language Acquisition and Communicative Choice*.
    Selected and introduced by A. S. Dil. Stanford: Stanford University
    Press.

Ferguson, C. A., and Slobin, D. I., eds. 1973. *Studies of Child Language De-
    velopment*. New York: Holt, Rinehart & Winston.

Fishman, J. A. 1971. *Sociolinguistics: A Brief Introduction*. Rowley, Mass.:
    Newbury House.

Gardner, R. C., and Lambert, W. E. 1972. *Attitudes and Motivation in Second-
    Language Learning*. Rowley, Mass.: Newbury House.

Hayes, J. R., ed. 1970. *Cognition and the Development of Language*. New
    York: John Wiley & Sons.

Hockett, C. 1961. "Grammar for the Hearer." In Jakobson, R., ed., *On the
    Structure of Language and Its Mathematical Aspects*. Providence, R.I.:
    American Mathematical Society, pp. 220–36.

Huey, E. B. 1968. *The Psychology and Pedagogy of Reading*. Cambridge,
    Mass.: The MIT Press. Original publication: Macmillan, 1908.

Joos, M. 1961. *The Five Clocks*. New York: Harcourt, Brace & World.

Lakoff, G. 1971. "On Generative Semantics." In Steinberg, D. D., and Jako-
    bovits, L. A., eds., *Semantics*. Cambridge, Eng.: Cambridge University
    Press, pp. 232–96.

————. 1972. "The Arbitrary Basis of Transformational Grammar." *Language*
    48: 76–87.

Lakoff, R. 1972. "Language in Context." *Language* 48:907–27.

Lambert, W. E. 1972. *Language, Psychology and Culture*. Selected and intro-
    duced by A. S. Dil. Stanford: Stanford University Press.

Langacker, R. W. 1967. *Language and Its Structure: Some Fundamental Lin-
    guistic Concepts*. New York: Harcourt, Brace & World.

Lyons, J. 1968. *Introduction to Theoretical Linguistics*. Cambridge, Eng.:
    Cambridge University Press.

Martinet, A. 1960. *Eléments de linguistique générale*. Paris: Colin. Nouv. éd.
    1973.

Maslow, A. H. 1970. *Motivation and Personality*. 2d ed. New York: Harper
    and Row.

Miller, G. A. 1967. *The Psychology of Communication: Seven Essays*. New
    York: Basic Books. Published 1969 as *Psychology and Communication*.
    London: Pelican.

————, ed. 1973. *Communication, Language, and Meaning: Psychological
    Perspectives*. New York: Basic Books.

Neisser, U. 1967. *Cognitive Psychology*. New York: Appleton-Century-Crofts.

Pimsleur, P., and Quinn, T., eds. 1971. *The Psychology of Second Language
    Learning. Cambridge,* Eng.: Cambridge University Press.

Politzer, R. L. 1972. *Linguistics and Applied Linguistics: Aims and Methods.*
    Philadelphia: Center for Curriculum Development.
Ruwet, N. 1967. *Introduction à la grammaire générative.* Paris: Plon.
————. 1972. *Théorie syntaxique et syntaxe du français.* Paris: Editions du
    Seuil.
Schare, S. A. 1968. *French Phonology and Morphology.* Cambridge, Mass.:
    The M.I.T. Press.
————, 1973. *Generative Phonology.* Englewood Cliffs, N.J.: Prentice-Hall.
Schlesinger, I. M. 1968. *Sentence Structure and the Reading Process.* The
    Hague: Mouton.
Searle, J. R. 1969. *Speech Acts: An Essay in the Philosophy of Language.*
    Cambridge, Eng.: Cambridge University Press.
Slama-Cazacu, T. 1972. *La Psycholinguistique.* Paris: Klinksieck.
Slobin, D. I. 1971. *Psycholinguistics.* Glenview, Ill.: Scott, Foresman.
Smith, Frank. 1971. *Understanding Reading.* New York: Holt, Rinehart &
    Winston.
Spearritt, D. 1962. *Listening Comprehension: A Factorial Analysis.* Melbourne:
    Australian Council for Educational Research.
Valdman, A., ed. 1972. *Papers in Linguistics and Phonetics in Memory of
    Pierre Delattre.* The Hague: Mouton.
Vygotsky, L. S. 1962. *Thought and Language.* Trans. E. Hanfmann and G.
    Vakar. Cambridge, Mass.: The MIT Press.

Index